READINGS
IN
AMERICAN
HISTORY

*A*MERICA
*A*FIRSTHAND

Volume II *FROM RECONSTRUCTION
TO THE PRESENT*

Second Edition

ROBERT D. MARCUS

State University of New York College at Brockport

and

DAVID BURNER

State University of New York at Stony Brook

ST. MARTIN'S PRESS
New York

Acquisitions Editor: Louise H. Waller
Project management: Sarah Troutt, Publication Services
Cover design: Judy Forster
Cover art: Jacob Lawrence, *The Libraries Are Appreciated*,
1943. The Philadelphia Museum of Art: The Louis
E. Stern Collection.

Library of Congress Catalog Card Number: 90-63550

Manufactured in the United States of America.
6543
fedc

For information, write:
St. Martin's Press, Inc.
175 Fifth Avenue
New York, NY 10010

ISBN: 0-312-04903-X

Preface

The second edition of *America Firsthand* is a response to the increasing difficulty of teaching and learning American history. In the four years since the publication of the first edition, the challenges of studying American history have continued to grow, as both historians and students have become more conscious of the voices that either have been silent or have remained outside the canon of the American past as it is studied in the present.

We believe that students need to find exemplars of themselves in the past. *America Firsthand* was written to help them discover how the diversities of past experience and recent scholarship can respond to that need. The focus is on people who speak directly of their own experiences. In this edition we have paid more attention to the voices of women, black and Native Americans, and those whose lifestyles have traditionally made them inaccessible to mainstream historians. Insofar as possible individuals are presented in their own words and in selections long enough to be memorable, personal, and immediate. The accounts of indentured servants, runaway slaves, cowboys, factory workers, civil rights activists, homeless people, and many others offer students opportunities to identify with a wide range of human experience.

We have retained enough political and military documents to maintain the traditional markers of United States history; these continue to provide a useful narrative framework. In this second edition, however, we have emphasized social history in the belief that personal remembrances create a sense of identification with the past. Readings include viewpoints as varied as John White's pre-Jamestown history of the lost colony of Roanoke, Joseph Plumb Martin's soldier's view of the fight at Yorktown, Harriet Jacobs' account of sexual exploitation at the hands of her white master, and Dolly Sumner Burge's diary entry on Sherman's army passing through her Southern plantation, all in Volume I. Volume II includes a variety of letters to Franklin Roosevelt by the "forgotten men and women" of the Great Depression, Charity Adams Earley's experience as an Afro-American WAC officer during World War II, and interviews with "new" Americans from Latin American. While the readings convey the experiences and forces of specific personalities, they include observations on the American Revolution and the Civil War, on Reconstruction, the Great Depression, and the war in Vietnam.

All teachers and students must struggle with the problem of connecting traditional chronology with the new materials of social history, and no formula for doing that is without its problems. We have offered a set of connections that, in combination with a good United States history textbook, will be workable for many courses. Careful headnotes and questions at the end of each section help make the essential links from the personalities to the times in which those personalities lived.

America Firsthand, second edition, explores in even greater concreteness than the preceding edition the many ways of being American and the multitudinous minds and characters that make up a diverse history and nation. We see the American experience through the perspective of many cultures and diverse people who have in common that, in some form, they have left behind a vivid record of the world they inhabited and the times they experienced. We hope these recollections serve as fertile ground in which students can begin to root their own interest in history, and their own perception of the times in which they live.

Acknowledgments

The authors wish to thank the following individuals who reviewed the second edition of *America Firsthand* for St. Martin's Press: Holly Baggett, University of Delaware; Karel D. Bicha, Marquette University; W. Marvin Dulaney, University of Texas—Arlington; John d'Entremont, Randolph-Macon Women's College; Harold Ferguson, Montclair State College; Henry C. Ferrell, East Carolina University; David Fuchs, Lehman College; Gretchen Green, College of William and Mary; Daniel Horowitz, Smith College; Thomas W. Jodziewicz, University of Dallas; David M. Kennedy, Stanford University; Michael L. Krenn, University of Miami; Jessica Kross, University of South Carolina; Donna McCaffrey, Providence College; John F. McClymer, Assumption College; Richard Orst, Colgate University; David Pivar, Cal State—Fullerton; Norman L. Rosenberg, Macalester College; Emily Rosenberg, Macalester College; Neil Sapper, Amarillo College; Sara Lee Silberman, Connecticut College; Donna L. Van Razphorst, Cuyahoga Community College; Richard Toskin, North Adams State College; and Ralph Weber, Marquette University.

Contents

v

PART I | RECONSTRUCTION AND THE WESTERN FRONTIER

The crisis provoked by slavery and sectionalism was resolved only by the Civil War. Much of the technology of the war was quite advanced, and it speeded the transformation of American life into something that we can recognize as modern.

Victory for the Union, though, did not resolve questions about the role of Afro-American men and women in American life. Three new amendments to the Constitution initiated a revolution that, more than a century later, is far from over. In the selections that follow, we see the first painful and difficult responses to these changes as black and white Southerners react to Reconstruction. We also witness how the revolution in race relations carried with it striking changes in the most important forms of property and economic relations: ownership of the land and the crops planted on it. By the 1880s, sharecropping, governed by instruments like the Grimes Sharecrop contract, had emerged as the principal replacement for slavery.

The completion of the first transcontinental railroad link in 1869, and the renewed movement westward that it generated, fundamentally altered the western United States. The destruction of western buffalo herds, as shown in the writings of W.S. Glenn, E.N. Andrews, and John R. Cook, meant the collapse of Native American culture on the plains, which was based on hunting the buffalo. The increasing number of white settlers delivered the final blow.

Industries such as buffalo hunting, the larger scale commercial raising of cattle, and mining—combined with the warfare between whites and Native Americans—made the late nineteenth century a legendary era of western violence. Nat Love's attitudes and adventures are representative of the more romantic views of the western cowboy. Famous as "Deadeye Dick," Love was one of the about 25 percent of cowboys who were black.

The main motive of cowboys, however, was less romantic violence popularized in Hollywood films than the pursuit of economic for-

1

tune, the search for new means of livelihood, or, simply a stable income. Bob Kennon's account of a cattle drive provides one example of the existence of routine in what was ordinarily thought of as an extraordinary, adventuresome life.

The late nineteenth century marked the final shunting of Native Americans to reservations often far distant from their ancestral homes. The struggles of Zitkala-Sä, a Dakota Sioux, to find her place in both the Native American and the white world indicates the complexity lurking behind the stereotypes of cowboys and Native Americans.

FELIX HAYWOOD ET AL.

1 | Blacks' Reactions to Reconstruction

The Reconstruction period remains a subject of intense historical debate. The Thirteenth, Fourteenth, and Fifteenth Amendments to the U.S. Constitution decreed an equality between the races that was not realized in fact. At first the federal government vigorously supported the Freedmen's Bureau and the efforts of Reconstruction governments in Southern states to help the freed slaves, but within about a decade those efforts were abandoned as the Northern public lost interest.

The social revolution brought about by emancipation caused severe problems for both Afro-Americans and whites. Just as the slaves' experiences had varied widely, so the newly freed Afro-Americans responded to their new situation in many different ways. Their needs were rarely understood by whites ill-prepared to accept Afro-Americans as equals or to support the long-term federal intervention that was required to make freedom an economic and social reality.

The interviews below were collected in the 1930s. Historians have found such accounts valuable sources for the history of slaves and Reconstruction.

FELIX HAYWOOD From San Antonio, Texas, Born in Raleigh, North Carolina. Age at Interview: 88.

The end of the war, it come just like that—like you snap your fingers. ...How did we know it! Hallelujah broke out—

> Abe Lincoln freed the nigger
>   With the gun and the trigger;
> And I ain't going to get whipped any more.
>   I got my ticket,
> Leaving the thicket,
>   And I'm a-heading for the Golden Shore!

Soldiers, all of a sudden, was everywhere—coming in bunches, crossing and walking and riding. Everyone was a-singing. We was all walking on golden clouds. Hallelujah!

Botkin, B.A. (editor), Lay My Burden Down: A Folk History of Slavery. (Chicago, University of Chicago Press, 1945), pp. 65–70, 223–224, 241–242, 246–247. Copyright 1989 by Curtis Brown, Ltd.

> *Union forever,*
>   *Hurrah, boys, hurrah!*
> *Although I may be poor,*
>   *I'll never be a slave—*
> *Shouting the battle cry of freedom.*

Everybody went wild. We felt like heroes, and nobody had made us that way but ourselves. We was free. Just like that, we was free. It didn't seem to make the whites mad, either. They went right on giving us food just the same. Nobody took our homes away, but right off colored folks started on the move. They seemed to want to get closer to freedom, so they'd know what it was—like it was a place or a city. Me and my father stuck, stuck close as a lean tick to a sick kitten. The Gudlows started us out on a ranch. My father, he'd round up cattle—unbranded cattle—for the whites. They was cattle that they belonged to, all right; they had gone to find water 'long the San Antonio River and the Guadalupe. Then the whites gave me and my father some cattle for our own. My father had his own brand—7 B)—and we had a herd to start out with of seventy.

We knowed freedom was on us, but we didn't know what was to come with it. We thought we was going to get rich like the white folks. We thought we was going to be richer than the white folks, 'cause we was stronger and knowed how to work, and the whites didn't, and they didn't have us to work for them any more. But it didn't turn out that way. We soon found out that freedom could make folks proud, but it didn't make 'em rich.

Did you ever stop to think that thinking don't do any good when you do it too late? Well, that's how it was with us. If every mother's son of a black had thrown 'way his hoe and took up a gun to fight for his own freedom along with the Yankees, the war'd been over before it began. But we didn't do it. We couldn't help stick to our masters. We couldn't no more shoot 'em than we could fly. My father and me used to talk 'bout it. We decided we was too soft and freedom wasn't going to be much to our good even if we had a education.

/   /   /

WARREN MCKINNEY, From Hazen, Akansas. Born in South Carolina. Age at Interview: 85.

I was born in Edgefield County, South Carolina. I am eighty-five years old. I was born a slave of George Strauter. I remembers hearing them say, "Thank God, I's free as a jay bird." My ma was a slave in the field. I was eleven years old when freedom was declared. When I was little, Mr. Strauter whipped my ma. It hurt me bad as it did her. I hated him. She was crying. I chunked him with rocks. He run after me, but he didn't catch me. There was twenty-five or thirty hands that worked in the field. They raised wheat, corn, oats, barley, and cotton. All the children that couldn't work stayed at one house. Aunt Mat kept the babies and small children that couldn't go to the field. He had a gin and a shop. The shop was at the fork of the roads. When the war come on, my papa went to built forts. He quit Ma and took another woman. When the war close, Ma took her four children, bundled 'em up and went to Augusta. The government give out rations there. My ma washed and ironed. People died in piles. I don't know till yet what was the matter. They said it was the change of living. I seen five or six wooden, painted coffins piled up on wagons pass by our house. Loads passed every day like you see cotton pass here. Some said it was cholera and some took consumption. Lots of the colored people nearly starved. Not much to get to do and not much houseroom. Several families had to live in one house. Lots of the colored folks went up North and froze to death. They couldn't stand the cold. They wrote back about them dying. No, they never sent them back. I heard some sent for money to come back. I heard plenty 'bout the Ku Klux. They scared the folks to death. People left Augusta in droves. About a thousand would all meet and walk going to hunt work and new homes. Some of them died. I had a sister and brother lost that way. I had another sister come to Louisiana that way. She wrote back.

I don't think the colored folks looked for a share of land. They never got nothing 'cause the white folks didn't have nothing but barren hills left. About all the mules was wore out hauling provisions in the army. Some folks say they ought to done more for the colored folks when they left, but they say they was broke. Freeing all the slaves left 'em broke.

That reconstruction was a mighty hard pull. Me and Ma couldn't live. A man paid our ways to Carlisle, Arkansas, and we come. We started working for Mr. Emenson. He had a big store, teams, and land. We liked it fine, and I been here fifty-six years now. There was so much wild game, living was not so hard. If a fellow could get a little bread and a place to stay, he was all right. After I come to this state, I voted some. I have farmed and worked at odd jobs. I farmed mostly. Ma went back to her old master. He persuaded her to come back home. Me and her went back and run a farm four or five years before she died. Then I come back here.

/   /   /

LEE GUIDON, *From South Carolina. Born in South Carolina. Age at Interview: 89.*

Yes, ma'am, I sure was in the Civil War. I plowed all day, and me and my sister helped take care of the baby at night. It would cry, and me bumping it [in a straight chair, rocking.] Time I git it to the bed where its mama was, it wake up and start crying all over again. I be so sleepy. It was a puny sort of baby. Its papa was off at war. His name was Jim Cowan, and his wife Miss Margaret Brown 'fore she married him.

Miss Lucy Smith give me and my sister to them. Then she married Mr. Abe Moore. Jim Smith was Miss Lucy's boy. He lay out in the woods all time. He say no need in him gitting shot up and killed. He say let the slaves be free. We lived, seemed like, on 'bout the line of York and Union counties. He lay out in the woods over in York County. Mr. Jim say all the fighting 'bout was jealousy. They caught him several times, but every time he got away from 'em. After they come home Mr. Jim say they never win no war. They stole and starved out the South. . . .

After freedom a heap of people say they was going to name theirselves over. They named theirselves big names, then went roaming round like wild, hunting cities. They changed up so it was hard to tell who or where anybody was. Heap of 'em died, and you didn't know when you hear about it if he was your folks hardly. Some of the names was Abraham, and some called theirselves Lincum. Any big name 'cepting their master's name. It was the fashion. I heard 'em talking 'bout it one evening, and my pa say, "Fine folks raise us and we gonna hold to our own names." That settled it with all of us. . . .

I reckon I do know 'bout the Ku Kluck. I knowed a man named Alfred Owens. He seemed all right, but he was a Republican. He said he was not afraid. He run a tanyard and kept a heap of guns in a big room. They all loaded. He married a Southern woman. Her husband either died or was killed. She had a son living with them. The Ku Kluck was called Upper League. They get this boy to unload all the guns. Then the white men went there. The white man give up and said, "I ain't got no gun to defend myself with. The guns all unloaded, and I ain't got no powder and shot." But the Ku Kluck shot in the houses and shot him up like lacework. He sold fine harness, saddles, bridles—all sorts of leather things. The Ku Kluck sure run them outen their country. They say they not going to have them round, and they sure run them out, back where they came from. . . .

For them what stayed on like they were, Reconstruction times 'bout like times before that 'cepting the Yankee stole out and tore up a scandalous heap. They tell the black folks to do something, and then come white folks you live with and say Ku Kluck whup you. They say leave, and white folks say better not listen to them old Yankees. They'll git you too far off to come back, and you freeze. They done give you all the use they got for you. How they do? All sorts of ways. Some stayed at their cabins glad to have one to live in and farmed on. Some running round begging, some hunting work for money, and nobody had no money 'cepting the Yankees, and they had no homes or land and mighty little work for you to do. No work to live on. Some going every day to the city. That winter I heard 'bout them starving and freezing by the wagon loads. I never heard nothing 'bout voting till freedom. I don't think I ever voted till I come to Mississippi. I votes Republican. That's the party of my color, and I stick to them as long as they do right. I don't dabble in white folks' business, and that white folks' voting is their business. If I vote, I go do it and go on home.

I been plowing all my life, and in the hot days I cuts and saws wood. Then when I gets outa cotton-picking, I put each boy on a load of wood and we sell wood. The last years we got $3 a cord. Then we clear land till next spring. I don't find no time to be loafing. I never missed a year farming till I got the Bright's disease [one of several kinds of kidney ailments] and it hurt me to do hard work. Farming is the best life there is when you are able. . . .

When I owned most, I had six head mules and five head horses. I rented 140 acres of land. I bought this house and some other land about. The anthrax killed nearly all my horses and mules. I got one big fine mule yet. Its mate died. I lost my house. My son give me one room, and he paying the debt off now. It's hard for colored folks to keep anything. Somebody gets it from 'em if they don't mind.

The present times is hard. Timber is scarce. Game is about all gone. Prices higher. Old folks cannot work. Times is hard for younger folks too. They go to town too much and go to shows. They going to a tent show now. Circus coming, they say. They spending too much money for foolishness. It's a fast time. Folks too restless. Some of the colored folks work hard as folks ever did. They spends too much. Some folks is lazy. Always been that way.

I signed up to the government, but they ain't give me nothing 'cepting powdered milk and rice what wasn't fit to eat. It cracked up and had black something in it. A lady said she would give me some shirts that was her husband's. I went to get them, but she wasn't home. These heavy shirts give me heat. They won't give me the pension, and I don't know why. It would help me buy my salts and pills and the other medicines like Swamp Root. They won't give it to me.

/   /   /

TOBY JONES, From Madisonville, Texas. Born in South Carolina. Age at Interview: 87.

I worked for Massa 'bout four years after freedom, 'cause he forced me to, said he couldn't 'ford to let me go. His place was near ruint, the fences burnt, and the house would have been, but it was rock. There was a battle fought near his place, and I taken Missy to a hideout in the mountains to where her father was, 'cause there was bullets flying everywhere. When the war was over, Massa come home and says, "You son of a gun, you's supposed to be free, but you ain't, 'cause I ain't gwine give you freedom." So I goes on working for him till I gits the chance to steal a hoss from him. The woman I wanted to marry, Govie, she 'cides to come to Texas with me. Me and Govie, we rides the hoss 'most a hundred miles, then we turned him a-loose and give him a scare back to his house, and come on foot the rest the way to Texas.

All we had to eat was what we could beg, and sometimes we went three days without a bite to eat. Sometimes we'd pick a few berries.

When we got cold we'd crawl in a brushpile and hug up close together to keep warm. Once in a while we'd come to a farmhouse, and the man let us sleep on cottonseed in his barn, but they was far and few between, 'cause they wasn't many houses in the country them days like now.

When we gits to Texas, we gits married, but all they was to our wedding am we just 'grees to live together as man and wife. I settled on some land, and we cut some trees and split them open and stood them on end with the tops together for our house. Then we deadened some trees, and the land was ready to farm. There was some wild cattle and hogs, and that's the way we got our start, caught some of them and tamed them.

I don't know as I' spected nothing from freedom, but they turned us out like a bunch of stray dogs, no homes, no clothing, no nothing, not 'nough food to last us one meal. After we settles on that place, I never seed man or woman, 'cept Govie, for six years, 'cause it was a long ways to anywhere. All we had to farm with was sharp sticks. We'd stick holes and plant corn, and when it come up we'd punch up the dirt round it. We didn't plant cotton, 'cause we couldn't eat that. I made bows and arrows to kill wild game with, and we never went to a store for nothing. We made our clothes out of animal skins.

WHY ADAM KIRK WAS A DEMOCRAT

(House Report no. 262, 43 Cong., 2 Sess., p. 106. Statement of an Alabama Negro. [1874])

A white man raised me. I was raised in the house of old man Billy Kirk. He raised me as a body servant. The class that he belongs to seems nearer to me than the northern white man, and actually, since the war, everything I have got is by their aid and their assistance. They have helped me raise up my family and have stood by me, and whenever I want a doctor, no matter what hour of the day or night, he is called in whether I have got a cent or not. And when I want any assistance I can get it from them. I think they have got better principles and better character than the republicans.

Walter L. Fleming (editor), Documentary History of Reconstruction, Volume Two. *(Glouces-ter, Massachusetts, Peter Smith, 1960), p. 87.*

B. R. GRATTAN ET AL.

2 | White Southerners' Reactions
| to Reconstruction

The Congressional Joint Committee of Fifteen, assembled to examine Southern
representation in Congress, was named in December 1865 and served as the
Republican response to President Andrew Johnson's lenient plan of Reconstruction. In 1866, the committee held hearings as part of its effort to develop the
Fourteenth Amendment. Congress had already, despite the President's veto, enlarged the scope of the Freedmen's Bureau to care for displaced ex-slaves and to
try by military commission those accused of depriving freedmen of civil rights.
    The testimony of white Southerners, three samples of which are presented
below, indicate how difficult it was for the white South to accept the idea of
Afro-American equality. Congress's reconstruction policy, more stringent than
Johnson's but still cautious, appeared radical, even unthinkable, to most white
Southerners and probably to many Northerners. Reading such testimony, one
begins to understand why the nation has found it so difficult to carry out the
mandate of the Fourteenth and Fifteenth Amendments.

B. R. GRATTAN

Washington, D.C., February 10, 1866

QUESTION: Where do you reside?
  ANSWER: Richmond, Virginia.
QUESTION: Are you a native of Virginia?
  ANSWER: Yes, sir: I was raised in the valley of Virginia.
QUESTION: Do you hold any public position?
  ANSWER: I am a member of the present house of delegates of Virginia.
QUESTION: Is that the only public position you have held?
  ANSWER: I held the office of reporter to the court of appeals since
          January, 1844.

The Report of the Committees of the House of Representatives Made During the First Session, Thirty-Ninth Congress, 1865–'66. *Volume II. (Washington, D.C., Government Printing
Office, 1866),* Grattan: pp. 161–164; Forshey: pp. 129–132; Sinclair: 168–171.
    *It is a violation of the law to reproduce this selection by any means whatsoever without the
written permission of the copyright holder.*

QUESTION: I speak of two classes of people in Virginia for the sake of convenience, not with a view of offending anybody. I speak of secessionists and Union men. By secessionists I mean those who have directly or indirectly favored the rebellion; and by Union men I mean those who opposed the rebellion; and by the rebellion I mean the war which has taken place between the two sections of the country. What is the general feeling among the secessionists of Virginia towards the government of the United States, so far as your observation extends?

ANSWER: So far as I know, the sentiment is universal that the war has decided the question of secession entirely, that it is no longer an open question, and that we are all prepared to abide by the Union and live under it.

QUESTION: You mean to be understood as saying that they suppose that the sword has settled the abstract right of secession?

ANSWER: Yes; we consider that we put it to the arbitrament of the sword, and have lost.

QUESTION: What proportion of the legislature of Virginia are original secessionists, have in view the definitions I gave?

ANSWER: I would suppose that there are few members of the legislature who are less able to judge of that matter than myself, for my acquaintance as a member is very limited; but I should suppose, from the general sentiments of the people of Virginia, that while probably a very large proportion of those who are now members of the legislature were not in favor of secession or a dissolution of the Union originally, yet nearly all of them went with their State when it went out. They went heartily with it.

QUESTION: How have the results of the war affected the feelings of Virginians generally? What is the sentiment left in their hearts in regard to satisfaction or dissatisfaction with the government of the United States—love or hatred, respect or contempt?

ANSWER: I cannot undertake to say generally; my intercourse is very limited. I would rather suppose, however, that while the feeling against the government was originally very strong, that feeling has been very much modified; it is nothing like as strong as it was, and is gradually declining.

QUESTION: You think that the feeling is gradually changing from dislike to respect?

ANSWER: Yes, I think so.

QUESTION: Have you any reason to suppose that there are persons in Virginia who still entertain projects of a dissolution of the Union?

ANSWER: None whatever. I do not believe that there is an intelligent man in the State who does.

/   /   /

QUESTION: What has been, in your judgment, the effect, in the main, of President Johnson's liberality in bestowing pardons and amnesties on rebels?

ANSWER: I think it has been very favorable; I think President Johnson has commended himself very heartily. There is a very strong feeling of gratitude towards President Johnson.

/   /   /

QUESTION: What, in your judgment, would be the consequences of such an infranchisement: would it produce scenes of violence between the two races?

ANSWER: I believe it would. I have very great apprehension that an attempt of that sort would lead to their extermination, not immediately, but to their gradual extinction. It would set up really an antagonistic interest, which would probably be used as a power, because I have no doubt that the negro vote would be under the influence of white people. You are to recollect that this is not simply a prejudice between the white and black races. It has grown to be a part of our nature to look upon them as an inferior; just as much a part of our nature as it is a part of the nature of other races to have enmity to each other; for instance, between the Saxon Irish and the Celtic Irish, or between the English and the French. You must change that nature, and it takes a long time to do it. I believe that if you place the negro on a footing of perfect equality with the white, it would actually increase the power of the white race, which would control the negro vote; yet it seems to me that nothing can reconcile the white people to that short of equal political power, and I fear, therefore, very much the consequences of any attempt of that sort upon the black race in Virginia.

QUESTION: Would not that prejudice become modified a great deal in case the blacks should be educated and rendered more intelligent than they are now?

ANSWER: You would have to change their skin before you can do it. I beg leave to say this, so far from there being any unkind feeling to the negro, I believe that there is, on the part of the white race, towards the negro, no feeling but that of kindness, sympathy, and pity, and that there is every disposition to ameliorate their condition and improve it as much as possible; but it is that difference which has existed so long in their obvious distinction of color and condition—

QUESTION: But suppose the condition of the negro should change?

ANSWER: The condition is annexed to the color. We are accustomed to see the color in the condition.

/   /   /

QUESTION: Is there a general repugnance on the part of whites to the acquisition and enjoyment of property by the blacks?

ANSWER: I do not know. I do not think there is. Far from it. We would be very glad to see them all doing well and improving their condition.

QUESTION: Do you find a similar repugnance to the acquisition of knowledge by blacks?

ANSWER: No, sir; far from it; on the contrary, we are trying, so far as we can, to educate them; but we are too poor ourselves to do much in educating other people, and they are certainly too poor to educate themselves.

QUESTION: You would, then, anticipate a struggle of races in case the right of suffrage was given to the blacks?

ANSWER: Yes, sir; I think so.

QUESTION: You would not anticipate it in case the blacks should vote in the interests of the white race?

ANSWER: As I said before, I believe that if the blacks are left to themselves, if all foreign influence were taken away, the whites would control their vote. It is not in that the difficulty lies, but it is in the repugnance which the white race would feel to that sort of political equality. It is the same sort of repugnance which a man feels to a snake. He does not feel any animosity to the snake, but there is a natural shrinking from it; that is my feeling. While I think I have as much sympathy for the black race, and feel as much interest in them as anybody else, while I can treat them kindly and familiarly, still the idea of equality is one which has the same sort of shrinking for me, and is as much a part of my nature, as was the antagonism between Saxon and Celt in Ireland.

QUESTION: You are aware that that state of feeling does not exist in Ireland, England, or Scotland towards the blacks?

ANSWER: No; because they never had them; because they never saw them in their constant condition. So that difference of alienation between Saxon and Celt does not exist here, but it exists in Ireland. It is where that has been the feeling operating for so long that it has become a part of our nature. It is not simple prejudice, but it becomes part of the nature of the man. . . .

QUESTION: You have not much reason to expect that the legislature of Virginia will adopt this constitutional amendment in case it shall pass both houses of Congress?

ANSWER: I cannot speak for others, but for myself I say certainly not. No political power would ever induce me to vote for it. That form is much more objectionable than even a proposition to make them voters. It is giving you all the advantages of numbers, while you are taking that from us which, according to the original constitution, we had—three-fifths of the slave population—and no political power will force me to consent to that.

CALEB G. FORSHEY

Washington, D.C., March 28, 1866

QUESTION: Where do you reside?

ANSWER: I reside in the State of Texas.

QUESTION: How long have you been a resident of Texas?

ANSWER: I have resided in Texas and been a citizen of that State for nearly thirteen years.

QUESTION: What opportunities have you had for ascertaining the temper and disposition of the people of Texas towards the government and authority of the United States?

ANSWER: For ten years I have been superintendent of the Texas Military Institute, as its founder and conductor. I have been in the confederate service in various parts of the confederacy; but chiefly in the trans-Mississippi department, in Louisiana and Texas, as an officer of engineers. I have had occasion to see and know very extensively the condition of affairs in Texas, and also to a considerable extent in Louisiana. I think I am pretty well-informed, as well as anybody, perhaps, of the present state of affairs in Texas.

QUESTION: What are the feelings and views of the people of Texas as to the late rebellion, and the future condition and circumstances of the State, and its relations to the federal government?

ANSWER: After our army had given up its arms and gone home, the surrender of all matters in controvsry was complete, and as nearly universal, perhaps, as anything could be. Assuming the matters in controversy to have been the right to secede, and the right to hold slaves, I think they were given up tee-totally, to use a strong Americanism. When you speak of feeling, I should discriminate a little. The feeling was that of any party who had been cast in a suit he had staked all upon. They did not return from feeling, but from a sense of necessity, and from a judgment that it was the only and necessary thing to be done, to give up the contest. But when they gave it up, it was without reservation; with a view to look forward, and not back. That is my impression of the manner in which the thing was done. There was a public expectation that in some very limited time there would be a restoration to former relations; and in such restoration they felt great interest, after the contest was given up. The expectation was, and has been up to the present time, that there would be a speedy and immediate restoration. It was the expectation of the people that, as soon as the State was organized as proposed by the President, they would be restored to their former relations, and things would go on as before.

/   /   /

QUESTION: What is your opinion of a military force under the authority of the federal government to preserve order in Texas and to protect those who have been loyal, both white and black, from the aggressions of those who have been in the rebellion?

ANSWER: My judgment is well founded on that subject: that wherever such military force is and has been, it has excited the very feeling it was intended to prevent; that so far from being necessary it is very pernicious everywhere, and without exception. The local authorities and public sentiment are ample for protection. I think no occasion would occur, unless some individual case that our laws would not reach. We had an opportunity to test this after the surrender and before any authority was there. The military authorities, or the military officers, declared that we were without laws, and it was a long time before the governor appointed arrived there, and then it was sometime before we could effect anything in the way of organization. We were a people without law, order, or anything; and it was a time for violence if it would occur. I think it is a great credit to our civilization that, in that state of affairs, there was nowhere any instance of violence. I am proud of it, for I expected the contrary; I expected that our soldiers on coming home, many of them, would be dissolute, and that many of them would oppress the class of men you speak of; but it did not occur. But afterwards, wherever soldiers have been sent, there have been little troubles, none of them large; but personal collisions between soldiers and citizens.

QUESTION: What is your opinion as to the necessity and advantages of the Freedmen's Bureau, or an agency of that kind, in Texas?

ANSWER: My opinion is that it is not needed; my opinion is stronger than that—that the effect of it is to irritate, if nothing else. While in New York city recently I had a conversation with some friends from Texas, from five distant points in the State. We met together and compared opinions; and the opinion of each was the same, that the negroes had generally gone to work since January; that except where the Freedmen's Bureau had interfered, or rather encouraged troubles, such as little complaints, especially between negro and negro, the negro's disposition was very good, and they had generally gone to work, a vast majority of them with their former masters.

I was very gratified to learn that from districts where I feared the contrary. Still this difference was made, particularly by Mr. Carpenter, from Jefferson, the editor of the Jefferson Herald. He said that in two or three counties where they had not been able to organize the Freedmen's Bureau, there had been no trouble at all; nearly all the negroes had gone to work. The impression in Texas at present is that the negroes under the influence of the Freedmens's Bureau do worse than without it.

I want to state that I believe all our former owners of negroes are the friends of the negroes; and that the antagonism paraded in the papers of the north does not exist at all. I know the fact is the very converse of that; and good feeling always prevails between the masters and the slaves. But the negroes went off and left them in the lurch; my own family was an instance of it. But they came back after a time, saying they had been free enough and wanted a home.

QUESTION: Do you think those who employ the negroes there are willing to make contracts with them, so that they shall have fair wages for their labor?

ANSWER: I think so; I think they are paid liberally, more than the white men in this country get; the average compensation to negroes there is greater than the average compensation of free laboring white men in this country. It seems to have regulated itself in a great measure by what each neighborhood was doing; the negroes saying, "I can get thus and so at such a place." Men have hired from eight to fifteen dollars per month during the year, and women at about two dollars less a month; house-servants at a great deal more.

QUESTION: Do the men who employ the negroes claim to exercise the right to enforce their contract by physical force?

ANSWER: Not at all; that is totally abandoned; not a single instance of it has occurred. I think they still chastise children, though. The negro parents often neglect that, and the children are still switched as we switch our own children. I know it is done in my own house; we have little house-servants that we switch just as I do our own little fellows.

QUESTION: What is your opinion as to the respective advantages to the white and black races, of the present free system of labor and the institution of slavery?

ANSWER: I think freedom is very unfortunate for the negro; I think it is sad; his present helpless condition touches my heart more than anything else I ever contemplated, and I think that is the common sentiment of our slaveholders. I have seen it on the largest plantations, where the negro men had all left, and where only women and children remained, and the owners had to keep them and feed them. The beginning certainly presents a touching and sad spectacle. The poor negro is dying at a rate fearful to relate.

I have some ethnological theories that may perhaps warp my judgment; but my judgment is that the highest condition the black race has ever reached or can reach, is one where he is provided for by a master race. That is the result of a great deal of scientific investigation and observation of the negro character by me ever since I was a man. The labor question had become a most momentous one, and I was studying it. I undertook to investigate the condition of the negro from statistics under various circumstances, to treat it purely as a matter of statistics from the census tables of this country of ours. I found that the free blacks of the north decreased 8 per cent.; the free blacks of the south increased 7 or 8 per cent., while the slaves by their sides increased 34 per cent. I inferred from the doctrines of political economy that the race is in the best condition when it procreates the fastest; that, other things being equal, slavery is of vast advantage to the negro. I will mention one or two things in connexion with this as explanatory of that result. The negro will not take care of his offspring unless required to do it, as compared with the whites. The little children will die; they do die, and hence the necessity of very rigorous regulations on our plantations which we have adopted in our nursery system.

Another cause is that there is no continence among the negroes. All the continence I have ever seen among the negroes has been enforced upon plantations, where it is generally assumed there is none. For the sake of procreation, if nothing else, we compel men to live with their wives. The discipline of the plantation was more rigorous, perhaps, in regard to men staying with their wives, than in regard to anything else; and I think the procreative results, as shown by the census tables, is due in a great measure to that discipline.

I think they are very much better off in having homes than the free blacks are. The free blacks in Louisiana, where we had 34,000, with a great deal of blood of the whites in them, and therefore a great deal of white sense, were nothing like so happy and so well off as our slaves are. My observation for many years leads me to this conclusion.

QUESTION: What is the prevailing inclination among the people of Texas in regard to giving the negroes civil or political rights and privileges?

ANSWER: I think they are all opposed to it. There are some men—I am not among them—who think that the basis of intelligence might be a good basis for the elective franchise. But a much larger class, perhaps nine-tenths of our people, believe that the distinctions between the races should not be broken down by any such community of interests in the management of the affairs of the State. I think there is a very common sentiment that the negro, even with education, has not a mind capable of appreciating the political institutions of the country to such an extent as would make him a good associate for the white man in the administration of the government. I think if the vote was taken on the question of admitting him to the right of suffrage there would be a very small vote in favor of it—scarcely respectable: that is my judgment.

/   /   /

REVEREND JAMES SINCLAIR

Washington, D.C., January 29, 1866

[James Sinclair, a Scottish born minister who served on the Freedmen's Bureau in 1865, had been living in North Carolina for nine years. Though a slaveholder himself, Sinclair opposed secession. This led to the loss of his church and his eventual arrest during the war. In contrast to the testimony of Caleb Forshey, Sinclair's description of relations between whites and blacks suggests that, in some cases, paternalism has been replaced by outright enmity. An outsider in the South both during and after the conflict, Sinclair offers a point of view that seems the most pessimistic in its assessment of whether the wounds of the war would heal in the near future.]

QUESTION: What is generally the state of feeling among the white people of North Carolina towards the government of the United States?

ANSWER: That is a difficult question to answer, but I will answer it as far as my own knowledge goes. In my opinion, there is generally among the white people not much love for the government. Though they are willing, and I believe determined, to acquiesce in what is inevitable, yet so far as love and affection for the government is concerned, I do not believe that they have any of it at all, outside of their personal respect and regard for President Johnson.

QUESTION: How do they feel towards the mass of the northern people— that is, the people of what were known formerly as the free States?

ANSWER: They feel in this way: that they have been ruined by them. You can imagine the feelings of a person towards one whom he regards as having ruined him. They regard the northern people as having destroyed their property or taken it from them, and brought all the calamaties of this war upon them.

QUESTION: How do they feel in regard to what is called the right of secession?

ANSWER: They think that it was right . . . that there was no wrong in it. They are willing now to accept the decision of the question that has been made by the sword, but they are not by any means converted from their old opinion that they had a right to secede. It is true that there have always been Union men in our State, but not Union men without slavery, except perhaps among Quakers. Slavery was the central idea even of the Unionist. The only difference between them and the others upon that question was, that they desired to have that institution under the aegis of the Constitution, and protected by it. The secessionists wanted to get away from the north altogether. When the secessionists precipitated our State into rebellion, the Unionists and secessionists went together, because the great object with both was the preservation of slavery by the preservation of State sovereignty. There was another class of Unionists who did not care anything at all about slavery, but they were driven by the other whites into the rebellion for the purpose of preserving slavery. The poor whites are to-day very much opposed to conferring upon the negro the right of suffrage; as much so as the other classes of the whites. They believe it is the intention of government to give the negro rights at their expense. They cannot see it in any other light than that as the negro is elevated they must proportionately go down. While they are glad that slavery is done away with, they are bitterly opposed to conferring the right of suffrage on the negro as the most prominent secessionists; but it is for the reason I have stated, that they think rights conferred on the negro must necessarily be taken from them, particularly the ballot, which was the only bulwark guarding their superiority to the negro race.

QUESTION: In your judgment, what proportion of the white people of North Carolina are really, and truly, and cordially attached to the government of the United States?

ANSWER: Very few, sir; very few.

QUESTION: Judging from what you have observed of the feelings of the people of that State, what would be their course in case of a war between the United States and a foreign government?

ANSWER: I can only tell you what I have heard young men say there; perhaps it was mere bravado. I have heard them say that they wished to the Lord the United States would get into a war

with France or England; they would know where they would
be. I asked this question of some of them: If Robert E. Lee
was restored to his old position in the army of the United
States, and he should call on you to join him to fight for the
United States, and against a foreign enemy, what would you
do? They replied, "Wherever old Bob would go we would
go with him."

QUESTION: Have you heard such remarks since the war is over, as that
they wished the United States would get into a war with
England and France?

ANSWER: Oh, yes, sir; such remarks are very common. I have heard
men say, "May my right hand wither and my tongue cleave
to the roof of my mouth if I ever lift my arm in favor of the
United States."

QUESTION: Did you ever hear such sentiments rebuked by bystanders?

ANSWER: No, sir; it would be very dangerous to do so.

QUESTION: Is the Freedmen's Bureau acceptable to the great mass of the
white people in North Carolina?

ANSWER: No, sir; I do not think it is; I think the most of the whites
wish the bureau to be taken away.

QUESTION: Why do they wish that?

ANSWER: They think that they can manage the negro for themselves:
that they understand him better than northern men do. They
say, "Let us understand what you want us to do with negro—
what you desire of us; lay down your conditions for our re-
admission into the Union, and then we will know what we
have to do, and if you will do that we will enact laws for
the government of these negroes. They have lived among
us, and they are all with us, and we can manage them better
than you can." They think it is interfering with the rights
of the State for a bureau, the agent and representative of
the federal government, to overslaugh the State entirely, and
interfere with the regulations and administration of justice
before their courts.

QUESTION: Is there generally a willingness on the part of the whites to
allow the freedmen to enjoy the right of acquiring land and
personal property?

ANSWER: I think they are very willing to let them do that, for this reason; to get rid of some portion of the taxes imposed upon
their property by the government. For instance, a white man
will agree to sell a negro some of his land on condition of
his paying so much a year on it, promising to give him a
deed of it when the whole payment is made, taking his note
in the mean time. This relieves that much of the land from
taxes to be paid by the white man. All I am afraid of is,
that the negro is too eager to go into this thing; that he will
ruin himself, get himself into debt to the white man, and be

forever bound to him for the debt and never get the land. I have often warned them to be careful what they did about these things.

QUESTION: There is no repugnance on the part of the whites to the negro owning land and personal property?

ANSWER: I think not.

QUESTION: Have they any objection to the legal establishment of the domestic relations among the blacks, such as the relation of husband and wife, of parent and child, and the securing by law to the negro the rights of those relations?

ANSWER: That is a matter of ridicule with the whites. They do not believe the negroes will ever respect those relations more than the brutes. I suppose I have married more than two hundred couples of negroes since the war, but the whites laugh at the very idea of the thing. Under the old laws a slave could not marry a free woman of color; it was made a penal offence in North Carolina for any one to perform such a marriage. But there was in my own family a slave who desired to marry a free woman of color, and I did what I conceived to be my duty, and married them, and I was presented to the grand jury for doing so, but the prosecuting attorney threw out the case and would not try it. In former times the officiating clergyman marrying slaves, could not use the usual formula: "Whom God has joined together let no man put asunder;" you could not say, "According to the ordinance of God I pronounce you man and wife; you are no longer two but one." It was not legal for you to do so.

QUESTION: What, in general, has been the treatment of the blacks by the whites since the close of hostilities?

ANSWER: It has not generally been of the kindest character, I must say that; I am compelled to say that.

QUESTION: Are you aware of any instance of personal ill treatment towards the blacks by the whites?

ANSWER: Yes, sir.

QUESTION: Give some instances that have occurred since the war.

ANSWER: [Sinclair describes the beating of a young woman across her buttocks in graphic detail.]

QUESTION: What was the provocation, if any?

ANSWER: Something in regard to some work, which is generally the provocation.

QUESTION: Was there no law in North Carolina at that time to punish such an outrage?

ANSWER: No, sir; only the regulations of the Freedmen's Bureau; we took cognizance of the case. In old times that was quite allowable; it is what was called "paddling."

QUESTION: Did you deal with the master?

ANSWER: I immediately sent a letter to him to come to my office, but he did not come, and I have never seen him in regard to the matter since. I had no soldiers to enforce compliance, and I was obliged to let the matter drop.

QUESTION: Have you any reason to suppose that such instances of cruelty are frequent in North Carolina at this time—instances of whipping and striking?

ANSWER: I think they are; it was only a few days before I left that a woman came there with her head all bandaged up, having been cut and bruised by her employer. They think nothing of striking them.

QUESTION: And the negro has practically no redress?

ANSWER: Only what he can get from the Freedmen's Bureau.

QUESTION: Can you say anything further in regard to the political condition of North Carolina—the feeling of the people towards the government of the United States?

ANSWER: I for one would not wish to be left there in the hands of those men; I could not live there just now. But perhaps my case is an isolated one from the position I was compelled to take in that State. I was persecuted, arrested, and they tried to get me into their service; they tried everything to accomplish their purpose, and of course I have rendered myself still more obnoxious by accepting an appointment under the Freedmen's Bureau. As for myself I would not be allowed to remain there. I do not want to be handed over to these people. I know it is utterly impossible for any man who was not true to the Confederate States up to the last moment of the existence of the confederacy, to expect any favor of these people as the State is constituted at present.

QUESTION: Suppose the military pressure of the government of the United States should be withdrawn from North Carolina, would northern men and true Unionists be safe in that State?

ANSWER: A northern man going there would perhaps present nothing obnoxious to the people of the State. But men who were born there, who have been true to the Union, and who have fought against the rebellion, are worse off than northern men. And Governor Holden will never get any place from the people of North Carolina, not even a constable's place.

QUESTION: Why not?

ANSWER: Because he identified himself with the Union movement all along after the first year of the rebellion. He has been a marked man; his printing office has been gutted, and his life has been threatened by the soldiers of the rebellion. He is killed there politically, and never will get anything from the people of North Carolina, as the right of suffrage exists there at present. I am afraid he would not get even the support of the negro, if they should be allowed to vote, because he did not stand right up for them as he should have done. In my opinion, he would have been a stronger man than ever if he had.

QUESTION: Is it your opinion that the feelings of the great mass of the white people of North Carolina are unfriendly to the government of the United States?

ANSWER: Yes, sir, it is; they have no love for it. If you mean by loyalty, acquiescence in what has been accomplished, then they are all loyal; if you mean, on the other hand, that love and affection which a child has for its parent even after he brings the rod of correction upon him, then they have not that feeling. It may come in the course of time.

/   /   /

QUESTION: In your judgment, what effect has been produced by the liberality of the President in granting pardons and amnesties to rebels in that State—what effect upon the public mind?

ANSWER: On my oath I am bound to reply exactly as I believe; that is, that if President Johnson is ever a candidate for re-election he will be supported by the southern States, particularly by North Carolina; but that his liberality to them has drawn them one whit closer to the government than before, I do not believe. It has drawn them to President Johnson personally, and to the democratic party, I suppose.

QUESTION: Has that clemency had any appreciable effect in recovering the real love and affection of that people for the government?

ANSWER: No, sir; not for the government, considered apart from the person of the Executive.

QUESTION: Has it had the contrary effect?

ANSWER: I am not prepared to answer that question, from the fact that they regard President Johnson as having done all this because he was a southern man, and not because he was an officer of the government.

/   /   /

3 | A Sharecrop Contract

The ending of slavery and the impoverishment of the South in the aftermath of the Civil War seriously disrupted Southern agriculture. Five years after the war's end, Southern cotton production was still only about half of what it had been in the 1850s. The large plantations, no longer tended by gangs of slaves or hired freedmen, were broken up into smaller holdings, but the capital required for profitable agriculture meant that control of farming remained centralized in a limited elite of merchants and larger landholders.

Various mechanisms arose to finance Southern agriculture. Tenants worked on leased land. Small landowners gave liens on their crops to get financing. But the most common method of financing agriculture was sharecropping. Agreements like the Grimes family's sharecrop contract determined the economic life of thousands of poor rural families in the southern United States after the Civil War. Families, black and white, lacking capital for agriculture, were furnished the seed, implements, and a line of credit for food and other necessities to keep them through the growing season. Accounts were settled in the winter after crops were in. Under these conditions a small number of farmers managed to make money and eventually became landowners, and the larger part found themselves in ever deeper debt at the end of the year with no choice but to contract again for the next year.

To every one applying to rent land upon shares, the following conditions must be read, and *agreed to.*

To every 30 or 35 acres, I agree to furnish the team, plow, and farming implements, except cotton planters, and I *do not* agree to furnish a cart to every cropper. The croppers are to have half of the cotton, corn and fodder (and peas and pumpkins and potatoes if any are planted) if the following conditions are compiled with, but—if not—they are to have only two fifths ($\frac{2}{5}$). Croppers are to have no part or interest in the cotton seed raised from the crop planted and worked by them. No vine crops of any description, that is, no watermelons, muskmelons, . . . squashes or anything of that kind, except peas and pumpkins, and

From the Grimes Family Papers (#3357), 1882. Held in the Southern Historical Collection, University of North Carolina, Chapel Hill.

potatoes, are to be planted in the cotton or corn. All must work under my direction. All plantation work to be done by the croppers. My part of the crop to be *housed* by them, and the fodder and oats to be hauled and put in the house. All the cotton must be topped about 1st August. If any cropper fails from any cause to save all the fodder from his crop, I am to have enough fodder to make it equal to one half of the whole if the whole amount of fodder had been saved.

For every mule or horse furnished by me there must be 1000 good sized rails . . . hauled, and the fence repaired as far as they will go, the fence to be torn down and put up from the bottom if I so direct. All croppers to haul rails and work on fence whenever I may order. Rails to be split when I may say. Each cropper to clean out every ditch in his crop, and where a ditch runs between two croppers, the cleaning out of that ditch is to be divided equally between them. Every ditch bank in the crop must be shrubbed down and cleaned off before the crop is planted and must be cut down every time the land is worked with his hoe and when the crop is "laid by," the ditch banks must be left clean of bushes, weeds, and seeds. The cleaning out of all ditches must be done by the first of October. The rails must be split and the fence repaired before corn is planted.

Each cropper must keep in good repair all bridges in his crop or over ditches that he has to clean out and when a bridge needs repairing that is outside of all their crops, then any one that I call on must repair it.

Fence jams to be done as ditch banks. If any cotton is planted on the land outside of the plantation fence, I am to have *three fourths* of all the cotton made in those patches, that is to say, no cotton must be planted by croppers in their home patches.

All croppers must clean out stables and fill them with straw, and haul straw in front of stables whenever I direct. All the cotton must be manured, and enough fertilizer must be brought to manure each crop highly, the croppers to pay for one half of all manure bought, the quantity to be purchased for each crop must be left to me.

No cropper to work off the plantation when there is any work to be done on the land he has rented, or when his work is needed by me or other croppers. Trees to be cut down on Orchard, House field & Evanson fences, leaving such as I may designate.

Road field to be planted from the *very edge of the ditch to the fence,* and all the land to be planted close up to the ditches and fences. *No stock of any kind* belonging to croppers to run in the plantation after crops are gathered.

If the fence should be blown down, or if trees should fall on the fence outside of the land planted by any of the croppers, any one or all that I may call upon must put it up and repair it. Every cropper must feed, or have fed, the team he works, Saturday nights, Sundays, and every morning before going to work, beginning to feed his team (morning, noon, and night *every day* in the week) on the day he rents and feeding it to and including the 31st day of December. If any cropper shall from any cause fail to repair his fence as far as 1000 rails will go, or shall fail to clean out any part of his ditches, or shall fail to leave his ditch banks, any part of them, well shrubbed and clean when his crop is laid by, or shall fail to clean out stables, fill them up and haul straw in front of them whenever he is told, he shall have only two-fifths ($\frac{2}{5}$) of the cotton, corn, fodder, peas and pumpkins made on the land he cultivates.

If any cropper shall fail to feed his team Saturday nights, all day Sunday and all the rest of the week, morning/noon, and night, for every time he so fails he must pay me five cents.

No corn nor cotton stalks must be burned, but must be cut down, cut up and plowed in. Nothing must be burned off the land except when it is *impossible* to plow it in.

Every cropper must be responsible for all gear and farming implements placed in his hands, and if not returned must be paid for unless it is worn out by use.

Croppers must sow & plow in oats and haul them to the crib, but *must have no part of them.* Nothing to be sold from their crops, nor fodder nor corn to be carried out of the fields until my rent is all paid, and all amounts they owe me and for which I am responsible are paid in full.

I am to gin & pack all the cotton and charge every cropper an eighteenth of his part, the cropper to furnish his part of the bagging, ties, & twine.

The sale of every cropper's part of the cotton to be made by me when and where I choose to sell, and after deducting all they owe me and all sums that I may be responsible for on their accounts, to pay them their half of the net proceeds. Work of every description, particularly the work on fences and ditches, to be done to my satisfaction, and must be done over until I am satisfied that it is done as it should be.

No wood to burn, nor light wood, nor poles, nor timber for boards, nor wood for any purpose whatever must be gotten above the house occupied by Henry Beasley—nor must any trees be cut down nor any wood used for any purpose, except for firewood, without my permission.

W. SKELTON GLENN ET AL.

4 | On Buffaloes and Indians

The great herds of buffalo on the western plains were essential to the Plains Indians, providing them with food, shelter, and fuel. In the twenty years after the Civil War, though, with buffalo hides in fashion in white society, professional hunters and so-called sportsmen nearly extinguished the species in one of the great ecological disasters in history. It has been estimated that thirteen million animals were exterminated by 1883, when extinction threatened and buffalo became too scarce to be hunted profitably. Ironically, it was principally the herds of buffalo saved for "wild west" shows, such as that of Buffalo Bill Cody, that allowed the limited survival of the species.

In the first reading, W. Skelton Glenn describes commercial buffalo hunting. His 1910 memoirs, which most likely describe a hunt taking place in Texas sometime in 1876 or 1877, provide an account of the buffalo's rapid decline. The second selection, by E. N. Andrews, documents the hunt of buffalo for sport. As Andrews documents the brutality of the kill, he is wistful and somewhat regretful about the encroachment of white civilization onto Native American lands. However, John Cook expresses little sentimental concern about the Native Americans. The fact that the decline of Native Americans was linked to the destruction of their food resources provided an incentive against the conservation of the buffalo herds. Influenced by the conservative Social Darwinism of the late nineteenth century, Cook saw the decline of the buffalo and the Native Americans as a process that not only was inevitable, but that would lead to the establishment of a more advanced civilization on the North American continent.

I have seen their bodies so thick after being skinned, that they would look like logs where a hurricane had passed through a forrest [sic]. If they were lying on a hillside, the rays of the sun would make it look like a hundred glass windows. These buffalo would lie in this way until warm weather, drying up, and I have seen them piled fifty or sixty in a pile where the hunter had made a stand. As the skinner commenced on the edge, he would have to roll it out of the way to have

From Strickland, Rex W., editor, "The Recollections of W. S. Glenn, Buffalo Hunter," Panhandle-Plains Historical Review 22 (1949), pp. 20–26. Courtesy of Panhandle-Plains Historical Society.

room to skin the next, and when finished they would be rolled up as thick as saw logs around a mill. In this way a man could ride over a field and pick out the camps that were making the most money out of the hunt.

These hides, like all other commodities would rise and fall in price and we had to be governed by the prices [in the] East. This man, J. R. Loganstein, that run the hunt, has known them to be shipped to New York, then to Liverpool and back again in order to raise the price or corner the market. . . .

We will now describe a camp outfit. They would range from six to a dozen men, there being one hunter who killed the buffalo and took out the tongues, also the tallow. As the tallow was of an oily nature, it was equal to butter; [it was used] for lubricating our guns and we loaded our own shells, each shell had to be lubricated and [it] was used also for greasing wagons and also for lights in camp. Often chunks as large as an ear of corn were thrown on the fire to make heat. The [i.e., the removal of the tallow] had to be done while the meat was fresh, the hunter throwing it into a tree to wind dry; if the skinner forgot it, it would often stay there all winter and still be good to eat in the spring and better to eat after hanging there in the wind a few days.

We will return to the wagon man. [There were] generally two men to the wagon and their business was to follow up the hunter, if they were not in sight after the hunter had made a killing, he would proceed in their direction until he had met them, and when they would see him, he would signal with his hat where the killing was. If they got to the buffalo when they were fresh, their duty was to take out all the humps, tongues and tallow from the best buffalo. The hunter would then hunt more if they did not have hides enough to make a load or finish their day's work.

A remarkable good hunter would kill seventy-five to a hundred in a day, an average hunter about fifty, and a common one twenty-five, some hardly enough to run a camp. It was just like in any other business. A good skinner would skin from sixty to seventy-five, an average man from thirty to forty, and a common one from fifteen to twenty-five. These skinners were also paid by the hide[,] about five cents less than the hunter was getting for killing, being furnished with a grind stone, knives and steel and a team and wagon. The men were furnished with some kind of a gun, not as valuable as Sharp's rifle, to kill cripples with, also kips and calves that were standing around. In several incidents [instances?] it has been known to happen while the skinner was busy, they would slip up and knock him over. Toward the latter part of the hunt, when all the big ones were killed, I have seen as many as five hundred up to a thousand in a bunch, nothing but calves and have ridden right up to them, if the wind was right.

/   /   /

E. N. ANDREWS*

Excursions over the "Plains" are becoming so common as to excite little or no attention. One can now ride over the broad expanse extending beyond the borders of civilization on the east, to and beyond the Rocky Mountains, in the most elegant coaches drawn by the untiring horse of iron.

In boyhood, when on some gunning excursion for game so infinitesimal as to be unworthy of mention, it was considered unwise to reveal a favorable resort, lest other Nimrods [hunters] should go and steal our honors. But on the occasion referred to in this sketch, having had our views philanthropic enlarged a little, we shall not hesitate to tell, from actual observations, something of the Indian hunting-grounds of the Plains, which form the open porch to the mountains. It will, however, be as impossible to describe the scenes we saw, or the impressions produced, as it is for the poet fully to paint with words all the finer emotions of his soul.

Although these excursions are of common occurrence since the laying of the rails, and will ever continue so, yet to the writer the trip revealed scenes and events altogether new and striking, and such as can never be forgotten. We played a little on the border-lands; while the limitless area, where roam the Indian and his counterpart the buffalo, together with the wolf, the prairie-dog and the antelope, swift of foot, extends hundreds of miles farther westward, and thousands northward and southward.

Our excursion party, organized for the benefit of a church in that place, and numbering about three hundred, left Lawrence, Kansas, Tuesday, A.M., at 10 o'clock, October 6, 1868, by the Kansas Pacific Railway. Our train consisted of five passenger coaches, one smoking car, one baggage and one freight car. The two latter were used for the commissary, although on our way back the freight car was devoted to another purpose.

The Lawrence Cornet Band, which went along, entertained us upon the platform while our large company were undergoing the slow process of shipment. Our engine (all honor to her for having "done what she could") being of rather a consumptive tendency, drew us not very rapidly toward the Occident, especially along the inevitably upward acclivities which lay in her track toward the Rocky Mountains. . . .

There were seventy-five or eighty guns on board, and the writer bagged the first game, namely, one quail, while the train stopped near a plowed field. He does not boast of this, however, as most of the guns were rifles, while he had a shot-and-rifle combined—the right kind for a variety of game. . . .

*From E. N. Andrews, "A Buffalo Hunt by Rail," Kansas Magazine 3 (May 1873), pp. 450–455.

It was now tea time; the day had been comfortable and pleasant. One of those rare sunset scenes which are not uncommon to the people of Kansas, greeted our sight, to describe which were impossible. Suffice it to say, that the golden flood which extended eastward along the northern horizon, gradually ended in a distinctly violet hue, while the dark clouds above seemed to compress this evening glory, as they shut down from above, within the compass of a narrow space, making the scene more intense. But as joy and beauty are often accompanied by tears, so did not this day close without a change. We went on to Ellsworth, where we spent the night, arranging our seats, (for there were no sleeping-cars,) as best we could for a night's rest. At nine o'clock the wind had changed from south to north, and howled frightfully, as if to blow the cars from the track. The rain came, beating through every crevice; the lightning flashed, the temperature became quite cold, and there was a prospect of an uncomfortable night. But fires were kindled, and we rested as well as we could, with feet as high as our heads, while we wished for day.

At 5 o'clock A.M., on Wednesday, we left Ellsworth, near which is Fort Harker, and proceeded. The all-important question, revealing very plainly the thought and desire of all, was: "Where shall we see the buffalo?" "Are there any buffalo about here?" These and similar interrogatories were put to everybody we could find, especially to the colored soldiers or guards at the various water-tanks. When told that we should soon see the "animals," all were on the *qui vive;* the rifles were made ready; all eyes were strained lest some object should escape our notice. And it is no wonder that there was this hopeful expectancy, for most of us had probably never seen the bison, the mythic autocrat of the Plains! Nor did we anticipate a very near proximity to any large number of those animals. For one, however, I ardently desired to see a buffalo, a single one, at least, before the close of my mortal existence, especially since this is so peculiarly an American animal. . . .

We now arrived at Fort Hays and Hays City, the latter a poor gambling-place. Indeed, these frontier towns seem mostly to have been inhabited for the purpose of gambling with and thus robbing men coming in from the mines, or with cattle from over the Plains.

Here we were informed that there were plenty of buffalo twenty-five miles ahead! Could we believe it? We rolled onward on the iron [railroad] track, but looked in vain on either side for the chief object of attraction. A few were seen in the dim distance; but this was an aggravation. We continued to shoot at prairie-dogs, and gathered, when the train stopped at the water-tanks, the cactus,—the kind called prickly-pear. There is also another kind, the sword-cactus, growing in this region. We met another train which had on board several quarters of buffalo-meat, also General Sheridan. But the latter seemed of little account to us buffalo-hunters, just then, since we had seen the tracks or evidences of the "animals." We were now told that ten miles farther on we should find them.

With minds still dubious on the subject, when near the 325th milestone, (counting from State Line on the Missouri River, where the road begins,) we began to see buffalo near at hand , or within a quarter of a mile of the track. But what a sight was gradually unfolded to our vision! In the distance, as if upon a gentle slope, we beheld at least a thousand buffalo feeding, though this was not a circumstance to that which followed. For ten miles vast numbers continued in sight; and not only for this short (?) distance, but for forty miles, buffalo were scattered along the horizon, some nearer and others more remote. In estimating the number, the only fitting word was "innumerable;" one hundred thousand was too small a number, a million would be more correct. Besides, who could tell how many miles those herds, or *the* herd, extended beyond the visible horizon? It were vain to imagine! Antelope and wolves continued to be seen here and there, the latter skulking near the carcasses of buffalo scattered all along the Plains near the track. . . .

Another thing noticeable: what gives to the telegraph-poles in this region that smooth, greasy appearance a few feet from the base? That is where the animals have rubbed themselves when passing. Thanks to you, O Telegraph Company, in behalf of the bison. This is a rare luxury for our shaggy-coated herds which inhabit where no trees are. But while noticing this appearance of the poles, a suggestive thought came into my mind. Is not this pushing and rubbing of the buffalo against the telegraph poles, in his onward march northward or southward over his own long-inhabited feeding-grounds, an effort of his nature to repel the encroachments of civilization, as fitly embodied in this pioneer agency of electricity? So it seemed. And is it strange that the herdsmen of these animals, the red men, should also refuse to stand and look with complacency upon the on-reaching iron trail of the white man, bearing the shrieking locomotive far out into the depths of his hunting-ground, and disturbing the quiet and sanctity of that boundless realm? Without apologizing for the cowardly depredations and hostile demonstrations of the Indian, who was then on the "war-path," we can yet see something that may, from his stand-point, look like a provocation sufficient to warrant all this hostility.

But to return to the actual sights and the sports of our party. At about 6:30 o'clock on Wednesday evening, October 7th, though not anticipating any sport at close quarters, (since we were told that on the morrow the train would return to the hunting-ground, so that we could have all day with the buffalo and hunt to our satisfaction,) when at the 365th mile-post we saw buffalo near at hand. Three bulls were on the left of the track, though nearly all that we had seen were on the right, or north of that barrier, while now on their southward course, feeding in their slow advance toward winter-quarters in Texas or New Mexico. Of those three noble wanderers, one was doomed to fall before the bullets of the excursionists. They all kept pace with the train for at least a quarter of a mile, while the boys blazed away at them without effect. It was their design to get ahead of the train and cross over to the main body of their fellows; and they finally accomplished their object. The cow-catcher, however, became almost a bull-catcher, for it seemed to graze one as he passed on the jump. As soon as the three were well over upon the right, they turned backward, at a small angle away from the train, and then it was that powder and ball were brought into requisition! Shots enough were fired to rout a regiment of men. Ah! see that bull in advance there; he has stopped a second; he turns a kind of reproachful look toward the train; he starts again on the lope a step or two; he hesitates; poises on the right legs; a pail-full of blood gushes warm from his nostrils; he falls flat upon the right side, dead. One of the remaining companions turns a farewell look upon the vanquished one, and then starts off over the prairie toward the herd. We had expected no such *coup d' essai* on that day, expecially so late in the evening, and the pleasure and excitement were all the greater because so unexpected. The engineer was kind enough to shut off the steam; the train stopped, and such a scrambling and screeching was never before heard on the Plains, except among the red men, as we rushed forth to see our first game lying in his gore. The writer had the pleasure of first putting hands on the dark locks of the noble monster who had fallen so bravely. Another distinguished himself by mounting the fallen brave. Then came the ladies; a ring was formed; the cornet band gathered around, and, as if to tantalize the spirits of all departed buffalo, as well as Indians, played Yankee Doodle. I thought that "Hail to the Chief," would have done more honor to the departed.

And now butcher-knives and butchers were in requisition. "Let us eviscerate and carry home this our first captive without further mutilation, that we may give our friends the pleasure of seeing the dimensions of the animal." This seemed a good plan, and we proceeded to carry it out. After the butchers had done their work, a rope was attached to the horns, and the animal, weighing about fifteen hundred pounds, was dragged to the cars and thence lifted on board the freight-car, a few of our party climbing upon the top of the car, the better to pull on the rope. It was now getting dark, and as the head of that huge horned creature was being drawn up to the car-door, I thought I had never before seen any object that came so near my idea of the Prince of Darkness, as it seemed to look out over the crowd who were uplifting him.

"Monstrum horrendum, ingens!"

Our game being thus, after much effort, well bagged, we moved on again with a general feeling of immense satisfaction. "Glory enough for one day," thought we; "now what shall the morrow reveal?" . . .

JOHN R. COOK*

That evening there was a general discussion in regard to the main subject in hunters' minds. Colorado had passed stringent laws that were practically prohibitory against buffalo-killing; the Legislature of Kansas did the same; the Indian Territory was patrolled by United States marshals. And all the venturesome hunters from eastern Colorado, western Kansas, the Platte, Solomon and Republican rivers country came to Texas to follow the chase for buffalo-hides.

The Texas Legislature, while we were here among the herds, to destroy them, was in session at Austin, with a bill drawn up for their protection. General Phil. Sheridan was then in command of the military department of the Southwest, with headquarters at San Antonio. When he heard of the nature of the Texas bill for the protection of the buffaloes, he went to Austin, and, appearing before the joint assembly of the House and Senate, so the story goes, told them that they were making a sentimental mistake by legislating in the interest of the buffalo. He told them that instead of stopping the hunters they ought to give them a hearty, unanimous vote of thanks, and appropriate a sufficient sum of money to strike and present to each one a medal of bronze, with a dead buffalo on one side and a discouraged Indian on the other.

He said: "These men have done in the last two years and will do more in the next year, to settle the vexed Indian question, than the entire regular army has done in the last thirty years. They are destroying the Indians' commissary; and it is a well-known fact that an army losing its base of supplies is placed at a great disadvantage. Send them powder and lead, if you will; but, for the sake of a lasting peace, let them kill, skin, and sell until the buffaloes are exterminated. Then your prairies can be covered with speckled cattle, and the festive cowboy, who follows the hunter as a second forerunner of an advanced civilization."

His words had the desired effect, and for the next three years the American bison traveled through a hail of lead.

The next morning our outfit pulled out south, and that day we caught up with and passed through many straggling bands of these solemn-looking but doomed animals. And thus we traveled by easy stages four days more.

Arriving on the breaks of the Salt fork of the Brazos river, we realized that we were in the midst of the vast sea of animals that caused us gladness and sorrow, joy, trouble and anxiety, but independence, for the succeeding three years. We drove down from the divide, and, finding a fresh spring of water, went into camp at this place. We decided to scout the country around for a suitable place for a permanent camp.

*John R. Cook, The Border and the Buffalo: An Untold Story of the Southwest Plains. (Topeka, Kansas, Crane and Company, 1907), pp. 112–115, 290–291.

/   /   /

I had killed wild turkeys in southwest Missouri, also in southeastern Kansas, and had always looked upon them as a wary game bird. But here, turkey, turkey! Manifesting at all times and places a total indifference to our presence. At first we killed some of them, but after cooking and attempting to eat them we gave it up. Their meat was bitter and sickening, from eating china-berries (the fruit of *Sapindus marginatus,* or soapberry trees).

So we passed and repassed them; and they did the same, and paid no attention whatever to us.

/   /   /

Deer were simply too easy to find; for they were ever present. The same with antelope, bear, panther, mountain lion or cougar, raccoon, polecat, swift coyotes and wolves—they were all here.

And at times I asked myself: "What would you do, John R. Cook, if you had been a child of this wonderfully prolific game region, your ancestors, back through countless ages, according to traditional history, having roamed these vast solitudes as free as the air they breathed? What would you do if some outside interloper should come in and start a ruthless slaughter upon the very soil you had grown from childhood upon, and that you believed you alone had all the rights by occupancy that could possibly be given one? Yes, what would you do?"

But there are two sides to the question. It is simply a case of the survival of the fittest. Too late to stop and moralize now. And sentiment must have no part in our thoughts from this time on. We must have these 3361 hides that this region is to and did furnish us inside of three months, within a radius of eight miles from this main camp. So at it we went. And Hart, whom we will hereafter call Charlie, started out, and in two hours had killed sixty-three bison.

/   /   /

The summer of 1877 is on record as being the last of the Comanches in the role of raiders and scalpers; and we hunters were justly entitled to credit in winding up the Indian trouble in the great State of Texas, so far as the Kiowas and Comanches were concerned. Those Indians had been a standing menace to the settlement of 90,000 square miles of territory in Texas and New Mexico.

And to-day, 1907, it is a pleasing thought to the few surviving hunters of the old Southwest to know that the entire country of the then vast unsettled region is now dotted over with thousands of peaceful, prosperous homes.

/   /   /

The last great slaughter of the buffaloes was during the months of December, 1877, and January, 1878, more than one hundred thousand buffalo-hides being taken by the army of hunters during that fall and winter. That winter and spring many families came onto the range and selected their future homes, and killed buffaloes for hides and meat. More meat was cured that winter than the three previous years all put together.

In the spring of 1877 but few buffalo went north of Red river. The last big band of these fast-diminishing animals that I ever saw was ten miles south of the Mustang Spring, going southwest. They never came north again. And I afterward learned that the remnant of the main herd that were not killed crossed the Rio Grande and took to the hills of Chihuahua in old Mexico. This last view was in February, 1878. During the rest of the time that I was on the range, the hunters could only see a few isolated bands of buffaloes. And if one heard of a herd which contained fifty head he would not only look, but be surprised.

/   /   /

BOB KENNON

5 | From the Pecos to the Powder,
A Cowboy's Autobiography

From the close of the Civil War until the end of the nineteenth century long cattle drives, such as the one Bob Kennon describes in his autobiography, were part of the romantic history of the West. The image of the cowboy with six-shooters and rugged clothes on the trail or in the tough saloons and cow towns is an enduring part of American mythology. And, indeed, even after the end of the era when the teenage Kennon took part in a long drive from Mexico to Montana, the romance survives to color today's view of raising cattle on ranches close to shipping routes. Kennon exemplifies the transition from the long drives to more economically profitable settled ranches; he decided to remain in Montana after making the trek with Don Luis Terrazas's cattle.

Don Luis Terrazas, the cattle king of Chihuahua, was the largest land-holder and cattle breeder in the world at that time. He owned about 1,000,000 head of cattle and branded as high as 200,000 calves in one year at one time. Before the revolution later broke him, he had over 3,000 head of horses in use on his more than 11,000,000 acres of ranches.

Bill Nort, one of the foremen, gave me a job wrangling horses. He was a kindly sort of man who understood and could talk with a kid like me. Taking this job was the turning point of my life. I had only been working there a few months when Mr. Broadus and Mr. Hysham, two cowmen from Montana, together with their foreman, Mr. Baker, came down to buy steers.

They bought two thousand Mexican steers from Terrazas, and Baker was to trail them north to Montana. Baker asked Bill Nort and Tom Cottrell, a Terrazas cowhand, myself, and a few others to come along up the trail. I was willing and anxious to go up the cattle trail at any time. This had been my hope and dream for months. If a fellow had never been up to Montana on a cattle drive, he wasn't considered much of a cowman. I held back, though, until Mr. Broadus agreed to pay me a monthly wage of forty dollars for the trip. Compared with the eighteen dollars I was getting, this seemed like a fortune to me and I told him I'd go all the way.

/   /   /

At last everything was in readiness, the cattle gathered, tallied, and turned over to Broadus and Hysham. With the transaction closed, the wagons loaded with supplies, beds, etc., and the cook fixed out with all his culinary needs, everything was complete for the long trip north. The remuda of horses was gathered, and every cowhand had his own saddle, chaps, and war-bag where he kept his personal belongings.

Early the next morning we crossed the Rio Grande under Terrazas' supervision. After crossing into Texas, Broadus and Hysham gave the orders. We didn't travel fast nor very far in a week's time, and camped at regular intervals, holding the steers on good feed all along the way. Cattle get footsore and leg weary if crowded too hard or handled roughly, and they wanted the steers to reach Montana in good condition.

/   /   /

We had a fine run of luck and were having no serious trouble with the herd. Only the lightning storms caused any worry. We were bound to get these storms, for the weather was getting very hot. You may not know that cattle stampede like hell in a lightning storm. First, they hate the heat and closeness before it breaks, and the distant rumble gets them all worked up. Then the fierce lightning finishes the job. Amid the dust and confusion, even the men get short tempered and go to pieces. Many an old hand claimed that cowboys were likely to go crazy at this time, though few did. Most of them could stand the test; it was a part of their life. The first storm on this drive was the worst, for we didn't seem to be organized just right when it hit us and it came up so quickly out of nowhere.

After the first run, we did our best to get the cattle to milling. If unable to keep them from scattering too much, we would have to ride miles and miles to round them up the next morning, so everyone worked hard. It was a bad thing to have a herd scatter on you and have to spend days rounding them up again.

As quickly as it came up, the storm passed over, and we very luckily got the cattle quieted down. Night passed somehow, and in the morning we hit the trail north again. We had other storms less severe, and we controlled things better.

On our trek north there were a number of rivers to cross. Every crossing was another struggle to get the cattle to take water and swim. The southern rivers were wide and sluggish, but not so with the northern ones. These were swift, with high, steep banks and mostly with clear water except the Missouri, which is always muddy, having many sand bars and treacherous holes because of the constant shifting of its course.

There were other things to worry about, too. Bands of rustlers used to raid just such outfits as ours. They got away with plenty of trail stock and were well organized throughout the years after the first drives came up.

We had a scare one night when a couple of the boys came in and declared they had spotted a bunch of riders waiting for us at the water hole ahead. We were sure they were rustlers. We prepared to shoot it out with them if we had to, but with two thousand steers in our herd, we didn't want any shooting if it could be avoided. They were nowhere in sight when we reached the water hole, nor did we later encounter any of them. For this we thanked our lucky stars. They laid off of us for some good reason. Maybe they thought us just a little outfit until they saw our riders, or perhaps they were waiting for some other outfit, or a more favorable night. Rustlers had a slick way of stampeding a herd, or they would pick a favorable night and surprise the herders. We always doubled our night guard in a dangerous area.

When the grass was good, we trailed the cattle; when it was poor, we shipped them on the railroad until the grass country got better. Baker was a marvel at this and seemed to sense things. I'll say he was the most wonderful trail boss I ever saw, and I've known a lot of them in my years.

The trail we took had been carefully mapped and planned by experienced cattlemen who certainly knew their business. Our trail was like a long rope with its coils and twists, and its tangles were always straightened out. The route shied away from the beaten track near towns except where it was necessary, at certain points, to put the steers in the railway cars.

Once we were properly outfitted, we kept the trail. We thought of nothing but Montana, night and day. We bedded down the cattle at night and then at daylight again started the trek over the prairie. What a sight those old steers would make if we could see them again! Horns tossing as they swam the flood of a swollen stream, they made an unforgettable sight as we pressed on and on toward the north—and Powder River. . . .

/   /   /

Once in a while some fellow would put up a kick to ride into a near-by town. Though we could hardly spare a rider and they'd always get drunk and into trouble when they did get to town, a few of them managed to go. Sometimes when we put the cattle on the cars we could spend a few hours in some little cow town at the bars and cafes. These places were all alike, having plenty of saloons, dance halls, a hotel or two, and a blacksmith shop. There were always buckboards and freight wagons and fine saddle horses tied to the hitching rails. We hated to leave all this, but we remained faithful to our promises and broke up when it was time to ride on. We had started out on a trail-herd job, hundreds of miles of it—the greatest adventure a cowboy could ever have.

Sometimes we'd catch sight of other herds, but we'd keep clear of them. There wasn't a man among us who wanted to mix all those brands. We'd be riding and cutting for days if the stock ever tangled on the trail. We were mighty careful to keep clear of each other, and were plenty tired when we'd graze those steers onto the bed-ground. We'd eat at the chuck wagon, then take turns with the night herd. All we asked was a turn at the bedroll and a chance to pull off our boots for a while. If there was a storm brewing, none of us got any sleep. Baker, as a good trail boss, was a sure judge of not only cattle, trails, and weather, but of the men themselves.

When we came to a crossing, Baker would have the lead steers strewn out free-like, so as not to cause a crowding of the herd. There was never a crush of animals in all that long trip north. One night we had a little trouble with a band of mustangs that somehow got separated from their main band, and they kept us worried for fear they would cause a stampede among our steers.

There was a herd of cattle a few hours ahead of us and we were keeping clear of them to avoid mixing the brands, and they were the ones that caused the trouble. We could see the dust of these critters all day, and that night after we had gotten our steers on the bed-ground these damned mustangs came crossing through the cattle at a great rate. They'd run and nicker, then gallop off with a thundering of hoofs in the night's quiet. We worked for hours keeping them off our territory until some of the riders ran them clear out of the country by morning.

Baker always picked good level ground for a bed-ground. Some inexperienced fellow might insist on running stock into some valley, onto a mountainside, or into a deep coulee, thinking perhaps of shelter, but a steer never picks such a place and neither does a good trail foreman.

He insisted that we not camp too close to the herd and that we keep the camp quiet, too, as far as sudden noises were concerned. We could sing, though, if we wanted to, and the more drony and melancholy it sounded, the better, as it seemed to lull the herd. We took the greatest pains each night on that long trail to water every head of those cattle and give them their fill of grass. It was all this that added up to success in the end.

The trail itself, as I've said, was well planned for us. It lay across the tablelands, or mesas, of West Texas and into Kansas, crossed part of the old Santa Fe Trail near Dodge City, then led onward to the North Platte, keeping clear of Ogallala, that big cow town full of fun and trouble for a bunch of cowboys on a trail drive. We skirted the Black Hills and went on into Montana. We varied somewhat in later drives as herd men found it was far better to avoid all towns unless there were stockyards there. At any rate, these shipping places were nearly all at a distance outside the towns themselves.

We unloaded the steers for the last time at Wichita, Kansas, and took them on across Kansas by trail, then across the North Platte River and the sand hills of Nebraska. On northwest of Deadwood, South Dakota, we traveled for about forty or fifty miles, going by Devils Tower and the Belle Fourche country. Belle Fourche was a cowman's country in the brakes of the Little Missouri where there was an abundance of fine feed.

We were getting excited by this time. No one seemed tired any more. In our minds we were already spending our pay in Miles City, and nothing could dampen our spirits. We were getting mighty tired of looking at those steers, and yet we had come so far together they seemed like old friends.

We came on down Little Cottonwood and at last crossed the Powder River. We were sure happy at the sight of it, and if we hadn't been trailing those two thousand steers and afraid of stampeding them, we'd have shot into the air to celebrate our arrival, for every cowman's slogan was "Powder River or bust." Though we'd been in Montana for several days, no one could really believe it until we had crossed the Powder.

After crossing, we went over to the Broadus holdings, which were in close on the other side. The town of Broadus was established here on the old site of this ranch. We crossed the Little Powder at the Half Circle Cross Ranch, then went down the Mizpah and on to Miles City. We were now nearing the end of our long trail and coming to the beautiful Yellowstone River. We had practically the same bunch of men we had started with from Mexico with the exception of cooks, for we had had about five different cooks since starting. They would begin drinking at stops along the way and the boss would fire one and hire another. We swam the herd and remuda across the Yellowstone while the wagons were ferried across, and our job was done. The steers were sold to different parties, some to a Mr. B. K. Holt, some to the Bow and Arrow outfit, and some to several others whom I cannot recall.

We were wild to have our freedom, and now, at last, we were one happy bunch of cowpunchers when Broadus and Hysham paid us off. Miles City was a wide-open town if I ever saw one, but cleaner than El Paso, and without such fights. We had plenty to drink, for there were many saloons, beer halls, and dance halls with girls. Our money melted like snow in the sun. There were some of the finest people living there in Miles City I ever saw.

6 | Deadwood Dick

While Afro-Americans rarely appear in "Westerns" as anything but cooks and clowns, about twenty to twenty-five percent of the cowboys who drove cattle on the long trails were black, as were a similar proportion of western cavalrymen in the United States Army during the taming of the last Native American frontier.

The most famous of the Afro-American cowboys—famous in part because he wrote a vivid autobiography—was Nat Love, who became known as Dead-wood Dick. Born a slave in 1854, he "struck out of Kansas" in 1869 to escape discrimination and the lack of schools for black children. On the cow trails, though, Nat found race to be no barrier. He shot and boasted with the best and became an expert "Indian fighter."

The era of the cattle trails was short. By the late 1880s, railroads had replaced cowpunchers in moving western beef to Eastern consumers. Nat Love quit the trails in 1890 and found that the best opportunity for a black man—even in the West—was as a Pullman car porter.

We arrived in Deadwood in good condition without having had any trouble with the Indians on the way up. We turned our cattle over to their new owners at once, then proceeded to take in the town. The next morning, July 4th, the gamblers and mining men made up a purse of $200 for a roping contest between the cow boys that were then in town, and as it was a holiday nearly all the cow boys for miles around were assembled there that day. It did not take long to arrange the details for the contest and contestants, six of them being colored cow boys, including myself. Our trail boss was chosen to pick out the mustangs from a herd of wild horses just off the range, and he picked out twelve of the most wild and vicious horses that he could find.

The conditions of the contest were that each of us who were mounted was to rope, throw, tie, bridle and saddle and mount the particular horse picked for us in the shortest time possible. The man accomplishing the feat in the quickest time to be declared the winner.

Nat Love, The Life and Adventures of Nat Love Better Known in the Cattle Country as "Deadwood Dick" by Himself (*Los Angeles, 1907*), pp. 91, 93, 95, 97–99, 101, 103–105.

It is a violation of the law to reproduce this selection by any means whatsoever without the written permission of the copyright holder.

It seems to me that the horse chosen for me was the most vicious of the lot. Everything being in readiness, the "45" cracked and we all sprang forward together, each of us making for our particular mustang.

I roped, threw, tied, bridled, saddled and mounted my mustang in exactly nine minutes from the crack of the gun. The time of the next nearest competitor was twelve minutes and thirty seconds. This gave me the record and championship of the West, which I held up to the time I quit the business in 1890, and my record has never been beaten. It is worthy of passing remark that I never had a horse pitch with me so much as that mustang, but I never stopped sticking my spurs in him and using my quirt on his flanks until I proved his master. Right there the assembled crowd named me Deadwood Dick and proclaimed me champion roper of the western cattle country.

The roping contest over, a dispute arose over the shooting question with the result that a contest was arranged for the afternoon, as there happened to be some of the best shots with rifle and revolver in the West present that day. Among them were Stormy Jim, who claimed the championship; Powder Horn Bill, who had the reputation of never missing what he shot at; also White Head, a half breed, who generally hit what he shot at, and many other men who knew how to handle a rifle or 45-Colt.

The range was measured off 100 and 250 yards for the rifle and 150 for the Colt 45. At this distance a bull's-eye about the size of an apple was put up. Each man was to have 14 shots at each range with the rifle and 12 shots with the Colts 45. I placed every one of my 14 shots with the rifle in the bulls-eye with ease, all shots being made from the hip; but with the 45-Colts I missed it twice, only placing 10 shots in the small circle, Stormy Jim being my nearest competitor, only placing 8 bullets in the bull's-eye clear, the rest being quite close, while with the 45 he placed 5 bullets in the charmed circle. This gave me the championship of rifle and revolver shooting as well as the roping contest, and for that day I was the hero of Deadwood, and the purse of $200 which I had won on the roping contest went toward keeping things moving, and they did move as only a large crowd of cattle men can move things. This lasted for several days when most of the cattle men had to return to their respective ranches, as it was the busy season, accordingly our outfit began to make preparations to return to Arizona.

In the meantime news had reached us of the Custer massacre (June 1876), and the indignation and sorrow was universal, as General Custer was personally known to a large number of the cattle men of the West. But we could do nothing now, as the Indians were out in such strong force. There was nothing to do but let Uncle Sam revenge the loss of the General and his brave command, but it is safe to say not one of us would have hesitated a moment in taking the trail in pursuit of the bloodthirsty red skins had the opportunity offered. Everything now being in readiness with us we took the trail homeward bound, and left Deadwood in a blaze of glory. On our way home we visited the Custer battle field in the Little Big Horn Basin.

There was ample evidence of the desperate and bloody fight that had taken place a few days before. We arrived home in Arizona in a short time without further incident, except that on the way back we met and talked with many of the famous Government scouts of that region, among them Buffalo Bill (William F. Cody), Yellowstone Kelley, and many others of that day, some of whom are now living, while others lost their lives in the line of duty, and a finer or braver body of men never lived than these scouts of the West. It was my pleasure to meet Buffalo Bill often in the early 70s, and he was as fine a man as one could wish to meet, kind, generous, true and brave.

Buffalo Bill got his name from the fact that in the early days he was engaged in hunting buffalo for their hides and furnishing U. P. Railroad graders with meat, hence the name Buffalo Bill. Buffalo Bill, Yellowstone Kelley, with many others were at this time serving under Gen. C. C. Miles.

The name of Deadwood Dick was given to me by the people of Deadwood, South Dakota [the Dakota Territory], July 4, 1876, after I had proven myself worthy to carry it, and after I had defeated all comers in riding, roping, and shooting, and I have always carried the name with honor since that time.

We arrived at the home ranch again on our return from the trip to Deadwood about the middle of September, it taking us a little over two months to make the return journey, as we stopped in Cheyenne for several days and at other places, where we always found a hearty welcome, especially so on this trip, as the news had preceded us, and I received enough attention to have given me the big head, but my head had constantly refused to get enlarged again ever since the time I sampled the demijohn in the sweet corn patch at home.

Arriving at home, we received a send off from our boss and our comrades of the home ranch, every man of whom on hearing the news turned loose his voice and his artillery in a grand demonstration in my honor.

But they said it was no surprise to them, as they had long known of my ability with the rope, rifle and 45 Colt, but just the same it was gratifying to know I had defeated the best men of the West, and brought the record home to the home ranch in Arizona. After a good rest we proceeded to ride the range again, getting our herds in good condition for the winter now at hand.

/   /   /

It was a bright clear fall day, October 4, 1876, that quite a large number of us boys started out over the range hunting strays which had been lost for some time. We had scattered over the range and I was riding along alone when all at once I heard the well known Indian war whoop and noticed not far away a large party of Indians making straight for me. They were all well mounted and they were in full war paint, which showed me that they were on the war path, and as I was alone and had no wish to be scalped by them I decided to run for it. So I headed for Yellow Horse Canyon and gave my horse the rein, but as I had considerable objection to being chased by a lot of painted savages without some remonstrance, I turned in my saddle every once in a while and gave them a shot by way of greeting, and I had the satisfaction of seeing a painted brave tumble from his horse and go rolling in the dust every time my rifle spoke, and the Indians were by no means idle all this time, as their bullets were singing around me rather lively, one of them passing through my thigh, but it did not amount to much. Reaching Yellow Horse Canyon, I had about decided to stop and make a stand when one of their bullets caught me in the leg, passing clear through it and then through my horse, killing him. Quickly falling behind him I used his dead body for a breast work and stood the Indians off for a long time, as my aim was so deadly and they had lost so many that they were careful to keep out of range.

But finally my ammunition gave out, and the Indians were quick to find this out, and they at once closed in on me, but I was by no means subdued, wounded as I was and almost out of my head, and I fought with my empty gun until finally overpowered. When I came to my senses I was in the Indians' camp.

My wounds had been dressed with some kind of herbs, the wound in my breast just over the heart was covered thickly with herbs and bound up. My nose had been nearly cut off, also one of my fingers had been nearly cut off. These wounds I received when I was fighting my captors with my empty gun. What caused them to spare my life I cannot tell, but it was I think partly because I had proved myself a brave man, and all savages admire a brave man and when they captured a man whose fighting powers were out of the ordinary they generally kept him if possible as he was needed in the tribe.

Then again Yellow Dog's tribe was composed largely of half breeds, and there was a large percentage of colored blood in the tribe, and as I was a colored man they wanted to keep me, as they thought I was too good a man to die. Be that as it may, they dressed my wounds and gave me plenty to eat, but the only grub they had was buffalo meat which they cooked over a fire of buffalo chips,* but of this I had all I wanted to eat. For the first two days after my capture they kept me tied hand and foot. At the end of that time they untied my feet, but kept my hands tied for a couple of days longer, when I was given my freedom, but was always closely watched by members of the tribe. Three days after my capture my ears were pierced and I was adopted into the tribe. The operation of piercing my ears was quite painful, in the method used, as they had a small bone secured from a deer's leg, a small thin bone, rounded at the end and as sharp as a needle. This they used to make the holes, then strings made from the tendons of a deer were inserted in place of thread, of which the Indians had none. Then horn ear rings

*Dried buffalo manure, commonly used as fuel

were placed in my ears and the same kind of salve made from herbs which they placed on my wounds was placed on my ears and they soon healed.

The bullet holes in my leg and breast also healed in a surprisingly short time. That was good salve all right. As soon as I was well enough I took part in the Indian dances. One kind or another was in progress all the time. The war dance and the medicine dance seemed the most popular. When in the war dance the savages danced around me in a circle, making gestures, chanting, with every now and then a blood curdling yell, always keeping time to a sort of music provided by stretching buffalo skins tightly over a hoop.

When I was well enough I joined the dances, and I think I soon made a good dancer. The medicine dance varies from the war dance only that in the medicine dance the Indians danced around a boiling pot, the pot being filled with roots and water and they dance around it while it boils. The medicine dance occurs about daylight.

I very soon learned their ways and to understand them, though our conversation was mostly carried on by means of signs. They soon gave me to understand that I was to marry the chief's daughter, promising me 100 ponies to do so, and she was literally thrown in my arms; as for the lady she seemed perfectly willing if not anxious to become my bride. She was a beautiful woman, or rather girl; in fact all the squaws of this tribe were good looking, out of the ordinary, but I had other notions just then and did not want to get married under such circumstances, but for prudence sake I seemed to enter into their plans, but at the same time keeping a sharp lookout for a chance to escape. I noted where the Indians kept their horses at night, even picking out the handsome and fleet Indian pony which I meant to use should opportunity occur, and I seemed to fall in with the Indians' plans and seemed to them so contented that they gave me more and more freedom and relaxed the strict watch they had kept on me, and finally in about thirty days from the time of my capture my opportunity arrived.

My wounds were now nearly well, and gave me no trouble. It was a dark, cloudy night, and the Indians, grown careless in their fancied security, had relaxed their watchfulness. After they had all thrown themselves on the ground and the quiet of the camp proclaimed them all asleep I got up and crawling on my hands and knees, using the greatest caution for fear of making a noise, I crawled about 250 yards to where the horses were picketed, and going to the Indian pony I had already picked out I slipped the skin thong in his mouth which the Indians use for a bridle, one which I had secured and carried in my shirt for some time for this particular purpose, then springing to his back I made for the open prairie in the direction of the home ranch in Texas, one hundred miles away. All that night I rode as fast as my horse could carry me and the next morning, twelve hours after I left the Indians camp I was safe on the home ranch again. And my joy was without bounds, and such a reception as I received from the boys.

They said they were just one day late, and if it hadn't been for a fight they had with some of the same tribe, they would have been to my relief. As it was they did not expect to ever see me again alive. But that they know that if the Indians did not kill me, and gave me only half a chance I would get away from them, but now that I was safe home again, nothing mattered much and nothing was too good for me.

It was a mystery to them how I managed to escape death with such wounds as I had received, the marks of which I will carry to my grave and it is as much a mystery to me as the bullet that struck me in the breast just over the heart passed clear through, coming out my back just below the shoulder. Likewise the bullet in my leg passed clear through, then through my horse, killing him.

Those Indians are certainly wonderful doctors, and then I am naturally tough as I carry the marks of fourteen bullet wounds on different part of my body, most any one of which would be sufficient to kill an ordinary man, but I am not even crippled. It seems to me that if ever a man bore a charm I am the man, as I have had five horses shot from under me and killed, have fought Indians and Mexicans in all sorts of situations, and have been in more tight places than I can number. Yet I have always managed to escape with only the mark of a bullet or knife as a reminder. The fight with the Yellow Dog's tribe is probably the closest call I ever had, and as close a call as I ever want.

The fleet Indian pony which carried me to safety on that memorable hundred mile ride, I kept for about five years. I named him "The Yellow Dog Chief." And he lived on the best the ranch afforded, until his death which occurred in 1881, never having anything to do except an occasional race, as he could run like a deer. I thought too much of him to use him on the trail and he was the especial pet of every one on the home ranch, and for miles around.

I heard afterwards that the Indians pursued me that night for quite a distance, but I had too much the start and besides I had the fastest horse the Indians owned. I have never since met any of my captors of that time. As they knew better than to venture in our neighborhood again. My wound healed nicely, thanks to the good attention the Indians gave me. My captors took everything of value I had on me when captured. My rifle which I especially prized for old associations sake; also my forty-fives, saddle and bridle, in fact my whole outfit leaving me only the few clothes I had on at the time.

My comrades did not propose to let this bother me long, however, because they all chipped in and bought me a new outfit, including the best rifle and revolvers that could be secured, and I had my pick of the ranch horses for another mount. During my short stay with the Indians I learned a great deal about them, their ways of living, sports, dances, and mode of warfare which proved of great benefit to me in after years. The oblong shields they carried were made from tanned buffalo skins and so tough were they made that an arrow would not pierce them although I have seen them shoot an arrow clean through a buffalo. Neither will a bullet pierce them unless the ball hits the shield square on, otherwise it glances off.

All of them were exceedingly expert with the bow and arrow, and they are proud of their skill and are always practicing in an effort to excel each other. This rivalry extends even to the children who are seldom without their bows and arrows.

They named me Buffalo Papoose, and we managed to make our wants known by means of signs. As I was not with them a sufficient length of time to learn their language, I learned from them that I had killed five of their number and wounded three while they were chasing me and in the subsequent fight with my empty gun. The wounded men were hit in many places, but they were brought around all right, the same as I was. After my escape and after I arrived home it was some time before I was again called to active duty, as the boys would not hear of me doing anything resembling work, until I was thoroughly well and rested up. But I soon began to long for my saddle and the range.

And when orders were received at the ranch for 2000 head of cattle, to be delivered at Dodge City, Kansas, I insisted on taking the trail again. It was not with any sense of pride or in bravado that I recount here the fate of the men who have fallen at my hand.

It is a terrible thing to kill a man no matter what the cause. But as I am writing a true history of my life, I cannot leave these facts out. But every man who died at my hands was either seeking my life or died in open warfare, when it was a case of killing or being killed.

ZITKALA-SÄ
(GERTRUDE SIMMONS BONNIN)

7 | The School Days of an Indian Girl

From the mid 1880s to the 1930s the thrust of American Indian policy was to assimilate Native Americans into the larger society. As part of this effort, boarding schools for Native American children became a common strategy for inducting promising young Native Americans into white culture. Zitkala-Sä, or Red Bird (1876–1938), a Sioux from the Yankton reservation in South Dakota, in describing her experiences at a Quaker missionary school for Native Americans in Wabash, Indiana, which she attended from ages eight to eleven, remarks ironically that she returned to the reservation "neither a wild Indian nor a tame one."

To resolve this painful cultural dislocation, Red Bird returned to the school four years later to complete the course of study and then attended Earlham College in Richmond, Indiana, acquiring somehow both the capacity to succeed in the white world and a firm grip on her Native American heritage. She wrote of her experience in a series of magazine articles, as well as a book, Old Indian Legends, *returned to the Sioux country, married a Sioux, and began a lifetime of work to improve the status and condition of Native Americans. In a long career that ended with her death in 1938, she played an influential role in the organization of the Native American communities that led to major reforms in the New Deal era of the 1930s.*

The first turning away from the easy, natural flow of my life occurred in an early spring. It was in my eighth year; in the month of March, I afterward learned. At this age I know but one language, and that was my mother's native tongue.

From some of my playmates I heard that two paleface missionaries were in our village. They were from that class of white men who wore big hats and carried large hearts, they said. Running direct to my mother, I began to question her why these two strangers were among us. She told me, after I had teased much, that they had come to take away Indian boys and girls to the East. My mother did not seem to want me to talk about them. But in a day or two, I gleaned many wonderful stories from my playfellows concerning the strangers.

Zitkala-Sä (Gertrude Simmons Bonnin), "The School Days of an Indian Girl," Atlantic Monthly, *Volume 89 (1900) January-March, pp. 45–47, 190, 192–194.*

"Mother, my friend Judéwin is going home with the missionaries. She is going to a more beautiful country than ours; the palefaces told her so!" I said wistfully, wishing in my heart that I too might go.

Mother sat in a chair, and I was hanging on her knee. Within the last two seasons my big brother Dawée had returned from a three years' education in the East, and his coming back influenced my mother to take a farther step from her native way of living. First it was a change from the buffalo skin to the white man's canvas that covered our wigwam. Now she had given up her wigwam of slender poles, to live, a foreigner, in a home of clumsy logs.

"Yes, my child, several others besides Judéwin are going away with the palefaces. Your brother said the missionaries had inquired about his little sister," she said, watching my face very closely.

My heart thumped so hard against my breast, I wondered if she could hear it.

"Did he tell them to take me, mother?" I asked, fearing lest Dawée had forbidden the palefaces to see me, and that my hope of going to the Wonderland would be entirely blighted.

With a sad, slow smile, she answered: "There! I knew you were wishing to go, because Judéwin has filled your ears with the white men's lies. Don't believe a word they say! Their words are sweet, but, my child, their deeds are bitter. You will cry for me, but they will not even soothe you. Stay with me, my little one! Your brother Dawée says that going East, away from your mother, is too hard an experience for his baby sister."

Thus my mother discouraged my curiosity about the lands beyond our eastern horizon; for it was not yet an ambition for Letters that was stirring me. But on the following day the missionaries did come to our very house. I spied them coming up the footpath leading to our cottage. A third man was with them, but he was not my brother Dawée. It was another, a young interpreter, a paleface who had a smattering of the Indian language. I was ready to run out to meet them, but I did not dare to displease my mother. With great glee, I jumped up and down on our ground floor. I begged my mother to open the door, that they would be sure to come to us. Alas! They came, they saw, and they conquered!

Judéwin had told me of the great tree where grew red, red apples; and how we could reach out our hands and pick all the red apples we could eat. I had never seen apple trees. I had never tasted more than a dozen red apples in my life; and when I heard of the orchards of the East, I was eager to roam among them. The missionaries smiled into my eyes, and patted my head. I wondered how mother could say such hard words against them.

"Mother, ask them if little girls may have all the red apples they want, when they go East," I whispered aloud in my excitement.

The interpreter heard me, and answered: "Yes, little girl, the nice red apples are for those who pick them; and you will have a ride on the iron horse if you go with these good people."

I had never seen a train, and he knew it.

"Mother, I'm going East! I like big red apples, and I want to ride on the iron horse! Mother, say yes!" I pleaded.

My mother said nothing. The missionaries waited in silence; and my eyes began to blur with tears, though I struggled to choke them back. The corners of my mouth twitched, and my mother saw me.

"I am not ready to give you any word," she said to them. "To-morrow I shall send you my answer by my son."

With this they left us. Alone with my mother, I yielded to my tears, and cried aloud, shaking my head so as not to hear what she was saying to me. This was the first time I had ever been so unwilling to give up my own desire that I refused to hearken to my mother's voice.

There was a solemn silence in our home that night. Before I went to bed I begged the Great Spirit to make my mother willing I should go with the missionaries.

The next morning came, and my mother called me to her side. "My daughter, do you still persist in wishing to leave your mother?" she asked.

"Oh, mother, it is not that I wish to leave you, but I want to see the wonderful Eastern land," I answered.

My dear old aunt came to our house that morning, and I heard her say, "Let her try it."

I hoped that, as usual, my aunt was pleading on my side. My brother Dawée came for mother's decision. I dropped my play, and crept close to my aunt.

"Yes, Dawée, my daughter, though she does not understand what it all means, is anxious to go. She will need an education when she is grown, for then there will be fewer real Dakotas, and many more pale-faces: This tearing her away, so young, from her mother is necessary, if I would have her an educated woman. The palefaces, who owe us a large debt for stolen lands, have begun to pay a tardy justice in offering some education to our children. But I know my daughter must suffer keenly in this experiment. For her sake, I dread to tell you my reply to the missionaries. Go, tell them that they may take my little daughter, and that the Great Spirit shall not fail to reward them according to their hearts."

Wrapped in my heavy blanket, I walked with my mother to the carriage that was soon to take us to the iron horse. I was happy. I met my playmates, who were also wearing their best thick blankets. We showed one another our new beaded moccasins, and the width of the belts that girdled our new dresses. Soon we were being drawn rapidly away by the white man's horses. When I saw the lonely fig-ure of my mother vanish in the distance, a sense of regret settled heavily upon me. I felt suddenly weak, as if I might fall limp to the ground. I was in the hands of strangers whom my mother did not fully trust. I no longer felt free to be myself, or to voice my own feel-ings. The tears trickled down my cheeks, and I buried my face in the folds of my blanket. Now the first step, parting me from my mother, was taken, and all my belated tears availed nothing.

Having driven thirty miles to the ferryboat, we crossed the Missouri in the evening. Then riding again a few miles eastward, we stopped before a massive brick building. I looked at it in amazement, and with a vague misgiving, for in our village I had never seen so large a house. Trembling with fear and distrust of the palefaces, my teeth chattering from the chilly ride, I crept noiselessly in my soft moccasins along the narrow hall, keeping very close to the bare wall. I was as frightened and bewildered as the captured young of a wild creature.

THE CUTTING OF MY LONG HAIR.

The first day in the land of apples was a bitter-cold one; for the snow still covered the ground, and the trees were bare. A large bell rang for breakfast, its loud metallic voice crashing through the belfry overhead and into our sensitive ears. The annoying clatter of shoes on bare floors gave us no peace. The constant clash of harsh noises, with an undercurrent of many voices murmuring an unknown tongue, made a bedlam within which I was securely tied. And though my spirit tore itself in struggling for its lost freedom, all was useless.

A paleface woman, with white hair, came up after us. We were placed in a line of girls who were marching into the dining room. These were Indian girls, in stiff shoes and closely clinging dresses. The small girls wore sleeved aprons and shingled hair. As I walked noiselessly in my soft moccasins, I felt like sinking to the floor, for my blanket had been stripped from my shoulders. I looked hard at the Indian girls, who seemed not to care that they were even more immodestly dressed than I, in their tightly fitting clothes. While we marched in, the boys entered at an opposite door. I watched for the three young braves who came in our party. I spied them in the rear ranks, looking as uncomfortable as I felt.

A small bell was tapped, and each of the pupils drew a chair from under the table. Supposing this act meant they were to be seated, I pulled out mine and at once slipped into it from one side. But when I turned my head, I saw that I was the only one seated, and all the rest at our table remained standing. Just as I began to rise, looking shyly around to see how chairs were to be used, a second bell was sounded. All were seated at last, and I had to crawl back into my chair again. I heard a man's voice at one end of the hall, and I looked around to see him. But all the others hung their heads over their plates. As I glanced at the long chain of tables, I caught the eyes of a paleface woman upon me. Immediately I dropped my eyes, wondering why I was so keenly watched by the strange woman. The man ceased his mutterings, and then a third bell was tapped. Every one picked up his knife and fork and began eating. I began crying instead, for by this time I was afraid to venture anything more.

But this eating by formula was not the hardest trial in that first day. Late in the morning, my friend Judéwin gave me a terrible warning. Judéwin knew a few words of English; and she had overhead the paleface woman talk about cutting our long, heavy hair. Our mothers had taught us that only unskilled warriors who were captured had their hair shingled by the enemy. Among our people, short hair was worn by mourners, and shingled hair by cowards!

We discussed our fate some moments, and when Judéwin said, "We have to submit, because they are strong," I rebelled.

"No, I will not submit! I will struggle first!" I answered.

I watched my chance, and when no one noticed I disappeared. I crept up the stairs as quietly as I could in my squeaking shoes,— my moccasins had been exchanged for shoes. Along the hall I passed, without knowing whither I was going. Turning aside to an open door, I found a large room with three white beds in it. The windows were covered with dark green curtains, which made the room very dim. Thankful that no one was there, I directed my steps toward the corner farthest from the door. On my hands and knees I crawled under the bed, and cuddled myself in the dark corner.

From my hiding place I peered out, shuddering with fear whenever I heard footsteps near by. Though in the hall loud voices were calling my name, and I knew that even Judéwin was searching for me, I did not open my mouth to answer. Then the steps were quickened and the voices became excited. The sounds came nearer and nearer. Women and girls entered the room. I held my breath and watched them open closet doors and peep behind large trunks. Some one threw up the curtains, and the room was filled with sudden light. What caused them to stoop and look under the bed I do not know. I remember being dragged out, though I resisted by kicking and scratching wildly. In spite of myself, I was carried downstairs and tied fast in a chair.

I cried aloud, shaking my head all the while until I felt the cold blades of the scissors against my neck, and heard them gnaw off one of my thick braids. Then I lost my spirit. Since the day I was taken from my mother I had suffered extreme indignities. People had stared at me. I had been tossed about in the air like a wooden puppet. And now my long hair was shingled like a coward's! In my anguish I moaned for my mother, but no one came to comfort me. Not a soul reasoned quietly with me, as my own mother used to do; for now I was only one of many little animals driven by a herder.

IRON ROUTINE.

A loud-clamoring bell awakened us at half past six in the cold winter mornings. From happy dreams of Western rolling lands and unlassoed freedom we tumbled out upon chilly bare floors back again into a paleface day. We had short time to jump into our shoes and clothes, and wet our eyes with icy water, before a small hand bell was vigorously rung for roll call.

There were too many drowsy children and too numerous orders for the day to waste a moment in any apology to nature for giving her children such a shock in the early morning. We rushed downstairs, bounding over two high steps at a time, to land in the assembly room.

A paleface woman, with a yellow-covered roll book open on her arm and a gnawed pencil in her hand, appeared at the door. Her small, tired face was coldly lighted with a pair of large gray eyes.

She stood still in a halo of authority, while over the rim of her spectacles her eyes pried nervously about the room. Having glanced at her long list of names and called out the first one, she tossed up her chin and peered through the crystals of the spectacles to make sure of the answer "Here."

Relentlessly her pencil black-marked our daily records if we were not present to respond to our names, and no chum of ours had done it successfully for us. No matter if a dull headache or the painful cough of slow consumption had delayed the absentee, there was only time enough to mark the tardiness. It was next to impossible to leave the iron routine after the civilizing machine had once begun its day's buzzing; and as it was inbred in me to suffer in silence rather than to appeal to the ears of one whose open eyes could not see my pain, I have many times trudged in the day's harness heavy-footed, like a dumb sick brute.

Once I lost a dear classmate. I remember well how she used to mope along at my side, until one morning she could not raise her head from her pillow. At her deathbed I stood weeping, as the paleface woman sat near her moistening the dry lips. Among the folds of the bedclothes I saw the open pages of the white man's Bible. The dying Indian girl talked disconnectedly of Jesus the Christ and the paleface who was cooling her swollen hands and feet.

I grew bitter, and censured the woman for cruel neglect of our physical ills. I despised the pencils that moved automatically, and the one teaspoon which dealt out, from a large bottle, healing to a row of variously ailing Indian children. I blamed the hard-working, well-meaning, ignorant woman who was inculcating in our hearts her superstitious ideas. Though I was sullen in all my little troubles, as soon as I felt better I was ready again to smile upon the cruel woman. Within a week I was again actively testing the chains which tightly bound my individuality like a mummy for burial.

The melancholy of those black days has left so long a shadow that it darkens the path of years that have since gone by. These sad memories rise above those of smoothly grinding school days. Perhaps my Indian nature is the moaning wind which stirs them now for their present record. But, however tempestuous this is within me, it comes out as the low voice of a curiously colored seashell, which is only for those ears that are bent with compassion to hear it.

INCURRING MY MOTHER'S DISPLEASURE.

In the second journey to the East I had not come without some precautions. I had a secret interview with one of our best medicine men, and when I left his wigwam I carried securely in my sleeve a tiny bunch of magic roots. This possession assured me of friends wherever I should go. So absolutely did I believe in its charms that I wore it through all the school routine for more than a year. Then, before I lost my faith in the dead roots, I lost the little buckskin bag containing all my good luck.

At the close of this second term of three years I was the proud owner of my first diploma. The following autumn I ventured upon a college career against my mother's will.

I had written for her approval, but in her reply I found no encouragement. She called my notice to her neighbors' children, who had completed their education in three years. They had returned to their homes, and were then talking English with the frontier settlers. Her few words hinted that I had better give up my slow attempt to learn the white man's ways, and be content to roam over the prairies and find my living upon wild roots. I silenced her by deliberate disobedience.

Thus, homeless and heavy-hearted, I began anew my life among strangers.

As I hid myself in my little room in the college dormitory, away from the scornful and yet curious eyes of the students, I pined for sympathy. Often I wept in secret, wishing I had gone West, to be nourished by my mother's love, instead of remaining among a cold race whose hearts were frozen hard with prejudice.

During the fall and winter seasons I scarcely had a real friend, though by that time several of my classmates were courteous to me at a safe distance.

My mother had not yet forgiven my rudeness to her, and I had no moment for letter-writing. By daylight and lamplight, I spun with reeds and thistles, until my hands were tired from their weaving, the magic design which promised me the white man's respect.

At length, in the spring term, I entered an oratorical contest among the various classes. As the day of competition approached, it did not seem possible that the event was so near at hand, but it came. In the chapel the classes assembled together, with their invited guests. The high platform was carpeted, and gayly festooned with college colors. A bright white light illumined the room, and outlined clearly the great polished beams that arched the domed ceiling. The assembled crowds filled the air with pulsating murmurs. When the hour for speaking arrived all were hushed. But on the wall the old clock which pointed out the trying moment ticked calmly on.

One after another I saw and heard the orators. Still, I could not realize that they longed for the favorable decision of the judges as much as I did. Each contestant received a loud burst of applause, and some were cheered heartily. Too soon my turn came, and I paused a moment behind the curtains for a deep breath. After my concluding words, I hear the same applause that the others had called out.

Upon my retreating steps, I was astounded to receive from my fellow students a large bouquet of roses tied with flowing ribbons. With the lovely flowers I fled from the stage. This friendly token was a rebuke to me for the hard feelings I had borne them.

Later, the decision of the judges awarded me the first place. Then there was a mad uproar in the hall, where my classmates sang and shouted my name at the top of their lungs; and the disappointed students howled and brayed in fearfully dissonant tin trumpets. In this excitement, happy students rushed forward to offer their congratulations. And I could not conceal a smile when they wished to escort me in a procession to the students' parlor, where all were going to calm themselves. Thanking them for the kind spirit which prompted them to make such a proposition, I walked alone with the night to my own little room.

A few weeks afterward, I appeared as the college representative in another contest. This time the competition was among orators from different colleges in our state. It was held at the state capital, in one of the largest opera houses.

Here again was a strong prejudice against my people. In the evening, as the great audience filled the house, the student bodies began warring among themselves. Fortunately, I was spared witnessing any of the noisy wrangling before the contest began. The slurs against the Indian that stained the lips of our opponents were already burning like a dry fever within my breast.

But after the orations were delivered a deeper burn awaited me. There, before that vast ocean of eyes, some college rowdies threw out a large white flag, with a drawing of a most forlorn Indian girl on it. Under this they had printed in bold black letters words that ridiculed the college which was represented by a "squaw." Such worse than barbarian rudeness embittered me. While we waited for the verdict of the judges, I gleamed fiercely upon the throngs of palefaces. My teeth were hard set, as I saw the white flag still floating insolently in the air.

Then anxiously we watched the man carry toward the stage the envelope containing the final decision.

There were two prizes given, that night, and one of them was mine!

The evil spirit laughed within me when the white flag dropped out of sight, and the hands which furled it hung limp in defeat.

Leaving the crowd as quickly as possible, I was soon in my room. The rest of the night I sat in an armchair and gazed into the crackling fire. I laughed no more in triumph when thus alone. The little taste of victory did not satisfy a hunger in my heart. In my mind I saw my mother far away on the Western plains, and she was holding a charge against me.

RETROSPECTION.

Leaving my mother, I returned to the school in the East. As months passed over me, I slowly comprehended that the large army of white teachers in Indian schools had a larger missionary creed than I had suspected.

It was one which included self-preservation quite as much as Indian education. When I saw an opium-eater holding a position as teacher of Indians, I did not understand what good was expected, until a Christian in power replied that this pumpkin-colored creature had a feeble mother to support. An inebriate paleface sat stupid in a doctor's chair, while Indian patients carried their ailments to untimely graves, because his fair wife was dependent upon him for her daily food.

I find it hard to count that white man a teacher who tortured an ambitious Indian youth by frequently reminding the brave changeling that he was nothing but a "government pauper."

Though I burned with indignation upon discovering on every side instances no less shameful than those I have mentioned, there was no present help. Even the few rare ones who have worked nobly for my race were powerless to choose workmen like themselves. To be sure, a man was sent from the Great Father to inspect Indian schools, but what he saw was usually the students' sample work *made* for exhibition. I was nettled by this sly cunning of the workmen who hoodwinked the Indian's pale Father at Washington.

My illness, which prevented the conclusion of my college course, together with my mother's stories of the encroaching frontier settlers, left me in no mood to strain my eyes in searching for latent good in my white co-workers.

At this stage of my own evolution, I was ready to curse men of small capacity for being the dwarfs their God had made them. In the process of my education I had lost all consciousness of the nature world about me. Thus, when a hidden rage took me to the small white-walled prison which I then called my room, I unknowingly turned away from my one salvation.

Alone in my room, I sat like the petrified Indian woman of whom my mother used to tell me. I wished my heart's burdens would turn me to unfeeling stone. But alive, in my tomb, I was destitute!

For the white man's papers I had given up my faith in the Great Spirit. For these same papers I had forgotten the healing in trees and brooks. On account of my mother's simple view of life, and my lack of any, I gave her up, also. I made no friends among the race of people I loathed. Like a slender tree, I had been uprooted from my mother, nature, and God. I was shorn of my branches, which had waved in sympathy and love for home and friends. The natural coat of bark which had protected my oversensitive nature was scraped off to the very quick.

Now a cold bare pole I seemed to be planted in a strange earth. Still, I seemed to hope a day would come when my mute aching head, reared upward to the sky, would flash a zigzag lightning across the heavens. With this dream of vent for a long-pent consciousness, I walked again amid the crowds.

At last, one weary day in the schoolroom, a new idea presented itself to me. It was a new way of solving the problem of my inner self. I liked it. Thus I resigned my position as teacher; and now I am in an Eastern city, following the long course of study I have set for myself. Now, as I look back upon the recent past, I see it from a distance, as a whole. I remember how, from morning till evening, many specimens of civilized peoples visited the Indian school. The city folks with canes and eyeglasses, the countrymen with sunburnt cheeks and clumsy feet, forgot their relative social ranks in an ignorant curiosity. Both sorts of these Christian palefaces were alike astounded at seeing the children of savage warriors so docile and industrious.

As answers to their shallow inquiries they received the students' sample work to look upon. Examining the neatly figured pages, and gazing upon the Indian girls and boys bending over their books, the white visitors walked out of the schoolhouse well satisfied: they were educating the children of the red man! They were paying a liberal fee to the government employees in whose able hands lay the small forest of Indian timber.

In this fashion many have passed idly through the Indian schools during the last decade, afterward to boast of their charity to the North American Indian. But few there are who have paused to question whether real life or long-lasting death lies beneath this semblance of civilization.

Questions for Part I

1 Based on the evidence you have read, what were some of the attitudes and expectations among the freedmen after the Civil War?

2 Did Southern whites accept the consequences of the Civil War? Explain.

3 What kind of life would a sharecropping family lead? Give details.

4 What, if anything, does the whites' style or manner of hunting buffalo say about the character of white civilization as it moved westward across America? Compare it with the Native Americans' way of life.

5 Describe the life of a cowboy as it is depicted by Bob Kennon and Nat Love. Which account seems more realistic? How do you account for the difference?

6 Contrast the life Zitkala-Sä had at home to the one she experienced at the missionary school. Why was her mother so reluctant to let her go to the school? Do you agree with the mother or with the stated aim of the missionary school?

PART II | AN AGE OF ECONOMIC EXPANSION

In pre-Civil War America a concept of "producerism" sought to define a common element in the economic contribution of workers, farmers, and entrepreneurs even though, among these groups, roles underwent so much shifting that men—and sometimes women—had multiple functions in the economy. Workers dreamed of operating small businesses. Farmers, as one commentator ironically noted, cultivated the soil and, increasingly (thinking of themselves as entrepreneurs going beyond self-sufficiency and selling their goods on the open market), "the main chance."

In the post-Civil War era, the harsher outlines of modern industrial society emerged. Different interests led to different ideologies. The labor movement grew on the recognition that "once a worker" most likely meant "always a worker," particularly when this was applied to women, children, immigrants, and members of other groups for whom opportunities for a different life would not often materialize. Farmers began to see themselves as distinct from an urbanizing and industrializing America. And some of the rich, like Frederick Martin Townsend, began to imagine themselves a separate aristocratic caste.

In the readings that follow, Andrew Carnegie articulates the emerging ideology of business—an ideology that stresses individual integrity and vision. However, while the owner of a business or an entrepreneur might be liberated from conventions of the past, large-scale enterprise carried with it restrictions on workers, even to the stunting of opportunity implied by child labor. In this era millions of children worked full-time for minimal wages, sacrificing both the pleasures of childhood and the chance for education toward a different way of life as adults. Some common folk found opportunities to advance, as for example Bethenia Owens-Adair. Others, such as the anonymous Afro-American woman interviewed in one of the readings, found their lives hemmed in by prejudice and the lack of personal freedom and economic opportunity. Midwestern farmers, trying to make their enterprises succeed against the backdrop of harsh climates and lonely surroundings, discovered that the family farm as a representative American institution had already begun its decline. The sentiments of struggling farmers are expressed in the letters of Halvor Harris and other supporters of late nineteenth-century populism.

Many Americans seeking to control a society apparently developing without boundaries turned to a variety of moral reforms such as prohibiting the use of alcohol, stamping out prostitution, eliminating gambling and other perceived vices, as well as to the general improvement of health and personal manners and morals. Carry A. Nation in her unique way served one of the largest of these reform movements.

Sharpening the tensions in American society were the massive surges of immigration in the 1880s and in the early years of the twentieth century. In contrast to earlier immigrants (from Northern and Western Europe), the new immigrants were, more frequently, from Southern and Eastern Europe. These people looked different, they sounded different, and their culture seemed very different.

The first victims of nativist resentment were the Chinese, whose economic role on the West coast (they supposedly took railroad and other jobs away from white Americans) led to a prohibition through federal legislation enacted in 1882 of new immigrants from China to the United States. The new European immigrants of the late nineteenth century raised further anti-nativist sentiment that was to continue well into the 1920s and 1930s and beyond. The children of these later immigrants doubted they could meld into American society as easily as did children in earlier generations. The painful manifestations of these fears are revealed in the series of letters to the Jewish Daily Forward.

ANDREW CARNEGIE

8 | Climbing the Ladder

Andrew Carnegie (1835–1919), the great steel manufacturer and philanthropist, delivered the following address in 1885 to students at a business school in Pittsburgh. Its optimism and measurement of success by character rather than circumstance or inherited advantages makes it typical of American success literature. As advice, it differs little from what one might have heard in a school commencement speech at any time in the past hundred years. Carnegie, though, gave the message authenticity because he was that rare case: the very rich man who actually did begin poor and without connections.

Movie buffs have applied Carnegie's advice to another class on the make, the gangsters of the depression era. Edward G. Robinson's "Little Rico," for instance, followed Carnegie to the line: In the opening of the movie Little Caesar *Rico robs a filling station, following Carnegie's advice to "begin at the beginning and occupy the most subordinate positions." After the gas station robbery, Rico goes to a diner with his pal and complains, "We're nobodies." "Be Somebody," he says, and dreams of being a big Chicago mobster. "Aim high," advises Carnegie. Rico becomes a professional of sorts, a professional killer. Rico never drank; Carnegie said, "The destroyer of young men is the drinking of alcohol." Rico avoids women, another Carnegie precept. Rico, too, was single-minded; Carnegie wrote, "And here is the great secret: concentrate your energy, thought and capital exclusively on the business in which you are engaged."*

THE ROAD TO BUSINESS SUCCESS: A TALK TO YOUNG MEN

It is well that young men should begin at the beginning and occupy the most subordinate positions. Many of the leading business men of Pittsburgh had a serious responsibility thrust upon them at the very threshold of their career. They were introduced to the broom, and spent the first hours of their business lives sweeping out the office. I notice we have janitors and janitresses now in offices, and our young men unfortunately miss that salutary branch of a business education. But if by chance the professional sweeper is absent any morning the boy who has the genius of the future partner in him will not hesitate to try his hand at the broom. The other day a fond fashionable mother in Michigan asked a young man whether he had ever seen a young lady

From an address to Curry Commercial College, Pittsburgh, June 23, 1885. Published in Andrew Carnegie, The Empire of Business. *(New York, Doubleday, Page, and Co., 1902) pp. 3–18.*

sweep in a room so grandly as her Priscilla. He said no, he never had, and the mother was gratified beyond measure, but then said he, after a pause, "What I should like to see her do is sweep out a room." It does not hurt the newest comer to sweep out the office if necessary. I was one of those sweepers myself, and who do you suppose were my fellow sweepers? David McCargo, now superintendent of the Alleghany Valley Railroad; Robert Pitcairn, Superintendent of the Pennsylvania Railroad, and Mr. Moreland, City Attorney. We all took turns, two each morning did the sweeping; and now I remember Davie was so proud of his clean white shirt bosom that he used to spread over it an old silk bandana handkerchief which he kept for the purpose, and we other boys thought he was putting on airs. So he was. None of us had a silk handkerchief.

Assuming that you have all obtained employment and are fairly started, my advice to you is "aim high." I would not give a fig for the young man who does not already see himself the partner or the head of an important firm. Do not rest content for a moment in your thoughts as head clerk, or foreman, or general manager in any concern, no matter how extensive. Say each to yourself. "My place is at the top." *Be king in your dreams.* Make your vow that you will reach that position, with untarnished reputation, and make no other vow to distract your attention, except the very commendable one that when you are a member of the firm or before that, if you have been promoted two or three times, you will form another partnership with the loveliest of her sex—a partnership to which our new partnership act has no application. The liability there is never limited.

Let me indicate two or three conditions essential to success. Do not be afraid that I am going to moralize, or inflict a homily upon you. I speak upon the subject only from the view of a man of the world, desirous of aiding you to become successful business men. You all know that there is no genuine, praiseworthy success in life if you are no honest, truthful, fair-dealing. I assume you are and will remain all these, and also that you are determined to live pure, respectable lives, free from pernicious or equivocal associations with one sex or the other. There is no creditable future for you else. Otherwise your learning and your advantages not only go for naught, but serve to accentuate your failure and your disgrace. I hope you will not take it amiss if I warn you against three of the gravest dangers which will beset you in your upward path.

The first and most seductive, and the destroyer of most young men, is the drinking of liquor. I am no temperance lecturer in disguise, but a man who knows and tells you what observation has proved to him; and I say to you that you are more likely to fail in your career from acquiring the habit of drinking liquor than from any, or all, the other temptations likely to assail you. You may yield to almost any other temptation and reform—may brace up, and if not recover lost ground, at least remain in the race and secure and maintain a respectable position. But from the insane thirst for liquor escape is almost impossible. I have known but few exceptions to this rule. First, then, you must not drink liquor to excess. Better if you do not touch it at all—much better; but if this be too hard a rule for you then take your stand firmly here:—Resolve never to touch it except at meals. A glass at dinner will not hinder your advance in life or lower your tone; but I implore you hold it inconsistent with the dignity and self-respect of gentlemen, with what is due from yourselves to yourselves, being the men you are, and especially the men you are determined to become, to drink a glass of liquor at a bar. Be far too much of the gentleman ever to enter a bar-room. You do not pursue your careers in safety unless you stand firmly upon this ground. Adhere to it and you have escaped danger from the deadliest of your foes.

The next greatest danger to a young business man in this community I believe to be that of speculation. When I was a telegraph operator here we had no Exchanges in the City, but the men or firms who speculated upon the Eastern Exchanges were necessarily known to the operators. They could be counted on the fingers of one hand. These men were not our citizens of first repute: they were regarded with suspicion. I have lived to see all of these speculators irreparably ruined men, bankrupt in money and bankrupt in character. There is scarcely an instance of a man who has made a fortune by speculation and kept it. Gamesters die poor, and there is certainly not an instance of a speculator who has lived a life creditable to himself, or advantageous to the community. The man who grasps the morning paper to see first how his speculative ventures upon the Exchanges are likely to result, unfits himself for the calm consideration and proper solution of business problems, with which he has to deal later in the day, and saps the sources of that persistent and concentrated energy upon which depend the permanent success, and often the very safety, of his main business.

The speculator and the business man tread diverging lines. The former depends upon the sudden turn of fortune's wheel; he is a millionaire to-day, a bankrupt to-morrow. But the man of business knows that only by years of patient, unremitting attention to affairs can he earn his reward, which is the result, not of chance, but of well-devised means for the attainment of ends. During all these years his is the cheering thought that by no possibility can he benefit himself without carrying prosperity to others. The speculator on the other hand had better never have lived so far as the good of others or the good of the community is concerned. Hundreds of young men were tempted in this city not long since to gamble in oil, and many were ruined; all were injured whether they lost or won....

The third and last danger against which I shall warn you in one which has wrecked many a fair craft which started well and gave promise of a prosperous voyage. It is the perilous habit of indorsing— all the more dangerous, inasmuch as it assails one generally in the garb of friendship. It appeals to your generous instincts, and you say, "How can I refuse to lend my name only, to assist a friend?" It is because there is so much that is true and commendable in that view that the practice is so dangerous. Let me endeavor to put you upon safe honourable grounds in regard to it. I would say to you to make it a rule now, *never indorse*: but this is too much like never taste wine, or never smoke, or any other of the "nevers." They generally result in exceptions. You will as business men now and then probably become security for friends. Now, here is the line at which regard for the success of friends should cease and regard for your own honour begins.

If you owe anything, all your capital and all your effects are a solemn trust in your hands to be held inviolate for the security of those who have trusted you. Nothing can be done by you with honour which jeopardizes these first claims upon you. When a man in debt indorses for another, it is not his own credit or his own capital he risks, it is that of his own creditors. He violates a trust. Mark you then, never indorse until you have cash means not required for your own debts, and never indorse beyond those means . . . .

I beseech you avoid liquor, speculation and indorsement. Do not fail in either, for liquor and speculation are the Scylla and Charybdis of the young man's business sea, and indorsement his rock ahead.

Assuming you are safe in regard to these your gravest dangers, the question now is how to rise from the subordinate position we have imagined you in, through the successive grades to the position for which you are, in my opinion, and, I trust, in your own, evidently intended. I can give you the secret. It lies mainly in this. Instead of the question, "What must I do for my employer?" substitute "What can I do?" Faithful and conscientious discharge of the duties assigned you is all very well, but the verdict in such cases generally is that you perform your present duties so well that you had better continue performing them. Now, young gentlemen, this will not do. It will not do for the coming partners. There must be something beyond this. We make Clerks, Bookkeepers, Treasurers, Bank Tellers of this class, and there they remain to the end of the chapter. The rising man must do something exceptional, and beyond the range of his special department. *He must attract attention.* A shipping clerk, he may do so by discovering in an invoice an error with which he has nothing to do, and which has escaped the attention of the proper party. If a weighing clerk, he may save for the firm by doubting the adjustment of the scales and having them corrected, even if this be the province of the master mechanic. If a messenger boy, even he can lay the seed of promotion by going beyond the letter of his instructions in order to secure the desired reply. There is no service so low and simple, neither any so high, in which the young man of ability and willing disposition cannot readily and almost daily prove himself capable of greater trust and usefulness, and, what is equally important, show his invincible determination to rise. Some day, in your own department, you will be directed to do or say something which you know will prove disadvantageous to the interest of the firm. Here is your chance. Stand up like a man and say so. Say it boldly, and give your reasons, and thus prove to your employer that, while his thoughts have been engaged upon other matters, you have been studying during hours when perhaps he thought you asleep, how to advance his interests. You may be right or you may be wrong, but in either case you have gained the first condition of success. You have attracted attention. Your employer has found that he has not a mere hireling in his service, but a man; not one who is content to give so many hours of work for so many dollars in return, but one who devotes his spare hours and constant thought to the business. Such an employee must perforce be thought of, and thought of kindly and well. It will not be long before his advice is asked in his special branch, and if the advice given be sound, it will soon be asked and taken upon questions of broader bearing. This means partnership; if not with present employers then with others. Your foot, in such a case, is upon the ladder; the amount of climbing done depends entirely yourself.

One false axiom you will often hear, which I wish to guard you against is "Obey orders if you break owners." Don't you do it. This is no rule for you to follow. Always break orders to save owners. There never was a great character who did not sometimes smash the routine regulations and make new ones for himself. The rule is only suitable for such as have no aspirations, and you have not forgotten that you are destined to be owners and to make orders and break orders. Do not hesitate to do it whenever you are sure the interests of your employer will be thereby promoted and when you are so sure of the result that you are willing to take responsibility. You will never be a partner unless you know the business of your department far better than the owners possibly can. When called to account for your independent action, show him the result of your genius, and tell him that you knew that it would be so; show him how mistaken the orders were. Boss your boss just as soon as you can; try it on early. There is nothing he will like so well if he is the right kind of boss; if he is not, the man for you to remain with—leave him whenever you can, even at a present sacrifice, and find one capable of discerning genius. Our young partners in the Carnegie firm have won their spurs by showing that we did not know half as well what was wanted as they did. Some of them have acted upon occasion with me as if they owned the firm and I was but some airy New Yorker presuming to advise upon what I knew very little about. Well, they are not interfered with much now. They were the true bosses—the very men we were looking for.

There is one sure mark of the coming partner, the future millionaire; his revenues always exceed his expenditures. He begins to save early, almost as soon as he begins to earn. No matter how little it may be possible to save, save that little. Invest it securely, not necessarily in bonds, but in anything which you have good reason to believe will be profitable, but no gambling with it, remember. A rare chance will soon present itself for investment. The little you have saved will prove the basis for an amount of credit utterly surprising to you. Capitalists trust the saving young man. For every hundred dollars you can produce as the result of hard-won savings, Midas, in search of a partner, will lend or credit a thousand; for every thousand, fifty thousand. It is not capital that your seniors require, it is the man who has proved that he has the business habits which create capital, and to create it in the best of all possible ways, as far as self-discipline is concerned, is, by adjusting his habits to his means. Gentlemen, it is the first hundred dollars saved which tells. Begin at once to lay up something. The bee predominates in the future millionnaire.

Of course there are better, higher aims than saving. As an end, the acquisition of wealth is ignoble in the extreme; I assume that you save and long for wealth only as a means of enabling you the better to do some good in your day and generation. Make a note of this essential rule: Expenditure always within income.

You may grow impatient, or become discouraged when year by year you float on in subordinate positions. There is no doubt that it is becoming harder and harder as business gravitates more and more to immense concerns, for a young man without capital to get a start for himself, and in this city especially where large capital is essential, it is unusually difficult. Still, let me tell you for your encouragement, that there is no country in the world, where able and energetic young men can so readily rise as this, nor any city where there is more room at the top. Young men give all kinds of reasons why in their cases failure was clearly attributable to exceptional circumstances which render success impossible. Some never had a chance, according to their own story. This is simply nonsense. No young man ever lived who had not a chance, and a splendid chance, too, if he ever was employed at all . . . .

The young man who never had a chance is the same young man who has been canvassed over and over again by his superiors, and found destitute of necessary qualifications, or is deemed unworthy of closer relations with the firm, owing to some objectionable act, habit, or association, of which he thought his employers ignorant . . . .

And here is the prime condition of success, the great secret: concentrate your energy, thought, and capital exclusively upon the business in which you are engaged. Having begun in one line, resolve to fight it out on that line, to lead in it; adopt every improvement, have the best machinery, and know the most about it.

The concerns which fail are those which have scattered their capital, which means that they have scattered their brains also. They have investments in this, or that, or the other, here, there and everywhere. "Don't put all your eggs in one basket" is all wrong. I tell you "put all your eggs in one basket, and then watch that basket." Look round you and take notice; men who do that do not often fail. It is easy to watch and carry the one basket. It is trying to carry too many baskets that breaks most eggs in this country. He who carried three baskets must put one on his head, which is apt to tumble and trip him up. One fault of the American business man is lack of concentration.

To summarize what I have said: Aim for the highest; never enter a bar-room; do not touch liquor, or if at all only at meals; never speculate; never indorse beyond your surplus cash fund; make the firm's interest yours; break orders always to save owners; concentrate; put all your eggs in one basket, and watch that basket; expenditure always within revenue; lastly, be not impatient, for, as Emerson says, "no one can cheat you out of ultimate success but yourselves."

BETHENIA OWENS-ADAIR

9 | Pioneer to Physician

Bethenia Owens-Adair was an extraordinary woman by any standards. From a family of nine that had migrated from Missouri to Oregon, she married at age fourteen, divorced at age eighteen (at a time when divorce was difficult and unusual), became a successful milliner and dressmaker, earned an education, and finally went east to study medicine and become a doctor at the age of forty. She even returned to the East several times for postgraduate training. As her memoirs indicate, Owens-Adair had to overcome many prejudices to achieve her ambitions. Hers is a fascinating story of both the possibilities, and the difficulties of realizing the opportunities western life offered to a nineteenth-century American woman.

I was born February 7th, 1840, in Van Buren Country, Missouri, being the second daughter of Thomas and Sarah Damron Owens.

My father and mother crossed the plains with the first emigrant wagons of 1843, and settled on Clatsop plains, Clatsop County, Oregon, at the mouth of the Columbia; the wonderful "River of the West," in sound of the ceaseless roar of that mightiest of oceans, the grand old Pacific. Though then very small and delicate in stature, and of a highly nervous and sensitive nature, I possessed a strong and vigorous constitution, and a most wonderful endurance and recuperative power.

/   /   /

I was a veritable "tom-boy," and gloried in the fact. It was father's custom to pat me on the head, and call me his "boy."

The regret of my life up to the age of thirty-five, was that I had not been born a boy, for I realized very early in life that a girl was hampered and hemmed in on all sides simply by the accident of sex.

Brother and I were always trying our muscular strength, and before I was thirteen, I bet him I could carry four sacks of flour, or two hundred pounds. I stood between a table and a box, on which we had put two sacks of flour each. Then brother placed a sack of flour on each of my

From Cathy Luchetti, Women of the West (*Antelope Island Press, 1982*), pp. 173–175, 177–186.

shoulders, and held them steady, while I managed to get the other two
sacks (one on the table and the other on the box on each side of me)
under each arm, and then I walked triumphantly off, carrying all four
sacks . . . !

I was the family nurse: and it was seldom that I had not a child in
my arms, and more clinging to me. Where there is a baby every two
years, there is always no end of nursing to be done; especially when
the mother's time is occupied, as it was then, every minute, from early
morning till late at night, with much outdoor as well as indoor work.
She seldom found time to devote to the baby, except to give it the breast.

/   /   /

In 1853, finding that his 640 acres on Clatsop could no longer supply feed for his rapidly increasing herds, father decided to remove to
Southern Oregon, where he could have an abundance of range for them.

/   /   /

Brother Flem and I, with the assistance of one man, who was not
half equal to either one of us for the purpose, drove the herd.

Father said we were worth more than any two men he could hire.
There was an abundance of grass; the weather was fine, and this part
of the journey was really a picnic for us all.

/   /   /

During the winter, Mr. Hill came to visit us. His parents and their
family had come to Oregon the year before, and settled in the Rogue
River valley, near the Siskiyou mountains.

It was now arranged that we should be married the next spring,
when father's house was far enough completed to move in. During the
winter and early spring, I put in all my spare time in preparing for my
approaching marriage.

I had four quilts already pieced, ready for the lining; mother had
given me the lining for them all, and the cotton for two, and we quilted
and finished them all. She also gave me muslin for four sheets, two
pairs of pillow-cases, two tablecloths, and four towels. I cut and made
two calico dresses for myself, and assisted mother in the making of my
wedding dress, which was a pretty, sky-blue figured lawn.

I had everything done, and neatly folded away long before the
wedding day arrived. Mr. Hill came early in April, and assisted us in
moving into the new house.

On May 4th, 1854, with only our old friends, the Perrys, and the
minister present, beside our own family, we were married. I was still
small for my age. My husband was five-feet eleven-inches in height,
and I could stand under his outstretched arm. I grew very slowly, and

did not reach my full stature until I was 25 years old, which is now 5-feet 4-inches.

/ / /

In the beginning of our married life, my father had advised my husband to begin at once to fell trees, and hew them, and put up a good house before winter set in. There was an abundance of suitable timber on our land, near by, but he was never in any hurry to get down to work. In one way and another he managed to idle away the summer, going to camp meetings, reading novels, and hunting.

/ / /

We moved into our new house in March, with the $150 mortgage hanging over us. On April 17th, 1856, our baby [George] was born, and then Aunt Kelley begged me to give him to her, addressing me thus:

"Now Bethenia, you just give him to me. I will take him, and educate him, and make him my heir. I will give him all I have, and that is more than his father will ever do for him. I know very well that Legrand will just fool around all his life, and never accomplish anything."

She seemed to think my consent to her having the child was all that was necessary. But my baby was too precious to give to anyone.

/ / /

My health was poor. I had not been strong since the baby came, and I could not seem to recover from the effects of the fever. The baby was ill and fretful, much of the time, and things were going anything but smoothly. A short time before the climax, I went home and told my parents that I did not think I could stand it much longer. Mother was indignant, and told me to come home, and let him go; that "any man that could not make a living with the good starts and help he has had, never will make one; and with his temper, he is liable to kill you at any time."

Father broke down, and shed tears, saying:

"Oh, Bethenia, there has never been a divorce in my family, and I hope there never will be. I want you to go back, and try again, and do your best. After that, if you cannot possibly get along, come home." I went back, greatly relieved, for I knew that if I had to leave, I would be protected.

Our trouble usually started over the baby, who was unusually cross. He was such a sickly, tiny mite, with an abnormal, voracious appetite, but his father thought him old enough to be trained and disciplined, and would spank him unmercifully because he cried. This I could not endure, and war would be precipitated at once. A few days before our separation, his father fed him six hard boiled eggs at supper, in spite of all I could do or say. I slept little that night, expecting that the child would be in convulsions before morning. And thus one thing led to another until the climax was reached.

Early one morning in March, after a tempestuous scene of this sort, Mr. Hill threw the baby on the bed, and rushed down in town. As soon as he was out of sight, I put on my hat and shawl, and gathering a few necessaries together for the baby, I flew over to father's.

/   /   /

And now, at eighteen years of age, I found myself, broken in spirit and health, again in my father's house, from which, only four short years before, I had gone with such a happy heart, and such bright hopes for the future. . . .

It seemed to me now that I should never be happy or strong again. I was, indeed, surrounded with difficulties seemingly insurmountable; a husband for whom I had lost all love and respect; a divorce, the stigma of which would cling to me all my future life, and a sickly babe of two years in my arms, all rose darkly before me.

At this time I could scarcely read or write, and four years of trials and hardships and privations sufficient to crush a mature woman, had wrought a painful change in the fresh, blooming child who had so buoyantly taken the duties and burdens of wifehood and motherhood on her young shoulders. I realized my position fully, and resolved to meet it bravely, and do my very best.

My little George, too, felt the beneficial change fully as I did; for my mother's idea of raising children could not be improved upon; simply give them sufficient wholesome food, keep them clean and happy, and let them live out of doors as much as possible.

George was such a tiny creature, and so active in his movements that my young brothers and sisters felt him no burden, and always had him out of doors; so after pondering the matter for some time, I said one day:

"Mother do you think I might manage to go to school?"

"Why yes," she answered: "go right along. George is no trouble. The children will take care of him."

I joyfully accepted this opportunity, and from that day on, I was up early and out to the barn, assisting with the milking, and doing all the work possible in the house, until 8:30, when I went to school with the children, my younger brothers and sisters. Saturdays, with the aid of the children, I did the washing and ironing of the family, and kept up with my studies.

At the end of my first four months' term I had finished the third reader, and made good progress with my other studies of spelling, writing, geography, and arithmetic. . . .

Before going to Clatsop, in the fall of 1859, with my sister, I applied for a divorce, and the custody of my child and petitioned for the restoration of my maiden name of Owens.... The suit was strongly contested on account of the child.... My father employed Hon. Stephen F. Chadwick on my behalf, and he won my suit.... After the decree of the court was rendered giving me custody of my child, and my father's name, which I have never since discarded, and never will, I felt like a free woman.

The world began to look bright once more, as with renewed vigor and reviving hope, I sought work in all honorable directions, even accepting washing, which was one of the most profitable occupations among the few considered "proper" for women in those days.

/ / /

Late in the fall of 1860, sister and I went over to Oysterville, Wash., to visit my old and much beloved girl friend, Mrs. S. S. Munson.... I told Mrs. Munson of my great anxiety for an education, and she immediately said:

"Why not, then, stay here with me, and go to school? We have a good school here, and I should like so much to have you with me, especially farther on."

To this generous offer I replied that I would gladly accept it if I could only find some way of earning my necessary expenses while attending school. Mrs. Munson replied:

"There are my brother and his hired man: I can get you their washing, which will bring you in from $1.00 to $1.50 per week, which will be all you will need."

To this I gratefully assented and I did their washing evenings. Work to me then was scarcely more than play.

Thus passed one of the pleasantest, and most profitable winters of my life, while, whetted by what it fed on, my desire for knowledge grew daily stronger. My sister, Mrs. Hobson, now urged me to come back to her, and I said to her: I am determined to get at least a common school education. I now know that I can support and educate myself and my boy, and I am resolved to do it: furthermore, I do not intend to do it over a washtub, either. Nor will I any longer work for my board and clothes alone. You need me, and I am willing to stay with you the next six months, if you will arrange for me to go to school in Astoria next winter. She agreed to this, and some time later I said to her: "Diane, don't you think I could teach a little summer school here on the plains? I can rise at four, and help with the milking, and get all the other work done by 8 a.m., and I can do the washing mornings and evenings, and on Saturdays."

She said: "You can try," so the following day I asked Mr. Hobson if he would not get up a little school for me.

He replied: "Take the horse and go around and among the neighbors and work it up yourself."

I lost no time in carrying out his suggestion, and succeeded in getting the promise of sixteen pupils, for which I was to receive $2 for three months.

This was my first attempt to instruct others. I taught my school in the old Presbyterian church, the first Presbyterian church building ever erected in Oregon. Of my sixteen pupils, there were three who were more advanced than myself, but I took their books home with me nights, and, with the help of my brother-in-law, I managed to prepare the lessons beforehand, and they never suspected my incompetency.

From this school I received my first little fortune of $25; and I added to this by picking wild blackberries at odd times, which found a ready sale at fifty cents a gallon.

Fall found me settled at the old Boelling Hotel in Astoria, with my nephew, Frank Hobson, and my little son George. Our board was paid, I taking care of our small room, and our clothes, with the privilege of doing our washing and ironing on Saturdays. And now I encountered one of my sharpest trials, for, on entering school, and being examined in mental arithmetic, I was placed in the primary class!

Mr. Deardorff, the principal, kindly offered to assist me in that study after school, and, later, permitted me to enter both classes. Words can never express my humiliation at having to recite with children of from eight to fourteen years of age. This, however, was of brief duration, for in a few weeks, I had advanced to the next class above, and was soon allowed to enter the third (and highest) class in mental arithmetic.

At the end of the term of nine months, I had passed into most of the advanced classes; not that I was an apt scholar, for my knowledge has always been acquired by the hardest labor, but by sheer determination, industry and perseverance. At 4 a.m. my lamp was always burning, and I was poring over my books, never allowing myself more than eight hours of sleep.

Nothing was permitted to come between me and this, the greatest opportunity of my life.

/   /   /

In 1870 I place my son in the University of California at Berkeley. I had always had a fondness for nursing, and had developed a special capacity in that direction by assisting my neighbors in illness. I was more and more besieged by the entreaties of my friends and doctors, which were hard to refuse, to come to their aid in sickness, often times to the detriment of business, and now that money came easily, a desire began to grow within me for a medical education. One evening I was sent for by a friend with a very sick child. The old physician in my presence attempted to use an instrument for the relief of the little sufferer, and, in his long, bungling, and unsuccessful attempt he severely lacerated the tender flesh of the poor little girl. At last, he laid down the instrument, to wipe his glasses. I picked it up saying, "Let me try, Doctor," and passed it instantly, with perfect ease, bringing immediate relief to the tortured child. The mother, who was standing by in agony at the sight of her child's mutilation, threw her arms around my neck, and sobbed out her thanks. Not so the doctor! He did not appreciate or approve of my interference, and he showed his displeasure at the time most emphatically. This apparently unimportant event really decided my future course.

A few days later, I called on my friend, Dr. Hamilton, and confiding to him my plans and ambitions, I asked for the loan of medical books. He gave me Gray's *Anatomy*. I came out of his private office into the drug-store, where I saw Hon. S.F. Chadwick, who had heard the conversation, and who came promptly forward and shook my hand warmly, saying: "Go ahead. It is in you; let it come out. You will win."

/ / /

...I now began in good earnest to arrange my business affairs so that I could leave for the East in one year from that time, meantime studying diligently to familiarize myself with the science of anatomy, the groundwork of my chosen profession....

In due time, I announced that in two weeks I would leave for Philadelphia, to enter a medical school. As I have said, I expected disapproval from my friends and relatives, but I was not prepared for the storm of opposition that followed. My family felt they were disgraced, and even my own child was influenced and encouraged to think I was doing him an irreparable injury, by my course. People sneered and laughed derisively. Most of my friends seemed to consider it their Christian duty to advise against, and endeavor to prevent me from taking this "fatal" step. I was literally kept on the rack. But as all things must have an end, the day of my departure was at last at hand....

I had taken the decisive step, and I would never turn back.... My decision was now irrevocably made, and I was comforted....

/ / /

Stage travel was no hardship for me, for, like the sailor on his ship, I felt at home in the stage. For several years I had gone to San Francisco spring and fall by land, when the nearest railroad connection was at Marysville, California....

On reaching Philadelphia, I matriculated in the Eclectic School of Medicine, and employed a private tutor. I also attended the lectures and clinics in the great Blockly Hospital twice a week, as did all the medical students of the city. In due time I received my degree, and returned to Roseburg to wind up my business, which I had left in charge of my sister. A few days after my return, an old man without friends died, and the six physicians who had all attended him at various times, decided to hold an autopsy. At their meeting, Dr. Palmer, who had not forgotten my former "impudence" in using his instrument, made a motion to invite the new "Philadelphia" doctor to be present. This was carried, and a messenger was dispatched to me with a written invitation. I knew this meant no honor for me, but I said: "Give the doctors my compliments, and say that I will be there in a few minutes." The messenger left, and I followed close behind him. I waited outside until he went in and closed the door. I heard him say, in excited tones: "She said to give you her compliments, and that she'd be here in a minute." Then came a roar of laughter, after which I quietly opened the door and walked in, went forward, and shook hands with Dr. Hoover, who advanced to meet me, saying:

"Do you know that the autopsy is on the genital organs?"

"No," I answered; "but one part of the human body should be as sacred to the physician as another."

Dr. Palmer here stepped back, saying: "I object to a woman's being present at a male autopsy, and if she is allowed to remain, I shall retire!"

"I came here by written invitation," I said; "and I will leave it to a vote whether I go or stay: but first I would like to ask Dr. Palmer what is the difference between the attendance of a woman at a male autopsy, and the attendance of a man at a female autopsy?"

Dr. Hoover said: "Well, I voted for you to come, and I will stick to it." Another said: "I voted yes, and I'll not go back on it. . . ."

One of the doctors opened an old medicine case, and offered it to me.

"You do not want me to do the work, do you?" I asked, in surprise.

"Oh, yes, yes, go ahead," he said. I took the case and complied. The news of what was going on had spread to every house in town, and the excitement was at fever-heat.

When I had at last finished the dissection, the audience (not the doctors) gave me three cheers. As I passed out and down on my way home, the street was lined on both sides with men, women and children, all anxious to get a look at "the woman who dared," to see what sort of a strange, anomalous being she was. The women were shocked and scandalized! The men were disgusted, but amused, thinking it "such a good joke on the doctors. . . ."

And now, as I look back, I believe that all that saved me was the fact that my brothers, Flem and Josiah, lived there, and although they disapproved of my actions quite as much as the rest of the community did, yet "blood is thicker than water," and they would have died in their tracks before they would have seen me subjected to indignities, or driven out of town. And as everyone knew they would shoot at the drop of a hat, good care was taken to lay no violent hands on me.

As soon as possible after that autopsy, I closed up my business, and, taking my sister, and the remnant of my store goods, I removed to Portland, Oregon.

I first occupied the ground-floor of a two-story brick building on the east side of First street, between Taylor and Yahhill. There were no brick buildings in Portland south of there at that time. I had two rooms fitted up for electrical and medicated baths. This was a new process of treatment, and it, in connection with my other practice, proved both attractive and remunerative. I obtained the knowledge in a New York institution, which had been open but a short time.

There was but one man, a German, in Portland who seemed to have any knowledge of electrical batteries, and he found much trouble in keeping my batteries in running order.

I was now well settled, and notwithstanding occasional rebuffs here and there, and frequent slights from my brother M.D.s, I went steadily on, gaining a step here, and a point there, and constantly advancing, with money coming in faster and faster.

My son George was now nineteen, and I entered him in the Medical Department of the Willamette University. It was certainly one of the proudest days of my life when he was graduated from it, two years later. From the beginning, I had set my heart on making a physician of him, and at last my life's ambition was crowned with success. . . .

Time passed on. I was successful and prosperous, but not yet satisfied.

Again I was beginning to pine for more knowledge.

My sister asked for a course in Mills College, which I gave her. My son had his profession. "I have done my duty to those depending on me," I thought, "and now I will treat myself to a full medical course in the old school, and a trip to Europe. I shall then be equipped for business on an advanced scale. . . .

Again my family and friends objected. They said: "You will soon be rich; why spend all you have for nothing. . . ."

But I was deaf to all entreaties—a better education I must have, and the best way to secure it was to go to the fountain head. . . .

/   /   /

It was my intention, if possible to gain admission to the then renowned Jefferson Medical College.

Armed with letters from U.S. Senators, Governers, Professors, and Doctors, on reaching Philadelphia, I at once called upon, and was entertained by Dr. Hannah Longshore, one of the first graduates of the Women's Medical School of Philadelphia, and sister of Professor Longshore, founder of and professor in the Eclectic Medical School of Philadelphia for men and women.

I told her plainly just what I desired.

"I have no faith that you can get into Jefferson College," she said, "but I want to see you try it. I believe the time will come when the doors of every medical school in our land will be forced open for women, as do the Eclectic and Homeopathic schools now. But the old schools, as you know, do not recognize them. If there is any man today who can open the doors of Jefferson College to women, it is Professor Gross."

"This is Saturday," I said, "and I will go at once to see him."

He received me with a gracious smile, requesting me to be seated, as I handed him the envelope containing my credentials.

While he was looking over the letters with a pleased expression on his fine face, I could scarcely realize that I was in the presence of the then greatest surgeon in the United States.

His slender, delicate hands were not suggestive of bloodletting.

I was lost in contemplation of this grand man, when he broke my reverie by saying, with the gentlest voice and manner:

"And now, my little lady, what can I do for you?"

"I have come to this grand old city in search of knowledge," I answered. "I hunger and thirst after it. I want to drink at the fountain-head. Can you not lead me into Jefferson College, you, her greatest professor?"

He gazed at me with moist and sympathetic eyes for an instant. Then, in the gentlest, softest tones, he said:

"My dear little woman, how gladly I would open the doors of Jefferson to you; but that privilege is denied to me. The deciding power lies in the hands of the board of regents, and they are a whole age behind the times. They would simply be shocked, scandalized, and enraged at the mere mention of admitting a woman into Jefferson College. Why not go to the Women's College? It is just as good. The examinations required to be passed are identically the same."

"I know that, Professor Gross," I responded, "but a Woman's College out West stands below par, and I must have a degree that is second to none."

"Then the University of Michigan is the school for you," he said. "It is a long-term school, and a mixed school, and it is second to none in America."

"Thanks, Professor, a thousand thanks!" I gratefully exclaimed; "I will follow your advice and go there at once. . . . "

/   /   /

After supper came "Quizzes," and then study till nine p.m., when I retired, to sleep soundly.

Between lectures, clinics, laboratory work, Quizzes, examinations, two good sermons on Sunday, and a church social now and then, the time was fully and pleasantly occupied. The constant change brought rest, and acted as a safety valve to our over heated brains.

At the close of the second year, in June, 1880, I received my degree. During all that time, I had not suffered from a day's sickness, and had been present at every class lecture save one, my absence from it being due to my having been so deeply absorbed in my studies that I failed to hear the bell. This lapse almost broke my heart, which had been set on being able to say, at the end of the course, that I had not missed a single lecture.

After graduating, having arranged for three years' absence from home, I went with one of my classmates to Chicago. Taking rooms, we devoted ourselves to hospital and clinical work.

While there, my son, Dr. Hill, joined me, and the first of October found us back at the University, where Dr. Hill entered for a post course, while I remained as a resident physician, which entitled me to all the lectures. I attended all the advanced lectures in my department, theory and practice in the Homeopathic School, and English literature and history in the Literary Department.

At the end of six months, with my son and two lady physicians, I sailed for Europe. We visited Glasgow, Hamburg, Berlin, Potsdam, Munich, Dresden, Paris, London, and other cities. . . .

When I landed at New York, the Customs Collector demanded $75 duty on my instruments, which I had purchased in Paris. I said: "These instruments are for my own use. I am a physician. Here is a letter from the President of the University of Michigan, and letters from U.S. Senators, Governers, etc. I know you have no right to collect duty on my instruments, and if you take my goods, I will employ an attorney."

"You stay right here," he said, "till I come back, and you'll find you will have to pay the duty." After two hours, he returned, and said: "Take your things, and go on."

I speedily obeyed, glad to get out of his clutches. In a few hours my ticket to San Francisco was secured and I was *en route* thither. . . .

A week or two after I was settled, Col. McC. called, and said:

"I am glad to welcome you back, and I thought I would take a few of your electrical medical baths. I have not really had an attack of rheumatism since that terrible time I had before, but I thought I had better take a few as a preventative."

I laughed again, saying: "I have no baths, and never expect to have again."

"Really; you have not lost faith in them, have you?"

"Oh, no, I fully realize their worth; but you see, Colonel, I am now a full-fledged University physician of the old school, and I cannot afford to attach to myself the odium of the epithet, "Bath Doctor." One dollar and a half was considered a large price for those baths, by some of my customers, but no one expects to get a prescription for less than $2.00. Oh no, I expect to carry my stock in trade in my head from this time on."

Thus passed three of the happiest and most prosperous years of my life. Health, hosts of friends, and unbroken prosperity. What more could I ask, or desire?

10 | Testimony on Child Labor

Children have been working in factories since the advent of the Industrial Revolution. The opportunity to provide work for women and children was one of the arguments made in favor of "manufacturing establishments" by Alexander Hamilton in his Report on Manufacturing *in 1791. Organized efforts to regulate and restrict child labor finally began in the 1880s but had limited success and that only in the North. The Progressive Movement worked to outlaw child labor, but in 1918 the Supreme Court declared federal law to that effect unconstitutional in* Hammer v. Dagenhart. *Federal efforts to outlaw child labor succeeded only in 1938.*

The three documents that follow illustrate the phenomenon of child labor. The first is from the important Report of the Committee of the U.S. Senate Upon the Relations Between Labor and Capital, Hearings Held in 1883; *the latter two are from a* New York State Legislative Committee Hearing *in 1896.*

Augusta, GA., November 23, 1883.*

    Otis G. Lynch sworn and examined.

    By the Chairman:

Q: What is your occupation?

A: I am superintendent of the Enterprise Manufacturing Company.

Q: How long have you been superintendent of that company?

A: I have been superintendent of the Enterprise Company for something over two and one-half years.

Q: Please state where you were born and what has been your experience in manufacturing?

A: I was born in Otsego County, New York, I came to Augusta twenty-eight years ago.

Q: Had you any knowledge of manufacturing when you came here?

A: Yes; I had worked some in the mills in Oneida County, New York. I commenced the business in the county in which I was born, at the age of about ten, and I have been in the same business ever since, except during short periods when I went to school about six months

---

*From Report of the Committee of the Senate Upon the Relations Between Labor and Capital and Testimony Taken by the Committee. *Volume IV, (Washington, D.C., Government Printing Office, 1885), pp. 748–749, 752–753.*

    It is a violation of the law to reproduce this selection by any means whatsoever without the written permission of the copyright holder.

at a time when I was a boy. For a good many years I was employed in a subordinate position in the Augusta factory and afterwards I got to be the overseer.

Q: You have worked your way up, as Mr. Hickman says a man will?
A: Yes, sir; as some men will.
Q: What is the capital stock of the Enterprise Company?
A: Five hundred thousand dollars.
Q: What is the annual product?
A: We run 602 looms at the present time.
Q: How many bales of lint cotton do you work up?
A: About 6,200 a year.
Q: How much help do you employ?
A: We have, I think, 485 on our pay-roll.
Q: How many of those are men?
A: I cannot answer that exactly; about one-seventh.
Q: The rest are women and children, I suppose?
A: Yes, sir.
Q: How many of them would you class as women and how many as children?
A: I think about one-third of the remainder would be children and two-thirds women. That is about the proportion.
Q: What is the average wages that you pay?
A: Eighty-two cents a day for the last six months, or in that neighbor-hood.
Q: What do the women make a day?
A: About $1.
Q: And the men?
A: Do you mean common laborers?
Q: Yes; the average wages of your laborers.
A: About $1 a day.
Q: What do the children make on an average?
A: About from 35 to 75 cents a day.
Q: You employ children of ten years and upward?
A: Yes, sir.
Q: Do you employ any below the age of ten?
A: No.
Q: About what proportion of the men in your employ can read and write; I mean who can read well enough to read the Constitution of the United States, or the New Testament, or a newspaper and understand what they are about?
A: I think about two-thirds of them can do it.
Q: What proportion of the women?
A: Not so large a proportion; I should think, probably, one-half of them.
Q: You think that one-half of the female operatives in your employ can read a common book, one of the novels of the day, or a history of the United States, and understand it?
A: I think that one-half of them may be said to know how to read, but that is a rough guess on my part.

Q: What proportion of the children can read or write?

A: Most of them can read. They nearly all go to Sunday school.

Q: Do they learn to read in the Sunday schools?

A: Yes sir; if they have not learned elsewhere before they come to the mill.

Q: Then, reading and writing are taught in the Sunday schools?

A: Yes; reading is. I think a larger proportion of the children than of the grown people can read intelligently....

Q: What is your experience as to the employment of child labor?

A: What do you mean?

Q: I mean is it a good thing according to your experience that children of from ten to fifteen years of age should work in the factories?

A: Yes, sir; I think it is.

Q: Do you think it is a good thing that they should work eleven hours a day all the year around?

A: I think it would be better for them if they were not compelled to work at all, but—

Q: (Interposing.) You would want them to work a part of the time in order to learn a business for life, would you not?

A: Yes, sir. Circumstances now force them into the mills. They come in with their mothers.

Q: I understand that as a matter of fact, in the present condition of these people it is a necessity that they shall have employment, and that the employment of the children of a family oftentimes prevents the whole family from becoming paupers; but setting aside this temporary necessity, do you think it well that children between the ages of say ten and fourteen years should be required to work more than about half the time in a factory?

A: Well, I don't know that I can answer that question satisfactorily. I don't know whether they should be compelled to work at all in the factory unless circumstances made it necessary.

Q: You think, I suppose, that it would be better for the children to have a chance to be outdoors?

A: Yes, sir.

Q: But the testimony is that many of those children seem to enjoy their work in the factory.

A: Oh, yes. It is not laborious work, and it is not continuous; there is more or less rest as they go along.

Q: Not much play, I suppose?

A: Some little; not much. Of course, we have discipline in the mill, but the labor is not continuous or excessive.

Q: Do the children remain in the mill during the whole eleven hours as the older operatives do?

A: Yes.

Q: How as to their chance of getting some education in your free schools?

A: Well, in individual cases they sometimes quit the mill and go to school—some of them do.

Q: For how long periods?
A: Indefinite periods. Some of the parents take their children out when they feel that they can do without them for a while and send them to school, and afterwards when it becomes necessary they send them back to the mill again. There is no rule about it.
Q: But most of them remain in the mill one year after another, I suppose.
A: Oh, yes; but they change a good deal out and in.

The following reading is part of a report of a committee of the Assembly of the State of New York. *

The inquiry into the condition of manufacturing places in the city of New York, and the condition and circumstances of the persons who worked therein, has involved the inquiry into branches of State and city government which are naturally and indissolubly connected therewith. The education and health of the persons who work in manufacturing establishments, as well as the sanitary arrangements and conditions existing therein, have necessarily become a part of the committee's inquiry, and the committee has found that the welfare of the working people depends not upon the wisdom, adequacy and enforcement of the Factory Law alone, but in addition upon proper and adequate education and health laws.

The opinion of the committee presented in its preliminary report, that large numbers of children were employed in manufacturing places contrary to law, has been amply confirmed by its further and fuller investigations. The committee stamps the employment of child labor under the statutory age as one of the most extensive evils now existing in the city of New York, and an evil which is a constant and grave menace to the welfare of its people. Many children were found by the diligent efforts of the committee's subpoena servers and brought before the committee, who were under the requisite age, and many others were seen by members of the committee upon their investigation tours. These children were undersized, poorly clad and dolefully ignorant, unacquainted with the simplest rudiments of a common school education, having no knowledge of the simplest figures and unable in many cases to write their own names in the native or any other language.

The following illustrations, of the many which could be cited, will suffice to corroborate the broad statement contained in the previous sentence:

Eva Lunsky testified as follows:

Q: When were you born?
A: I don't know.

* From Documents of the Assembly of the State of New York, *119th Session, 1896, Volume 23, No. 97, Part I (Albany, Wynkoop Hallenback Crawford Company, 1896), pp. 5–7, 460–465.*

Q: Nobody has ever told you?
A: No, sir.
Q: Did your mamma ever tell you when you were born?
A: She told me, but I have forgotten.
Q: You don't know whether you ever had a birthday part or not?
A: Yes, sir; I have had a birthday party.
Q: When?
A: Last year.
Q: How old were you last year?
A: I was 15
Q: Was it in the winter time?
A: It was in the summer time?
Q: And you don't know the month?
A: No, sir.
Q: Do you know when the Fourth of July is?
A: No, sir.
Q: Do you know when the summer time is when they fire off fire crack-
   ers; don't they have any down your way? (The witness gave no an-
   swer.)
Q: Did you ever go to school in this country?
A: I went only three months.
Q: When was that, Eva?
A: That was last summer.
Q: What time in the summer was it that you went there; what months,
   do you know?
A: No.
Q: Do you know the names of the summer months?
A: No, sir.
Q: What month is this; do you know what month this is?
A: No.

Again, Fannie Harris, who earned two dollars per week, of which
her mother allowed her two cents a week for spending money, testified:

Q: Now, have you been to school in this country?
A: No.
Q: Can you read?
A: I can read a little, not much.
Q: What can you read—can you read "dog?"
A: No, sir.
Q: Do you know how to spell dog?
A: I went to night school.
Q: Do you know how to spell dog?
A: I have forgotten it since night school stopped.
Q: Can you spell "cat?"
A: Yes, sir.
Q: How do you spell it?
A: I have forgot.

Q: When did you have a birthday; did you have a birthday lately?
A: No, sir.
Q: Did you ever have a birthday?
A: No, sir.
Q: You know what a birthday is, don't you, Fannie?
A: Yes, sir.
Q: What is that?
A: The day that you were born.
Q: Now, didn't you have a birthday?
A: I never had a birthday because we have not any money to make a birthday.
Q: That is, you never had a little party?
A: No, sir.
Q: A birthday is a day when you have a little party, is it not?
A: Yes, sir.
Q: Does your mamma work?
A: Now she ain't working, because I am working, but before, when I didn't work, she worked.
Q: Your mamma is not sick, is she?
A: No, sir.
Q: And your mamma wants you to go to work?
A: Yes, sir; sure she does; and I want to go to work myself.
Q: And if you don't go to work then your mamma will have to go to work?
A: Sure.
Q: Now, Fannie, when will you be 15 years of age?
A: I don't know.
Q: Are you 15 now?
A: No, sir.
Q: And this paper (showing age certificate) your mamma gave you, did she?
A: I went to a lawyer and paid twenty-five cents and he gave me it....

Abraham Rose, having been called as a witness (not sworn) testified as follows:
Examination by Mr. Mayer:

Q: You are not afraid of me, are you?
A: I can't understand English.
Q: You are not afraid of me, are you?
A: No.
Q: Will you tell me the truth in everything I ask you?
A: I will.
Q: What is going to happen to you if you do not tell the truth? (The examination of this witness was conducted with the aid of an interpreter.)
A: He knows that; he knows he will be punished if he don't tell the truth.
Q: Where do you live?

A: Five Norfolk street.
Q: Where do you work?
A: By Mr. Levi.
Q: Where is his place of business?
A: Thirty-one Hester street.
Q: Where were you born?
A: I don't know.
Q: Where were you born.
A: I was born in Gallacia.
Q: Is your papa alive?
A: Yes, sir.
Q: What does he do?
A: My father is living and working; he is a peddler.
Q: How much does Levi pay you every week.
A: He pays me two dollars a week.
Q: When do you go to work in the morning?
A: At seven o'clock.
Q: When do you go home?
A: At six o'clock.
Q: Do you get any time for dinner in the middle of the day?
A: Yes, sir.
Q: Do you go home for dinner?
A: I go home to dinner.
Q: Do you take dinner with your mother?
A: I live with my mother, and my mother gives me to eat.
Q: What do you do with the two dollars you get every week?
A: I give it to my mother.
Q: Does your mother give you any money to spend?
A: She don't give me nothing but one penny.
Q: One penny every week?
A: Every week one penny.
Q: When were you confirmed?
A: One year.
Q: Now, who told you to tell us that?
A: Nobody told me.
Q: What synagogue were you confirmed in?
A: I was confirmed in Europe—not here.
Q: When did you come from Europe?
A: About six months I am here.
Q: And is your father here only the same time?
A: My father and mother came here with me.
Q: What time of the year was it that you were confirmed?
A: He was confirmed about the fall or winter, he was confirmed about
   December.
Q: Last December?
A: Before that—about a couple of weeks before that; I was confirmed a
   year previous to last December.
Q: Now, you must be 13 years old to be confirmed, must you not?

A: I was 13 years old when I was confirmed.
Q: How old must a body be when he is confirmed?
A: Thirteen years old.
Q: How long have you been working for Levi?
A: Two months and a half I am working for Mr. Levi.
Q: Did you work for anybody else in this country?
A: Yes, sir; someone else.
Q: Who else—where does he live?
A: His name was Levi too.
Q: Where does he live?
A: In Montgomery street, but I don't remember the number.
Q: How much did this man pay you—the first Levi?
A: One dollar and a half a week.
Q: And did you work just as long as you are working now?
A: Yes, sir; I did.
Q: What do you do now—what is the kind of work you do?
A: I am pulling bastings.
Q: And you do that all day long?
A: Sometimes if there is nothing why I do nothing, but all the time there is nothing but bastings pulling.
Q: He keeps you busy all day long?
A: There is only one finisher present and she can't give me work enough to pull bastings out.
Q: Can you write your name in English.
A: I can read it in Polish.
Q: Can you write your name in English?
A: I don't know whether I could or not.
Q: You can not, can you?
A: No.
Q: Now, do you know what day to-day is?
A: Yes, sir.
Q: What day is today?
A: Monday.
Q: What month is this month?
A: I don't know what month it is.
Q: Can you write anything in Polish?
A: Yes, sir; I can write in Polish my name, my address, etc.
Q: Anything else?
A: I can write a little, but not very good.
Q: Can you add up?
A: I could, but I have forgotten.
Q: Do you know how much two and three make?
A: Yes, sir.
Q: How much?
A: Five.
Q: How much does five and seven make?
A: Five and seven makes twelve.
Q: Were you ever in school in this country?

A: No, sir; I was not.

Q: Who told you that you were 14 years old?

A: I know that by when I was confirmed; I am 13 years old, and I am confirmed one year, and therefore I know I am 14 years old; that is the only reason I know I am 14 years old.

Q: Did you and Levi have a talk before you came down here today?

A: No, sir. I have not spoken to Mr. Levi before I came here.

Q: Who told you how to get here?

A: My boss brought me here.

Q: What did he say to you on the way down from the shop?

A: A man brought me here to-day that came for me—a man that brought me here.

Q: You were down in the other building last Saturday, were you not?

A: I was last Saturday with my boss in the other building.

Q: Did he say anything to you last Saturday?

A: No; he said nothing to me last Saturday.

Nathan Levi, having been called as a witness and duly sworn by the chairman, testified as follows:

Examination by Mr. Mayer:

Q: What is you full name?

A: Nathan Levi.

Q: Where do you live?

A: Thirty-one Hester street.

Q: Now, Levi, this little boy Abraham Rose who was on the stand is employed by you, is he not?

A: Yes, sir.

Q: How old is he?

A: His father told me—

Q: How old is he?

A: I don't know.

Q: When did the father tell you that?

A: He told me that.

Q: Talk so we can understand you.

A: Yes, sir; when he came to me to work I asked him how old he was and he told me he was 14 years old, and I take him to work.

Q: He told you he was 14 years old; when was he 14?

A: About ten weeks ago.

Q: Was he 14 years old just before the Jewish holiday?

A: Yes, sir.

Q: Before what holiday?

A: Ten weeks before; he came up to me to work and I asked him how old he was and he told me 14 years.

Q: Now, when was he 14 years old; did the father tell you that?

A: No, sir; I don't ask him for that.

Q: Did you not ask the father to go before a notary public; you didn't ask him to swear to the boy's age?

A: No, sir.
Q: Have you done anything else except ask the father how old he was?
A: I told him to bring me a ticket.
Q: Has he brought you any ticket?
A: No, sir.
Q: Have you done anything else to find our how old he is?
A: No, sir.
Q: How long has he been with you?
A: Ten weeks.
Q: How much would you have to pay a boy 16 years old to do the same work that this little boy is doing?
A: All the same.
Q: You would pay a boy 16 years old two dollars, would you?
A: For this work I don't pay any more.

By Mr. Wilks:

Q: Can you get a boy 16 years old to work for that?
A: Yes, sir.

By Mr. Mayer:

Q: Did you ever have one?
A: Yes sir; I had a boy 16 years old.
Q: What was his name?
A: I couldn't remember his name.
Q: When did you keep him?
A: When I lived in East New York.
Q: When did you keep the boy that was 16 years old?
A: Before my present boy came to me.
Q: So you had this 16-year-old boy about two months ago, did you?
A: Yes, sir.
Q: What did he leave you for?
A: I don't know why.
Q: What were you paying when he left?
A: Two dollars a week.
Q: How old was he?
A: Sixteen years old.
Q: How do you know he was 16?
A: He brought me a ticket.
Q: He brought you a ticket, did he?
A: Yes, sir.
Q: Why didn't you ask for a ticket from this little boy?
A: I asked him for a ticket.
Q: You never asked for one, did you?
A: I asked the father for a ticket.
Q: He has been with you for ten weeks?
A: Yes, sir.

Q: Was there never a factory inspector in your place?
A: No, sir.
Q: How long have you been doing business where you are now?
A: Five years.
Q: And there never has been a factory inspector there?
A: No, sir.
Q: Do you know what a factory inspector is?
A: Yes, sir.
Q: There never was a factory inspector to see you?
A: No, sir.
Q: Not in five years?
A: I don't live there five years.
Q: How long have you been in this place, No. 11 Norfolk street?
A: Only about four months.
Q: In No. 11 Norfolk street; that is where you have your workshop now?
A: Yes, sir.
Q: Where were you before that?
A: In East New York.
Q: How long were you there?
A: About a year and a half.
Q: What do you mean by telling me nobody hs been to see you for five years?
A: There was a lady in East New York.
Q: But there has been nobody here in Norfolk street?
A: No, sir.
Q: Do you know what can be done to you for employing this boy?
A: No, sir; I don't know.
Q: Did you ever try to find out?
A: No, sir.
Q: Do you know whether you have a right to employ that boy?
A: I asked for a ticket.
Q: Do you know whether you have a right to employ that boy?
A: If he is 14 years old then I can take him to work.
Q: Is that all you know; if he is under 16 years of age and can not write a sentence in English can you employ him?
A: I don't know that.
Q: Did the factory inspector tell you that?
A: No, sir.
Q: Has there ever been an inspector from the board of health where you are now?
A: No, sir.

11 | Letters from Six Farm Men and Women

Hard times on the farm fueled the Populist movement of the late nineteenth century. You can see the reality behind the political slogans of the era in letters written by farm men and women to Populist newspapers or Populist politicians. The first letter is from Minnesota; the second from Nebraska; the third from North Dakota; the fourth from a Nebraskan preparing to move to the Oklahoma Territory; and the fifth and sixth are from Kansas. Although the spelling and grammar in the letters are far from exemplary, the farmers' concerns—the cost of land, railroad rates, credit rates, drought—are real and compelling. The farmers found expression not only in the Populist or People's party, but in the 1896 capture of the Democratic party by the followers of William Jennings Bryan.

HALVOR HARRIS*

In the minds of the forlorne and the unprotected Poor People of this and other states I might say I am one of those Poor and unprotected. One of those which have settled upon the socalled Indemnity Land of the Minn St Paul and Manitoba now the great Northern [Railroad]. I settled on this Land in good Faith Built House and Barn Broken up Part of the Land. Spent years of hard Labor in grubing fencing and Improving are they going to drive us out like tresspassers wife and children a sickly wife with Poor Health enough Before and give us away to the Corporations how can we support them. When we are robed of our means. they will shurely not stand this we must Decay and Die from Woe and Sorrow We are Loyal Citicens and do Not Intend to Intrude on any R.R. Corporation we Believed and still do Believe that the RR Co has got No Legal title to this Land in question We Love our wife and children just as Dearly as any of you But how can we protect them give them education as they should wen we are driven from sea to sea. . . .

Halvor Harris to Ignatius Donnelly, January 29, 1891, Donnelly Papers, Minnesota Historical Society.

W. M. TAYLOR*

This season is without a parallel in this part of the country. The hot winds burned up the entire crop, leaving thousands of families wholly destitute, many of whom might have been able to run through this crisis had it not been for the galling yoke put on them by the money loaners and sharks—not by charging 7 per cent. per annum, which is the lawful rate of interest, or even 10 per cent. ,but the unlawful and inhuman country destroying rate of 3 per cent. a month, some going still farther and charging 50 per cent per annum. We are cursed, many of us financially, beyond redemption, not by the hot winds so much as by the swindling games of the bankers and money loaners, who have taken the money and now are after the property, leaving the farmer moneyless and homeless.... I have borrowed for example $1,000. I pay $25 besides to the commission man. I give my note and second mortgage of 3 per cent of the $1,000, which is $30 more. Then I pay 7 per cent. on the $1,000 to the actual loaner. Then besides all this I pay for appraising the land, abstract, recording, etc., so when I have secured my loan I am out the first year $150. Yet I am told by the agent who loans me the money, he can't stand to loan at such low rates. This is on the farm, but now comes the chattel loan. I must have $50 to save myself. I get the money; my note is made payable in thirty or sixty days for $35, secured by chattel of two horses, harness and wagon, about five times the value of the note. The time comes to pay, I ask for a few days. No I can't wait; must have the money. If I can't get the money, I have the extreme pleasure of seeing my property taken and sold by this iron handed money loaner while my family and I suffer.

W. T. McCULLOCH**

As We are about to have our first great Battle in this State between Corporate Greed, and the great Plain People, the Strugle will be a Desperate one, and must be fought to a finish. Determining, whether it shall be Masters, and Slaves, or a free People. in fact as well as in Name. And few, Reading thinking Men in America, Deny the Slavery of the Masses. to the Money Power of our Country, and a large Portion of our People, having lost all faith in our present Political Parties. for any Reforms. that would wrest the Masses of our People from Corporate Greed. Or give them any Rights, that Corporate Greed would have to respect It does

---

*W. M. *Taylor to editor,* Farmer's Alliance *(Lincoln), January 10, 1891, Nebraska Historical Society.*
**W. T. McCulloch to Ignatius Donnelly, April, 1892, Donnelly Papers, Minnesota Historical Society.*

11 / HARRIS ET AL.: LETTERS FROM SIX FARM MEN AND WOMEN   91

not appear, that we are Destined to Slavery of one Kind or another,
For the Slavery of to Day. Is but of a little different Kind from that
of old. While in former Days it was necessary, that the Masters Keep
within reach of their Slaves. in order to reap the Profits of their Toil. . . .
And there is no Denying. that the Masses have literally slept, the Sleep
that brings on Tenantry and Serfdom. and the Partizan Hireling Press
have depended upon our Ignorance, and their Power to fool us, and
have taken unto themselves. leases, for Prevarication. Missrepresenta-
tion and Slander. which is a Menace. to the Moral. Social and financial
welfare of every Honest Citizen, and Bodes the Destruction of this Republic. and our People must be put on their guard. Taught not, only the
remedy but how to apply it, in order to rid our Land of this Blighting.
Blasting Curse, which is undermining. Honest true Manhood in every
Department of Life. where they Will not be made Jumping Jacks, at
their Beck or call.

M. F. BLANKENSHIP*

I had a mortgage on my team, like all my brother farmers, of $64.50.
I was given to understand that this must be paid. To borrow money
was out of the question. Nothing was left for me to do but haul off
corn, hogs, etc., and pay it. I went to work, hauled off my corn and
hogs and sold my hay and paid it. I had made calculations and found I
would have no feed, seed, or even bread and meat. . . . I did not know
what to do. I received a letter from my uncle in Oklahoma, stating there
was plenty of work here at good wages. There was no work, as you all
know, in Custer county. After taking all things in careful consideration
I concluded I would come to Oklahoma where I could get work. Before
reaching this conclusion it cost me many a bitter tear and sleepless night.

SUSAN ORCUTT**

I take my Pen In hand to let you know that we are Starving to death It
is Pretty hard to do without any thing to Eat hear in this God for saken
country we would of had Plenty to Eat if the hail hadent cut our rye
down and ruined our corn and Potatoes I had the Prettiest Garden that
you Ever seen and the hail ruined It and I have nothing to look at My
Husband went a way to find work and came home last night and told

*M. F. Blankenship to editor, Custer County Beacon (Broken Bow, Nebraska), March 24, 1892, Nebraska Historical Society.
**Susan Orcutt to Lorenzo D. Lewelling, June 29, 1894, Lewelling Papers, Kansas State Historical Society.

It is a violation of the law to reproduce these selections by any means whatsoever without the written permission of the copyright holder.

me that we would have to Starve he has bin in ten countys and did not Get no work It is Pretty hard for a woman to do with out any thing to Eat when She dosent no what minute She will be confined to bed If I was In Iowa I would be all right I was born there and raised there I havent had nothing to Eat to day and It is three oclock[.]

W. R. CHRISTY*

We are worried over what our Poor People of our county are to do for fuel to keep them warm this winter. . . . there are at least $\frac{2}{3}$ of the People that have to depend on Cow chips for fuel & as the cattle had to be Sold off verry close that its been difficult to get them. Some have went as far as 13 miles to get them. the thermometer this morning was 16 below zero & .4 or 5 inches of snow on the ground, under those circumstances what are the People to do. at this time our coal dealers have not all told more than 100 bushels of coal on hand & it cant be bought for less than 40¢ per hundred in Less than ton lots.

*W. R. Christy to L. P. Broad, December 28, 1894, Lewelling Papers, Kansas State Historical Society.

12 | Breaking Up a Bar in Kansas

Carry A. Nation (1846–1911) and her hatchet became familiar symbols of the battle against alcohol consumption from 1899 until her death. A hero to some and a laughingstock to others, she went on "hatchetations" of bars. Armed, she claimed, with divine guidance as well as bricks and a hatchet, she would enter a saloon, sing hymns, shout denunciations and passages from the Bible, then smash bottles, furniture, mirrors, and risqué decorations. Occasionally she would be mobbed or beaten, although at nearly six feet and 175 pounds she was a formidable adversary. Not until near the end of her life, after having been beaten by the woman owner of a Montana saloon, did she abandon her trademark hatchet.

Carry Nation became an embarrassment to the temperance movement, and she soon had no political champions. Yet she continued to receive thousands of small donations which indicated that she remained a hero to many. Campaigns against drink have punctuated American history and have always generated controversy. Whether Nation's dramatic tactics helped or hindered the cause is a debatable question.

At the time these dives were open, contrary to the statutes of our state, the officers were really in league with this lawless element. I was heavily burdened and could see "the wicked walking on every side, and the vilest men exalted." (Ps. 12:8.) I was ridiculed, was called "meddler," "crazy," was pointed to as a fanatic. I spent much time in tears, prayer and fasting. I would fast days at a time. One day I was so sad; I opened the Bible with a prayer for light, and saw these words: "Arise, shine, for thy light is come and the glory of the Lord is risen upon thee." (Isa. 60:1.) These words gave me unbounded delight.

I ran to a sister and said: "There is to be a change in my life."

As Jail Evangelist for the W. C. T. U. in Medicine Lodge, I would ask the men in prison, young and old, why are you here? The answer was, it was "drink," "drink." I said, why do you get drunk in Kansas where we have no saloons? They told me that they got their drink in

Carry A. Nation, The Use and Need of the Life of Carry A. Nation. *(Topeka, F.M. Steves & Sons, 1909), pp. 126–135.*

It is a violation of the law to reproduce this selection by any means whatsoever without the written permission of the copyright holder.

Kiowa. This town was in Barber county, a county right on the border of Oklahoma. I went to Mr. Sam Griffen, the County Attorney, time after time, telling him of these men being in jail from drink. He would put the matter off and seem very much annoyed because I asked him to do what he swore he would do, for he was oath bound to get out a warrant and put this in the hands of the sheriff who was oath bound to arrest these dive-keepers, and put them in jail and the place or dive was to be publicly abated or destroyed. Mr. Griffen was determined that these dive-keepers should not be arrested. I even went down to Kiowa myself and went into these places and came back asking this County Attorney to take my evidence and he would not do it. Then I wrote to Mr. A. A. Godard of Topeka, the State's Attorney, whose duty it was to see that all the County Attorneys did their duties. I saw he did not intend to do anything, then I went to William Stanley the Governor at Topeka. I told him of the prisoners in jail in our county from the sale of liquor in the dives of Kiowa, told him of the broken families and trouble of all kinds in the county, told him of two murders that had been committed in the county, one alone costing the tax payers $8,000.00, told him of the broken hearted women and the worse than fatherless children as the result. I found out that he would not do his duty. I had gone from the lowest to the chief-executive of the state, and after appealing to the governor in vain I found that I could go to no other authority on earth.

Now I saw that Kansas was in the power of the bitter foe to the constitution, and that they had accomplished what the whiskey men and their tools, the Republican party and politicians had schemed and worked for. When two thirds of the voters of Kansas said at the ballot box—about 1880, I think it was—"We will not have a saloon in our state." This was made constitutional by the two-thirds majority. Nothing could change this or take it out of the constitution except by having the amendment re-submitted and two-thirds of the people voting to bring the saloons back. They intended then with their bribes and otherwise to buy votes. The first act was to organize the state into what they called the "Mystic Order of Brotherhood." Of course this was kept very quiet and few of the people in the towns knew of this order and organization. When the Devil wants to carry out his deepest plots he must do, through a secret order, what he cannot otherwise do. He does his work through, by, and in, the kingdom of darkness. For this one reason he must hoodwink the people to make them his tools.

God has given me a mean fight, a dirty and dangerous fight; for it is a war on the hidden things of darkness. I am, in this book throwing all the light I can on the dangerous foe to liberty, free speech and Christianity, the Masonic Lodge, which is the father of all the other secret orders. Through this Mystic Order of Brotherhood managing the primaries and elections, they got into office from constable up to the governor, the tools of the liquor power. The great question that was then discussed was "re-submission." Every representative to congress at Topeka was in favor of the re-submission without an exception. Money was sent into Kansas by the thousands from brewers and distillers to be used by politicians for the purpose of bringing about re-submission. Kansas was the storm center. If the liquor men could bring back saloons into Kansas then a great blow would be struck against prohibition in all the states. This would discourage the people all over. Their great word was, "you can't," "prohibition will not prohibit." I do not belong to the "can't" family. When I was born my father wrote my name Carry A. Moore, then later it was Nation, which is more still. C. A. N. are the initials of my name, then C. (see) A. Nation! And all together Carry A. Nation! This is no accident but Providence. This does not mean that I will carry a nation, but that the roused heart and conscience will, as I am the roused heart and conscience of the people in operation. There are just two crowds, God's crowd and the Devil's crowd. One gains the battle by *can*, and the other loses it by *can't*.

My Christian experience will give you the secret of my life. It is God indwelling. When I found I could effect nothing through the officials, I was sad, indeed. I saw that Kansas homes, hearts and souls were to be sacrificed. I had lost all the hopes of my young life through drink, I saw the terrible results that would befall others. I felt that I had rather die than see the saloons come back into Kansas. I felt desperate. I took this to God daily, feeling that He only, could rescue. On the 5th of June, 1899, before retiring, I threw myself face downward at the foot of my bed in my home in Medicine Lodge. I poured out my grief and agony to God, in about this strain: "Oh Lord you see the treason in Kansas, they are going to break the mothers' hearts, they are going to send the boys to drunkards' graves and a drunkard's hell. I have exhausted all my means, Oh Lord, you have plenty of ways. You have used the base things and the weak things, use me to save Kansas. I have but one life to give you, If I had a thousand, I would give them all, please show me something to do." The next morning I was awakened by a voice which seemed to be speaking in my heart, these words, "Go to Kiowa," and my hands were lifted and thrown down and the words, "I'll stand by you." The words, "Go to Kiowa," were spoken in a murmuring, musical tone, low and soft, but, "I'll stand by you," was very clear, positive and emphatic. I was impressed with a great inspiration, the interpretation was very plain, it was this: "Take something in your hands, and throw at these places in Kiowa and smash them." I was very much relieved and overjoyed and was determined to be, "obedient to the heavenly vision." (Acts 20:19.) I told no one what I heard or what I intended to do.

I was a busy home keeper, did all my house work, was superintendent of two Sunday schools, one in the country, was jail evangelist, and president of the W. C. T. U. and kept open house for all of God's people, where all the Christian workers were welcome to abide at my house.

When no one was looking I would walk out in the yard and pick up brick bats and rocks, would hide them under my kitchen apron, would take them in my room, would wrap them up in newspapers one by one. I did this until I got quite a pile. A very sneaking degenerate druggist in Medicine Lodge named Southworth, had for years been selling intoxicating liquors on the sly. I had gotten in his drug store four bottles of Schlitz Malt. I was going to use them as evidence to convict this wily dive keeper.

One of the bottles I took to a W. C. T. U. meeting and in the presence of the ladies I opened it and drank the contents. Then I had two of them to take me down to a Doctor's office. I fell limp on the sofa and said: "Doctor, what is the matter with me?"

He looked at my eyes, felt my heart and pulse, shook his head and looked grave.

I said: "Am I poisoned?" "Yes, said the Doctor."

I said: "What poisoned me is that beer you recommended Bro. — — to take as a tonic." I resorted to this strategem, to show the effect that beer has upon the system. This Doctor was a kind man and meant well, but it must have been ignorance that made him say beer could ever be used as a medicine.

There was another, Dr. Kocile, in Medicine Lodge who used to sell all the whiskey he could. He made a drunkard of a very prominent woman of the town, who took the Keeley cure. She told the W. C. T. U. of the villainy of this doctor and she could not have hated any one more Oh! the drunkards the doctors are making! No physician, who is worthy of the name will prescribe it as a medicine, for there is not one medical quality in alcohol. It kills the living and preserves the dead. Never preserves anything but death. It is made by a rotting process and it rots the brain, body and soul; it paralyzes the vascular circulation and increases the action of the heart. This is friction and friction in any machinery is dangerous, and the cure is not hastened but delayed.

Any physician that will prescribe whiskey or alcohol as a medicine is either a fool or a knave. A fool because he does not understand his business, for even saying that alcohol does arouse the action of the heart, there are medicines that will do that and will not produce the fatal results of alcoholism, which is the worst of all diseases. He is a knave because his practice is a matter of getting a case, and a fee at the same time, like a machine agent who break the machine to get the job of mending it. Alcohol destroys the normal condition of all the functions of the body. The stomach is thrown out of fix, and the patient goes to the doctor for a stomach pill, the heart, liver, kidneys, and in fact, the whole body is in a deranged condition, and the doctor has a perpetual patient. I sincerely believe this to be the reason why many physicians prescribe it.

At half past three that day I was ready to start, hitched up the horse to the buggy, drove out of the stable, down a hill and over a bridge that was just outside the limits of Medicine Lodge. I saw in the middle of the road perhaps a dozen or so creatures in the forms of men leaning towards the buggy as if against a rope which prevented them from coming nearer. Their faces were those of demons and the gestures of their hands as if they would tear me up. I did not know what to do, but I lifted my hands, and my eyes to God, saying: "Oh! Lord, help me, help me." When I looked down these diabolical creatures were not in front of the buggy, but they were off to the right fleeing as if they were terrified. I did not know or think what this meant. My life was so full of strange, peculiar things at that time that I could not understand the meaning. Not for years did I interpret the meaning of this vision. I know now what those creatures were. They were real devils that knew more of what I was going to do than I did. The devil is a prophet, he reads scripture, he knew Jesus when He was here, and he knew that I came to fulfill prophecy, and that this was a death blow to his kingdom.

The peoples' consciences were asleep while these dreadful burglars of saloons were robbing the homes and God had to shock them to rouse them up. God cannot work with a people whose conscience is dead. The devil cannot continue with an awakened conscience. I expected to stay all night with a dear friend, Sister Springer, who lived about half way to Kiowa. When I arrived near her home the sun was almost down, but I was very eager to go to Kiowa and I said: "Oh, Lord, if it is Thy will for me to go to Kiowa tonight, have Prince, (my horse,) pass this open gate," which I knew he would never do unless God ordered it. I gave him the reins and when I got opposite the open gate my horse jumped forward as if some one had struck him a blow. I got to Kiowa at half past eight, stayed all night. Next morning I had my horse hitched and drove to the first dive kept by a Mr. Dobson, whose brother was then sheriff of the county. I stacked up these smashers on my left arm, all I could hold. They looked like packages wrapped in paper. I stood before the counter and said: "Mr. Dobson, I told you last spring to close this place, you did not do it, now I have come down with another remonstrance, get out of the way, I do not want to strike you, but I am going to break this place up." I threw as hard, and as fast as I could, smashing mirrors and bottles and glasses and it was astonishing how quickly this was done. These men seemed terrified, threw up their hands and backed up in the corner. My strength was that of a giant. I felt invincible. God was certainly standing by me.

I will tell you of a very strange thing. As the stones were flying against this "wonderful and horrible" thing, I saw Mr. McKinley, the President, sitting in an old fashion arm chair and as the stones would strike I saw them hit the chair fell to pieces, and I saw Mr. McKinley fall over. I did not understand this until very recently, now I know that the smashing in Kansas was intended to strike the head of this nation the hardest blow, for every saloon I smashed in Kansas had a license from the head of this government which made the head of the government more responsible than the dive-keeper. I broke up three of these dives that day, broke the windows on the outside to prove that the man who rents his house is a partner also with the man who sells. The party who licenses and the paper that advertises, all have a hand in this and are *particeps criminis*, I smashed five saloons with rocks, before I ever took a hatchet.

In the last place, kept by Lewis, there was quite a young man behind the bar. I said to him: "Young man, come from behind that bar, your mother did not raise you for such a place." I threw a brick at the mirror, which was a very heavy one, and it did not break, but th brick fell and broke everything in its way. I began to look around for something that would break it. I was standing by a billiard table on which there was one ball. I said: "Thank God," and picked it up, threw it, and it made a hole in the mirror.

By this time, the streets were crowded with people; most of them seemed to look puzzled. There was one boy about fifteen years old who seemed perfectly wild with joy, and he jumped, skipped and yelled with delight. I have since thought of that as being a significant sign. For to smash saloons will save the boy.

I stood in the middle of the street and spoke in this way: "I have destroyed three of your places of business, and if I have broken a statute of Kansas, put me in jail; if I am not a law-breaker your mayor and councilmen are. You must arrest one of us, for if I am not a criminal, they are."

One of the councilmen, who was a butcher, said: "Don't you think we can attend to our business?"

"Yes," I said, "You can, but you won't. As Jail Evangelist of Medicine Lodge, I know you have manufactured many criminals and this county is burdened down with taxes to prosecute the results of these dives. Two murders have been committed in the last five years in this county, one in a dive I have just destroyed. You are a butcher of hogs and cattle, but they are butchering men, women and children, positively contrary to the laws of God and man, and the mayor and councilmen are more to blame than the jointist, and now if I have done wrong in any particular arrest me." When I was through with my speech I got into my buggy and said: "I'll go home."

13 | The Bradley Martin Ball

The Bradley Martin Ball, which took place at the Waldorf Hotel in New York City on the night of February 10, 1897, was described in a newspaper as "the most splendid private entertainment ever given in this country." Eight hundred socialites spent about $400,000 imitating kings and queens. At a midnight champagne supper they dined on twenty-eight courses—including "Sorbet Fin de Siécle."

The ball was both a triumph and a disaster. "It may not be surpassed in another hundred years," oozed one society reporter; "it was a gorgeous, superb, and wonderful spectacle." Yet a prominent Episcopalian rector warned that such an occasion in a time of depression and social tension was "ill advised." He was right. Newspapers condemned the Bradley Martins for their extravagance; clergymen preached sermons against them; college debating societies resolved their iniquity. And the New York Assessor doubled their taxes. The Bradley Martins permanently retreated to England after a final and characteristic gesture: a farewell dinner for eighty-six intimate friends which, the newspapers faithfully reported, cost $116.28 a plate.

Every year my brother Bradley and his wife spent their winters in New York, when they entertained largely. One morning at breakfast my brother remarked—

"I think it would be a good thing if we got up something; there seems to be a great deal of depression in trade; suppose we send out invitations for a concert."

"And pray, what good will that do?" asked my sister-in-law, "the money will only benefit foreigners. No, I've a far better idea; let us give a costume ball at so short notice that our guests won't have time to get their dresses from Paris. That will give an impetus to trade that nothing else will."

Directly Mrs. Martin's plan became known, there was a regular storm of comment, which arose in the first instance from the remarks made by a clergyman who denounced the costume ball from the pulpit.

"Yes," he raged, "you rich people put next to nothing in the collection plate, and yet you'll spend thousands of dollars on Mrs. Bradley Martin's ball."

Frederick Martin Townsend, Things I Remember. (London, E. Nash, 1913), pp. 238–243.

The newspapers then took up the subject, and we were besieged by reporters, but my brother and his wife invariably refused to discuss the matter. Threatening letters arrived by every post, debating societies discussed our extravagance, and last, but not least, we were burlesqued unmercifully on the stage.

I was highly indignant about my sister-in-law being so cruelly attacked, seeing that her object in giving the ball was to stimulate trade, and, indeed, she was perfectly right, for, owing to the short notice, many New York shops sold out brocades and silks which had been lying in their stock-rooms for years.

The ball was fixed for February 10, 1897, and a day or two before Mrs. Martin met Theodore Roosevelt in the street. "I'm very pleased that you and Mrs. Roosevelt are coming to the ball," she said.

"Oh," he replied, "my wife's going because she's got her costume, but, as one of the commissioners, I shall be outside looking after the police!"

I think every one anticipated a disturbance, but nothing of the kind took place, and the evening passed without any untoward incident.

The best way I can describe what is always known as the "Bradley Martin Ball," is to say that it reproduced the splendour of Versailles in New York, and I doubt if even the Roi Soleil himself ever witnessed a more dazzling sight. The interior of the Waldorf-Astoria Hotel was transformed into a replica of Versailles, and rare tapestries, beautiful flowers and countless lights made an effective background for the wonderful gowns and their wearers. I do not think there has ever been a greater display of jewels before or since; in many cases the diamond buttons worn by the men represented thousands of dollars, and the value of the historic gems worn by the ladies baffles description.

My sister-in-law personated Mary Stuart, and her gold embroidered gown was trimmed with pearls and precious stones. Bradley, as Louis XV, wore a Court suit of brocade, and I represented a gentleman of the period. The whole thing appealed most strongly to my imagination, and my mind constantly reverted to the friend of my childhood, the dear grandmother who would have been so keenly interested in it all. I remember that Mrs. James Beekman, as Lady Teazle, wore a lovely dress, which formerly belonged to an ancestress, and Mrs. Henry Burnet's satin petticoat was another family heirloom which left the scented seclusion of a cedar-wood chest for this interesting occasion.

Anne Morgan lent a touch of barbaric colour with her wonderful Pochahontas costume which had been made by Indians, and the suit of gold inlaid armour worn by Mr. Belmont was valued at ten thousand dollars. The power of wealth with its refinement and vulgarity was everywhere. It gleamed from countless jewels, and it was proclaimed by the thousands of orchids and roses, whose fragrance that night was like incense burnt on the altar of the Golden Calf.

I cannot conceive why this entertainment should have been condemned. We Americans are so accustomed to display that I should have thought the ball would not have been regarded as anything very unusual. Every one said it was the most brilliant function of the kind ever seen in America, and it certainly was the most talked about.

After the ball the authorities promptly raised my brother's taxes quite out of proportion to those paid by any one else, and the matter was only settled after a very acrimonious dispute. Bradley and his wife resented intensely the annoyance to which they had been subjected, and they decided to sell their house in New York and buy a residence in London.

Four years previously their only daughter, Cornelia, had married Lord Craven, and my brother felt that the family affections were now implanted in the Old World. His grandson, who was born in the year of the famous ball, was such a source of pride to us all that I believe the advent of the boy finally decided the Bradley Martins about leaving New York.

14 | The Threat to the "White Goddess"

"Unguarded Gates," written in 1885, is a poetic expression of opposition to unrestricted immigration. Its author, Thomas Bailey Aldrich, was a member of the social elite of New York and Boston who, although he lived near the immigrants' ghettos, never sought to understand their culture, ignored their economic contributions, and saw them only as a social problem. Aldrich reflected the concerns felt by many Americans over the so-called new immigration from southern and eastern Europe. Beginning in the 1880s, this human tide exceeded immigration from northern and western Europe. As this influx reached its peak in the period from 1905 to 1914, sentiments like Aldrich's became more prominent and led ultimately to the immigration restriction "quota" laws of 1921 and 1924.

Unguarded Gates

Wide open and unguarded stand out gates,
    Named of the four winds, North, South, East, and
West;
Portals that lead to an enchanted land
    Of cities, forests, fields of living gold,
Vast prairies, lordly summits touched with snow,
    Majestic rivers sweeping proudly past
The Arab's date-palm and the Norseman's pine—
    A realm wherein are fruits of every zone,
Airs of all climes, for lo! throughout the year
    The red rose blossoms somewhere—a rich land,
A later Eden planted in the wilds,
    With not an inch of earth within its bound
But if a slave's foot press it sets him free.
    Here, it is written, Toil shall have its wage,
And Honor honor, and the humblest man
    Stand level with the highest in the law.
Of such a land have men in dungeons dreamed,
    And with the vision brightening in their eyes

Thomas Bailey Aldrich, Unguarded Gates and Other Poems, (Boston, Houghton, Mifflin and Company, 1895), pp. 15–17.

Gone smiling to the fagot and the sword.
  Wide open and unguarded stand our gates,
And through them presses a wild motley throng—
  Men from the Volga and the Tartar steppes,
Featureless figures of the Hoang-Ho,
  Malayan, Scythian, Teuton, Kelt, and Slav,
Flying the Old World's povery and scorn;
  These bringing with them unknown gods and
  rites,
Those, tiger passions, here to stretch their claws.
  In street and alley what strange tongues are loud,
Accents of menace alien to our air,
  Voices that once the Tower of Babel knew!
O Liberty, white Goddess! is it well
  To leave the gates unguarded? On thy breast
Fold Sorrow's children, soothe the hurts of fate,
  Lift the down-trodden, but with hand of steel
Stay those who to thy sacred portals come
  To waste the gifts of freedom. Have a care
Lest from thy brow the clustered stars be torn
  And trampled in the dust. For so of old
The thronging Goth and Vandal trampled Rome,
  And where the temples of the Caesars stood
The lean wolf unmolested made her lair.

ABRAHAM CAHAN

15 | A Bintel Brief

*Years before "Ann Landers" and "Dear Abby," there was "A Bintel Brief."
In 1906 the Jewish* Daily Forward, *a Yiddish-language newspaper addressing
the large community of Jewish immigrants in New York City, began running
an advice column, "A Bintel Brief" [bundle of letters]. The paper's editor was
Abraham Cahan, who also wrote several novels about immigrant life. Cahan
contributed some of the letters as well as the responses. "A Bintel Brief" gave
advice on all kinds of personal problems. The following excerpts from the early
years of the column offer fascinating glimpses into Jewish immigrant life at
the turn of the century, particularly the tensions resulting from the desire to
enjoy full equality and opportunity in a new land, and the need—for at least
some immigrants—to maintain continuity with traditions and beliefs of the old
country.*

Worthy Editor,

We are a small family who recently came to the "Golden Land." My
husband, my boy and I are together, and our daughter lives in another
city.

I had opened a grocery store here, but soon lost all my money. In
Europe we were in business; we had people working for us and paid
them well. In short, there we made a good living but here we are badly
off.

My husband became a peddler. The "pleasure" of knocking on
doors and ringing bells cannot be known by anyone but a peddler.
If anybody does buy anything "on time," a lot of the money is lost,
because there are some people who never intend to pay. In addition,
my husband has trouble because he has a beard, and because of the
beard he gets beaten up by the hoodlums.

Also we have problems with our boy, who throws money around.
He works every day till late at night in a grocery for three dollars a
week. I watch over him and give him the best because I'm sorry that

Isaac Metzker, A Bintel Brief: Sixty Years of Letters from the Lower East Side to the *Jewish*
Daily Forward. *(New York, Doubleday and Company, 1971), pp. 42–44, 49–51, 54–55, 58–59,
63–64, 68–70, 109–110, 117–118. Copyright by the Jewish Daily Forward. Used by permission.*

*It is a violation of the law to reproduce this selection by any means whatsoever without the
written permission of the copyright holder.*

he has to work so hard. But he costs me plenty and he borrows money from everybody. He has many friends and owes them all money. I get more and more worried as he takes here and borrows there. All my talking doesn't help. I am afraid to chase him away from home because he might get worse among strangers. I want to point out that he is well versed in Russian and Hebrew and he is not a child any more, but his behavior is not that of an intelligent adult.

I don't know what to do. My husband argues that he doesn't want to continue peddling. He doesn't want to shave off his beard, and it's not fitting for such a man to do so. The boy wants to go to his sister, but that's a twenty-five-dollar fare. What can I do? I beg you for a suggestion.

Your Constant reader,
F.L.

ANSWER:

Since her husband doesn't earn a living anyway, it would be advisable for all three of them to move to the city where the daughter is living. As for the beard, we feel that if the man is religious and the beard is dear to him because the Jewish law does not allow him to shave it off, it's up to him to decide. But if he is not religious, and the beard interferes with his earnings, it should be sacrificed.

Dear Editor,

For a long time I worked in a shop with a Gentile girl, and we began to go out together and fell in love. We agreed that I would remain a Jew and she a Christian. But after we had been married for a year, I realized that it would not work.

I began to notice that whenever one of my Jewish friends comes to the house, she is displeased. Worse yet, when she sees me reading a Jewish newspaper her face changes color. She says nothing, but I can see that she has changed. I feel that she is very unhappy with me, though I know she loves me. She will soon become a mother, and she is more dependent on me than ever.

She used to be quite liberal, but lately she is being drawn back to the Christian religion. She gets up early Sunday mornings, runs to church and comes home with eyes swollen from crying. When we pass a church now and then, she trembles.

Dear Editor, advise me what to do now. I could never convert, and there's no hope for me to keep her from going to church. What can we do now?

Thankfully,
A Reader

ANSWER:

Unfortunately, we often hear of such tragedies, which stem from marriages between people of different worlds. It's possible that if this couple were to move to a Jewish neighborhood, the young man might have more influence on his wife.

Dear Friend Editor,

Since your worthy newspaper has made it a policy in the "Bintel Brief" to allow everyone to state his opinions, ask questions and request advice, I hope you will allow me, too, to convey some part of my tragic life.

Thirteen years ago I loved and married a quiet young girl, and even in bad times we lived in peace and serenity. I worked hard. My wife devoted herself to our three children and the housekeeping.

A few years ago a brother of mine came to America too, with a friend of his. I worked in a shop, and as I was no millionaire, my brother and his friend became our boarders. Then my trouble began. The friend began earning good money. He began to mix in the household affairs and to buy things for my wife.

Neighbors began to whisper that my wife was carrying on an affair with this boarder, but I had no suspicions of my wife, whom I loved as life itself. I didn't believe them. Nevertheless I told her that people were talking. She swore to me that it was a lie, and evil people were trying to make bad blood between us. She cried as she spoke to me, and I believed her.

But people did not stop talking, and as time went on I saw that my wife was a common liar and that it was all true. My brother took it badly, because he had brought trouble into my home, and in remorse and shame, shot himself. He wounded himself and is left paralyzed on one side of his body. It was a terrible scandal. Good friends mixed in, made peace between us, and for the children's sake we remained together. I promised never to mention the tragic story and she promised to be a loyal wife to me and a good mother to the children she still loves deeply.

Again I worked long and hard, and with the aid of money I borrowed from friends I opened a stationery store. But my wife couldn't restrain herself and betrayed me again. She didn't give up her lover, but ran around with him day and night. I was helpless, because I had to be in the store at all times so she did as she pleased.

Again there was a scandal and her lover fled to Chicago. This was of little avail, because when my wife went to the country for the summer she left the children with the woman who rented her rooms, and went to him for two weeks.

In short, I sold the store and everything is ruined. I gave her a thousand dollars and all her household effects. She and the children are now with him.

I know, dear Editor, that you cannot advise me now, but for me it's enough that I can pour out my suffering on paper. I can't find a place for myself. I miss the children. Life is dark and bitter without them. I hope that my wife will read my letter in the *Forward* and that she will blush with shame.

> With respect, your reader who longs
> for his wife and dear children,
> B.R.

Dear Editor,

I, too, want to take advantage of this opportunity to tell about my troubles, and I ask you to answer me.

Eight months ago I brought my girlfriend from Russia to the States. We had been in love for seven years and were married shortly after her arrival. We were very happy together until my wife became ill. She was pregnant and the doctors said her condition was poor. She was taken to the hospital, but after a few days was sent home. At home, she became worse, and there was no one to tend her.

You can hardly imagine our bitter lot. I had to work all day in the shop and my sick wife lay alone at home. Once as I opened the door when I came home at dinnertime, I heard my wife singing with a changed, hoarse voice. I was terror-stricken, and when I ran to her I saw she was out of her head with fever.

Imagine how I felt. My wife was so ill and I was supposed to run back to the shop because the last whistle was about to blow. Everybody was rushing back to work, but I couldn't leave. I knew that my boss would fire me. He had warned me the day before that if I came late again he wouldn't let me in. But how could I think of work now, when my wife was so ill? Yet without the job what would happen? There would not be a penny coming into the house. I stayed at my wife's bedside and didn't move till four o'clock.

Suddenly I jumped up and began to run around the room, in despair. My wife's singing and talking drove me insane. Like a madman I ran to the door and locked it. I leaped to the gas jet, opened the valve, then lay down in the bed near my wife and embraced her. In a few minutes I was nearer death than she.

Suddenly my wife called out, "Water! water!" I dragged myself from the bed. With my last ounce of strength I crept to the door and opened it, closed the gas valve, and when I came to, gave her milk instead of water. She finished a glassful and wanted more, but there wasn't any more so I brought her some seltzer. I revived myself with water, and both of us slowly recovered.

The next morning they took my wife to the hospital, and after a stay of fourteen days she got well. Now I am happy that we are alive, but I keep thinking of what almost happened to us. Until now I never told anyone about it, but it bothers me. I have no secrets from my wife, and I want to know whether I should now tell her all, or not mention it. I beg you to answer me.

The Newborn

ANSWER:

This letter depicting the sad life of the worker is more powerful than any protest against the inequality between rich and poor. The advice to the writer is that he should not tell his wife that he almost ended both their lives. This secret may be withheld from his beloved wife, since it is clear he keeps it from her out of love.

/   /   /

Dear Editor,

I am a girl from Galicia and in the shop where I work I sit near a Russian Jew with whom I was always on good terms. Why should one worker resent another?

But once, in a short debate, he stated that all Galicians were no good. When I asked him to repeat it, he answered that he wouldn't retract a word, and that he wished all Galician Jews dead.

I was naturally not silent in the face of such a nasty expression. He maintained that only Russian Jews are fine and intelligent. According to him, the *Galitzianer* are inhuman savages, and he had the right to speak of them so badly.

Dear Editor, does he really have a right to say this? Have the Galician Jews not sent enough money for the unfortunate sufferers of the pogroms in Russia? When a Gentile speaks badly of Jews, it's immediately printed in the newspapers and discussed hotly everywhere. But that a Jew should express himself so about his own brothers is nothing? Does he have a right? Are Galicians really so bad? And does he, the Russian, remain fine and intelligent in spite of such expressions?

As a reader of your worthy newspaper, I hope you will print my letter and give your opinion.

With thanks in advance,
B.M.

ANSWER:

The Galician Jews are just as good and bad as people from other lands. If the Galicians must be ashamed of the foolish and evil ones among them, then the Russians, too, must hide their heads in shame because among them there is such an idiot as the acquaintance of our letter writer.

Worthy Editor,

I am eighteen years old and a machinist by trade. During the past year I suffered a great deal, just because I am a Jew.

It is common knowledge that my trade is run mainly by the Gentiles and, working among the Gentiles, I have seen things that cast a dark shadow on the American labor scene. Just listen:

I worked in a shop in a small town in New Jersey, with twenty Gentiles. There was one other Jew besides me, and both of us endured the greatest hardships. That we were insulted goes without saying. At times we were even beaten up. We work in an area where there are many factories, and once, when we were leaving the shop, a group of workers fell on us like hoodlums and beat us. To top it off, we and one of our attackers were arrested. The hoodlum was let out on bail, but we, beaten and bleeding, had to stay in jail. At the trial, they fined the hoodlum eight dollars and let him go free.

After that I went to work on a job in Brooklyn. As soon as they found out that I was a Jew they began to torment me so that I had to leave the place. I have already worked at many places, and I either have to leave, voluntarily, or they fire me because I am a Jew.

Till now, I was alone and didn't care. At this trade you can make good wages, and I had enough. But now I've brought my parents over, and of course I have to support them.

Lately I've been working on one job for three months and I would be satisfied, but the worm of anti-Semitism is beginning to eat at my bones again. I go to work in the morning as to Gehenna, and I run away at night as from a fire. It's impossible to talk to them because they are common boors, so-called "American sports." I have already tried in various ways, but the only way to deal with them is with a strong fist. But I am too weak and there are too many.

Perhaps you can help me in this matter. I know it is not an easy problem.

Your reader,
E.H.

ANSWER:

In the answer, the Jewish machinist is advised to appeal to the United Hebrew Trades and ask them to intercede for him and bring up charges before the Machinists Union about this persecution. His attention is also drawn to the fact that there are Gentile factories where Jews and Gentiles work together and get along well with each other.

Finally it is noted that people will have to work long and hard before this senseless racial hatred can be completely uprooted.

Worthy Editor,

I was born in America and my parents gave me a good education. I studied Yiddish and Hebrew, finished high school, completed a course in bookkeeping and got a good job. I have many friends, and several boys have already proposed to me.

Recently I went to visit my parents' home in Russian Poland. My mother's family in Europe had invited my parents to a wedding, but instead of going themselves, they sent me. I stayed at my grandmother's with an aunt and uncle and had a good time. Our European family, like my parents, are quite well off and they treated me well. They indulged me in everything and I stayed with them six months.

It was lively in the town. There were many organizations and clubs and they all accepted me warmly, looked up to me—after all, I was a citizen of the free land, America. Among the social leaders of the community was an intelligent young man, a friend of my uncle's, who took me to various gatherings and affairs.

He was very attentive, and after a short while he declared his love for me in a long letter. I had noticed that he was not indifferent to me, and I liked him as well. I looked up to him and respected him, as did all the townsfolk. My family became aware of it, and when they spoke to me about him, I could see they thought it was a good match.

He was handsome, clever, educated, a good talker and charmed me, but I didn't give him a definite answer. As my love for him grew, however, I wrote to my parents about him, and then we became officially engaged.

A few months later we both went to my parents in the States and they received him like their own son. My bridegroom immediately began to learn English and tried to adjust to the new life. Yet when I introduced him to my friends they looked at him with disappointment. "This 'greenhorn' is your fiancé?" they asked. I told them what a big role he played in his town, how everyone respected him, but they looked at me as if I were crazy and scoffed at my words.

At first I thought, Let them laugh, when they get better acquainted with him they'll talk differently. In time, though, I was affected by their talk and began to think, like them, that he really was a "greenhorn" and acted like one.

In short, my love for him is cooling off gradually. I'm suffering terribly because my feelings for him are changing. In Europe, where everyone admired him and all the girls envied me, he looked different. But, here, I see before me another person.

I haven't the courage to tell him, and I can't even talk about it to my parents. He still loves me with all his heart, and I don't know what to do. I choke it all up inside myself, and I beg you to help me with advice in my desperate situation.

Respectfully,
A Worried Reader

ANSWER:

The writer would make a grave mistake if she were to separate from her bridegroom now. She must not lose her common sense and be influenced by the foolish opinions of her friends who divided the world into "greenhorns" and real Americans.

We can assure the writer that her bridegroom will learn English quickly. He will know American history and literature as well as her friends do, and be a better American than they. She should be proud of his love and laugh at those who call him "greenhorn."

/   /   /

Dear Editor,

We, the unfortunates who are imprisoned on Ellis Island, beg you to have pity on us and print our letter in your worthy newspaper, so that our brothers in America may know how we suffer here.

The people here are from various countries, most of them are Russian Jews, many of whom can never return to Russia. These Jews are deserters from the Russian army and political escapees, whom the Czar would like to have returned to Russia. Many of the families sold everything they owned to scrape together enough for passage to America. They haven't a cent but they figured that, with the help of their children, sisters, brothers and friends, they could find means of livelihood in America.

You know full well how much the Jewish immigrant suffers till he gets to America. First he has a hard enough time at the borders, then with the agents. After this he goes through a lot till they send him, like baggage, on the train to a port. There he lies around in the immigrant sheds till the ship finally leaves. Then follows the torment on the ship, where every sailor considers a steerage passenger a dog. And when, with God's help, he has endured all this, and he is at last in America, he is given for "dessert" an order that he must show that he possesses twenty-five dollars.

But where can we get it? Who ever heard of such an outrage, treating people so? If we had known before, we would have provided for it somehow back at home. What nonsense this is! We must have the money on arrival, yet a few hours later (when relatives come) it's too late. For this kind of nonsense they ruin so many people and send them back to the place they escaped from.

It is impossible to describe all that is taking place here, but we want to convey at least a little of it. We are packed into a room where there is space for two hundred people, but they have crammed in about a thousand. They don't let us out into the yard for a little fresh air. We lie about on the floor in the spittle and filth. We're wearing the same shirts for three or four weeks, because we don't have our baggage with us.

Everyone goes around dejected and cries and wails. Women with little babies, who have come to their husbands, are being detained. Who can stand this suffering? Men are separated from their wives and children and only when they take us out to eat can they see them. When a man wants to ask his wife something, or when a father wants to see his child, they don't let him. Children get sick, they are taken to a hospital, and it often happens that they never come back.

Because today is a holiday, the Fourth of July, they didn't send anyone back. But Tuesday, the fifth, they begin again to lead us to the "slaughter," that is, to the boat. And God knows how many Jewish lives this will cost, because more than one mind dwells on the thought of jumping into the water when they take him to the boat.

All our hope is that you, Mr. Editor, will not refuse us, and print out letter which is signed by many immigrants. The women have not signed, because they don't let us get to them.

This letter is written by one of the immigrants, a student from Petersburg University, at Castle Garden, July 4, 1909, on the eve of the fast day of *Shivah Asar B'Tamuz* [the seventeenth day of the month of *Tamuz*, when Jews fast in memory of Nebuchadnezzar's siege and destruction of Jerusalem].

Alexander Rudnev

One hundred immigrants, aged from eight to fifty-eight, had signed this letter (each one had included his age). To stir up public opinion and the Jewish organizations, the letter was printed on page 1 with an appeal for action to help the unfortunates. To affirm the authenticity of the facts in the letter, the *Forward* stated that in the English press it had been announced that during the previous week six hundred detained immigrants had been sent back. And on the day the letter from the one hundred was printed, they were sending back two hundred and seventy people.

The *Forward* had previously printed many protests against the unjust treatment of the immigrants confined on Ellis Island, also against the fact that masses were being sent back, and the *Forward* was not silent on this letter.

Dear Editor,

Since I do not want my conscience to bother me, I ask you to decide whether a married woman has the right to go to school two evenings a week. My husband thinks I have no right to do this.

I admit that I cannot be satisfied to be just a wife and mother. I am still young and I want to learn and enjoy life. My children and my house are not neglected, but I go to evening high school twice a week. My husband is not pleased and when I come home at night and ring the bell, he lets me stand outside a long time intentionally, and doesn't hurry to open the door.

Now he has announced a new decision. Because I send out the laundry to be done, it seems to him that I have too much time for myself, even enough to go to school. So from now on he will count out every penny for anything I have to buy for the house, so I will not be able to send out the laundry any more. And when I have to do the work myself there won't be any time left for such "foolishness" as going to school. I told him that I'm willing to do my own washing but that I would still be able to find time for study.

When I am alone with my thoughts, I feel I may not be right. Perhaps I should not go to school. I want to say that my husband is an intelligent man and he wanted to marry a woman who was educated. The fact that he is intelligent makes me more annoyed with him. He is in favor of the emancipation of women, yet in real life he acts contrary to his beliefs.

Awaiting your opinion on this, I remain,

Your reader,
The Discontented Wife

ANSWER:

Since this man is intelligent and an adherent of the women's emancipation movement, he is scolded severely in the answer for wanting to keep his wife so enslaved. Also the opinion is expressed that the wife absolutely has the right to go to school two evenings a week.

Dear Editor,

I plead with you to open your illustrious newspaper and take in my "Bintel Brief" in which I write about my great suffering.

A long gloomy year, three hundred and sixty-five days, have gone by since I left my home and am alone on the lonely road of life. Oh, my poor dear parents, how saddened they were at my leaving. The leave-taking, their seeing me on my way, was like a silent funeral.

There was no shaking of the alms box, there was no grave digging and no sawing of boards, but I, myself, put on the white shirt that was wet with my mother's tears, took my pillow, and climbed into the wagon. Accompanying me was a quiet choked wail from my parents and friends.

The wheels of the wagon rolled farther and farther away. My mother and father wept for their son, then turned with heavy hearts to the empty house. They did not sit *shive* even though they had lost a child.

I came to America and became a painter. My great love for Hebrew, for Russian, all of my other knowledge was smeared with paint. During the year that I have been here I have had some good periods, but I am not happy, because I have no interest in anything. My homesickness and loneliness darken my life.

Ah, home, my beloved home. My heart is heavy for my parents whom I left behind. I want to run back, but I am powerless. I am a coward, because I know that I have to serve under *"Fonie"* [the Czar] for three years. I am lonely in my homesickness and I beg you to be my counsel as to how to act.

Respectfully,
V.A.

ANSWER:

The answer states that almost all immigrants yearn deeply for dear ones and home at first. They are compared with plants that are transplanted to new ground. At first it seems that they are withering, but in time most of them revive and take root in the new earth.

The advice to this young man is that he must not consider going home, but try to take root here. He should try to overcome all these emotions and strive to make something of himself so that in time he will be able to bring his parents here.

ANONYMOUS

16 | Memoirs of "A Negro Nurse"

At the beginning of the twentieth century few white American married women worked in public places, although it was common for women to do sewing, laundry, take in boarders, and undertake other such paying activities while remaining at home. And the labors of running a house and rearing children (if one lacked servants) were even more time-consuming than they are in the present. Afro-American women, however, had a very different lot in life, with a large percentage of them working outside the home. Domestic service, such as this anonymous "Negro Nurse" describes, was the most common employment. The hardships of that life and its demeaning character as measured by employers' treatment and sexual exploitation stand out vividly even in this sanitized account written by a magazine reporter.

[The following thrilling story was obtained by a representative of *The Independent* especially commissioned to gather the facts. The reporting is, of course, our representation but the facts are those given by the nurse—Editor.]

I am a negro woman, and I was born and reared in the South. I am now past forty years of age and am the mother of three children. My husband died nearly fifteen years ago, after we had been married about five years. For more than thirty years—or since I was ten years old—I have been a servant in one capacity or another in white families in a thriving Southern city, which has at present a population of more than 50,000. In my early years I was at first what might be called a "house-girl," or, better, a "house-boy." I used to answer the doorbell, sweep the yard, go on errands and do odd jobs. Later on I became a chambermaid and performed the usual duties of such a servant in a home. Still later I was graduated into a cook, in which position I served at different times for nearly eight years in all. During the last ten years I have been a nurse. I have worked for only four different families during all these thirty years. But, belonging to the servant class, which is the majority class among my race at the South, and associating only with

"More Slavery at the South: by a Negro Nurse," The Independent, Volume 72 (January 25, 1912), pp. 196–200.

servants, I have been able to become intimately acquainted not only with the lives of hundreds of household servants, but also with the lives of their employers. I can, therefore, speak with authority on the so-called servant question; and what I say is said out of an experience which covers many years.

To begin with, then, I should say that more than two-thirds of the negroes of the town where I live are menial servants of one kind or another, and besides that more than two-thirds of the negro women here, whether married or single, are compelled to work for a living—as nurses, cooks, washerwomen, chambermaids, seamstresses, hucksters, janitresses, and the like. I will say, also, that the condition of this vast host of poor colored people is just as bad as, if not worse than, it was during the days of slavery. Tho today we are enjoying nominal freedom, we are literally slaves. And, not to generalize, I will give you a sketch of the work I have to do—and I'm only one of many.

I frequently work from fourteen to sixteen hours a day. I am compelled by my contract, which is oral only, to sleep in the house. I am allowed to go home to my own children, the oldest of whom is a girl of 18 years, only once in two weeks, every other Sunday afternoon—even then I'm not permitted to stay all night. I not only have to nurse a little white child, now eleven months old, but I have to act as playmate or "handy-andy," not to say governess, to three other children in the home, the oldest of whom is only nine years of age. I wash and dress the baby two or three times each day; I give it its meals, mainly from a bottle; I have to put it to bed each night; and, in addition, I have to get up and attend to its every call between midnight and morning. If the baby falls to sleep during the day, as it has been trained to do every day about eleven o'clock, I am not permitted to rest. It's "Mammy, do this," or "Mammy, do that," or "Mammy, do the other," from my mistress, all the time. So it is not strange to see "Mammy" watering the lawn in front with the garden hose, sweeping the sidewalk, mopping the porch and halls, dusting around the house, helping the cook, or darning stockings. Not only so, but I have to put the other three children to bed each night as well as the baby, and I have to wash them and dress them each morning. I don't know what it is to go to church; I don't know what it is to go to a lecture or entertainment or anything of the kind; I live a treadmill life; and I see my own children only when they happen to see me on the streets when I am out with the children, or when my children come to the "yard" to see me, which isn't often, because my white folks don't like to see their servants' children hanging around their premises. You might as well say that I'm on duty all the time—from sunrise to sunrise, every day in the week. I am the slave, body and soul, of this family. And what do I get for this work—this lifetime bondage? The pitiful sum of ten dollars a month! And what am I expected to do with these ten dollars? With this money I'm expected to pay my house rent, which is four dollars per month, for a little house of two rooms, just big enough to turn round in; and I'm expected, also, to feed and clothe myself and three children. For two years my oldest child, it is true, has helped a little toward our support by taking in a little washing at home. She does the washing and ironing of two white families, with a total of five persons; one of these families pays her $1.00 per week, and the other 75 cents per week, and my daughter has to furnish her own soap and starch and wood. For six months my youngest child, a girl about thirteen years old, has been nursing, and she receives $1.50 per week but has no night work. When I think of the low rate of wages we poor colored people receive, and when I hear so much said about our unreliability, our untrustworthiness, and even our vices, I recall the story of the private soldier in a certain army who, once upon a time, being upbraided by the commanding officer because the heels of his shoes were not polished, is said to have replied: "Captain, do you expect all the virtues for $13 per month?"

Of course, nothing is being done to increase our wages, and the way things are going at present it would seem that nothing could be done to cause an increase of wages. We have no labor unions or organizations of any kind that could demand for us a uniform scale of wages for cooks, washerwomen, nurses, and the like; and, for another thing, if some negroes did here and there refuse to work for seven and eight and ten dollars a month, there would be hundreds of other negroes right on the spot ready to take their places and do the same work, or more, for the low wages that had been refused. So that, the truth is, we have to work for little or nothing or become vagrants! And that, of course, in this State would mean that we would be arrested, tried, and despatched to the "State Farm," where we would surely have to work for nothing or be beaten with many stripes!

Nor does this low rate of pay tend to make us efficient servants. The most that can be said of us negro household servants in the South—and I speak as one of them—is that we are to the extent of our ability willing and faithful slaves. We do not cook according to scientific principles because we do not know anything about scientific principles. Most of our cooking is done by guesswork or by memory. We cook well when our "hand" is in, as we say, and when anything about the dinner goes wrong, we simply say, "I lost my hand today!" We don't know anything about scientific food for babies, nor anything about what science says must be done for infants at certain periods of their growth or when certain symptoms of disease appear; but somehow we "raise" more of the children than we kill, and, for the most part, they are lusty chaps— all of them. But the point is, we do not go to cooking-schools nor to nurse-training schools, and so it cannot be expected that we should make as efficient servants without such training as we should make were such training provided. And yet with our cooking and nursing, such as it is, the white folks seem to be satisfied—perfectly satisfied. I sometimes wonder if this satisfaction is the outgrowth of the knowledge that more highly trained servants would be able to demand better pay!

Perhaps some might say, if the poor pay is the only thing about which we have to complain, then the slavery in which we daily toil and struggle is not so bad after all. But the poor pay isn't all—not by any means! I remember very well the first and last place from which I was dismissed. I lost my place because I refused to let the madam's husband kiss me. He must have been accustomed to undue familiarity with his servants, or else he took it as a matter of course, because without any love-making at all, soon after I was installed as cook, he walked up to me, threw his arms around me, and was in the act of kissing me, when I demanded to know what he meant, and shoved him away. I was young then, and newly married, and didn't know then what has been a burden to my mind and heart ever since: that a colored woman's virtue in this part of the country has no protection. I at once went home, and told my husband about it. When my husband went to the man who had insulted me, the man cursed him, and slapped him, and—had him arrested! The police judge fined my husband $25. I was present at the hearing, and testified on oath to the insult offered me. The white man, of course, denied the charge. The old judge looked up and said: "This court will never take the word of a nigger against the word of a white man." Many and many a time since I have heard similar stories repeated again and again by my friends. I believe nearly all white men take, and expect to take, undue liberties with their colored female servants—not only the fathers, but in many cases the sons also. Those servants who rebel against such familiarity must either leave or expect a mighty hard time, if they stay. By comparison, those who tamely submit to these improper relations live in clover. They always have a little "spending change," wear better clothes, and are able to get off from work at least once a week—and sometimes oftener. This moral debasement is not at all times unknown to the white women in these homes. I know of more than one colored woman who was openly importuned by white women to become the mistresses of their white husbands, on the ground that they, the white wives, were afraid that, if their husbands did not associate with colored women, they would certainly do so with outside white women, and the white wives, for reasons which ought to be perfectly obvious, preferred to have their husbands do wrong with colored women in order to keep their husbands *straight*! And again, I know at least fifty places in my small town where white men are positively raising two families—a white family in the "Big House" in front, and a colored family in a "Little House" in the backyard. In most cases, to be sure, the colored women involved are the cooks or chambermaids or seamstresses, but it cannot be true that their real connection with the white men of the families is unknown to the white women of the families. The results of this concubinage can be seen in all of our colored churches and in all of our colored public schools in the South, for in most of our churches and schools the majority of the young men and women and boys and girls are light-skinned mulattoes. The real, Simon-pure, blue-gum, thick-lip, coal-black negro is passing away—certainly in the cities; and the fathers of the new generation of negroes are white men, while their mothers are unmarried colored women.

Another thing—it's a small indignity, it may be, but an indignity just the same. No white person, not even the little children just learning to talk, no white person at the South ever thinks of addressing any negro man or woman as *Mr.*, or *Mrs.*, or *Miss.* The women are called, "Cook," or "Nurse," or "Mammy," or "Mary Jane," or "Lou," or "Dilcey," as the case might be, and the men are called "Bob," or "Boy," or "Old Man," or "Uncle Bill," or "Pate." In many cases our white employers refer to us, and in our presence, too, as their "niggers." No matter what they call us—no matter what they teach their children to call us—we must tamely submit, and answer when we are called; we must enter no protest; if we did object, we should be driven out without the least ceremony, and, in applying for work at other places, we should find it very hard to procure another situation. In almost every case, when our intending employers would be looking up our record, the information would be given by telephone or otherwise that we were "impudent," "saucy," "dishonest," and "generally unreliable." In our town we have no such thing as an employment agency or intelligence bureau, and, therefore, when we want work, we have to get out on the street and go from place to place, always with hat in hand, hunting for it.

Another thing. Sometimes I have gone on the street cars or the railroad trains with the white children, and, so long as I was in charge of the children, I could sit anywhere I desired, front or back. If a white man happened to ask some other white man, "What is that nigger doing in here?" and was told, "Oh, she's the nurse of those white children in front of her!" immediately there was the hush of peace. Everything was all right, so long as I was in the white man's part of the street car or in the white man's coach as a servant—a slave—but as soon as I did not present myself as a menial, and the relationship of master and servant was abolished by my not having the white children with me, I would be forthwith assigned to the "nigger" seats or the "colored people's coach." Then, too, any day in my city, and I understand that it is so in every town in the South, you can see some "great big black burly" negro coachman or carriage driver huddled up beside some aristocratic Southern white woman, and nothing is said about it, nothing is done about it, nobody resents the familiar contact. But let that same colored man take off his brass buttons and his high hat, and put on the plain livery of an average American citizen, and drive one block down any thoroughfare in any town in the South with that same white woman, as her equal or companion or friend, and he'd be shot on the spot!

You hear a good deal nowadays about the "service pan." The "service pan" is the general term applied to "left-over" food, which in many a Southern home is freely placed at the disposal of the cook, or, whether so placed or not, it is usually disposed of by the cook. In my town, I know, and I guess in many other towns also, every night when the cook starts for her home she takes with her a pan or a plate or cold victuals. The same thing is true on Sunday afternoons after dinner—and most cooks have nearly every Sunday afternoon off. Well, I'll be frank with you, if it were not for the service pan, I don't know what the majority of our Southern colored families would do. The service pan is the mainstay in many a home. Good cooks in the South receive on an average

$8 per month. Porters, butlers, coachmen, janitors, "office boys" and the like receive on an average $16 per month. Few and far between are the colored men in the South who receive $1 or more per day. Some mechanics do; as, for example, carpenters, brick masons, wheelwrights, blacksmiths, and the like. The vast majority of negroes in my town are serving in menial capacities in homes, stores and offices. Now taking it for granted, for the sake of illustration, that the husband receives, $16 per month and the wife $8. That would be $24 between the two. The chances are that they will have anywhere from five to thirteen children between them. Now, how far will $24 go toward housing and feeding and clothing ten or twelve persons for thirty days? And, I tell you, with all of us poor people the service pan is a great institution; it is a great help to us, as we wag along the weary way of life. And then most of the white folks expect their cooks to avail themselves of these perquisities; they allow it; they expect it. I do not deny that the cooks find opportunity to hide away at times, along with the cold "grub," a little sugar, a little flour, a little meal, or a little piece of soap; but I indignantly deny that we are thieves. We don't steal; we just "take" things—they are a part of the oral contract, exprest or implied. We understand it, and most of the white folks understand it. Others may denounce the service pan, and say that it is used only to support idle negroes, but many a time, when I was a cook, and had the responsibility of rearing my three children upon my lone shoulders, many a time I have had occasion to bless the Lord for the service pan!

I have already told you that my youngest girl was a nurse. With scores of other colored girls who are nurses, she can be seen almost any afternoon, when the weather is fair, rolling the baby carriage or lolling about on some one of the chief boulevards of our town. The very first week that she started out on her work she was insulted by a white man, and many times since has been improperly approached by other white men. It is a favorite practice of young white sports about town—and they are not always young, either—to stop some colored nurse, inquire the name of the "sweet little baby," talk baby talk to the child, fondle it, kiss it, make love to it, etc., etc., and in nine of ten cases every such white man will wind up by making love to the colored nurse and seeking an appointment with her.

I confess that I believe it to be true that many of our colored girls are as eager as the white men are to encourage and maintain these improper relations; but where the girl is not willing, she has only herself to depend upon for protection. If their fathers, brothers or husbands seek to redress their wrongs, under our peculiar conditions, the guiltless negroes will be severely punished, if not killed, and the white blackleg will go scot-free!

Ah, we poor colored women wage-earners in the South are fighting a terrible battle, and because of our weakness, our ignorance, our poverty, and our temptations we deserve the sympathies of mankind. Perhaps a million of us are introduced daily to the privacy of a million chambers thruout the South, and hold in our arms a million white children, thousands of whom, as infants, are suckled at our breasts—during my lifetime I myself have served as "wet nurse" to more than a dozen white children. On the one hand, we are assailed by white men, and, on the other hand, we are assailed by black men, who should be our natural protectors; and, whether in the cook kitchen, at the washtub, over the sewing machine, behind the baby carriage, or at the ironing board, we are but little more than pack horses, beasts of burden, slaves! In the distant future, it may be, centuries and centuries hence, a monument of brass or stone will be erected to the Old Black Mammies of the South, but what we need is present help, present sympathy, better wages, better hours, more protection, and a chance to breathe for once while alive as free women. If none others will help us, it would seem that the Southern white women themselves might do so in their own defense, because we are rearing their children—we feed them, we bathe them, we teach them to speak the English language, and in numberless instances we sleep with them—and it is inevitable that the lives of their children will in some measure be pure or impure according as they are affected by contact with their colored nurses.

Questions for Part II

1   What advice does Carnegie give? What aim does he consider to be higher than accumulating money?

2   What difficulties did Owens-Adair have to overcome to make the life she wanted for herself? Were you acquainted with her story before reading about her here? If not, why do you think that is so?

3   Why would the use of child labor have appealed to employers? What are some negative consequences of child labor?

4   Discuss the problems the farm people cite in their letters. Compare them with what Bryan said in his Cross of Gold speech in 1896 (your textbook covers that speech). What solutions to these problems did the Populists propose?

5   Why do you think Carry Nation embarrassed the establishment yet continued to draw support from people all over the United States? Give your reasons in detail.

6   Contrast the attitudes and culture of the Bradley Ball with one of the other readings in this part—Lynch or Harris. Was the image the same as the reality?

7   What does the "melting pot" image mean? What reasons does Aldrich give for opposing the "new" immigration? What do you think of these reasons?

8   What kinds of problems are discussed in the "Bintel Brief" reading? How different are they from the problems in the personal advice column in the newspaper you read?

9   What do you think was the influence of the Afro-American nurse on the privileged children of the South? How do you think she affected their adult lives?

PART *III* | *ROOTS OF THE MODERN ERA*

Historians have interpreted the first decades of the twentieth century as an era in which Americans struggled to reorganize a rapidly changing society. While the United States was becoming a major political and military influence in the world at large, its leaders and citizens tried to understand a country that was becoming increasingly diverse in the composition of its population, more bureaucratic and urban, and increasingly dependent on new technologies like the automobile.

In the readings that follow on the Progressive Era (1901–1917), an American of the late twentieth century will find descriptions of many social ills and problems that have been recurrent concerns in recent United States history. George Washington Plunkitt, an urban political-machine "boss," offers a view of the political process as a matter of who gets what. Upton Sinclair pits workers against new technologies and consumers against products whose dangers they do not necessarily understand. Finally, even though it may seem that descriptions of the Triangle Shirtwaist Factory Fire of 1911 depict workplace hazards of a sort that since have largely been eliminated by elementary safety inspection laws, problems of workplace safety remain. Modern problems with substances like asbestos and other carcinogens are more subtle, long-term, and difficult to remedy.

Although all wars generate uncertainty and turmoil, some in American history have ended in great clarity about national mission and purpose. World War I, however, like the Korean and Vietnamese Wars, encouraged social discontent. The war had to be sold to the American people; it raised the questions of who was a hyphenated American (Irish-American, German-American, and so on), and who was loyal and who was not. While some soldiers such as Dick O'Neill went to war rather innocently, they came back less innocent. At home, the battle over the meaning of the war and of American loyalty engaged much of American society. Dissenters were silenced; and some, like Emma Goldman, were deported.

The First World War brought other major domestic changes. Fresh opportunities in war industries and the depredations of the boll weevil on cotton crops combined to stimulate the great migration of African-Americans into the northern cities, a migration that would be further fueled by the next great war and the era of Cold War prosperity that followed it. World War I was one of many forces inducing a higher degree of economic organization in American society as it moved into the age of the "expert." People no longer produced goods for an apparently limitless market; they turned to advertising experts to define both the goods and the market. The role of advertising in American life, defended in the Calkins reading, became an issue of debate in the 1920s; and the argument is not over yet. Americans were developing doubts about whether what had worked for a previous generation would work for them. These doubts fueled modern movements in the arts such as the Harlem Renaissance, as well as the more sinister reactions of the Ku Klux Klan.

The assumption that American life meant unending growth, expansion, and prosperity came into question once again during the Great Depression of the 1930s. As Studs Terkel's interviews show, everyone was reacting to the same overwhelming set of events, yet the degree to which different people were affected by the Depression was quite variable. Some people ruminated over lost fortunes on the stock markets; others organized workers; still others drifted from place to place. Many wrote plaintive letters to the President and the First Lady.

World War II helped pull the economy out of the Depression. This war focused the American sense of mission rather than eroding it. Yet as in World War I, civil liberties were violated on a massive scale, this time for Japanese-Americans; and racial prejudice remained a painful issue, sometimes confronted, more often avoided or ignored as the memoirs of an African-American woman in the United States army suggest. Americans followed the course of the war not only with concern for "the boys" overseas but also with pride in the nation's role in the world. Few suggested that these men had died in vain.

17 | Honest and Dishonest Graft

Reformers such as Lincoln Steffens blamed most of the ills of large cities on the political organizations or "machines" that often ran them. In New York City, the most powerful machine was the Democratic Party's "Tammany Hall." The following selection, by Tammany politician George Washington Plunkitt (1843–1924), offers a view of the political machine that differs from that presented by Steffens.

Plunkitt's reflections of his political experience were published, edited, and perhaps embroidered upon by newspaperman William L. Riordon in 1905. Plunkitt's view of American politics directly contravened the opinions typical of the Progressive Era. While the thrust of reformers, through civil service laws and other programs, was to limit the power of political parties and their machines, Plunkitt argued that parties and political machines performed vital functions. "Honest graft" was, he said, the oil that kept the machines, and government, in motion.

HONEST GRAFT AND DISHONEST GRAFT

"Everybody is talkin' these days about Tammany men growin' rich on graft, but nobody thinks of drawin' the distinction between honest graft and dishonest graft. There's all the difference in the world between the two. Yes, many of our men have grown rich in politics. I have myself. I've made a big fortune out of the game, and I'm gettin' richer every day, but I've not gone in for dishonest graft—blackmailin' gamblers, saloonkeepers, disorderly people, etc.—and neither has any of the men who have made big fortunes in politics.

"There's an honest graft, and I'm an example of how it works. I might sum up the whole thing by sayin': 'I seen my opportunities and I took 'em.'

"Just let me explain by examples. My party's in power in the city, and it's goin' to undertake a lot of public improvements. Well, I'm tipped off, say, that they're going to lay out a new park at a certain place.

"I see my opportunity and I take it. I go to that place and I buy up all the land I can in the neighborhood. Then the board of this or that

William L. Riordon, Plunkitt of Tammany Hall. *(New York, McClure, Phillips, and Company, 1905), pp. 3–10, 19–28, 46–55.*

It is a violation of the law to reproduce this selection by any means whatsoever without the written permission of the copyright holder.

makes its plan public, and there is a rush to get my land, which nobody cared particular for before.

"Ain't it perfectly honest to charge a good price and make a profit on my investment and foresight? Of course, it is. Well, that's honest graft.

"Or, supposin' it's a new bridge they're goin' to build. I get tipped off and I buy as much property as I can that has to be taken for approaches. I sell at my own price later on and drop some more money in the bank.

"Wouldn't you? It's just like lookin' ahead in Wall Street or in the coffee or cotton market. It's honest graft, and I'm lookin' for it every day in the year. I will tell you frankly that I've got a good lot of it, too.

"I'll tell you of one case. They were goin' to fix up a big park, no matter where. I got on to it, and went lookin' about for land in that neighborhood.

"I could get nothin' at a bargain but a big piece of swamp, but I took it fast enough and held on to it. What turned out was just what I counted on. They couldn't make the park complete without Plunkitt's swamp, and they had to pay a good price for it. Anything dishonest in that?

"Up in the watershed I made some money, too. I bought up several bits of land there some years ago and made a pretty good guess that they would be bought up for water purposes later by the city.

"Somehow, I always guessed about right, and shouldn't I enjoy the profit of my foresight? It was rather amusin' when the condemnation commissioners came along and found piece after piece of the land in the name of George Plunkitt of the Fifteenth Assembly District, New York City. They wondered how I knew just what to buy. The answer is—I seen my opportunity and I took it. I haven't confined myself to land; anything that pays is in my line.

"For instance, the city is repavin' a street and has several hundred thousand old granite blocks to sell. I am on hand to buy, and I know just what they are worth.

"How? Never mind that. I had a sort of monopoly of this business for a while, but once a newspaper tried to do me. It got some outside men to come over from Brooklyn and New Jersey to bid against me.

"Was I done? Not much. I went to each of the men and said: 'How many of these 250,000 stones do you want?' One said 20,000, and another wanted 15,000, and another wanted 10,000. I said: 'All right, let me bid for the lot, and I'll give each of you all you want for nothin'.

"They agreed, of course. Then the auctioneer yelled: 'How much am I bid for these 250,000 fine pavin' stones?'

"Two dollars and fifty cents,' says I.

" 'Two dollars and fifty cents!' screamed the auctioneer. 'Oh, that's a joke! Give me a real bid.'

"He found the bid was real enough. My rivals stood silent. I got the lot for $2.50 and gave them their share. That's how the attempt to do Plunkitt ended, and that's how all such attempts end.

'I've told you how I got rich by honest graft. Now, let me tell you that most politicians who are accused of robbin' the city get rich the same way.

"They didn't steal a dollar from the city treasury. They just seen their opportunities and took them. That is why, when a reform administration comes in and spends a half million dollars in tryin' to find the public robberies they talked about in the campaign, they don't find them.

"The books are always all right. The money in the city treasury is all right. Everything is all right. All they can show is that the Tammany heads of departments looked after their friends, within the law, and gave them what opportunities they could to make honest graft. Now, let me tell you that's never goin' to hurt Tammany with the people. Every good man looks after his friends, and any man who doesn't isn't likely to be popular. If I have a good thing to hand out in private life, I give it to a friend. Why shouldn't I do the same in public life?

"Another kind of honest graft. Tammany has raised a good many salaries. There was an awful howl by the reformers, but don't you know that Tammany gains ten votes for every one it lost by salary raisin'?

"The Wall Street banker thinks it shameful to raise a department clerk's salary from $1500 to $1800 a year, but every man who draws a salary himself says: 'That's all right. I wish it was me.' And he feels very much like votin' the Tammany ticket on election day, just out of sympathy.

"Tammany was beat in 1901 because the people were deceived into believin' that it worked dishonest graft. They didn't draw a distinction between dishonest and honest graft, but they saw that some Tammany men grew rich, and supposed they had been robbin' the city treasury or levyin' blackmail on disorderly houses, or workin' in with the gamblers and lawbreakers.

"As a matter of policy, if nothing else, why should the Tammany leaders go into such dirty business, when there is so much honest graft lyin' around when they are in power? Did you ever consider that?

"Now, in conclusion, I want to say that I don't own a dishonest dollar. If my worst enemy was given the job of writin' my epitaph when I'm gone, he couldn't do more than write:

" 'George W. Plunkitt. He Seen His Opportunities, and He Took 'Em.' "

THE CURSE OF CIVIL SERVICE REFORM

"This civil service law is the biggest fraud of the age. It is the curse of the nation. There can't be no real patriotism while is lasts. How are you goin' to interest our young men in their country if you have no offices to give them when they work for their party? Just look at things in this city to-day. There are ten thousand good offices, but we can't get at more than a few hundred of them. How are we goin' to provide

for the thousands of men who worked for the Tammany ticket? It can't
be done. These men were full of patriotism a short time ago. They
expected to be servin' their city, but when we tell them that we can't
place them, do you think their patriotism is goin' to last? Not much.
They say: 'What's the use of workin' for your country anyhow? There's
nothin' in the game.' And what can they do? I don't know, but I'll tell
you what I do know. I know more than one young man in past years
who worked for the ticket and was just overflowin' with patriotism, but
when he was knocked out by the civil service humbug he got to hate
his country and became an Anarchist.

"This ain't no exaggeration. I have good reason for sayin' that most
of the Anarchists in this city to-day are men who ran up against civil
service examinations. Isn't it enough to make a man sour on his country
when he wants to serve it and won't be allowed unless he answers a
lot of fool questions about the number of cubic inches of water in the
Atlantic and the quality of sand in the Sahara desert? There was once a
bright young man in my district who tackled one of these examinations.
The next I heard of him he had settled down in Herr Most's saloon
smokin' and drinkin' beer and talkin' socialism all day. Before that time
he had never drank anything but whisky. I knew what was comin' when
a young Irishman drops whisky and takes to beer and long pipes in a
German saloon. That young man is to-day one of the wildest Anarchists
in town. And just to think! He might be a patriot but for that cussed
civil service.

"Say, did you hear about the Civil Service Reform Association
kickin' because the tax commissioners want to put their fifty-five
deputies on the exempt list, and fire the outfit left to them by Low?
That's civil service for you. Just think! Fifty-five Republicans and mug-
wumps holdin' $3000 and $4000 and $5000 jobs in the tax department
when 1555 good Tammany men are ready and willin' to take their places!
It's an outrage! What did the people mean when they voted for Tammany? What is representative government, anyhow? Is it all a fake that
this is a government of the people, by the people and for the people?
If it isn't a fake, then why isn't the people's voice obeyed and Tammany
men put in all the offices?

"When the people elected Tammany, they knew just what they were
doin'. We didn't put up any false pretences. We didn't go in for humbug civil service and all that rot. We stood as we have always stood,
for rewardin' the men that won the victory. They call that the spoils
system. All right; Tammany is for the spoils system, and when we go
in we fire every anti-Tammany man from office that can be fired under
the law. It's an elastic sort of law and you can bet it will be stretched
to the limit. Of course the Republican State Civil Service Board will
stand in the way of our local Civil Service Commission all it can; but
say!—suppose we carry the State some time won't we fire the up-State
Board all right? Or we'll make it work in harmony with the local board,
and that means that Tammany will get everything in sight. I know that

the civil service humbug is stuck into the constitution, too, but, as Tim Campbell said: 'What's the constitution among friends?'

"Say, the people's voice is smothered by the cursed civil service law; it is the root of all evil in our government. You hear of this thing or that thing goin' wrong in the nation, the State or the city. Look down beneath the surface and you can trace everything wrong to civil service. I have studied the subject and I know. The civil service humbug is underminin' our institutions and if a halt ain't called soon this great republic will tumble down like a Park-avenue house when they were buildin' the subway, and on its ruins will rise another Russian government.

"This is an awful serious proposition. Free silver and the tariff and imperialism and the Panama Canal are triflin' issues when compared to it. We could worry along without any of these things, but civil service is sappin' the foundation of the whole shootin' match. Let me argue it out for you. I ain't up on sillygisms, but I can give you some arguments that nobody can answer.

"First, this great and glorious country was built up by political parties; second, parties can't hold together if their workers don't get the offices when they win; third, if the parties go to pieces, the government they built up must go to pieces, too; fourth, then there'll be h___ to pay.

"Could anything be clearer than that? Say, honest now; can you answer that argument? Of course you won't deny that the government was built up by the great parties. That's history, and you can't go back of the returns. As to my second proposition, you can't deny that either. When parties can't get offices, they'll bust. They ain't far from the bustin' point now, with all this civil service business keepin' most of the good things from them. How are you goin' to keep up patriotism if this thing goes on? You can't do it. Let me tell you that patriotism has been dying out fast for the last twenty years. Before then when a party won, its workers got everything in sight. That was somethin' to make a man patriotic. Now, when a party wins and its men come forward and ask for their reward, the reply is, 'Nothin' doin', unless you can answer a list of questions about Egyptian mummies and how many years it will take for a bird to wear out a mass of iron as big as the earth by steppin' on it once in a century?'

"I have studied politics and men for forty-five years, and I see how things are driftin'. Sad indeed is the change that has come over the young men, even in my district, where I try to keep up the fire of patriotism by gettin' a lot of jobs for my constituents, whether Tammany is in or out. The boys and men don't get excited any more when they see a United States flag or hear the 'Star Spangled Banner.' They don't care no more for fire-crackers on the Fourth of July. And why should they? What is there in it for them? They know that no matter how hard they work for their country in a campaign, the jobs will go to fellows who can tell about the mummies and the bird steppin' on the iron. Are you surprised then that the young men of the country are beginnin' to look coldly on the flag and don't care to put up a nickel for fire-crackers?

"Say, let me tell of one case. After the battle of San Juan Hill, the Americans found a dead man with a light complexion, red hair and blue eyes. They could see he wasn't a Spaniard, although he had on a Spanish uniform. Several officers looked him over, and then a private of the Seventy-first Regiment saw him and yelled, 'Good Lord, that's Flaherty.' That man grew up in my district, and he was once the most patriotic American boy on the West Side. He couldn't see a flag without yellin' himself hoarse.

"Now, how did he come to be lying dead with a Spanish uniform on? I found out all about it, and I'll vouch for the story. Well, in the municipal campaign of 1897, that young man, chockful of patriotism, worked day and night for the Tammany ticket. Tammany won, and the young man determined to devote his life to the service of the city. He picked out a place that would suit him, and sent in his application to the head of department. He got a reply that he must take a civil service examination to get the place. He didn't know what these examinations were, so he went, all lighthearted, to the Civil Service Board. He read the questions about the mummies, the bird on the iron, and all the other fool questions—and he left that office an enemy of the country that he had loved so well. The mummies and the bird blasted his patriotism. He went to Cuba, enlisted in the Spanish army at the breakin' out of the war, and died fightin' his country.

"That is but one victim of the infamous civil service. If that young man had not run up against the civil examination, but had been allowed to serve his country as he wished, he would be in a good office today, drawin' a good salary. Ah, how many young men have had their patriotism blasted in the same way!

"Now, what is goin' to happen when civil service crushes out patriotism? Only one thing can happen: the republic will go to pieces. Then a czar or a sultan will turn up, which brings me to the fourthly of my argument—that is, there will be h___ to pay. And that ain't no lie."

/   /   /

TO HOLD YOUR DISTRICT—STUDY HUMAN NATURE AND ACT ACCORDIN'

"There's only one way to hold a district; you must study human nature and act accordin'. You can't study human nature in books. Books is a hindrance more than anything else. If you have been to college, so much the worse for you. You'll have to unlearn all you learned before you can get right down to human nature, and unlearnin' takes a lot of time. Some men can never forget what they learned at college. Such men may get to be district leaders by a fluke, but they never last.

"To learn real human nature you have to go among the people, see them and be seen. I know every man, woman, and child in the Fifteenth District, except them that's been born this summer—and I know some of them, too. I know what they like and what they don't like, what they are strong at and what they are weak in, and I reach them by approachin' at the right side.

"For instance, here's how I gather in the young men. I hear of a young feller that's proud of his voice, thinks that he can sing fine. I ask him to come around to Washington Hall and join our Glee Club. He comes and sings, and he's a follower of Plunkitt for life. Another young feller gains a reputation as a baseball player in a vacant lot. I bring him into our baseball club. That fixes him. You'll find him workin' for my ticket at the polls next election day. Then there's the feller that likes rowin' on the river, the young feller that makes a name as a waltzer on his block, the young feller that's handy with his dukes—I rope them all in by givin' them opportunities to show themselves off. I don't trouble them with political arguments. I just study human nature and act accordin'.

"But you may say this game won't work with the high-toned fellers, the fellers that go through college and then join the Citizens' Union. Of course it wouldn't work. I have a special treatment for them. I ain't like the patent medicine man that gives the same medicine for all diseases. The Citizens' Union kind of a young man! I love him! He's the daintiest morsel of the lot, and he don't often escape me.

"Before telling you how I catch him, let me mention that before the election last year, the Citizens' Union said they had four hundred or five hundred enrolled voters in my district. They had a lovely headquarters, too, beautiful roll-top desks and the cutest rugs in the world. If I was accused of havin' contributed to fix up the nest for them, I wouldn't deny it under oath. What do I mean by that? Never mind. You can guess from the sequel, if you're sharp.

"Well, election day came. The Citizens' Union's candidate for Senator, who ran against me, just polled five votes in the district, while I polled something more than 14,000 votes. What became of the 400 or 500 Citizens' Union enrolled voters in my district? Some people guessed that many of them were good Plunkitt men all along and worked with the Cits just to bring them into the Plunkitt camp by election day. You can guess that way, too, if you want to. I never contradict stories about me, especially in hot weather. I just call your attention to the fact that on last election day 395 Citizens' Union enrolled voters in my district were missin' and unaccounted for.

"I tell you frankly, though, how I have captured some of the Citizens' Union's young men. I have a plan that never fails. I watch the City Record to see when there's civil service examinations for good things. Then I take my young Cit in hand, tell him all about the good thing and get him worked up till he goes and takes an examination. I don't bother about him any more. It's a cinch that he comes back to me in a few days and asks to join Tammany Hall. Come over to Washington Hall some night and I'll show you a list of names on our rolls marked 'C. S.' which means, 'bucked up against civil service.'

"As to the older voters, I reach them, too. No, I don't send them campaign literature. That's rot. People can get all the political stuff they want to read—and a good deal more, too—in the papers. Who reads speeches, nowadays, anyhow? It's bad enough to listen to them. You ain't goin' to gain any votes by stuffin' their letter boxes with campaign documents. Like as not you'll lose votes, for there's nothin' a man hates more than to hear the letter-carrier ring his bell and go to the letter-box expectin' to find a letter he was lookin' for, and find only a lot of printed politics. I met a man this very mornin' who told me he voted the Democratic State ticket last year just because the Republicans kept crammin' his letter-box with campaign documents.

"What tells in holdin' your grip on your district is to go right down among the poor families and help them in the different ways they need help. I've got a regular system for this. If there's a fire in Ninth, Tenth, or Eleventh Avenue, for example, any hour of the day or night, I'm usually there with some of my election district captains as soon as the fire-engines. If a family is burned out I don't ask whether they are Republicans or Democrats, and I don't refer them to the Charity Organization Society, which would investigate their case in a month or two and decide they were worthy of help about the time they are dead from starvation. I just get quarters for them, buy clothes for them if their clothes were burned up, and fix them up till they get things runnin' again. It's philanthropy, but it's politics, too—mighty good politics. Who can tell how many votes one of the fires bring me? The poor are the most grateful people in the world, and, let me tell you, they have more friends in their neighborhoods than the rich have in theirs.

"If there's a family in my district in want I know it before the charitable societies do, and me and my men are first on the ground. I have a special corps to look up such cases. The consequence is that the poor look up to George W. Plunkitt as a father, come to him in trouble—and don't forget him on election day.

"Another thing, I can always get a job for a deservin' man. I make it a point to keep on the track of jobs, and it seldom happens that I don't have a few up my sleeve ready for use. I know every big employer in the district and in the whole city, for that matter, and they ain't in the habit of sayin' no to me when I ask them for a job.

"And the children—the little roses of the district! Do I forget them? Oh, no! They know me, every one of them, and they know that a sight of Uncle George and candy means the same thing. Some of them are the best kind of vote-getters. I'll tell you a case. Last year a little Eleventh Avenue rosebud whose father is a Republican, caught hold of his whiskers on election day and said she wouldn't let go till he'd promise to vote for me. And she didn't.

ON THE SHAME OF THE CITIES

"I've been readin' a book by Lincoln Steffens on *The Shame of the Cities.* Steffens means well but, like all reformers, he don't know how to make distinctions. He can't see no difference between honest graft and dishonest graft and, consequent, he gets things all mixed up. There's the biggest kind of a difference between political looters and politicians who make a fortune out of politics by keepin' their eyes wide open. The looter goes in for himself alone without considerin' his organization or his city. The politician looks after his own interests, the organization's interests, and the city's interests all at the same time. See the distinction? For instance, I ain't no looter. The looter hogs it. I never hogged. I made my pile in politics, but, at the same time, I served the organization and got more big improvements for New York City than any other livin' man. And I never monkeyed with the penal code."

18 | *Conditions at the Slaughterhouse*

The publication of Upton Sinclair's The Jungle *in 1906 was one of the major events of the Progressive Era. Intended as a plea for socialism, the book was read by a shocked public as an exposé not of the economic system but of the sanitary conditions in Chicago meatpacking houses. Sinclair himself said that he had taken aim at America's heart and hit instead its stomach. Evidently the empty stomachs of the book's immigrant workers Jurgis and Ona mattered less to the public than its own, which it feared might be filled with packinghouse wastes that were mixed with food. Sinclair's book and President Theodore Roosevelt's leadership persuaded Congress to enact the nation's first national pure food and drug and meat inspection laws.*

"They don't waste anything here," said the guide, and then he laughed and added a witticism, which he was pleased that his unsophisticated friends should take to be his own: "They use everything about the hog except the squeal." In front of Brown's General Office building there grows a tiny plot of grass, and this, you may learn, is the only bit of green thing in Packingtown; likewise this jest about the hog and his squeal, the stock in trade of all the guides, is the one gleam of humor that you will find there.

/   /   /

Entering one of the Durham buildings, they found a number of other visitors waiting; and before long there came a guide, to escort them through the place. They make a great feature of showing strangers through the packing plants, for it is a good advertisement. But *ponas* Jokubas whispered maliciously that the visitors did not see any more than the packers wanted them to.

They climbed a long series of stairways outside of the building, to the top of its five or six stories. Here was the chute, with its river of hogs, all patiently toiling upward; there was a place for them to rest to cool off, and then through another passageway they went into a room from which there is no returning for hogs.

It was a long, narrow room, with a gallery along it for visitors. At the head there was a great iron wheel, about twenty feet in circumference, with rings here and there along its edge. Upon both sides of this wheel there was a narrow space, into which came the hogs at the end of their journey; in the midst of them stood a great burly Negro, bare-armed and bare-chested. He was resting for the moment, for the wheel had stopped while men were cleaning up. In a minute or two, however, it began slowly to revolve, and then the men upon each side of it sprang to work. They had chains which they fastened about the leg of the nearest hog, and the other end of the chain they hooked into one of the rings upon the wheel. So, as the wheel turned, a hog was suddenly jerked off his feet and borne aloft.

At the same instant the ear was assailed by a most terrifying shriek; the visitors started in alarm, the women turned pale and shrank back. The shriek was followed by another, louder and yet more agonizing— for once started upon that journey, the hog never came back; at the top of the wheel he was shunted off upon a trolley, and went sailing down the room. And meantime another was swung up, and then another, and another, until there was a double line of them, each dangling by a foot and kicking in frenzy—and squealing. The uproar was appalling, perilous to the eardrums; one feared there was too much sound for the room to hold—that the walls must give way or the ceiling crack. There were high squeals and low squeals, grunts, and wails of agony; there would come a momentary lull, and then a fresh outburst, louder than ever, surging up to a deafening climax. It was too much for some of the visitors—the men would look at each other, laughing nervously, and the women would stand with hands clenched, and the blood rushing to their faces, and the tears starting in their eyes.

Meantime, heedless of all these things, the men upon the floor were going about their work. Neither squeals of hogs nor tears of visitors made any difference to them; one by one they hooked up the hogs, and one by one with a swift stroke they slit their throats. There was a long line of hogs, with squeals and lifeblood ebbing away together; until at last each started again, and vanished with a splash into a huge vat of boiling water.

It was all so very businesslike that one watched it fascinated. It was porkmaking by machinery, porkmaking by applied mathematics. And yet somehow the most matter-of-fact person could not help thinking of the hogs;

/   /   /

One could not stand and watch very long without becoming philosophical, without beginning to deal in symbols and similes, and to hear the hog squeal of the universe. Was it permitted to believe that there was nowhere upon the earth, or above the earth, a heaven for hogs, where they were requited for all this suffering? Each one of these hogs was a separate creature. Some were white hogs, some were black; some were brown, some were spotted; some were old, some young; some were long and lean, some were monstrous. And each of them had an individuality of his own, a will of his own, a hope and a heart's desire; each was full of self-confidence, of self-importance, and a sense of dignity. And trusting and strong in faith he had gone about his business, the while a black shadow hung over him and a horrid Fate waited in his pathway. Now suddenly it had swooped upon him, and had seized him by the leg. Relentless, remorseless, it was; all his protests, his screams, were nothing to it—it did its cruel will with him, as if his wishes, his feelings, had simply no existence at all; it cut his throat and watched him gasp out his life. And now was one to believe that there was nowhere a god of hogs, to whom this hog personality was precious, to whom these hog squeals and agonies had a meaning? Who would take this hog into his arms and comfort him, reward him for his work well done, and show him the meaning of his sacrifice? Perhaps some glimpse of all this was in the thoughts of our humble-minded Jurgis, as he turned to go on with the rest of the party, and muttered: "*Dieve*—but I'm glad I'm not a hog!"

The carcass hog was scooped out of the vat by machinery, and then it fell to the second floor, passing on the way through a wonderful machine with numerous scrapers, which adjusted themselves to the size and shape of the animal, and sent it out at the other end with nearly all of its bristles removed. It was then again strung up by machinery, and sent upon another trolley ride; this time passing between two lines of men, who sat upon a raised platform, each doing a certain single thing to the carcass as it came to him. One scraped the outside of a leg; another scraped the inside of the same leg. One with a swift stroke cut the throat; another with two swift strokes severed the head, which fell to the floor and vanished through a hole. Another made a slit down the body; a second opened the body wider; a third with a saw cut the breastbone; a fourth loosened the entrails; a fifth pulled them out—and they also slid through a hole in the floor. There were men to scrape each side and men to scrape the back; there were men to clean the carcass inside, to trim it and wash it. Looking down this room, one saw, creeping slowly, a line of dangling hogs a hundred yards in length; and for every yard there was a man, working as if a demon were after him. At the end of this hog's progress every inch of the carcass had been gone over several times; and then it was rolled into the chilling room, where it stayed for twenty-four hours, and where a stranger might lose himself in a forest of freezing hogs.

Before the carcass was admitted here, however, it had to pass a government inspector, who sat in the doorway and felt of the glands in the neck for tuberculosis. This government inspector did not have the manner of a man who was worked to death; he was apparently not haunted by a fear that the hog might get by him before he had finished his testing. If you were a sociable person, he was quite willing to enter into conversation with you, and to explain to you the deadly nature of the ptomaines which are found in tubercular pork; and while he was talking with you you could hardly be so ungrateful as to notice that a dozen carcasses were passing him untouched. This inspector wore a blue uniform, with brass buttons, and he gave an atmosphere of authority to the scene, and, as it were, put the stamp of official approval upon the things which were done in Durham's.

Jurgis went down the line with the rest of the visitors, staring open-mouthed, lost in wonder. He had dressed hogs himself in the forest of Lithuania; but he had never expected to live to see one hog dressed by several hundred men. It was like a wonderful poem to him, and he took it all in guilelessly—even to the conspicuous signs demanding immaculate cleanliness of the employees. Jurgis was vexed when the cynical Jokubas translated these signs with sarcastic comments, offering to take them to the secret rooms where the spoiled meats went to be doctored.

The party descended to the next floor, where the various waste materials were treated. Here came the entrails, to be scraped and washed clean for sausage casings; men and women worked here in the midst of a sickening stench, which caused the visitors to hasten by, gasping. To another room came all the scraps to be "tanked," which meant boiling and pumping off the grease to make soap and lard; below they took out the refuse, and this, too, was a region in which the visitors did not linger. In still other places men were engaged in cutting up the carcasses that had been through the chilling rooms. First there were the "splitters," the most expert workmen in the plant, who earned as high as fifty cents an hour, and did not a thing all day except chop hogs down the middle. Then there were "cleaver men," great giants with muscles of iron; each had two men to attend him—to slide the half carcass in front of him on the table, and hold it while he chopped it, and then turn each piece so that he might chop it once more. His cleaver had a blade about two feet long, and he never made but one cut; he made it so neatly, too, that his implement did not smite through and dull itself—there was just enough force for a perfect cut, and no more. So through various yawning holes there slipped to the floor below—to one room hams, to another forequarters, to another sides of pork. One might go down to this floor and see the pickling rooms, where the hams were put into vats, and the great smoke rooms, with their airtight iron doors. In other rooms they prepared salt pork—there were whole cellars full of it, built up in great towers to the ceiling. In yet other rooms they were putting up meat in boxes and barrels, and wrapping hams and bacon in oiled paper, sealing and labeling and sewing them. From the doors of these rooms went men with loaded trucks, to the platform where freight cars were waiting to be filled; and one went out there and realized with a start that he had come at last to the ground floor of this enormous building.

Then the party went across the street to where they did the killing of beef—where every hour they turned four or five hundred cattle into meat. Unlike the place they had left, all this work was done on one floor; and instead of there being one line of carcasses which moved to the workmen, there were fifteen or twenty lines, and the men moved from one to another of these. This made a scene of intense activity, a picture of human power wonderful to watch. It was all in one great room, like a circus amphitheater, with a gallery for visitors running over the center.

Along one side of the room ran a narrow gallery, a few feet from the floor; into which gallery the cattle were driven by men with goads which gave them electric shocks. Once crowded in here, the creatures were prisoned, each in a separate pen, by gates that shut, leaving them no room to turn around; and while they stood bellowing and plunging, over the top of the pen there leaned one of the "knockers," armed with a sledge hammer, and watching for a chance to deal a blow. The room echoed with the thuds in quick succession, and the stamping and kicking of the steers. The instant the animal had fallen, the "knocker" passed on to another; while a second man raised a lever, and the side of the pen was raised, and the animal, still kicking and struggling, slid out to the "killing bed." Here a man put shackles about one leg, and pressed another lever, and the body was jerked up into the air. There were fifteen or twenty such pens, and it was a matter of only a couple of minutes to knock fifteen or twenty cattle and roll them out. Then once more the gates were opened, and another lot rushed in; and so out of each pen there rolled a steady stream of carcasses, which the men upon the killing beds had to get out of the way.

The manner in which they did this was something to be seen and never forgotten. They worked with furious intensity, literally upon the run—at a pace with which there is nothing to be compared except a football game. It was all highly specialized labor, each man having his task to do; generally this would consist of only two or three specific cuts, and he would pass down the line of fifteen or twenty carcasses, making these cuts upon each. First there came the "butcher," to bleed them; this meant one swift stroke, so swift that you could not see it— only the flash of the knife; and before you could realize it, the man had darted on to the next line, and a stream of bright red was pouring out upon the floor. This floor was half an inch deep with blood, in spite of the best efforts of men who kept shoveling it through the holes; it must have made the floor slippery, but no one could have guessed this by watching the men at work.

The carcass hung for a few minutes to bleed; there was no time lost, however, for there were several hanging in each line, and one was always ready. It was let down to the ground, and there came the "headsman," whose task it was to sever the head, with two or three swift strokes. Then came the "floorsman," to make the first cut in the skin; and then another to finish ripping the skin down the center; and then half a dozen more in swift succession, to finish the skinning. After they were through, the carcass was again swung up; and while a man with a stick examined the skin, to make sure that it had not been cut, and another rolled it up and tumbled it through one of the inevitable holes in the floor, the beef proceeded on its journey. There were men to cut it, and men to split it, and men to gut it and scrape it clean inside. There were some with hose which threw jets of boiling water upon it, and others who removed the feet and added the final touches. In the end, as with the hogs, the finished beef was run into the chilling room, to hang its appointed time.

The visitors were taken there and shown them, all neatly hung in rows, labeled conspicuously with the tags of the government inspectors—and some, which had been killed by a special process, marked with the sign of the *kosher* rabbi, certifying that it was fit for sale to the orthodox. And then the visitors were taken to the other parts of the building, to see what became of each particle of the waste material that had vanished through the floor; and to the pickling rooms, and the salting rooms, the canning rooms, and the packing rooms, where choice meat was prepared for shipping in refrigerator cars, destined to be eaten in all the four corners of civilization. Afterward they went outside, wandering about among the mazes of buildings in which was done the work auxiliary to this great industry.

/   /   /

The packers had secret mains, through which they stole billions of gallons of the city's water. The newspapers had been full of this scandal—once there had even been an investigation, and an actual uncovering of the pipes; but nobody had been punished, and the thing went right on. And then there was the condemned meat industry, with its endless horrors. The people of Chicago saw the government inspectors in Packingtown, and they all took that to mean that they were protected from diseased meat; they did not understand that these hundred and sixty-three inspectors had been appointed at the request of the packers, and that they were paid by the United States government to certify that all the diseased meat was kept in the state. They had no authority beyond that; for the inspection of meat to be sold in the city and state the whole force in Packingtown consisted of three henchmen of the local political machine! And shortly afterward one of these, a physician, made the discovery that the carcasses of steers which had been condemned as tubercular by the government inspectors, and which therefore contained ptomaines, which are deadly poisons, were left upon an open platform and carted away to be sold in the city; and so he insisted that these carcasses be treated with an injection of kerosene—and was ordered to resign the same week! So indignant were the packers that they went farther, and compelled the mayor to abolish the whole bureau of inspection; so that since then there has not been even a pretense of any interference with the graft. There was said to be two thousand dollars a week hush money from the tubercular steers alone; and as much again from the hogs which had died of cholera on the trains, and which you might see any day being loaded into boxcars and hauled away to a place called Globe, in Indiana, where they made a fancy grade of lard.

Jurgis heard of these things little by little, in the gossip of those who were obliged to perpetrate them. It seemed as if every time you met a person from a new department, you heard of new swindles and new crimes. There was, for instance, a Lithuanian who was a cattle butcher for the plant where Marija had worked, which killed meat for canning only; and to hear this man describe the animals which came to his place would have been worth while for a Dante or a Zola. It seemed that they must have agencies all over the country, to hunt out old and crippled and diseased cattle to be canned. There were cattle which had been fed on "whisky-malt," the refuse of the breweries, and had become what the men called "steerly"—which means covered with boils. It was a nasty job killing these, for when you plunged your knife into them they would burst and splash foul-smelling stuff into your face; and when a man's sleeves were smeared with blood, and his hands steeped in it, how was he ever to wipe his face, or to clear his eyes so that he could see? It was stuff such as this that made the "embalmed beef" that had killed several times as many United States soldiers as all the bullets of the Spaniards; only the army beef, besides, was not fresh canned, it was old stuff that had been lying for years in the cellars.

/   /   /

There were the men in the pickle rooms, for instance, where old Antanas had gotten his death; scarce a one of these that had not some spot of horror on his person. Let a man so much as scrape his finger pushing a truck in the pickle rooms, and he might have a sore that would put him out of the world; all the joints in his fingers might be eaten by the acid, one by one. Of the butchers and floorsmen, the beef-boners and trimmers, and all those who used knives, you could scarcely find a person who had the use of his thumb; time and time again the base of it had been slashed, till it was a mere lump of flesh against which the man pressed the knife to hold it. The hands of these men would be criss-crossed with cuts, until you could no longer pretend to count them or to trace them. They would have no nails,—they had worn them off pulling hides; their knuckles were swollen so that their fingers spread out like a fan. There were men who worked in the cooking rooms, in the midst of steam and sickening odors, by artificial light; in these rooms the germs of tuberculosis might live for two years, but the sup-ply was renewed every hour. There were the beef-luggers, who carried two-hundred-pound quarters into the refrigerator-cars; a fearful kind of work, that began at four o'clock in the morning, and that wore out the most powerful men in a few years. There were those who worked in the chilling rooms, and whose special disease was rheumatism; the time limit that a man could work in the chilling rooms was said to be five years. There were the wool-pluckers, whose hands went to pieces even sooner than the hands of the pickle men; for the pelts of the sheep had to be painted with acid to loosen the wool, and then the pluckers had to pull out this wool with their bare hands, till the acid had eaten their fingers off. There were those who made the tins for the canned meat; and their hands, too, were a maze of cuts, and each cut represented a chance for blood poisoning. Some worked at the stamping machines, and it was very seldom that one could work long there at the pace that was set, and not give out and forget himself, and have a part of his hand chopped off. There were the "hoisters," as they were called, whose task it was to press the lever which lifted the dead cattle off the floor. They ran along upon a rafter, peering down through the damp and the steam; and as old Durham's architects had not built the killing room for the convenience of the hoisters, at every few feet they would have to stoop under a beam, say about four feet above the one they ran on; which got them into the habit of stooping, so that in a few years they would be walking like chimpanzees. Worst of any, however, were the fertilizer men, and those who served in the cooking rooms. These people could not be shown to the visitor,—for the odor of a fertilizer man would scare any ordinary visitor at a hundred yards, and as for the other men, who worked in tank rooms full of steam, and in some of which there were open vats near the level of the floor, their peculiar trouble was that they fell into the vats; and when they were fished out, there was never enough of them left to be worth exhibiting,—sometimes they would be overlooked for days, till all but the bones of them had gone out to the world as Durham's Pure Leaf Lard!

/   /   /

It was only when the whole ham was spoiled that it came into the department of Elzbieta. Cut up by the two-thousand-revolutions-a-minute flyers, and mixed with half a ton of other meat, no odor that ever was in a ham could make any difference. There was never the least attention paid to what was cut up for sausage; there would come all the way back from Europe old sausage that had been rejected, and that was moldy and white—it would be dosed with borax and glycerine, and dumped into the hoppers, and made over again for home consumption. There would be meat that had tumbled out on the floor, in the dirt and sawdust, where the workers had tramped and spit uncounted billions of consumption germs. There would be meat stored in great piles in rooms; and the water from leaky roofs would drip over it, and thousands of rats would race about on it. It was too dark in these storage places to see well, but a man could run his hand over these piles of meat and sweep off handfuls of the dried dung of rats. These rats were nuisances, and the packers would put poisoned bread out for them; they would die, and then rats, bread, and meat would go into the hoppers together. This is no fairy story and no joke; the meat would be shoveled into carts, and the man who did the shoveling would not trouble to lift out a rat even when he saw one—there were things that went into the sausage in comparison with which a poisoned rat was a tidbit. There was no place for the men to wash their hands before they ate their dinner, and so they made a practice of washing them in the water that was to be ladled into the sausage. There were the butt-ends of smoked meat, and the scraps of corned beef, and all the odds and ends of the waste of the plants, that would be dumped into old barrels in the cellar and left there. Under the system of rigid economy which the packers enforced, there were some jobs that it only paid to do once in a long time, and among these was the cleaning out of the waste barrels. Every spring they did it; and in the barrels would be dirt and rust and old nails and stale water—and cartload after cartload of it would be taken up and dumped into the hoppers with fresh meat, and sent out to the public's breakfast. Some of it they would make into "smoked" sausage—but as the smoking took time and was therefore expensive, they would call upon their chemistry department, and preserve it with borax and color it with gelatine to make it brown. All of their sausage came out of the same bowl, but when they came to wrap it they would stamp some of it "special," and for this they would charge two cents more a pound.

Such were the new surroundings in which Elzbieta was placed, and such was the work she was compelled to do. It was stupefying, brutalizing work; it left her no time to think, no strength for anything. She was part of the machine she tended, and every faculty that was not needed for the machine was doomed to be crushed out of existence. There was only one mercy about the cruel grind—that it gave her the gift of insensibility. Little by little she sank into a torpor—she fell silent. She would meet Jurgis and Ona in the evening, and the three would walk home together, often without saying a word. Ona, too, was falling into a habit of silence—Ona, who had once gone about singing like a bird. She was sick and miserable, and often she would barely have strength enough to drag herself home. And there they would eat what they had to eat, and afterward, because there was only their misery to talk of, they would crawl into bed and fall into a stupor and never stir until it was time to get up again, and dress by candlelight, and go back to the machines. They were so numbed that they did not even suffer much from hunger, now; only the children continued to fret when the food ran short.

Yet the soul of Ona was not dead—the souls of none of them were dead, but only sleeping; and now and then they would waken, and these were cruel times. The gates of memory would roll open—old joys would stretch out their arms to them, old hopes and dreams would call to them, and they would stir beneath the burden that lay upon them, and feel its forever immeasurable weight. They could not even cry out beneath it; but anguish would seize them, more dreadful than the agony of death. It was a thing scarcely to be spoken—a thing never spoken by all the world, that will not know its own defeat.

They were beaten; they had lost the game, they were swept aside. It was not less tragic because it was so sordid, because it had to do with wages and grocery bills and rents. They had dreamed of freedom; of a chance to look about them and learn something; to be decent and clean, to see their child grow up to be strong. And now it was all gone— it would never be! They had played the game and they had lost. Six years more of toil they had to face before they could expect the least respite, the cessation of the payments upon the house; and how cruelly certain it was that they could never stand six years of such a life as they were living! They were lost, they were going down—and there was no deliverance for them, no hope; for all the help it gave them the vast city in which they lived might have been an ocean waste, a wilderness, a desert, a tomb. So often this mood would come to Ona, in the nighttime, when something wakened her; she would lie, afraid of the beating of her own heart, fronting the blood-red eyes of the old primeval terror of life. Once she cried aloud, and woke Jurgis, who was tired and cross. After that she learned to weep silently—their moods so seldom came together now! It was as if their hopes were buried in separate graves.

Jurgis, being a man, had troubles of his own. There was another specter following him. He had never spoken of it, nor would he allow any one else to speak of it—he had never acknowledged it existence to himself. Yet the battle with it took all the manhood that he had—and once or twice, alas, a little more. Jurgis had discovered drink.

He was working in the steaming pit of hell; day after day, week after week—until now there was not an organ of his body that did its work without pain, until the sound of ocean breakers echoed in his head day and night, and the buildings swayed and danced before him as he went down the street. And from all the unending horror of this there was a respite, a deliverance—he could drink! He could forget the pain, he could slip off the burden; he would see clearly again, he would be master of his brain, of his thoughts, of his will. His dead self would stir in him, and he would find himself laughing and cracking jokes with his companions—he would be a man again, and master of his life.

19 | The Triangle Fire

In 1909 the shirtwaist dress makers in New York went on strike for better wages, improved sanitary conditions, and more safety precautions in their workplaces. The strike failed but left in its wake the International Ladies Garment Workers Union. On March 25, 1911, the issues of the strike received renewed meaning when fire broke out in the shop of the Triangle Shirtwaist Company, on the eighth, ninth, and tenth floors of a modern "fireproof" loft building in lower Manhattan. The number of exits was inadequate, doors were locked to prevent pilfering, other doors opened inward, and the stairwell had no exit to the roof; thus, hundreds of workers were trapped. Within half an hour, one-hundred forty-six people had died. They did not, however, die wholly in vain. After the tragedy, New York City created the Bureau of Fire Prevention, and New York State created a Factory Investigation Commission, making New York the most advanced state in the nation in the protection of factory workers. In the first excerpt, Pauline Newman, who became one of the leaders of the garment workers union, recounted what it was like to work at the Triangle Company. The second excerpt is the coverage of the fire in the following morning's edition of the New York World.

PAULINE NEWMAN*

I'd like to tell you about the kind of world we lived in 75 years ago because all of you probably weren't even born then. Seventy-five years is a long time, but I'd like to give you at least a glimpse of that world because it has no resemblance to the world we live in today, in any respect.

That world 75 years ago was a world of incredible exploitation of men, women, and children. I went to work for the Triangle Shirtwaist Company in 1901. The corner of a shop would resemble a kindergarten because we were young, eight, nine, ten years old. It was a world of greed; the human being didn't mean anything. The hours were from 7:30 in the morning to 6:30 at night when it wasn't busy. When the

*From We Were There: The Story of Working Women in America, by Barbara Wertheimer. Copyright © 1977 by Barbara Wertheimer, pp. 294–295. Reprinted by permission of Pantheon Books, a Division of Random House, Inc.

It is a violation of the law to reproduce this selection by any means whatsoever without the written permission of the copyright holder.

season was on we worked until 9 o'clock. No overtime pay, not even supper money. There was a bakery in the garment center that produced little apple pies the size of this ashtray [*holding up ashtray for group to see*] and that was what we got for our overtime instead of money.

My wages as a youngster were $1.50 for a seven-day week. I know it sounds exaggerated, but it isn't; it's true. If you worked there long enough and you were satisfactory you got 50 cents a week increase every year. So by the time I left the Triangle Waist Company in 1909, my wages went up to $5.50, and that was quite a wage in those days.

All shops were as bad as the Triangle Waist Company. When you were told Saturday afternoon, through a sign on the elevator, "If you don't come in on Sunday, you needn't come in on Monday," what choice did you have? You had no choice.

I worked on the 9th floor with a lot of youngsters like myself. Our work was not difficult. When the operators were through with sewing shirtwaists, there was a little thread left, and we youngsters would get a little scissors and trim the threads off.

And when the inspectors came around, do you know what happened? The supervisors made all the children climb into one of those crates that they ship material in, and they covered us over with finished shirtwaists until the inspector had left, because of course we were too young to be working in the factory legally.

The Triangle Waist Company was a family affair, all relatives of the owner running the place, watching to see that you did your work, watching when you went into the toilet. And if you were two or three minutes longer than foreman or foreladies thought you should be, it was deducted from your pay. If you came five minutes late in the morning because the freight elevator didn't come down to take you up in time, you were sent home for half a day without pay.

Rubber heels came into use around that time and our employers were the first to use them; you never knew when they would sneak up on you, spying, to be sure you did not talk to each other during working hours.

Most of the women rarely took more than $6.00 a week home, most less. The early sweatshops were usually so dark that gas jets (for light) burned day and night. There was no insulation in the winter, only a pot-bellied stove in the middle of the factory. If you were a finisher and could take your work with you (finishing is a hand operation) you could sit next to the stove in winter. But if you were an operator or a trimmer it was very cold indeed. Of course in the summer you suffocated with practically no ventilation.

There was no drinking water, maybe a tap in the hall, warm, dirty. What were you going to do? Drink this water or none at all. Well, in those days there were vendors who came in with bottles of pop for 2 cents, and much as you disliked to spend the two pennies you got the pop instead of the filthy water in the hall.

The condition was no better and no worse than the tenements where we lived. You got out of the workshop, dark and cold in winter, hot in summer, dirty unswept floors, no ventilation, and you would go home. What kind of home did you go to? You won't find the tenements *we* lived in. Some of the rooms didn't have any windows. I lived in a two-room tenement with my mother and two sisters and the bedroom had no windows, the facilities were down in the yard, but that's the way it was in the factories too. In the summer the sidewalk, fire escapes, and the roof of the tenements became bedrooms just to get a breath of air.

We wore cheap clothes, lived in cheap tenements, ate cheap food. There was nothing to look forward to, nothing to expect the next day to be better.

Someone once asked me; "How did you survive?" And I told him, what alternative did we have? You stayed and you survived, that's all.

THE NEW YORK WORLD*

At 4:35 o'clock yesterday afternoon fire springing from a source that may never be positively identified was discovered in the rear of the eighth floor of the ten-story building at the northwest corner of Washington place and Greene street, the first of three floors occupied as a factory of the Triangle Shirtwaist Company.

At 11:30 o'clock Chief Croker made this statement:

"Every body has been removed. The number taken out, which includes those who jumped from windows, is 141 . . .

At 2 o'clock this morning Chief Croker estimated the total dead as one hundred and fifty-four. He said further: "I expect something of this kind to happen in these so-called fire-proof buildings, which are without adequate protection as far as fire-escapes are concerned."

More than a third of those who lost their lives did so in jumping from windows. The firemen who answered the first of the four alarms turned in found 30 bodies on the pavements of Washington place and Greene street. Almost all of these were girls, as were the great majority of them all. . . .

Inspection by Acting Superintendent of Buildings Ludwig will be made the basis for charges of criminal neglience on the ground that the fire-proof doors leading to one of the inclosed tower stairways were locked. . . .

It was the most appalling horror since the Slocum disaster and the Iroquois Theater fire in Chicago. Every available ambulance in Manhattan was called upon to cart the dead to the morgue—bodies charred to unrecognizable blackness or reddened to a sickly hue—as was to be seen by shoulders or limbs protruding through flame-eaten cloth-

*From New York World, *March 26, 1911.*

ing. Men and women, boys and girls were of the dead that littered the street; that is actually the condition—the streets were littered.

The fire began in the eighth story. The flames licked and shot their way up through the other two stories. All three floors were occupied by the Triangle Waist Company. The estimate of the number of employees at work is made by Chief Croker at about 1,000. The proprietors of the company say 700 men and girls were in their place. . . .

Before smoke or flame gave signs from the windows, the loss of life was fully under way. The first signs that persons in the street knew that these three top stories had turned into red furnaces in which human creatures were being caught and incinerated was when screaming men and women and boys and girls crowded out on the many window ledges and threw themselves into the streets far below.

They jumped with their clothing ablaze. The hair of some of the girls streamed up aflame as they leaped. Thud after thud sounded on the pavements. It is a ghastly fact that on both the Green Street and Washington Place sides of the building there grew mounds of the dead and dying.

And the worst horror of all was that in this heap of the dead now and then there stirred a limb or sounded a moan.

Within the three flaming floors it was as frightful. There flames enveloped many so that they died instantly. When Fire Chief Croker could make his way into these three floors, he found sights that utterly staggered him, that sent him, a man used to viewing horrors, back and down into the street with quivering lips.

The floors were black with smoke. And then he saw as the smoke drifted away bodies burned to bare bones. There were skeletons bending over sewing machines.

The elevator boys saved hundreds. They each made twenty trips from the time of the alarm until twenty minutes later when they could do no more. Fire was streaming into the shaft, flames biting at the cables. They fled for their own lives.

Some, about seventy, chose a successful avenue of escape. They clambered up a ladder to the roof. A few remembered the fire escape. Many may have thought of it but only as they uttered cries of dismay.

Wretchedly inadequate was this fire escape—a lone ladder running down to a rear narrow court, which was smoke filled as the fire raged, one narrow door giving access to the ladder. By the score they fought and struggled and breathed fire and died trying to make that needle-eye road to self-preservation. . . .

Shivering at the chasm below them, scorched by the fire behind, there were some that still held positions on the window sills when the first squad of firemen arrived.

The nets were spread below with all promptness. Citizens were commandeered into service, as the firemen necessarily gave their attention to the one engine and hose of the force that first arrived.

The catapult force that the bodies gathered in the long plunges made the nets utterly without avail. Screaming girls and men, as they

fell, tore the nets from the grasp of the holders, and the bodies struck
the sidewalks and lay just as they fell. Some of the bodies ripped big
holes through the life-nets. . . .

Concentrated, the fire burned within. The flames caught all the
flimsy lace stuff and linens that go into the making of spring and summer shirtwaists and fed eagerly upon the rolls of silk.

The cutting room was laden with the stuff on long tables. The
employees were toiling over such material at the rows and rows of
machines. Sinisterly the spring day gave aid to the fire. Many of the
window panes facing south and east were drawn down. Draughts had
full play.

The experts say that the three floors must each have become a
whirlpool of fire. Whichever way the entrapped creatures fled they met
a curving sweep of flame. Many swooned and died. Others fought their
way to the windows or the elevator or fell fighting for a chance at the
fire escape, the single fire escape leading into the blind court that was
to be reached from the upper floors by clambering over a window sill!

On all of the three floors, at a narrow window, a crowd met death
trying to get out to that one slender fire escape ladder.

It was a fireproof building in which this enormous tragedy occurred. Save for the three stories of blackened windows at the top,
you would scarcely have been able to tell where the fire had happened.
The walls stood firmly. A thin tongue of flame now and then licked
around a window sash. . . .

On the ledge of a ninth-story window two girls stood silently
watching the arrival of the first fire apparatus. Twice one of the girls
made a move to jump. The other restrained her, tottering in her foothold
as she did so. They watched firemen rig the ladders up against the wall.
They saw the last ladder lifted and pushed in place. They saw that it
reached only the seventh floor.

For the third time, the more frightened girl tried to leap. The bells of
arriving fire wagons must have risen to them. The other girl gesticulated
in the direction of the sounds. But she talked to ears that could no longer
hear. Scarcely turning, her companion dived head first into the street.

The other girl drew herself erect. The crowds in the street were
stretching their arms up at her shouting and imploring her not to leap.
She made a steady gesture, looking down as if to assure them she
would remain brave. But a thin flame shot out of the window at her
back and touched her hair. In an instant her head was aflame. She tore
at her burning hair, lost her balance, and came shooting down upon
the mound of bodies below.

From opposite windows spectators saw again and again pitiable
companionships formed in the instant of death—girls who placed their
arms around each other as they leaped. In many cases their clothing
was flaming or their hair flaring as they fell. . . .

By eight o'clock the available supply of coffins had been exhausted,
and those that had already been used began to come back from the

morgue. By that time bodies were lowered at the rate of one a minute, and the number of patrol wagons became inadequate, so that four, sometimes six, coffins were loaded upon each.

At intervals throughout the night the very horror of their task overcame the most experienced of the policemen and morgue attendants at work under the moving finger of the searchlight. The crews were completely changed no less than three times . . .

20 | The Automobile Comes to Cooperstown

Charles Zabriskie's letters to his son in 1909 and 1910 about the purchase of the first family automobile suggest the transformation wrought in the course of less than a century by the private motor car. In 1910 fewer than 500,000 automobiles were registered in the entire United States. But they were a popular item among the affluent and, as is plain from the letters, demand far exceeded supply. Owning a car carried with it a sense of technological adventure paralleled today, perhaps, by the purchase of a personal computer. Zabriskie was fascinated by technology of all sorts: he was an avid photographer while this hobby was relatively young, and his letters were written on a typewriter—an unusual household item.

[New York City]
Wednesday, Oct. 13. 1909.

My dearest Boy,

Alea Jacta Est, which meant when I was a boy, the Die is Cast. In other words, The Auto is OURS. Monday morning I went to the Cadillac Office, and paid $250. down, the remainder to be paid on delivery of auto, and thus secured the auto for next May 1st. I was afraid that they might have such a rush of orders that they could not fill them, and I might get left. I send you a copy of the contract. You will see there are quite a lot of extras. But they are necessary. The slips are quite expensive, and some say they are useless. Dr. King says, "No good," and Lily Mitchell never has any. Also the speedometer is variable according to selection. They prefer the Stewart. While I have ordered the lowest price, I may change to the $50. one, as the latter has a clock and an electric bulb to use at night. I examined a model auto at the store. It certainly is very handsome. I think you will be pleased with it.

I sent you two pairs of Sun-garters by mail on Monday, and hope you have received them. Yesterday I sent you a box by express, in which

Copy of Charles Zabriskie's contract with the Detroit Cadillac Motor Company, typed by Zabriskie for inclusion in his letter of October 13, 1909. Zabriskie Papers, New York State Historical Association, Cooperstown.

I put all the different things you asked for. You will find a list under the copy of contract of auto I enclose. This morning I printed your films and will enclose them in this letter. I think they are very good, especially the groups. The landscapes are good also....I have a bill from the Cooperstown electric Co. for taking down wires and removing poles from Mrs. Brady's stable. I am glad that so much is done, towards next year. And the work of laying out the grounds for the new stable and GARAGE has also begun. Hurrah!

Your loving Father,
Charles F.

[New York City]
Wednesday, Jan. 12. 1910.

My dearest Boy,

Yesterday I went to the Auto show. the Cadillac looked fine, and I got some books with specifications describing it. I send you one, with some other pamphlets that are of interest. The Goodyear detachable-demountable tire was a wonder. You merely pushed the whole thing on the rim, gave it a kick, and it was all right. Some springs held it in position. Nothing could be simpler and easier. I send you a little comic book about autos and Goodyear tires, which I think you will enjoy. I bought still another guage [sic] for tires, quite an original thing, so now I have three, enough to test all the tires in the country. The Wintons looked very handsome, and I hope some time to get one. Down in the basement were about 50 or 100 Motor-cycles, more than I ever saw together before. I see in the Cadillac catalogue that they give you a generator. I always thought *that* was a tank for holding acetylene gas. But their catalogue says, Prest-o-lite tanks $25. extra. I suppose I must get one, but then, what is a generator? And they mention only Jones Speedometres. When will they sell you a car quite complete including all extras? I saw some nice chains for tires, where the cross-links were independent and slipped on with a spring at each end, so if one should break it would be easy to take it off and slip another on. Most of the supplies were the same as we saw at the other show.... Your loving Father,

Charles F.

[New York City]
Friday, Jan. 21/10

My dearest Boy,

....I see by this morning's papers that Edison has at last completed his storage battery, and yesterday they tried it on a trolley car, with much success. This means that there is no need of any overhead or underground wires, but each car will carry a storage-battery with it, and run on its own power. The cost is One cent a mile. If this is really true,

(Copy).

Detroit Cadillac Motor Co.
  59 St., Broadway, and Columbus Circle.
                      NEw York. Oct.11.1909.
I hereby order one (1) Cadillac Standard Touring Car
to be delivered if possible by April 20.1910.],Price
$1600.F.O.B.Factory.Deposit $250.Balance due (including extras as specified below) to be paid upon notif-
ication that the car is ready for delivery.

Model or Type:-1910 Touring Car 30. Regular.$1630.
Magneto, , ,   Regular.
Top, Mohair,,, , . $95.
Lamps. . Regular
Speedometer. Stewart. 25.
Coat and Foot Rail. . 3.50
Slip Covers. (not yet ordered. $75.)
Extra Shoe,Goodyear, 46.80
Extra Tubes. 9.80
Tire Case. 4.00
Wind Shield. . . $30.

              Total $1844.10
Deposit   ,   . .   250.

       Balance due. $1594.10

Salesman,,,Welch.

          Signature, Charles F.Zabriskie.

The $30. in the 1630 is for freight from Detroit to NY

        Contents of box sent to you Oct.12.
Camphor Pills for Cold.
3 Corks of Thumb-Tacks.
1 Thermometer.
2 Boxes of xxggggVanilla Wafers.
1 Box Letter paper.
1 Box Envelopes.
100 ₿2cent Stamps.
1 Film Pack.

[Copy of Charles Zabriskie's contract with the Detroit Cadillac Motor Company typed by Zabriskie for inclusion in his letter of October 13, 1909, Zabriskie Papers, New York State Historical Association, Cooperstown.]

it will be applied to autos and boats, and traveling will be delightful. . . .
Your loving Father,

Charles F.

[New York City]
Sunday, January 23. 1910.

My dearest Boy,

I am writing this letter on a new Oliver type writer, as you may
doubtless notice by the improved type. I was always dissatisfied with
the old type, from the very beginning, and I made up my mind to get
a new set of type put in. But after considering, I thought of a better
plan. So yesterday morning a man from the office called on me, and I
asked him how much he would allow me for the old type writer and
sell me a new one. He offered so much that I at once agreed to it,
and in the afternoon the new one came. I am delighted with it. It has
one very important improvement, that of back-spacing, which the old
one lacked. I forgot to tell you one very nice feature of the Goodyear
or Goodrich demountable-detachable rim. When you are about to put
it on, you open the rim a little, so that it will slip on easily. After it
is on, you easily screw it up again and there you are. Nice, isn't it? I
have heard of a man who is very anxious to come to us this summer to
work at the stable. He is a very experienced chauffer [sic] from Chicago,
but wants to come to the city, but no one will take him without any
reference, and he knows no one here. He will come to us reasonably
for the summer for the sake of a reference I will give him in the Fall. He
will keep the auto clean, and show you anything you want to learn. But
this is all in the air. He may not come after all. Only talk, just now. . . . I
see the Y.M.C.A. auto school give out of door lessons, demonstrations
in the street. That will be nice to try when you come to us at Easter.
They have about ten teachers. Any profit they make is put into new
autos, or other things connected with them. We all send love and best
wishes.

Your loving Father,
Charles F.

[New York City]
Tuesday, March 15. 1910.

My dearest Boy,

. . . . I went last week to the R. R. depot about getting the Auto
up to the country. They will allow it in the Horse-car, but charge One
Dollar a hundred pounds extra for allowing it in. As it weighs 2600
pounds, that means $26. extra. And as the space in the car is limited,

one of the carriages will have to go up some otherway. I then went to the Cadillac Office, to get the size and weight of the auto. They told me I would get it when promised, at the end of April, or to be exact, on the 20th. The wind-shield has been improved. Where it bends in two, there is usually a piece of brass to keep the air from rushing in between. Now the two pieces of glass come together without any metal between. So I ordered the change. Your loving Father,

Charles F.

[New York City]
Thursday, March 17. 1910

My dearest Boy,

. . . . Colgan spent most of the morning about making arrangements for taking the auto up to the country. He found that although the auto could put its nose, so to say, in the side door, yet it was so long that the whole body could not follow. So they would have to get a car that had a door at the end, and yet stalls for the horses. The car man said he would try to get the best he could. There are also two carriages to go, and there is room for only one, which will have to go in another car. For a while we thought that perhaps the Cadillac people could ship the auto direct from Detroit to Cooperstown, but inquiry at the Cadillac office showed that that could not be done. The express man will however put us through. . . . Your loving Father,

Charles F.

[New York City]
Sunday, March 20. 1910.

Dearest Boy,

This is Monday, and we will have you again with us on Wednesday afternoon. It seems almost too good to be true. . . . The Rosses are having trouble with their chauffer [sic]. This is confidential. He says their Thomas Car is all worn out, although they have had it only a short time, and he wants them to get another. I call it almost a fraud. He probably wants a big commission for a new car. A Cadillac will last for years; almost too long. . . . When you come, we will go to Bloomingdale's or Wanamaker's for auto goods, and I will have to make out quite a list of the things we need. Tichenor-Grand has sold out to the Maxwell auto Co., and it will be turned into an auto store. This is the last letter I shall write to you for a while, so I hope you will get it all right. Good-bye.

Your loving Father,
Charles F.

[New York City]
Sunday morning, April 24, 1910.

My dearest Boy,

I awoke early this morning, and as I could not get to sleep again, I thought the best way of passing the time until breakfast would be to write to you. So here I am at it. The other day I was passing the Rochelle Apartments when I noticed a man putting on a new shoe [i.e. tire] and inner tube. So I stopped and watched him. It was evidently a Clincher, and he was nearly an hour doing it. It was a very good object lesson in that kind of tire. Moral:—avoid clinchers. The only thing else that I learnt was the way in which he filled the inner tube. He used a copper tank, filled with compressed air or gas, and by simply connecting a tube with the tire, he turned on a tap and the air rushed in nicely, without the trouble of pumping at all. It was very interesting and instructive. I have an ad. about it. It is called the Liquid Gas Tire Inflator, and is filled with liquid carbon gas. It weighs 24 pounds, and inflates 25 to 50 tires, and may be refilled at the gas factory for $2.00. Price, $20. It also has a guage [sic] on it. I shall have to get one. Somewhere else I saw a man pumping up an inner tube, and it was hard work, and slow, and he wiped the perspiration off his heated brow very frequently. . . . Your loving Father,

Charles F.

[Cooperstown, N.Y.]
Monday, May 16. 1910.

My dearest Boy,

. . . . I think I wrote to you about our arriving here . . . Thursday evening, finding the weather quite cold. The next morning I wrote to you, and after breakfast I went around to take a look at the stable. At first I was somewhat disappointed in it, but the general effect is very nice. The carriage-room is very large and fresh-looking, the horses' stalls roomy, and upstairs the rooms for Colgan fine. But soon I discovered a number of flaws. Think of an architect building a hay loft over the horses and not putting any opening for the hay to come down! The horses would not like that. Then the box-stall is of no use, one of the four stalls being quite good enough for the purpose. Then the faucet for water for washing the carriages is put behind the harness door, so that you cannot open the door wide while watering. But the greatest fault is the position of the Garage. In the rear of the stable is a manure pit, at one corner, made of thick concrete, the walls one foot thick. (By the way, there is no way of getting the manure out of the stable and into the pit except by shovelling it out of the rear door, shovel by shovel, in a sideways movement, instead of simply pushing it out with a broom directly into the pit). In running an auto into the garage you have to make a very sudden sharp turn around this pit, which has a very sharp corner, then suddenly turn the auto the other way and put on full force to run it up the hill into the garage. The floor of the garage is about one and a half feet above the ground, so you see the danger you would run of not stopping quickly enough and going right through the garage and out of the rear. I have made a little diagram of the situation on the opposite page. After talking the matter over with several people I have decided to move the garage across to the other side of the lot, and thus you can run the auto in a straight line directly into the building, and run no risk of breaking your shoe every time you do it. . . .

To-morrow is the all-important day when the auto is to arrive in the city. Then I will be notified of that fact and will send on the money and soon receive it. Perhaps? Your loving Father,

Charles F.

[Cooperstown, N. Y.
Thursday, May 19. 1910.

My dearest Boy,

I was in hopes that I would write you another long letter, but the sudden changes in the weather from warm to very cold, has quite upset me, and I am feeling very mean. No news of auto yet. I shall write soon about it, but what is the use? I am getting discouraged. . . . At the stable they have made the concrete drive up to the entrance, and now we can drive straight in nicely. The masons are busy getting ready for the foundation of the new place for the garage. This will take some time, about two weeks, but as there is no auto it makes no difference . . .

Your loving Father,
Charles F.

[Cooperstown, N. Y.]
Tuesday, May 24. 1910.

My dearest Boy,

Last Friday I got very impatient, and finally wired to New York, asking how soon I might expect the AUTO. Soon after, I received the following answer:—"Received nothing but demis expect touring next week will wire." We all puzzled over the word demis and could make nothing out of it, until I pronounced the word differently from the way it looked, and then solved the mystery. Demis is the plural of Demi, which means "half," like a demi-tasse of coffee after dinner, meaning a small or half cup, and this demi meant a half tonneau or in other words a small car. According to this message I should expect a touring car this week. Well! perhaps! I have been disappointed so often that I am learning to expect nothing till it comes, but it may come, after all. At any rate, let's hope so. . . . Your loving Father,

Charles F.

[Cooperstown, N. Y.]
Wednesday, June 1. 1910.

My dearest Boy,

Hurrah! Hurrah!—No! The auto has not yet arrived, but the Company has just written to me that they hope to ship it to me this week, and I feel much encouraged. You may remember that I wrote to you that I had telegraphed to them last Friday, and had received no answer. They state that they had written to the Crist Co. here, to notify me by telephone that they expected to ship the Car very soon. But the Crist Co. paid no attention to it whatever. Pretty mean, wasn't it. And I suppose because I did not order the Car through them. You may [be] sure they will gain nothing by it.

The weather has been beastly here for a long time, cold and rainy every day, so that I shiver and freeze constantly. . . . Mr. Woodman is desperate, nothing to do. He cannot run his Packard on these muddy roads, and his chauffer [sic] has nothing to do. It seems that John, who was sent to an auto school to learn, does not know much yet, so Woodman has to keep a chauffer [sic] to help John. He keeps the machine in a corner of his dirty barn, and all looks very ugly. A few days ago I commenced taking photos, for lack of something to do, and am now started and want to take something all the time. How would it do to take the auto——when it comes. . . . I gave Bissell a copy of the auto contract, and he says he will try his pull with the Detroit Company, but that is not necessary now. We are able now to drive along the Lake Shore, on the new road, and it is very good, but makes a lot of dust. Think how nice it will be in the—but, no, I will not torment you about it. You can imagine what I mean. . . . Your loving Father

Charles F.

[Cooperstown, N. Y.]
Wednesday, June 8. 1910.

My dearest Boy,

I did not expect to write to you to-day, but have just heard by telephone from Amos Bissell, that the Car Co. have my car now, and are waiting for the money before putting on the equipment. They will send it Friday, and I should receive it Saturday. Isn't that jolly? I enclose a copy of the Co's letter that I got yesterday, as I thought you might like to read it. I shall write to you again, and it will probably be my last letter before seeing you. I note about your having Tommy for a room-mate next year. Be very sure that you have a very nice and pure-minded boy, as a bad boy can do a lot of damage to a whole school. But I am in a hurry to mail this, so must stop.

Your loving Father,
Charles F.

(Copy)

Dear Sir:—We are pleased to inform you that your touring car is at last on the way, having left Detroit on the 2nd inst., and if it will be of any assistance to you to have the number of the engine for the purpose of securing your license, insurance, etc., it is 47161.

This car should reach here Tuesday or Wednesday of this week, and as soon as it is received we will attach the speedometer, foot-rail, wind-shield, etc., and send it by the American Express as instructed. Itemized bill for this will be sent you as soon as the car is received and before the equipment is put on.

Yours very truly,
Detroit Cadillac Motor Car Co.

[Cooperstown, N. Y.]
Thursday, June 9. 1910. 6 P. M.

My dearest Boy,

. . . . It is so uncertain about getting our auto and putting it in running order, that I shall get a Cadillac at Crist's, and meet you with that. There seems to be a hoodoo about our car. To-day I got a letter from Bissell, in which he says that the auto people find that in the specifications I have ordered slip covers for the seats, and they have to get an experienced upholsterer to do the work, which may delay it somewhat. Isn't that enough to make one fairly dance with rage. I particularly said that I did *not* want slips, and they were not charged on the contract. They cost $75 and I will take them right off if they come on the seats. How they could make that mistake I cannot imagine. I wrote again to Bissell (really I am giving him a lot of trouble) sending him the contract, showing that there are no slips ordered or charged. If the Company make me pay for them, well—what would *you* do? On the other hand I want the auto in a tremendous hurry, and told Bissell I would pay the money if it would hurry the car any. Anything to get it! Hang it! It should be here Saturday morning, and how the express people are going to deliver it to the Garage I don't know. I talked to Gallup and he proposed that the Crist people should take some gasoline to the train, and fill the tank and run the auto on its own power. But the Crist people have treated me badly and I don't want to ask them for anything more than I can help. However, it will get to the Garage somehow, so I shall not worry. I look with envy at Dr. Dewer's beautiful Cadillac, as it runs around the streets, so silently and quickly! That has only a rumble at the back. . . . Chapman is very slow in grading the road leading up to the Garage, working one day, and then going off to the Cooper House and working there. It is exasperating. I shall be so glad when the stable is completely done—and the bills paid. They will be quite heavy. The road to Middlefield is being widened and improved, so that when done, it will be fine for autos. And that is the way to Cherry Valley. I ordered quite a lot of things for the auto to-day. I am looking over an ad. about small electric bulbs with the Howard Mazda Tungsten Lamps. They look very pretty, and may be of use, when you make electric light. But I must say Good-bye.

> Your loving Father,
> Charles F.

Cooperstown
Saturday, June 11 1910

My dearest Boy,

Just a last word. The Auto has come at last and is now in the Garage. Besides the mistake of the slip covers, they have put a folding or rolling upwind-shield of mica, which is fastened to the canopy top, so when the canopy top is put down there is no wind-shield at all. I ordered and paid for a glass one, with what is called clear vision. When I first discovered this I felt quite sick. But I think that possibly the Crist people may be able to put a glass wind shield on. It is very important. I shall bring the car to Colliers Tuesday if the weather and roads are fit, and *you* can run it home. . . .

> Your loving Father,
> Charles F.

RICHARD W. O'NEILL

21 | A War Hero

About two million Americans served in the American Expeditionary Force in World War I, and no single person's experience can be called "typical." The war-time experience left some, in Gertrude Stein's words, "a lost generation" whose moorings in the past had been cut loose. The war solidified the patriotism of others. These two visions collided in the 1930s, as the country argued about involvement in another European war. When the writer Henry Berry sought out veterans of World War I in the mid–1970s, he found mostly men who saw the war as the central test of the prime of their lives. Memoirs like those of Richard W. O'Neill, a winner of the Congressional Medal of Honor, give the reader a feel for the war-time experience of many who fought. Surely for many of the "doughboys," as the infantrymen were called, the war was the first experience for them of the intimate mixing of American ethnic groups, a theme repeated in memoirs—and motion pictures—about World War II.

SERGEANT RICHARD W. O'NEILL

B Company 165th Infantry (69th NYNG), 42nd (Rainbow) Division; Holder of the Congressional Medal of Honor

> It is only natural, I suppose, to be proud of being the recipient of our glorious nation's highest military award, but it has always been my honest contention that when an individual is chosen to be the recipient of that award, it is a grateful nation's way of recognizing the overall fighting qualities and selfless sacrifices of *all members* of the Unit in which the recipient served, especially the *sacred combat dead.*

> Dick O'Neill

Henry Berry, Make the Kaiser Dance. *(Doubleday and Company, Garden City, New York, 1978)* pp. 327–338. Copyright 1978 Henry Berry. Reprinted by permission of the author.
    It is a violation of the law to reproduce this selection by any means whatsoever without the written permission of the copyright holder.

What an outfit we had! Of course, I'm bound to be biased, understand. But really, there was something a little special about the old 69th. Maybe it was because of the large amount of Irish-born in the regiment. They had known how hard it was in Ireland, and they had a particularly strong feeling toward America. I think most of those who had come from the other side felt that way. My mother was a native New Yorker, but my father was a County Clare man. When he first left Ireland, he went to Liverpool, England. Hell, he used to work fourteen, sixteen hours a day, trying to make ends meet there. He did much better in this country, and he appreciated it. And so did most of the men who came over.

Of course, they felt they were a little special. Oh they accepted those who had been born here, but they did call us narrow backs. And were they characters! I remember one time in France, before we went into the trenches. I had just received several packages from home. One of these was a carton of cigarettes. Now, I didn't smoke, and these four or five Irishmen eying me and the cigarettes knew it. They turned their backs and started to talk in hush-hush tones—they sounded like people who had learned to whisper in a boiler factory.

"That Dick O'Neill, he's the finest sergeant in the 69th."

"The 69th, yuh say—in the whole goddamn division, I say!"

"The two of yuh are wrong—it's in the whole American Army. He's a fair man, and a brave one at that. He could chase these damn Heinies back to Germany all alone."

Then they turned around with these surprised looks on their faces.

"Oh Sergeant, darlin', we didn't know yuh were there. But we mean it."

"Indeed, indeed, sure and we do!"

Now, what could you say about men like these? I knew they were putting one over on me. But what the hell could I do? I threw them the cigarettes.

Well, I wanted to tell you that so you'd have some kind of an idea what the 69th was like: I think all of New York's Irish were proud of it. As for myself, I was nineteen when the rumors started about the regiment going down to the Mexican border. It sounded great to me, so I joined up. It was May 22, 1916. And do you know it was exactly three years later to the day—May 22, 1919—that I was mustered out. And what a three years they were!

You see, our regiment was a little different. Most of the National Guard outfits had some time off between the border and the World War. Not the 69th. We stayed in right through.

In March of '17 we went to Washington, D.C., to be in Wilson's Inaugural Parade. By then it seemed quite obvious that Uncle Sam was going to go to war with Germany, so I guess the government felt what the hell, there's no sense in discharging these men now. We went back to New York to guard reservoirs and what have you. I think we even had some men guarding Grand Central Station. Washington was afraid that with all the German Americans we had in this country, there was bound to be some trouble. I can't remember that there was, though.

The border itself was a huge letdown. We ended up spending all those months hiking up and down the Rio Grande. We got in great shape, all right, but if anyone was killed, it was by boredom. The poor newspapermen were just as badly off as we were. They're getting all this pressure from back in New York to get some battle stories.

Then they got a big break. Some nut on the other side of the river took a potshot at one of our patrols. Oh this was great! Our men could shoot back, anything for a little excitement. But it was all over in a few minutes, with no one getting hit. Well, Jeez, one of the papers, I think it was the *Journal*, broke out these huge headlines, "69th in Big Battle with the Mexicans." You can imagine what concern this caused back home. What a mess! Even the governor was upset. It took a long time to straighten that out.

There was one other incident to relieve our boredom. I can't remember the name of the Mexican town this happened in, but it was directly across the river from us. I had binoculars, so I really had a front-row seat.

Well, this band of rebels attacked the town. It wasn't much of a battle—a lot of firing, then the rebels rode away, leaving one of their group stretched out on the ground. Then I'll be damned if every one in the town didn't come out and take a shot at the poor guy. He must have looked like a piece of Swiss cheese; it was sickening.

All in all, though, you have to call the whole border thing a farce except for one thing: It gave the National Guard outfits a military feeling that helped a great deal when Congress did declare war on Germany. Remember, four of the six divisions to be in France by the first of March 1918 were Guard outfits.

Ours was the 42nd, soon to be called the Rainbow. And we owed that name to none other than Douglas MacArthur. What an officer he was, a peach! He commanded the Rainbow, you know, at the very end. But back at the beginning he was chief of staff for the division.

Now, the government wanted to get a division, made up of men from states throughout the country, to France as soon as possible. At that time we had the old square divisions with four infantry regiments, three artillery ones, three machine-gun battalions, and all these other units such as MPs, medical groups, etc.—there were a total of twenty-six different organizations in each division.

Well, according to what we heard, MacArthur and Newton Baker [the Secretary of War] were deciding on how they would set the division up when Mac came up with the name.

"Mr. Secretary," he said, "the 42nd will have National Guard outfits from all these states; it will cross the country like a rainbow. Why not call it 'the Rainbow Division'—a rainbow across the land." And that was it.

We were to be one of the infantry regiments, along with the 4th Ohio, 3rd Iowa, and the 4th Alabama. And we all got along fine. I know that movie *The Fighting 69th* shows us having some trouble with the Alabama boys. Maybe so, but I don't remember it. And that movie was the biggest phony that ever came down the pike anyway! None of the old 69th people gave a damn about it.

We were now the 165th U. S. Infantry. Along with the 166th (the Ohioans) we made up the 83rd Brigade—that's the way we did it then, two regiments to a brigade. Hell, we had over seven thousand men in our brigade—it was almost as big as some of the French and British divisions all by itself.

Our gathering place was Camp Mills, Long Island. It was here that they started to turn us into a division. And it was here that I got to know our battalion commander, Major William Joseph Donovan. Now, let me point out that my son is named William Donovan O'Neill; that should tell you what I thought about him. But he surely worked us that summer at Mills. But I ask you, was there any other way to get us ready for what was coming? And it came fast enough. We started our trip for France in September 1917, finally landing at Le Havre on November 1. There'll always be a big controversy over which National Guard division landed first, ours or the 26th. They always told us we were the first complete one there. But what difference does it make? Both the Rainbow and the Yankee were there with plenty of time for the war. And that 26th was a good outfit also.

After we landed they shipped us over to Alsace-Lorraine, and it was here that our troubles really began. The hell of it was the foulup in clothing. Here we were in the Vosges Mountain area, with what was to be one of the worst winters in French history beginning, and half the men didn't have their overcoats. Can you imagine that? Hardly any of them had winter brogans—many were walking around in those light shoes you'd wear in a dress parade during the summer. Why, the next thing you knew a lot of the boys had rags on their feet. And the blankets—we had lightweight summer ones until the first of the year.

I can't say the food supplies were much better. Here, look, this is a diary I kept that winter:

"December 7: hiked 10 kilometers. Food—coffee like water, luke-warm—a few strips of bacon—all we had that day. December 10: hiked ten kilometers—many of the men without shoes—weather freezing. One meal, some kind of stew."

Now, it wasn't that we didn't have equipment in France. They just had trouble getting it to us, that's all. But how the boys did suffer! Nothing was worse than Christmas. We went to Mass in a cathedral Christmas Eve and the next day had one tiny meal, that rotten coffee again, and some kind of meat, and a small portion at that.

At about this time I was sent to a place called Mission. My job was to set up barns and sheds for the enlisted men, and houses, if possible, for the officers. I don't know how far it was but because of the weather, it took me ten days. Most of the time I had to walk, even though I did hitch a ride or two on farmers' wagons. Once I even jumped up on

a French caisson for a few miles. All in all, that trip had to be one of
the low points of the war for me. At least when we were doing all that
marching down at the border, we didn't have to worry about frozen
feet.

Well, I set things up as best I could, even recruiting many of the
French women to help with the food until the rolling kitchen arrived. A
while later the first battalion arrived. There was a little improvement in
the weather and we did get a chance for some real training. We needed
it.

Then in March we moved into a place called Luneville for our first
spell in the trenches. We were to spend our next four months here and
over at Baccarat going in and out of the trenches.

I can't say this was pleasant, but the real brutal stuff, for D Company anyway, was still a while away. One of our companies took a real
pasting at a place called Rouge Bouquet, where they lost twenty-four
men in a cave-in, but all in all, the worst thing about it was the living
conditions—the mud, the cooties, the rats—just lousy living, that's all.

One of the few good things about our trench tours was the opportunity it allowed me to really establish a friendship with Major Donovan.
It was a friendship that would last through two World Wars until 1959,
when Bill died.

You know, they always called him "Wild Bill," but not because he
was irrational. There had been a manager of the New York Highlanders
[later the Yankees] named "Wild Bill" Donovan—that's where Bill got
the nickname. In reality, he was anything but. Actually, he was the
calmest man under fire I ever saw. Oh you'd think he was standing at
the corner of Broadway and Forty-second Street, not in the middle of a
barrage.

And he was always in the middle of everything—Bill was no dugout
officer. That's why he was such a great leader. Once the men realized
that the major was going to keep calm no matter what happened, they
began to count on him to do the right thing.

I'll never forget a conversation we had later on when I had to take
over command of the company.

"O'Neill," he said to me, "these are great soldiers; they'll take hell
with bayonets if they're properly led." And with Donovan leading us,
we might have done just that.

Well, after our time in the trenches, we moved into the Champagne
sector, where we really got to fight the war. First, we played our part in
stopping the last German drive, then we attacked in an area around the
Ourcq River. From then on, the Germans were on the defensive until
the Armistice.

First came the Champagne defense. Here we were part of
Gouraud's Fourth French Army, holding the center of the line. Gouraud
was a real old campaigner, with an empty sleeve and a stiff leg from
wounds. I think he lost the arm at Gallipoli.

Now, the way we heard it was that MacArthur gave the French the
idea for the defense. We knew the Germans were going to attack, so

Mac told the French to leave just a few men in the frontline trenches, but to beef up the second line. The Rainbow was right in the middle, with French on either side. None of our battalion was actually in the first trench line; our job was to wait and see what happened. And that waiting was bad business, particularly when the shelling started.

While we had no way of knowing it, this was to be the end of Ludendorrf's final offensive. If we could stop them here, at the road to Chalons-sur-Marne, we could start the counterattack that Foch had planned.

Well, I think it was about seven o'clock the morning of July 15 that the Germans came over. Naturally, they had no trouble at first. Most of our men got out of the first-line trenches in a hurry as planned. And were those Germans happy! They thought they'd won a big battle, you see. We could hear them laughing, cheering, singing—it was really a little sad.

Then our concentrated barrage opened up. Oh my Christ, did it ever shock those Heinies! Our artillery had a field day. They'd measured the exact position of the trenches and knew just where those Germans had stopped. It was like ducks in a shooting gallery.

But these were the Prussian Guards. They weren't quite stopped yet. What was left of them kept coming at us. It varied up and down the line depending on the amount of troops. In several areas they reached the second-line trenches, where it turned into a real vicious hand-to-hand affair.

I think it was our second battalion that took it the worse in the 69th. They had some real rough stuff. And they had a couple of great stories to tell.

In one of them four Germans, each with this huge red cross on his arm, were toting a stretcher up to the lines. When they got close enough to us, they threw this blanket off the stretcher and opened up with a machine gun. You can bet those four never saw ze Father in ze Father-land again. Still another group tried to infiltrate our lines dressed in French uniforms. They were also shot down. All in all, I think the Rainbow held its own that day.

Of course, I've been just talking about our regiment because a front-line soldier rarely gets involved with anything larger. And that's pretty high up at that—usually your thinking doesn't go any higher than your battalion.

My point is that there were probably over two hundred thousand Germans attacking along a line of several miles. In some areas I heard they'd made small breakthroughs, but were shortly driven back. From then on until November 11 the Boche were headed the other way. Let me add one more thing before I go into our move to the Ourcq River—I really should tell you this, as it was just about the most incredible thing I saw in France. I can't tell you the day and the hour, but it did happen while we were there in the Champagne sector.

Now, I'll bet you very few Americans realize that we fought along-side of Polish troops in 1918. Well, we did. They were called the

Paderewski Brigade because he had raised them. I guess they figured they could have an independent country of their own if they ended up on the winning side. It did turn out that way, but very few of the Polish soldiers that we saw lived to see it—not if what they did at Champagne was any indication of their officers, anyway.

I was standing in a trench when I heard a sound of marching men. I looked over and saw these Polish soldiers moving up the Chalons road. My God, you'd think they were strutting down Fifth Avenue on the seventeenth of March—why, they were actually in close formation in broad daylight. How in the hell they ever thought they'd get away with it I'll never know.

The Germans spotted them, of course, probably from a balloon or a plane. Then they opened up with their artillery. It was plain suicide— I doubt like hell if more than 10 per cent of them weren't hit. And the saddest part was they accomplished absolutely nothing. What a waste!

Well, as I've said, our next stop was over near the Ourcq. Oh we had a few days to recuperate, but the first thing we knew they loaded us on those 40 and 8's for a short ride down near Château-Thierry. They'd been fighting like hell here just a few days before, and we had a first-hand view of the destruction. The area looked as if a cyclone had hit it.

I can't remember where they let us off, but wherever it was they piled us onto these camions for our jaunt to where the Germans were. These camions seemed to be a cross between a bus and a truck. They were driven by Vietnamese. Naturally, we called them Chinks—I doubt if any of the boys had even heard of Vietnamese then.

Now, the Ourcq itself was what we'd call a creek back home. I can particularly remember one of our boys taking one look at it with disgust.

"If this is a river, "he croaked,"the Hudson must be an ocean."

River or not, the Germans thought enough of it to have some very tough *hombres*, including the 4th Imperial Prussian Footguard, trying to hold it. Between working our way up to it and finally crossing the damn thing, the 69th experienced just about as tough a fight as it ever had. It was attack, face their counterattack, and attack again. It may be almost sixty years ago, but there are many little things that still stick in my mind about that last week in July of '18.

One of them concerns this grand old Irish sergeant, Tom O'Malley. It happened at Dead Man's Curve just as we were ready to hit the Germans, not far from Meurcy Farm. We were taking a little rest when a couple of officers came by and asked Tom for Company D's commanding officer.

"Sure and there're no officers here," O'Malley told them. "Oh we'd see them all the time back at the camp; Christ, you'd be tripping over 'em! But here, none at all."

"Then we'd better give you a temporary commission, O'Malley. These men can't go against the Germans without an officer."

"What, Tom O'Malley an officer, the devil you say? No Sam Browne belt for me! Now, take that nice young man Dick O'Neill—we'll make Dick the acting captain. I'll see the boys do what he says."

And that's how I was given temporary command of Company D. I was twenty years of age. Hell, O'Malley knew much more about soldiering than I did—I wanted him to have command myself. But we all got a kick out of his crack, "No Sam Browne belt for me!"

Of course, it's the events of the thirtieth of July that have stayed with me the longest, even though my actual fight with the twenty-five Germans is a little hazy. Then again, it always was. When you keep getting hit with bullets and you're fighting as hard as you can to stay alive, you're reacting by instinct.

Strangely enough, one of the things that stands out in my mind is what a beautiful morning it was and how nice it would have been to take a walk through that French countryside. What a contrast between the scenic beauty and the shelling! I said to myself, "Dick, this is a hell of a morning to pick to get killed!"

My pessimism was due to the job Donovan had given us. We knew there were machine guns up ahead but not how many or where. We were to find out where they had them so our artillery could zero in. It was, however, the major's final words that stuck in my mind.

"Dick," he said, "it would be a lot better if your boys could knock out those guns. We could move faster."

Well, we found their machine guns soon enough and went after them; I had thirty-two men with me.

It didn't take the Germans long to open up on us. Christ, there were bullets flying all around. One of them knocked the rifle out of my hand, but being a sergeant, I still had my pistol. I didn't realize it at the time, but I was running so fast that I was way out in front of the men I was leading.

The first thing I knew I climbed this ridge and almost fell into this large gravel pit. Then I got the shock of my life. The hole was filled with about twenty-five Germans and several machine guns. The only thing that saved me was the fact that they were as surprised as I was. I threw a grenade or two and started firing my pistol—of course, they started firing at the same time. They hit me with four or five shots, maybe six, but they weren't bad enough to knock me over; amazingly enough, they were all flesh wounds.

I knew I'd been doing better against them because I could see these gray-clad figures falling over. They later told me there were five dead Germans in the gravel pit—two of them being noncoms. I guess this panicked the rest because they all started to surrender.

Oh, it all sounds great, all right, but put yourself in my place. Here I am with twenty or so Heinie prisoners smack on top of the German lines. They're all jabbering away a mile a minute while I'm pointing a pistol at them that probably didn't have any rounds left in it. I was the one in a hell of a spot, but I guess these Krauts didn't know it.

Anyway, I figured the only thing to do was hike them back to our lines. It seemed like a good idea at the time, but Jeez, we'd no sooner started when whack, a couple of other German machine gunners over on my left opened up on us. They knocked the bejesus out of me, but they also chopped down their own men like cordwood.

Hell, I'd already been hit in one of my legs in the gravel pit— now they really punctured the other one. I couldn't walk, couldn't even crawl. But I could roll—so over and over I barreled down the ridge with their machine-gun fire bouncing all around me. And two more of those damn German bullets didn't miss!

I finally reached the cover of some woods, where some of our men grabbed me. One of my Irish buddies, named Pat, took one look at me and sighed.

"Jee-sus, Dick me boy, you're leaking all over the place! I should carry yuh back on me back."

Well, I knew he wanted to get out of the fighting. Then another Irishman came over.

"And where the hell do yuh think you're going?"

"Oh I want to take care of the sergeant."

"And not yourself, Pat—get back over there. Someone will get the sergeant."

So poor Pat went back over where he belonged, and wouldn't you know it, Pat was killed within the hour.

A short time later two men rolled me in a blanket and headed for a dressing station. Oh I wanted to get patched up, all right, but not before I told Major Donovan precisely where those German machine guns were. The 2nd Battalion was going to attack in that area, and I figured they wouldn't spot them until they'd lost a lot of men. The boys carrying me in the blanket started to argue with me about it.

"I'm not going anywhere," I told them," until I tell the major where those machine guns are." So they took me to Donovan. I gave him a report, and then I think I collapsed.

My next step landed me in a damn good hospital run by a Jewish group from back home. I think it was connected with New York Hospital. And what a great job they did on me! I was lucky in one respect: None of the bullets had really injured a vital spot. I was also young and healthy, which greatly aided my recovery. The first thing I knew I reached a point where I was really itching to get back with the 69th. When the word came back on how rough things were up in the Argonne, I couldn't take it any longer, so I concerned my doctor.

"Look," I told him, "I could go ten rounds with Jess Williard; I want to get back with my outfit."

"Oh for Christ's sake, O'Neill," he answered, "you looked like a pincushion when they brought you in. You've had your war!"

Well, it went on like this for a few days until I wore him down; then he finally gave up.

"All right, all right," he said, "you're driving us all nuts. If you want to kill yourself, go ahead, but I won't be responsible for you." I moved out as quickly as I could and headed for the 69th.[1]

I joined the boys sometime in October, right in the middle of that donneybrook called the Meuse-Argonne. I was shocked to find so few of the old-timers left. And with that nasty grinding-out stuff, it was fewer every day. The Germans even badly wounded my old friend Sergeant Tom O'Malley. There he was, lying there calmly smoking his pipe.

"Don't worry none about me, boys," he said. "I'll be foine, just foine." And he did make it back home.

It was beginning to get to me also. I took some shrapnel wounds up there, but compared to what happened at the Ourcq, I always figured they didn't count. I did start to occasionally get dizzy spells, but I was determined to stick it out.

Then, on November 8, when we were all tangled up in that mess to see who was going to take Sedan, I collapsed and was out cold for days. When I finally woke up, I was in a hospital bed with clean white sheets, looking out a window right into a beautifully bright dawning. When I turned my head, I saw this smiling nurse with a sparkling starched white uniform.

"Well, holy Christ," I said to myself. "I'm finally dead, and here's an angel. Thank God I'm in heaven and not the other place!" Then the angel started to talk.

"Good morning, Sergeant, I know you'll be glad to know it's all over."

"What's over?"

"Why, the war, of course."

"It is not. Why . . . " Then I began to realize where I was.

---

1. One report says that the sergeant went AWOL to get back to the 69th. Dick did not say this, only that they did not want him to go back.

EMMA GOLDMAN

22 | *Opposing the Draft*

Emma Goldman, who emigrated from Lithuania to the United States in 1885, was a major influence among American literary and political radicals from the early 1890s until her arrest in 1917 and her subsequent deportation. With her fellow anarchist, Alexander Berkman ("Sasha" in the excerpt below), her publications and lectures became an important conduit for European ideas of political anarchism and literary modernism as well as for a variety of related reforms, such as birth control and social welfare issues. Leon Czolgosz, who assassinated President McKinley in 1901, claimed to have been inspired by her speeches.

Goldman's opposition to the draft after the entry of the United States into World War I led to her arrest, conviction, and deportation, despite the lack of evidence that any of her activities had interfered with conscription. Her fate was more highly publicized than that of many others who criticized America's role in the war. The nation, sharply divided about entry into the European conflict, nonetheless showed scant tolerance for dissent even from speakers far more conservative than Emma Goldman.

In the spirit of her military preparations America was rivalling the most despotic countries of the Old World. Conscription, resorted to by Great Britain only after eighteen months of war, was decided upon by Wilson within one month after the United States had decided to enter the European conflict. Washington was not so squeamish about the rights of its citizens as the British Parliament had been. The academic author of *The New Freedom* [Woodrow Wilson] did not hesitate to destroy every democratic principle at one blow. He had assured the world that America was moved by the highest humanitarian motives, her aim being to democratize Germany. What if he had to Prussianize the United States in order to achieve it? Free-born Americans had to be forcibly pressed into the military mould, herded like cattle, and shipped across the waters to fertilize the fields of France. Their sacrifice would earn them the glory of having demonstrated the superiority of *My Country, 'Tis of Thee* over *Die Wacht am Rhein*. No American president had ever before succeeded in so humbugging the people as Woodrow Wilson, who wrote and talked democracy, acted despotically, privately and officially, and yet managed to keep up the myth that he was championing humanity and freedom.

We had no illusions about the outcome of the conscription bill pending before Congress. We regarded the measure as a complete denial of every human right, the death-knell to liberty of conscience, and we determined to fight it unconditionally. We did not expect to be able to stem the tidal wave of hatred and violence which compulsory service was bound to bring, but we felt that we had at least to make known at large that there were some in the United States who owned their souls and who meant to preserve their integrity, no matter what the cost.

We decided to call a conference in the *Mother Earth* office to broach the organization of a No-Conscription League and draw up a manifesto to clarify to the people of America the menace of conscription. We also planned a large mass meeting as a protest against compelling American men to sign their own death-warrants in the form of forced military registration.

Because of previously arranged lecture dates in Springfield, Massachusetts, I was unfortunately not able to be present at the conference, set for May 9. But as Sasha, Fitzi*, Leonard D. Abbott, and other clear-headed friends would attend, I felt no anxiety about the outcome. It was suggested that the conference should take up the question of whether the No-Conscription League should urge men not to register. *En route* to Springfield I wrote a short statement giving my attitude on the matter. I sent it with a note to Fitzi asking her to read it at the gathering. I took the position that, as a woman and therefore myself not subject to military service, I could not advise people on the matter. Whether or not one is to lend oneself as a tool for the business of killing should properly be left to the individual conscience. As an anarchist I could not presume to decide the fate of others, I wrote. But I could say to those who refused to be coerced into military service that I would plead their cause and stand by their act against all odds.

By the time I returned from Springfield the No-Conscription League had been organized and the Harlem River Casino rented for a mass meeting to take place on May 18. Those who had participated at the conference had agreed with my attitude regarding registration.

Almost ten thousand people filled the place, among them many newly rigged-out soldiers and their woman friends, a very boisterous lot indeed. Several hundred policemen and detectives were scattered through the hall. When the session opened, a few young "patriots" tried to rush the stage entrance. Their attempt was foiled, because we had prepared for such a contingency.

Leonard D. Abbott presided, and on the platform were Harry Weinberger, Louis Fraina, Sasha, myself, and a number of other opponents of forced military service. Men and women of varying political views sup-

---

* [M. Eleanor Fitzgerald, Office Secretary]

ported our stand on this occasion. Every speaker vigorously denounced the conscription bill which was awaiting the President's signature. Sasha was particularly splendid. Resting his injured leg on a chair and supporting himself with one hand on the table, he breathed strength and defiance. Always a man of great self-control, his poise on this occasion was remarkable. No one in the vast audience could have guessed that he was in pain, or that he gave a single thought to his helpless condition if we should fail to carry the meeting to a peaceful end. With great clarity and sustained power Sasha spoke as I had never heard him before.

The future heroes were noisy all through the speeches, but when I stepped on the platform, pandemonium broke loose. They jeered and hooted, intoned *The Star-Spangled Banner*, and frantically waved small American flags. Above the din the voice of a recruit shouted: "I want the floor!" The patience of the audience had been sorely tried all evening by the interrupters. Now men rose from every part of the house and called to the disturber to shut up or be kicked out. I knew what such a thing would lead to, with the police waiting for a chance to aid the patriotic ruffians. Moreover, I did not want to deny free speech even to the soldier. Raising my voice, I appealed to the assembly to permit the man to speak. "We who have come here to protest against coercion and to demand the right to think and act in accordance with our consciences," I urged, "should recognize the right of an opponent to speak and we should listen quietly and grant him the respect we demand for ourselves. The young man no doubt believes in the justice of his cause as we do in ours, and he has pledged his life for it. I suggest therefore that we all rise in appreciation of his evident sincerity and that we hear him out in silence." The audience rose to a man.

The soldier had probably never before faced such a large assembly. He looked frightened and he began in a quavering voice that barely carried to the platform, although he was sitting near it. He stammered something about "German money" and "traitors," got confused, and came to a sudden stop. Then, turning to his comrades, he cried: "Oh, hell! Let's get out of here!" Out the whole gang slunk, waving their little flags and followed by laughter and applause.

Returning from the meeting home we heard newsboys shouting extra night editions—the conscription bill had become a law! Registration day was set for June 4. The thought struck me that on that day American democracy would be carried to its grave.

/   /   /

Streams of callers besieged our office from morning till late at night; young men, mostly, seeking advice on whether they should register. We knew, of course, that among them were also decoys sent to trick us into saying that they should not. The majority, however, were frightened youths, fearfully wrought up and at sea as to what to do. They were helpless creatures about to be sacrificed to Moloch. Our sympathies were with them, but we felt that we had no right to decide the vital issue for them. There were also distracted mothers, imploring us to save their boys. By the hundreds they came, wrote, or telephoned. All day long our telephone rang; our offices were filled with people, and stacks of mail arrived from every part of the country asking for information about the No-Conscription League, pledging support and urging us to go on with the work. In this bedlam we had to prepare copy for the current issues of *Mother Earth* and the *Blast*, write our manifesto, and send out circulars announcing our forthcoming meeting. At night, when trying to get some sleep, we would be rung out of bed by reporters wanting to know our next step.

Anti-conscription meetings were also taking place outside of New York and I was busy organizing branches of the No-Conscription League. At such a gathering in Philadelphia the police came down with drawn clubs and threatened to beat up the audience if I dared mention conscription. I proceeded to talk about the freedom the masses in Russia had gained. At the close of the meeting fifty persons retired to a private place, where we organized a No-Conscription League. Similar experiences were repeated in many cities.

/ / /

The June issue of *Mother Earth* appeared draped in black, its cover representing a tomb bearing the inscription: "IN MEMORIAM—AMERICAN DEMOCRACY." The sombre attire of the magazine was striking and effective. No words could express more eloquently the tragedy that turned America, the erstwhile torch-bearer of freedom, into a grave-digger of her former ideals.

We strained our capital to the last penny to issue an extra large edition. We wanted to mail copies to every Federal officer, to every editor, in the country and to distribute the magazine among young workers and college students. Our twenty thousand copies barely sufficed to supply our own needs. It made us feel our poverty more than ever before. Fortunately an unexpected ally came to our assistance: the New York newspapers! They had reprinted whole passages from our anti-conscription manifesto, some even reproducing the entire text and thus bringing it to the attention of millions of readers. Now they copiously quoted from our June issue and editorially commented at length on its contents.

The press throughout the country raved at our defiance of law and presidential orders. We duly appreciated their help in making our voices resound through the land, our voices that but yesterday had called in vain. Incidentally the papers also gave wide publicity to our meeting scheduled for June 4.

/ / /

When we got within half a dozen blocks of Hunt's Point Palace, our taxi had to come to a stop. Before us was a human dam, as far as the eye could see, a densely packed, swaying mass, counting tens of thousands. On the outskirts were police on horse and on foot, and great numbers of soldiers in khaki. They were shouting orders, swearing, and pushing the crowd from the sidewalks to the street and back again. The taxi could not proceed, and it was hopeless to try to get Sasha to the hall on his crutches. We had to make a detour around vacant lots until we reached the back entrance of the Palace. There we came upon a score of patrol wagons armed with search-lights and machine-guns. The officers stationed at the stage door, failing to recognize us, refused to let us pass. A reporter who knew us whispered to the police sergeant in charge. "Oh, all right," he shouted, "but nobody else will be admitted. The place is overcrowded."

The sergeant had lied; the house was only half filled. The police were keeping the people from getting in, and at seven o'clock they had ordered the doors locked. While they were denying the right of entry to workers, they permitted scores of half-drunken sailors and soldiers to enter the hall. The balcony and the front seats were filled with them. They talked loudly, made vulgar remarks, jeered, hooted, and otherwise behaved as befits men who are preparing to make the world safe for democracy.

In the room behind the stage were officials from the Department of Justice, members of the Federal attorney's office, United States marshals, detectives from the "Anarchist Squad," and reporters. The scene looked as if set for bloodshed. The representatives of law and order were obviously keyed up for trouble.

When the meeting was opened and Leonard D. Abbott took the chair, he was greeted by the soldiers and sailors with catcalls, whistles, and stamping of feet. This failing of the desired effect, the uniformed men in the gallery began throwing on the platform electric lamps which they had unscrewed from the fixtures. Several bulbs struck a vase holding a bunch of red carnations, sending vase and flowers crashing to the floor. Confusion followed, the audience rising in indignant protest and demanding that the police put the ruffians out. John Reed, who was with us, called on the police captain to order the disturbers removed, but that official declined to intervene.

After repeated appeals from the chairman, supported by some women in the audience, comparative quiet was restored. But not for long. Every speaker had to go through the same ordeal. Even the mothers of prospective soldiers, who poured out their anguish and wrath, were jeered by the savages in Uncle Sam's uniform.

Stella was one of the mothers to address the audience. It was the first time she had to face such an assembly and endure insults. Her own son was still too young to be subject to conscription, but she shared the woe and grief of other, less fortunate, parents, and she could articulate the protest of those who had no opportunity to speak. She held her own against the interruptions and carried the audience with her by the earnestness and fervour of her talk.

Sasha was the next speaker; others were to follow him, and I was to speak last. Sasha refused to be helped to the platform. Slowly and with great effort he managed to climb up the several steps and then walked across the stage to the chair placed for him near the footlights. Again, as on May 18, he had to stand on one leg, resting the other on the chair and supporting himself with one hand on the table. He stood erect, his head held high, his jaw set, his eyes clear and unflinchingly turned on the disturbers. The audience rose and greeted Sasha with prolonged applause, a token of their appreciation of his appearance in spite of his injury. The enthusiastic demonstration seemed to enrage the patriots, most of whom were obviously under the influence of drink. Renewed shouts, whistles, stamping, and hysterical cries of the women accompanying the soldiers greeted Sasha. Above the clamour a hoarse voice cried: "No more! We've had enough!" But Sasha would not be daunted. He began to speak, louder and louder, berating the hoodlums, now reasoning with them, now holding them up to scorn. His words seemed to impress them. They became quiet. Then, suddenly, a husky brute in front shouted; "Let's charge the platform! Let's get the slacker!" In an instant the audience were on their feet. Some ran up to grab the soldier. I rushed to Sasha's side. In my highest pitch I cried: "Friends, friends—wait, wait!" The suddenness of my appearance attracted everyone's attention. "The soldiers and sailors have been sent here to cause trouble," I admonished the people, "and the police are in league with them. If we lose our heads there will be bloodshed, and it will be our blood they will shed!" There were cries of "She's right!" "It's true!" I took advantage of the momentous pause. "Your presence here," I continued, "and the presence of the multitude outside shouting their approval of every word they can catch, are convincing proof that you do not believe in violence, and it equally proves that you understand that war is the most fiendish violence. War kills deliberately, ruthlessly, and destroys innocent lives. No, it is not we who have come to create a riot here. We must refuse to be provoked to it. Intelligence and a passionate faith are more convincing than armed police, machine-guns, and rowdies in solders' coats. We have demonstrated it tonight. We still have many speakers, some of them with illustrious American names. But nothing they or I could say will add to the splendid example you have given. Therefore I declare the meeting closed. File out orderly, intone our inspiring revolutionary songs, and leave the soldiers to their tragic fate, which at present they are too ignorant to realize."

The strains of the *Internationale* rose above the approval shouted by the audience, and the song was taken up by the many-throated mass outside. Patiently they had waited for five hours and every word that had reached them through the open windows had found a strong echo in their hearts. All through the meeting their applause had thundered back to us, and now their jubilant song.

In the committee room a reporter of the New York *World* rushed up to me. "Your presence of mind saved the situation," he congratulated me. "But what will you report in your paper?" I asked. "Will you tell of the rough-house the soldiers tried to make, and the refusal of the police to stop them?" He would, he said, but I was certain that no truthful report would be published, even if he should have the courage to write it.

The next morning the *World* proclaimed that "Rioting accompanied the meeting of the No-Conscription League at Hunt's Point Palace. Many were injured and twelve arrests made. Soldiers in uniform sneered at the speakers. After adjournment the real riot began in the adjacent streets."

The alleged riot was of editorial making and seemed a deliberate attempt to stop further protests against conscription. The police took the hint. They issued orders to the hall-keepers not to rent their premises for any meeting to be addressed by Alexander Berkman or Emma Goldman. Not even the owners of places we had been using for years dared disobey. They were sorry, they said; they did not fear arrest, but the soldiers had threatened their lives and property. We secured Forward Hall, on East Broadway, which belonged to the Jewish Socialist Party. It was small for our purpose, barely big enough to seat a thousand people, but no other place was to be had in entire New York. The awed silence of the pacifist and anti-military organizations which followed the passing of the registration bill made it doubly imperative for us to continue the work. We scheduled a mass meeting for June 14.

It was not necessary for us to print announcements. We merely called up the newspapers, and they did the rest. They denounced our impudence in continuing anti-war activities, and they sharply criticized the authorities for failing to stop us. As a matter of fact, the police were working overtime waylaying draft-evaders. They arrested thousands, but many more had refused to register. The press did not report the actual state of affairs; it did not care to make it known that large numbers of Americans had the manhood to defy the government. We knew through our own channels that thousands had determined not to shoulder a gun against people who were as innocent as themselves in causing the world-slaughter.

EMMETT J. SCOTT

23 | *Letters from the Great Migration*

The following letters, collected by Emmett J. Scott, a distinguished Afro-American educator and editor, reflect one of the great events of American social history: the "great migration" of blacks from southern to northern cities during World War I. The war-fueled economy created opportunities, and the widespread circulation of Chicago newspapers, particularly the Chicago Defender, *gave southern Afro-Americans a picture of the opportunities in Chicago and other northern cities. The letters are, for the most part, practical requests to the* Defender *for information about jobs and the treatment of Afro-Americans.*

The "Great Migration" was dwarfed by the similar, but far larger, migration of blacks to the northern cities between 1940 and 1965. During the twentieth century, Afro-Americans went from being preponderantly the most rural Americans to the most urban. This had enormous consequences for American politics, cities, and culture.

Sherman, Ga., Nov. 28, 1916.

Dear Sir: This letter comes to ask for all infirmations concerning employment in your connection in the warmest climate. Now I am in a family of (11) eleven more or less boys and girls (men and women) mixed sizes who want to go north as soon as arrangements can be made and employment given places for shelter and so on (etc) now this are farming people they were raised on the farm and are good farm hands I of course have some experience and qualefication as a coman school teacher and hotel waiter and along few other lines.

I wish you would write me at your first chance and tell me if you can give us employment at what time and about what wages will you pay and what kind of arrangement can be made for our shelter. Tell me when can you best use us now or later.

Will you send us tickets if so on what terms and at what price what is the cost per head and by what route should we come. We are Negroes and try to show ourselves worthy of all we may get from any friendly source we endeavor to be true to all good causes, if you can we thank you to help us to come north as soon as you can.

From Scott, Emmett J. "Letters of Negro Migrants of 1916–1918," in The Journal of Negro History. *Copyrighted by and reprinted with the permission of the Association for the Study of Afro-American Life and History.*

/   /   /

Sanford, Fla., April 27, 1917.

Dear sir: I have seen through the Chicago Defender that you and
the people of Chicago are helping newcomers. I am asking you for some
information about conditions in some small town near Chicago.

There are some families here thinking of moving up, and are desirous of knowing what to expect before leaving. Please state about
treatment, work, rent and schools. Please answer at some spare time.

Anniston, Ala., April 23, 1917.

Dear sir: Please gave me some infamation about coming north i can
do any kind of work from a truck gardin to farming i would like to leave
here and i cant make no money to leave I ust make enough to live one
please let me here from you at once i want to get where i can put my
children in schol.

Cedar Grove, La., April 23, 1917.

Dear sir: to day I was advise by the defendent offices in your city
to communicate with you in regards to the labor for the colored of the
south as I was lead to beleave that you was in position of firms of your
city & your near by surrounding towns of Chicago. Please state me
how is the times in & around Chicago place to locate having a family
dependent on me for support. I am informed by the Chicago Defender
a very valuable paper which has for its purpose the Uplifting of my
race, and of which I am a constant reader and real lover, that you were
in position to show some light to one in my condition.

Seeking a Northern Home. If this is true Kindly inform me by next
mail the next best thing to do Being a poor man with a family to care
for, I am not coming to live on flowry Beds of ease for I am a man who
works and wish to make the best I can out of life I do not wish to come
there hoodwinked not knowing where to go or what to do so I Solicite
your help in this matter and thanking you in advance for what advice
you may be pleased to Give I am yours for success.

P. S. I am presently imployed in the I C RR. Mail Department at
Union Station this city.

Brookhaven, Miss., April 24, 1917.

Gents: The cane growers of Louisiana have stopped the exodus from
New Orleans, claiming shortage of labor which will result in a sugar
famine.

Now these laborers thus employed receive only 85 cents a day and
the high cost of living makes it a serious question to live.

There is a great many race people around here who desires to come
north but have waited rather late to avoid car fare, which they have not

got. isnt there some way to get the concerns who wants labor, to send passes here or elsewhere so they can come even if they have to pay out of the first months wages? Please done publish this letter but do what you can towards helping them to get away. If the R. R. Co. would run a low rate excursion they could leave that way. Please ans.

Savannah, Ga., April 24, 1917.

Sir: I saw an advertisement in the Chicago Ledger where you would send tickets to any one desireing to come up there. I am a married man with a wife only, and I am 38 years of age, and both of us have so far splendid health, and would like very much to come out there provided we could get good employment regarding the advertisement.

Fullerton, La., April 28, 1917

Dear sir: I was reading about you was neading labor ninety miles of Chicago what is the name of the place and what R R extends ther i wants to come north and i wants a stedy employment ther what doe you pay per day i dont no anything about molding works but have been working around machinery for 10 years. Let me no what doe you pay for such work and can you give me a job of that kind or a job at common labor and let me no your prices and how many hours for a day.

De Ridder, La., April 29, 1917.

Dear sir: there is lots of us southern mens wants transportation and we want to leave ratway as soon as you let us here from you some of us is married mens who need work we would like to bring our wife with us there is 20 head of good mens want transportation and if you need us let us no by return mail we all are redy only wants here from you there may be more all of our peoples wont to leave here and i want you to send as much as 20 tickets any way I will get you up plenty hands to do most any kind of work all you have to do is to send for them. looking to here from you. This is among us collerd.

Atlanta, Ga., April 30, 1917.

Dear Sir: In reading the Chicago Defender I find that there are many jobs open for workmen, I wish that you would or can secure me a position in some of the northern cities; as a workman and not as a loafer. One who is willing to do any kind of hard in side or public work, have had broad experience in machinery and other work of the kind. A some what alround man can also cook, well trained devuloped man; have travel extensively through the western and southern states; A good strong *morial religious* man no habits. I will accept transportation on advance and deducted from my wages later. It does not matter where, that is; as to city, country, town or state since you secure the positions.

I am quite sure you will be delighted in securing a position for a man of this description. I'll assure you will not regret of so doing. Hoping to hear from you soon.

Houston, Tx. April 30, 1917

Dear Sir: wanted to leave the South and Go any Place where a man will be any thing Except a Ker I thought would write you for Advise as where would be a Good Place for a Comporedly young man That want to Better his Standing who has a very Promising young Family.

I am 30 years old and have Good Experience in Freight Handler and Can fill Position from Truck to Agt.

would like Chicago or Philadelphia But I dont Care where so long as I Go where a man is a man.

Beaumont, Texas, May 7, 1917.

Dear Sir: I see in one of your recent issue of collored men woanted in the North I wish you would help me to get a position in the North I have no trade I have been working for one company eight years and there is no advancement here for me and I would like to come where I can better my condition I woant work and not affraid to work all I wish is a chance to make good. I believe I would like machinist helper or Molder helper. If you can help me in any way it will be highly appreciate hoping to hear from you soon

EARNEST ELMO CALKINS

24 | Advertising, the Civilizer

Americans seriously began worrying about the effects of advertising in the 1920s, the era in which advertising became a profession, and that fear has never quite been stilled. In the following reading, from the period, an advertising professional offers a defense of his industry. Calkins argues that advertising helps create a market for the labor-saving devices of the modern age. Advertising creates better-educated consumers, who, by their support of industry, encourage even more new products and, through the volume of their demand, help provide incentive for cheaper, more efficient means of production.

THE RISING GENERATION ASKS A QUESTION

A young man who had just joined the staff of one of the larger advertising agencies sought his boss in some perturbation. "I wish you would tell me the truth about this advertising business, chief. Is it all bunk?" To which his employer replied, "There is just as much bunk in advertising as there is in law or medicine, or for that matter, in literature and life, but it is never necessary to use bunk to practise advertising successfully."

That young man's state of mind was the natural result of his reading. He had been recruited from the profession of writing, and he still followed the ultra-intellectual world, which has lately concerned itself with the inconsistencies, the waste, and the smugness of advertising. In short, with the bunk.

The pages of those delightful magazines which are distinguished by good writing, distinctive typography, small circulation, and no advertising, offer some interesting points of view to the professional advertising man—who unfortunately does not as a rule read them.

/   /   /

William McFee finds the floor of his post office at Westport littered knee-deep with circulars cast off by disdainful recipients, and deplores the destruction of forests to make the paper for so futile an end. And

Earnest Elmo Calkins, Business the Civilizer (Boston, Atlantic Monthly Press Publication, Little, Brown, and Company, 1928) pp. 1–3, 12–18.

181

Joseph Pennell, who was pleased with few things apparently despised advertising more cordially and with stronger adjectives than any other manifestation of our commercial civilization.

Then there are the fiction makers, with less restriction and more imagination. The younger men, most of them after brief experiences inside advertising organizations, have seized the excellent opportunity for satire which modern business affords, and we have . . . Scott Fitzgerald's *The Great Gatsby*, Christopher Morley's *Ginger Cubes*, Sinclair Lewis's *Babbitt*, Sherwood Anderson's *Story-teller's Story*, and *Bunk, Lottery*, and *Bread and Circuses* by William Woodward, all presenting advertising as a sort of gigantic conspiracy, fostered and maintained by highly paid advertising men whose interests, like those of the priests of ancient religions, lie in keeping up the great illusion, and who go about their work with their tongues in their cheeks. Sometimes the conspiracy is imagined as directed against the business man, but the popular conception is that the public is the victim, and that manufacturer and agent are working together to put something over. This something may be higher prices for worthless goods, creating unnecessary wants and desires, or exterminating a competitor, making a better article at a lower price, but generally just misleading people with bunk about memory courses, or hair restorers, or correspondence universities.

/   /   /

The slogan "It pays to advertise" acquired its currency from George M. Cohan's play. Admitting that advertising pays, whom does it pay? It pays the professional advertising man, beyond doubt. It also pays the manufacturer who uses it to increase his business. But the crucial question is, does it pay the public? Are the people as a whole better off for it? Is it a benefit to mankind? And who pays for it? Is it added to the cost of the goods? Would it be desirable, as writers have suggested, to remove advertising from our commercial fabric, and would we be better off without it?

/   /   /

THE AMELIORATION OF THE HOUSEWIFE'S LOT

When I was a boy, about fifty years ago more or less, mother used to buy a bar of Castile soap half a yard long and four inches square and saw it up into cakes an inch thick. The cake was hard as Stonehenge, the corners sharper than a serpent's tooth. It took weeks of use to wear it down so that it comfortably fitted the hand.

Today we have a cake of toilet soap—a great many of them, in fact— just the right shape to fit the hand, just as pure as Castile, scented if we like, tinted to match the bathroom decorations if we prefer, reasonable in price; and when we want another cake we go to the nearest grocery or drug store, and there it is.

And not only toilet soap. We have seen the evolution of shaving creams, safety razors, and tooth pastes, as well as soap powders, laundry chips, washing machines, vegetable shortenings, self-rising flours, electric sadirons, vacuum cleaners, hot-water taps, aluminum cooking utensils, refrigerators, kitchen cabinets—everything, in short, that constitutes the difference between our mothers' kitchens and our wives'.

The amount of sheer drudgery that has been taken out of housekeeping in fifty years can be realized only by comparison, by drawing the illuminating parallel. An iron, soft-coal cook-stove; a reservoir at the back the only source of hot-water supply; the green-painted iron pump in the wooden corner sink for cold; drinking water from the pump outside; saleratus instead of baking powder; hog lard instead of vegetable shortening; butter and milk hung down the well by a string to keep them cold; heavy iron pots and skillets to be lifted, to say nothing of the coalhod; dishes washed by hand; no device to alleviate the frightful labor—no rubber scrapers, scouring mops, metal-ring dishrags, no wire brushes, or drying racks, or cleansing powders; baked beans an eighteen-hour job; oatmeal an overnight operation; sugar, salt, dried fruit, pickles, crackers, rice, coffee, pepper, spices, lard, bought in bulk, scooped out of open boxes or barrels or tierces, exposed until sold, dumped on a sheet of paper laid on the scales. Molasses and vinegar drawn from the wood, and between whiles the gallon measures standing around, proving the adage that molasses attracts more flies than vinegar. Food was unclean, there was no sponsor for its quality, and it came to the kitchen almost in a state of nature. The housemother became a miniature manufacturing plant before the food was ready for the family to eat. And the preparation of meals was but a small portion of the housewife's burden. There was cleaning with no other implements but a rag, a broom, and a turkey wing. Clothes were washed with a rub-rub-rub that wore the zinc from the washboard.

Put such a kitchen beside the one pictured in most advertisements selling kitchen equipment, or those complete ones shown in the housekeeping departments of the women's magazine, "How to Furnish the Ideal Kitchen." Better still, take a modern housewife, not the delicatessen and can-opener type, but a real housekeeper, who keeps her house and takes pride in it—there are such even today—and put her in an old-fashioned kitchen like that described above. She could not do in a week what my mother did every day of her toil-bound life. To keep house with what was available half a century ago was an art handed down from generation to generation, which happily has been lost, except among the newly arrived foreign-born.

/   /   /

The amelioration that has come about in fifty years is due directly and indirectly to advertising. These things did not come into existence because women demanded them. Women did not know that they were possible. They exist because there was a method of distributing them, of teaching possible buyers what a help they would be, of educating the housewife while offering her the means of applying what she learned, and of doing it on a large scale. And the strongest urge to invent desirable labor-saving devices has been this same possibility of distributing them—that is, selling enough of them to make it worth while.

Sometimes advertising supplies a demand, but in most cases it creates demand for things that were beyond even the imagination of those who would be most benefited by them. A woman knew the use of a broom, but she could not imagine a vacuum cleaner. Therefore she could not demand one, save with that vague unspoken desire which has existed from the beginning for some lightening of the terrible drudgery of keeping a house livable. The vacuum cleaner was introduced by educational advertising. The advertising was done partly by manufacturers anxious to sell vacuum cleaners, and partly by electric-light companies anxious to sell current. The spread of electrical housekeeping devices has followed the increase in the number of houses wired for electricity, and that too has been brought about by advertising, by the selfish desire to do more business, to sell more goods. But the result has been a public benefit, an increasing willingness to spend money to lighten the human burden, to cut down the waste of human energy spent in the operation of living.

No vacuum-cleaner factory could do business as a neighborhood proposition. Only a national market would furnish enough business to make the manufacture economically possible. And a national market is possible only through advertising. And that advertising must be educational. It must teach the sound economy of paying more to get the greater benefit. The woman's time and health and strength are worth more than the difference in cost between a broom and a cleaner. But not all of these improvements are in the vacuum-cleaner class. Most of them add nothing to the cost of upkeep. The greater number lower it. They teach the use of something better that costs less.

I do not think I am claiming too much in giving to advertising the credit of the great change in housekeeping that we have seen. I have had to observe it very closely for thirty years, and I have to some extent helped to bring it about. Some may be inclined to think it is due to the women's magazines. It is true that they have directed their editorial energies to the same ends and with remarkable results.

But it should not be forgotten that it is advertising that makes such magazines possible. It is the revenue from the advertisers that pays for the services of domestic economists, physicians, interior decorators, cooks, dressmakers, and other experts who teach women better ways of doing things. More than that, while such departments are conducted with the primary purpose of being helpful to readers, they furnish an excellent background for the advertising. Magazines with constructive departments on the care of babies, cooking, furnishing, housekeeping, dressmaking, laundry work, and all the other activities which go into home-making are preparing audiences to listen to manufacturers who sell sanitary nursing bottles, infants' wear, prepared foods, salad oils, paints, fabrics, wall papers, electric mangles, and washing powders.

/   /   /

Behind the successful and intelligently conducted magazine is the advertiser, who buys space and makes the magazine profitable; and so the educational work of home-making magazines should be credited largely to him.

Advertising is not an end. It is a means to an end. So the question is not, Is advertising desirable, but Are those ends desirable, and is advertising too great a price to pay for them? To those who look upon advertising as merely the selfish effort of manufacturers to induce them to buy more goods it seems that the world could easily do without it. People say to themselves, "I do not want to be persuaded to buy more goods," and that should settle it. As far as they are concerned advertising is unnecessary. For the manufacturer who uses it, advertising is a means of selling goods, but its present proportions are due not to the manufacturer's desire to sell goods, but to the real public need it supplies.

A familiar paradox is the man who tells you with much earnestness that he never reads advertising, and does not believe in it. And as he sits there he is dressed from head to foot in advertised goods. His office is equipped and his home is furnished with advertised goods. How did they get there? Because they were the things most accessible, the ones for sale in the stores where he bought, the ones the salesman showed him, and the ones that most exactly met his needs. It was not necessary for him to read the advertising. The advertising he did not read distributed the goods, brought them within his reach geographically and financially, and keeps them there for his benefit—better things than he could buy for the same money were it not for the tremendous savings that quantity production brings about. And most of them would not even exist, to say nothing of being distributed, if there had not been advertising.

But advertising adds to the cost of the goods! You still hear that. So does production add to the cost of the goods, and traveling salesmen, and retail stores, and jobbers' percentages. Everything that is done to a manufactured article and all handling of natural products must be added to the price that the customer pays. But nothing is so well established as the simple fact that the more you make the less the cost of each. And not only is cost of making lessened, but also the cost of selling, including cost of advertising. And the cost of selling can be and is lessened until the advertising costs nothing. Why does a tailor-made suit cost more than a ready-made? Why do custom-made shoes cost more than the product of the factories? It is difficult to prove these things by tables of statistics because prices of all things have advanced so in the years since the war.

But consider the motor car. Nearly everyone is interested in this product of advertising. Nearly everyone is aware of the continual improvement in the cars and the steady lowering of price, due to quantity production. Some are as much concerned over the congestion of motor cars as they are over the congestion of advertising. They feel that there is too much of both. Granted in both cases; but the only alternative is to turn back the page to mediaeval times, when each village was self-contained, or forward to one of the many Utopias which promise enough of everything and not too much of anything.

The point is that we cannot eat our cake of accessible and convenient apparatus of living and still have our cake of freedom from advertising, freight trains, industrial villages, steel and cement construction, riveting hammers, congested highways, and the many other annoyances of a prosperous, material, and mercantile age. It's a fair question whether or not our modern life is worth while, but it has nothing to do with this question, which is, If our modern life is worth while and we want to continue it, is advertising necessary to that end?

NAOMI WASHINGTON ET AL.

25 | Black New York in the
     Teens and Twenties

Beginning around 1900 Manhattan's Afro-Americans began moving north from the tenements in San Juan Hill and the Tenderloin—both on the west side of Manhattan—into the more spacious neighborhood of Harlem. By World War I Harlem had become the cultural capital of black America. In the 1920s, despite the poverty and the prejudice that most Harlemites encountered every day, this New York neighborhood centering on 125th Street was a vital and exciting place to live, to work, and particularly to create. In literature, in art, in music, and in political movements Harlem was, in many ways, the center of New York and for many people the center of the world. For an oral history of Manhattan from the 1890s to World War II, You Must Remember This *published in 1989, Jeff Kisseloff interviewed old-timers who remembered the Harlem of the teens and twenties. While they do not gloss over the difficulties of black people's lives, their accounts capture the excitement of the age of the Harlem Renaissance.*

NAOMI WASHINGTON: Now 125th Street didn't come into colored until much later. At the Loew's they'd tell you it was sold out even though it wasn't. Even the theaters that would admit you were segregated. At Hurtig and Seamon's, which later became the Apollo, you had to go 'round 126th Street and go up the back stairway. They tried to get fancy with it and call it the upper mezzanine, but everybody knew it as "nigger heaven," and it was built for that. If you look at the Apollo today, you'll see now they got a stairway, of course, but there's no connection. The only way you can get from the second balcony down to the theater, you have to jump down. The Alhambra was built the same way.

Before the Lafayette, the only other theaters open to colored were little dumps. There was one across 125th Street on the corner, a little frame shack that somebody turned into a little movie house. The Lincoln was a colored theater run by a white couple. That was a dump on 132nd Street. Then, Leo Brecher and some of his friends built a 3,000-seat house on 145th Street and Seventh Avenue. That was the Roosevelt.

He built a 3,000-seat house, the Douglas, on 142nd Street and Lenox Avenue, where the Cotton Club was later built over the lobby.

HAYWOOD BUTT: Despite the problems, Harlem was a beautiful place in which to live before the war. I was born in Elizabeth City, North Carolina, in 1897. My father was an upholsterer and a cabinetmaker for the fabulous sum of nine dollars a week. His parents had been slaves. I didn't know any of them, except for my grandmother. Though they were slaves, they were from a moderate section of the country, and they didn't get the full pinch of slavery as some of the others did from further south. They were originally from Guinea, in Africa. I knew that because they used a term in regard to my grandfather, called "Guinea niggers," which is a term the colored people assumed from the whites.

We came up here in 1912 partly because they had segregation down there. They were supposed to be separate but equal, but there's no such animal. There were also a lot of lynchings down south. That wasn't a problem in North Carolina, but it was further down south, and it had an effect on all black people at the time.

In 1913, there was quite a bit of sentiment about the Negro participation in the country's defense. They were limited to four regiments, the 24th and 25th Infantry and the 9th and 10th Cavalry. They weren't invited and sometimes they were prohibited from joining the state national guards. A Negro boy couldn't even join the Boy Scouts. Actually, they had to start their own Boy Scouts. the United States Boy Scouts.

I thought there was a deficiency in the Negroes' participation in civic affairs and that they should go in and prove that they were really worthy citizens. That was my train of thought at the time, and it hasn't changed very much. We have participated in all of the wars of the country, even the Revolution. The first blood that was shed in the war for independence was that of a Negro—Crispus Attucks. Then we had Peter Salem, who fought in Salem, Mass. They were fighting for America, and America should recognize that, but they seem to ignore that part of history. One of the black regiments was really the saviors of Colonel Roosevelt's regiment in the Spanish-American War.

Our unit started in 1913. There wasn't much to it at first. Boys used to drill with broomsticks up on 63rd Street, at St. Cyprian's Church. We drilled once a week in front of Lafayette Hall or on Seventh Avenue. The Boy Scouts gave us some military training. They showed us various soldier's positions. We didn't get any heavy combat training until we shipped out of the city up to Peekskill and Camp Whitman upstate. I was in the First Battalion of the 15th New York. In August 1917, when we shipped out of the city, we became the 369th.

DOLL THOMAS: I was a damn young foolish American. About eight or ten of us enlisted, and that was unheard of. We embarrassed the white folks. They didn't know what the hell to do with us. The last incident was in Chillicothe, Ohio. They put me on guard duty out there, and there was one particular officer that I couldn't stand anyhow. He was the only person in the world that ever called me a nigger that really riled me, just the way he could say it, just like you were filth or dirt. "You don't have any business in this army, nigger. I hope I'm relievin' some fellas, and you're around 'cause, whether you're in the war or not, you're gonna get shot." All that shit all the time.

Anyway, they told us Army regulations—you stop a guy and tell him to halt three times to get the countersign. If he don't say anything you shoot. I knew who it was, but I blasted him in the shoulder, and all hell broke loose. So they immediately put us on a ship and shipped us to Europe with the contingents of soldiers that were goin' over to make way for Pershing.

HAYWOOD BUTT: The camps were segregated. We objected to a certain extent, but we generally accepted it as our lot. The chefs were colored and they knew how to cook the kind of food we liked. There was a little resentment, but not very much toward the white officers. The fact is, the officers that really pushed us, we considered it our due.

In the camps, they had officers' clubs, but the ranks below major were excluded because we had very few Negro majors. We had quite a few captains, but no majors. This was all over.

We were discriminated against by the Red Cross. They would serve cocoa and doughnuts. A black man would get on the line, and the doughnuts and the cocoa would suddenly become exhausted. They couldn't replace it until the black man got out of the line.

The YMCAs were just about as bad. They were the chief offender at that time. They were supposed to supply us with cigarettes, but we couldn't go in there to get them. We resented it, but there was nothing we could do about it, so we accepted it. But then the Second and Third Battalions went down to Spartanburg, South Carolina, for training. One Sunday morning, Lieutenant Noble Sissle went into one of the hotels to buy some cigars and New York papers and someone in there told him. "Take your hat off. nigger."

They kicked them out, and the boys took that quite seriously. They organized themselves to make a raid on Spartanburg, but somebody got to the colonel, and the colonel and several of the officers persuaded them to let them handle it.

NAOMI WASHINGTON: Our older brother was drafted. I remember we went down to see him off. They left from St. Philip's Church. He was kissing us good-bye, and my father cried. That was the time that Lawrence said, "Pop, don't send me away like this." He couldn't stand to see him cry.

It was very sad there. People were crying. War is one of those things, you're saying good-bye, and for many of those saying good-bye, it *was* good-bye.

DR. HERMAN WARNER: From the middle of 1916 to 1918 I was in the British West Indies Forces. I saw combat on the Western Front, in Belgium, for the most part, where some of the fiercest fighting was. The British West Indies sent eleven battalions. We had white officers. It wasn't the custom to give officer rank to black soldiers. You went as far as sergeant major.

In general, I didn't have any difficulty with the whites. What problems we had was when America got into the war and their white soldiers came in. Anytime they met us in the cafes there was trouble. They wanted to get us out, and there would be a fight. Then, a group of West Indian soldiers would decide "if we have any more trouble from the soldiers, we're gonna kill 'em." That's what they did. If another incident occurred, the soldiers would be marked, and they waylaid and butchered them.

HAYWOOD BUTT: Pershing wanted us to become laborers and to take our arms from us. That would have been sort of a disgrace, to disarm us. We went over to a New York regiment, and they didn't want us. None of the white units did, so we went around to the French. We fought side by side with the French. We were in five engagements. We fought in the Champagne. I was on the front lines for 191 straight days.

HERMAN WARNER: I saw hand-to-hand combat. You get scared. Anybody who tells you that he was not scared is a liar. There is a line of demarcation between fear and cowardice. When your buddy falls next to you, you regret it, but you're glad it wasn't you. You mourn for the person, but the French have an expression, *sauve qui peut*—"save yourself if you can."

I thought about the idea of killing another man. I came from a religious background, and at times you would feel, "What am I doing here?" Just the thought of killing a person. But you then get completely conditioned, not only to the environment but to that way of life. So many times, you were so taken up with escape, just trying to get away, that you didn't have enough time to look at the individuals you were fighting. And you didn't always kill. Sometimes you would maim, and then you go on about your business, depending on your situation. It's horrible, but it then shows you how complex a human being is. You know, I am the most peaceful man in the world.

HAYWOOD BUTT: I took the communique that apprised us of the armistice. I was relieved, because we were going over the top the next day. I daresay I wouldn't be here, because we were in Alsace, and all of that terrain was mined.

I didn't get back until February. We were taken to the Battery, and people were waiting for us there. Our band, with James Reese Europe as the conductor, led us. We were the first ones to pass through that victory arch at Washington Square, then up Fifth Avenue. People were five or ten deep on the sidewalk, and they were throwing money down at us.

NAOMI WASHINGTON: As God would have it, Lawrence did come back, and he wasn't injured. When they came back, they came up Lenox Avenue. People were watching from the roofs. The young kids were running with them and cheering. I never recognized my brother, but my mother recognized her child. "That's my son. That's my son." She was so glad, because there were a lot of boys who didn't come back.

HERMAN WARNER: When the war was over, I applied for a leave of absence to come to America for maybe six months or a year. The leave was granted. But after I was in New York for six months, I decided I'd stay here, because, frankly. I was fed up with colonialism and I wanted to see what America was all about.

You cannot for a moment imagine what Harlem was like in those days. It was the most beautiful spot. The houses were some of the best houses in New York, and the people were of one class. Everybody seemed to know everybody else. It's hard to describe the feeling you got from belonging to that little space.

You know, Harlem then was a state of mind. It was more than just a physical place. There was something that it represented—a consciousness, if you will, feeling that from there you could go anywhere. There were people who were middle-class and upper-middle-class who wouldn't live anywhere but Harlem. It just had so much to offer, sociologically and psychologically. It was the place to live. It represented the best. You would go into an apartment house, and the elevator man would have a doctorate. It was a common thing—a Ph.D. who couldn't get work.

HAROLD ELLIS: When I was working at a hotel on Central Park West, one of the residents was a graduate of McGill, and he convinced me to apply there. I graduated McGill with an M.D. in '20—five years. I worked through the influenza epidemic of 1918. It was so bad that four or five of my classmates came to class one day and then died the next. Aspirin hadn't come out yet. In twenty-four hours, you got it and you were gone. There wasn't anything you could do. They gave you poultices, maybe some mercury preparation, all that sort of primitive medicine.

Since I didn't have any money to start up, I went to work as a cook's assistant up in Massachusetts. In those days, you didn't come by a job in a hospital so easily. They weren't hiring black doctors. I came back to New York to the hotel on Central Park West, and I went back to work as an elevator operator. With a medical license!

Anatole Longfellow, alias the Scarlet Creeper, strutted aimfully down the east side of Seventh Avenue. He wore a tight-fitting suit of shepherd's plaid which thoroughly revealed his lithe, sinewy figure to all who gazed upon him, and all gazed. A great diamond, or some less valuable stone which aped a diamond, glistened in his fuchsia cravat. The uppers of his highly polished tan boots were dove-coloured suede and the buttons were pale blue. His black hair was sleek under his straw hat set at a jaunty angle. When he saluted a friend—and his acquaintanceship seemed to be wide—two rows of pearly teeth gleamed from his seal-brown countenance.

—Carl Van Vechten, *Nigger Heaven*

RICHARD BRUCE NUGENT: That sounds like me in my monkey suit, looking like all of those other dickty niggers. We all wore those monkey-backed suits, bell-bottomed trousers, pinch-backed suits. I had one made when I was in England. I shall never forget that suit. It was blue-brown. It was *British*, and Seventh Avenue was the Fifth Avenue of Harlem.

ELTON FAX: I first came up to Harlem on an Easter Sunday, and that was something. I was out there in the parade. I'll never forget it, because I was with Hamtree Harrington, Bojangles, and all these people. Lofton Mitchell mentions this in black drama. He said, "Man, we *strolled* in Harlem. This was our turf." That was the feeling you got. There were people in the parade who were quite seriously elegant, in top hat, tails, cutaway coat, spats, cane—anything that mimicked white upper-class living, mimicry of that which was opulent, that which was approved, that which white folks aspired to be—J. P. Morgan.

NORA MAIR: Lofton Mitchell was right—we didn't walk, we strolled. I loved it when my brother-in-law would take me strolling on Seventh Avenue. You walked with your nose in the air, especially coming from Jamaica. Everybody was dressed to the teeth. You would wear the finest you had, like chiffon dresses, white hats, new shoes, and everything matched, from your pocketbook on down. We had a friend who was an African. On Easter Sunday, he would wear cutaway, striped pants, top hat, white spats, and cane, and he strolled Fifth Avenue. He *had* to be there. Everybody was out there. They would say if you stood at the corner of 135th Street and Lenox Avenue, you would see every important person you ever knew.

ISABEL WASHINGTON POWELL: While Adam and I were married, every Sunday morning after church, he would walk down Seventh Avenue wearing tails and an ascot. He was immaculate. He was fantastic. I had my own milliner who did my hats. I had a lady that made my dresses. My whole deal was getting ready for church on Sunday and strutting down the aisle of Abyssinian Baptist Church, oh, sure. He would walk from 138th Street to 125th Street. The people would come around and greet him. This was before he ran for anything, but he was getting ready then. You know how there are people who are always standing back. He would break from me and walk over and throw his arms around them. "Hi, friend." Those were the people who put him in.

BRUCE NUGENT: I came to New York from Washington, D. C. In Washington, black society imitated white society with tragic fidelity. Of course, they didn't think it was tragic fidelity. They just thought, White folks take sabbaticals, I'll take sabbaticals. On the sabbatical, they looked it up to see what a sabbatical was.

You didn't trust yourself enough to innovate, and if you did, you got called outrageous. That's the name that's been applied to me all my life. I've always been sort of an exception to the rule. I have always said, "Well, I'm a Bruce. I can do whatever I please. I have the divine right of kings." It was always tongue-in-cheek, but I always meant it.

We came to New York after my father died. Mother came to get a job to take care of us. She had first worked for the National Geographic, but that didn't pan out, so she became a waitress. My brother was dancing at the time on Broadway. I worked at the Martha Washington Hotel. It was a women's hotel, and it was the A-number-one first-class hotel. I loved that hotel. There was a woman in the hotel who, around her bathtub, had quart bottles of perfumes, so whenever she took a bath, she put this perfume on. She always smelled so good. I used to go up with little bottles and steal the perfume, so I always smelled so good. She said, "You don't have to steal my perfume. I'll give it to you. Always take what you want. I like the way you smell like I smell."

Then I got a job as an assistant to an iceman. That was a thrill, because you stuck a pick in the ice, and it split so perfectly. It was like being a diamond cutter. I loved that.

When I first saw Harlem, I was scared to death. I had never seen so many black people in my life. It was the longest time before black was beautiful. I'm very much like a cat or dog. I go around a place before I settle down. After I got up there, I had to see the neighborhood, and I fell in love with 138th Street because of the trees—and Goat Hill.

Who could help but notice that great big rock? I had a predilection for Mediterranean people, so I got to know these Italians that lived on the hill. I was so sad when they blasted and blasted that rock to get the hill out of the way. These people had goats. They drank goat's milk and they ate goat. I learned a lot of Italian foods from them, but they never could get me to eat an eye of the goat.

ELTON FAX: When I think of the Renaissance, the Harlem Renaissance, I think of the basketball team of that name. The Rennies were a forerunner of the Globetrotters. They were a great advertisement for Harlem in those days.

HOWARD "STRETCH" JOHNSON: The Renaissance basketball team was owned by Bob Douglas, who was a very militant black entrepreneur. He owned the Renaissance Casino and the Renaissance Bar & Grill. When he took over the Renaissance Theater and Ballroom, he saw it as an entertainment center in line with the poetry and literary explosion, which was known as the Harlem Renaissance. The Renaissance Big Five basketball team was a part of that surge, which some called the advent of the New Negro.

My father was a very fine professional basketball player. He played with a group called the Puritans, which later became the Renaissance Big Five, with Fats Jenkins and Pappy Ricks. My father taught Pappy Ricks how to make his carom shot from the side.

Paul Robeson played with Alpha fraternity against my father when my father was playing with St. Christopher's, another semi-pro team that was popular in the '20s. Paul was a great figure. People used to swarm around him when he walked out on the street. He was the inspiration in every walk of life. Those blacks who went in for law had respect for his being a Phi Beta Kappa at Columbia University. Those who aspired to be successful in the athletic field had him as an exemplar with his record at Rutgers, where he got fifteen varsity letters—more varsity A's than any individual who ever went to Rutgers—in football, basketball, track, and baseball.

My father played baseball for some of the black barnstorming teams against all-star white teams which were composed of people like Babe Ruth and other top stars from the big leagues, and most often they would beat 'em.

Before World War I, he played on a team that was comprised of the redcaps at Grand Central, half of whom were Ph.D.s who couldn't get work in the white world, so they smashed baggage at Grand Central Station. They formed a very talented team called the Grand Central Redcaps.

He also played with the Lincoln Giants, who later became the New York Black Yankees. He would take me to Catholic Protectory Oval, which was over behind where Harlem Hospital is located now. That's where the Lincoln Giants used to play. I don't think the bleachers held more than 500 people. They played against the Wilmington Potomacs, the Pittsburgh Crawfords, the Baltimore Elite Giants, the Hillsdale Giants. There were some great teams at that time.

BRUCE NUGENT: There was a woman in Washington who was fantastic. She was a very good poet, Georgia Douglas Johnson, and she had salons. I met Langston [Hughes] at her home. We took to each other immediately. Someone wrote once that Langston and I were lovers. It is at least hinted that I had a crush on Langston. And the hint may have more truth to it than I used to think, because, as I look back on it, Langston had a physical appearance that was everything I liked at the time. He looked Latin, and he looked like me complexion-wise. Yes, I had quite a crush on Langston. Years later, I discovered Langston had a very strange kind of unnecessary envy of me, that I seemed to be so free and easy sexually, and apparently he wasn't. We kind of had a crush on each other.

We spent that whole night walking from his mother's house to my grandmother's house. They were only four blocks away, but we weren't anywhere near through talking, so we just walked each other back and forth all night long. That was the thing that was beautiful about Langston. There were always things to talk about. That's the night *Fire!!* was born. Hall Johnson, at whose house I was living, had written a spiritual called "Fire!":

> *Fire, fire, Lawd fire burn my soul.*
> *Fire, fire, Lawd fire burn my soul.*
> *I ain't been good. I ain't been clean.*
> *I been stinkin' low down mean*
> *But fire, fire, Lawd fire burn my soul.*

Both Langston and I were very fond of that. As we were walking back and forth, I think it was Langston who said we—by *we* I mean blacks—should have a magazine of our own, in which they could have art, in which they could express themselves however they felt.

He was going to be coming to New York to receive a Krigwa Award—that was the award the *Crisis* used to give—and he invited me along. After the ceremony, Langston said the best food in New York was at the YWCA, so into the YWCA went we, and I must say that the smell of those biscuits and corn bread was wonderful. As we were walking along, Langston said, "Oh, there's Wallie Thurman." There were only two newspapers that I really cared for at that time, the St. Louis *Dispatch* and *Christian Science Monitor*. Then I heard that the editor of the *Monitor* was black, and it was Wallie Thurman, but I was so disappointed when I saw him. I was brought up in Washington, where you can't be black and be any good. So my heart went down into my shoes. I was so disappointed. I said, "You mean that black boy with the sneering nose?"

I was awful, and I was so ashamed of myself afterwards, because I prided myself on having no prejudice. Later, I went to Wallie and apologized.

Anyway, there was a wonderful woman named Iolanthe Sydney who ran an unemployment office. She owned two houses, one on 136th Street and one on Lenox Avenue, and the one on 136th Street she, in essence, turned over to artists who were all indigent. She told me to go over there, at 267. "Because," she said, "you'll never be able to pay any rent."

I went there. Wallie was living there. It was bohemian—267 was a house that just felt free to be in, because she saw to it that you were free. She thought all artists needed to be indigent, so they didn't have to pay like other people did, and she elected herself to be one who did pay.

HELEN BROWN: When I first came to Harlem, Bruce was living down in the Village, which was a magnificent bohemian place. He said he was sleeping under the fountain at Washington Square. He was just living day to day. He was very much bohemian. I didn't find Harlem to be bohemian at all.

I was born February 4, 1898, in Quincy, Illinois. I went to Howard University, in Washington, where I majored in business administration. The other course I took was music.

In Harlem, I met people who had homes where we read poetry. The younger people who were doing things would meet and sit on the floor and have peanuts, and they'd read their plays and poems. You'd meet all types of people, and you'd see how knowledgeable they were. At Hall Johnson's, the door was always open, and people just dropped in. There was nothing special about it.

If you met anybody, Langston Hughes, let's say, "C'mon, we're going up to Countee's" or "We're going here." Everybody was there. Zora Neale Hurston was a classmate of mine, and she'd just say, "C'mon along."

They were hoping that they could constructively help each other. They had to push, push, and push to even get their works read by the publishers. They were fresh from school, and they were trying to sell their wares. They were hoping against hope.

26 | *In Its Own Words*

The "platform" of the Ku Klux Klan of the 1920s consisted of organized bigotry against Catholics, Jews, blacks, Orientals, and southern- and eastern-European immigrants. For the small-town and small-city inhabitants who made up its ranks, though, membership was also an expression of piety and a badge of respectability. In this sense, the Klan was a descendant of the fraternal orders that had been popular, particularly since the 1870s. These orders compensated for a disruptive, modernizing social environment and allowed men an opportunity to relate to one another and to find a social home. The name "Ku Klux Klan" was the same as that of Southern vigilante groups during Reconstruction, which were organized to intimidate blacks and preserve political power for whites. The new Klan, however, was a national anti-Catholic and anti-Jewish group, a product of the cultural changes that World War I and the new consumer society had brought about. In addition, the new Klan was a business that, through modern advertising and enterprise, was highly profitable for its promoters. The Klansman's Manual *and* Klan Komment *illustrate these different but closely intertwined tendencies.*

KLANSMAN'S MANUAL, 1925

The Order

    I. *The Name*
       "Knights of the Ku Klux Klan."
       "Forever hereafter it shall be known as KNIGHTS OF THE KU KLUX KLAN."

    II. *Its Divisions*

       "There shall be four Kloranic Orders of this Order, namely:
       1. "The order of citizenship or K-UNO (Probationary)."
       2. "Knight Kamellia or K-DUO (Primary Order of Knighthood)."
       3. "Knights of the great Forrest or K-TRIO (The Order of American Chivalry)."
       4. "Knights of the Midnight Mystery or K-Quad (Superior Order of Knighthood and Spiritual Philosophies)."

197

III. *Its Nature*

1. *Patriotic.*One of the paramount purposes of this order is to "exemplify a pure patriotism toward our country." Every Klansman is taught from the beginning of his connection with the movement that it is his duty "to be patriotic toward our country."

2. *Military.*This characteristic feature applies to its form of organization and its method of operations. It is so organized on a military plan that the whole power of the whole order, or of any part of it, may be used in quick, united action for the execution of the purposes of the order.

3. *Benevolent.*This means that the movement is also committed to a program of sacrificial service for the benefit of others. As a benevolent institution, the Knights of the Ku Klux Klan must give itself to the task of relieving and helping the suffering and distressed, the unfortunate and oppressed.

4. *Ritualistic.*In common with other orders, the Knights of the Ku Klux Klan confers ritualistic degrees and obligations, and commits its grips, signs, words, and other secret work to those persons who so meet its requirements as to find membership in the order. The ritualistic devices become the ceremonial ties that bind Klansmen to one another.

5. *Social.*The Knights of the Ku Klux Klan endeavors to unite in companionable relationship and congenial association those men who possess the essential qualifications for membership. It is so designed that kinship of race, belief, spirit, character, and purpose will engender a real, vital, and enduring fellowship among Klansmen.

6. *Fraternal.*The order is designed to be a real brotherhood. Klansmen have committed themselves to the practice of "Klannishness toward fellow-Klansmen." By this commitment they have agreed to treat one another as brothers. Fraternal love has become the bond of union. And this requires the development of such a spirit of active good will as will impel every Klansman to seek to promote the well-being of his fellow-Klansmen "socially, physically, morally, and vocationally."

IV. *Its Government*

The Constitution provides for and establishes that form of government that will best further the interests of the movement and develop to the highest possible efficiency all of its component elements.

1. *This form of government is military in character.* It will suffice to compare the Klan's form of government to the government of an army. As the United States Army is duly organized with its various officers and troops, so is the Knights of the Ku

Klux Klan welded together as an organized force for the fulfill-
ment of its patriotic mission. The Commander-in-Chief is the
Imperial Wizard. The Divisional Commanders are the Grand
Dragons. The Brigade Commanders are the Great Titans. The
Regimental Commanders are the Exalted Cyclops. All of these
Commanders have their respective staffs and other subordi-
nate officers and aides.

2. *This form of government is necessary.*(a) For efficient administration: (b) For effectiveness in method and operation: (c) For the
preservation of the order.

Fraternal order history records the failure of many patriotic societies that were organized on a so-called democratic basis. Without this
feature of the military form of government which is designed to provide
efficient leadership, effective discipline, intelligent cooperation, active
functioning, uniform methods, and unified operation, quickly respon-
sive to the call to put over the immediate task at hand, even the Knights
of the Ku Klux Klan would degenerate into a mere passive, inefficient,
social order. The military form of government must and will be preserved for the sake of true, patriotic Americanism, because it is the
only form of government that gives any guarantee of success. We must
avoid the fate of the other organizations that have split on the rock of
democracy.

V. *Its Authority*

Is "Vested primarily in the Imperial Wizard." The organization of
the Knights of the Ku Klux Klan provides, and its principle of government demands, that there shall always be *one* individual, senior in
rank to all other Klansmen of whatever rank, on whom shall rest the
responsibility of command, and whose leadership will be recognized
and accepted by all other loyal Klansmen.

The whole movement, fraught with its tremendous responsibilities and rich in its magnificent possibilities, make stirring appeal to
redblooded American manhood. Every Klansman is an important, necessary, and vital factor in the movement. In this crusade there are few
occasions for "individual plays." Success is possible only through the
most unselfish "playing for the team."

Objects And Purposes (Article II, The Constitution)

I. *Mobilization*

This is its primary purpose: "To unite white male persons, nativeborn,
Gentile citizens of the United States of America, who owe no allegiance
of any nature or degree to any foreign government, nation, institution,
sect, ruler, person, or people; whose morals are good; whose reputa-
tions and vocations are respectable; whose habits are exemplary; who

are of sound minds and eighteen years or more of age, under a common oath into a brotherhood of strict regulations."

II. *Cultural*

The Knights of the Ku Klux Klan is a movement devoting itself to the needed task of developing a genuine spirit of American patriotism. Klansmen are to be examples of pure patriotism. They are to organize the patriotic sentiment of native-born white, Protestant Americans for the defense of distinctively American institutions. Klansmen are dedicated to the principle that American shall be made American through the promulgation of American doctrines, the dissemination of American ideals, the creation of wholesome American sentiment, the preservation of American institutions.

III. *Fraternal*

The movement is designed to create a real brotherhood among men who are akin in race, belief, spirit, character, interest, and purpose. The teachings of the order indicate very clearly the attitude and conduct that make for real expression of brotherhood, or, "the practice of Klannishness."

IV. *Beneficient*

"To relieve the injured and the oppressed; to succor the suffering and unfortunate, especially widows and orphans."

The supreme pattern for all true Klansmen is their Criterion of Character, Jesus Christ, "who went about doing good." The movement accepts the full Christian program of unselfish helpfulness, and will seek to carry it on in the manner commanded by the one Master of Men, Christ Jesus.

V. *Protective*

1. *The Home.* "*To shield the sanctity of the home.*" The American home is fundamental to all that is best in life, in society, in church, and in the nation. It is the most sacred of human institutions. Its sanctity is to be preserved, its interests are to be safeguarded, and its well-being is to be promoted. Every influence that seeks to disrupt the home must itself be destroyed. The Knights of the Ku Klux Klan would protect the home by promoting whatever would make for its stability, its betterment, its safety, and its inviolability.
2. *Womanhood.* The Knights of the Ku Klux Klan declare that it is committed to "the sacred duty of protecting womanhood"; and announces that one of its purposes is "to shield . . . the chastity of womanhood.

   The degradation of women is a violation of the sacredness of human personality, a sin against the race, a crime against society, a menace to our country, and a prostitution of all that is best, and noblest, and highest in life. No race, or society, or country, can rise higher than its womanhood.

3. *The Helpless.* "To protect the weak, the innocent, and the defenseless from the indignities, wrongs, and outrages of the lawless, the violent, and the brutal."

   Children, the disabled and other helpless ones are to know the protective, sheltering arms of the Klan.

4. *American Interests.* "To protect and defend the Constitution of the United States of America, and all laws passed in conformity thereto, and to protect the states and the people thereof from all invasion of their right from any source whatsoever."

VI. *Racial*

"To maintain forever white supremacy." "To maintain forever the God-given supremacy of the white race."

Every Klansman has unqualifiedly affirmed that he will "faithfully strive for the eternal maintenance of white supremacy."

Offenses and Penalties

I. *Two Classes of Offenses*

"Offenses against this order shall be divided into two classes — major and minor offenses."

II. *Major Offenses*

"Major offenses shall consist of:

1. *"Treason against the United States of America."*
2. *"Violating the oath of allegiance to this order or any supplementary oath of obligation thereof."*
3. *"Disrespect of virtuous womanhood."*

III. *"Violation of the Constitution or laws of this order."*

(a) By conspiracy:
(b) Relinquishment or forfeiture of citizenship:
(c) Support of any foreign power against the United States of America:
(d) Violating the bylaws of a Klan of this Order.
(e) Habitual drunkenness:
(f) Habitual profanity or vulgarity:
5. *Unworthy racial or Klan conduct:* "Being responsible for the polluting of Caucasian blood through miscegenation, or the commission of any act unworthy of a Klansman."

   White men must not mix their blood with that of colored or other inferior races.

6. *The repeated commission of a minor offense:* "The repeated commission of a minor offense shall in itself constitute a major offense."

Minor Offenses

1. *Drunkenness.*
2. *Profanity or vulgarity.*
3. *Actions inimical to interests of the order.*
4. *Refusal or failure to obey.*
5. *Refusal or failure to respond.*
6. *Refusal or failure to surrender credentials.*

/   /   /

KLAN KOMMENT, 1923

At a recent meeting addressed by two members of the Imperial Kloncilium at Kansas City, MO., and which was attended by ten thousand Klansmen a novel feature was introduced. Powerful searchlights suddenly illuminated a white-robed horseman, on a white steed standing on a hill near the meeting while an airplane bearing a huge fiery cross swooped low above the celebration.

/   /   /

A great Klan meeting was held at Clinton, Mo., a few days ago when Senator Zach Harris addressed seventy-five hundred people on the principles of the order. The meeting was under the direction of Clinton Klan, a very progressive organization.

/   /   /

Jacksonville Klan, Realm of Florida, is now one of the most active Klans in that section of the country. A few days ago representatives of the Klan called at the Calvary Baptist Church revival tent and expressed appreciation on the part of the order of the work of Evangelist Allen C. Shuler.

Bloxom Klan, Realm of Virginia, a few days ago presented an American Flag and a forty-foot flagpole to Bloxom High School. The presentation speech was made by a local minister and the flag was accepted by the principal of the school.

/   /   /

Members of the Quincy, Ill., Klan visited Woodlawn Cemetery on the night of May 30 with the fiery cross and American flag. They laid a cross of red carnations on the grave of Virgil Johnson as hundreds of people watched them. York Klan Number I, Realm of Pennsylvania, recently conducted the funeral services of Horace H. Heiney, a prominent and respected citizen and the first member of their Klan to pass on into the empire invisible. At the graveside a committee of Klansmen bore fiery crosses of roses, and one of the members in full regalia, who is a well-known York minister, offered prayer. The services in the cemetery were witnessed by a large number of people.

Klansmen Should Stop at the Sisson Hotel

Klansmen who visit Chicago will make no mistake if they register at the Hotel Sisson, Lake Michigan at Fifty-third Street.

When the Unity League recently published a list of alleged Chicago Klansmen the name of Harry W. Sisson, proprietor of the hotel, appeared upon it.

As a consequence his hotel is boycotted by Jews and Catholics.

SIDNEY J. WEINBERG ET AL.

27 | Experiences of the Great Depression

The journalist Studs Terkel has spent much of an interesting lifetime talking to Americans and recording what they say. Hard Times, *from which the following selections are taken, is his oral history of the Great Depression. The people he interviewed with a portable tape recorder in the late 1960s talk about experiences they had more than thirty years earlier, and allowance must be made for the tricks an individual's memory can play with historical fact. Nonetheless, the memories of participants offer unique, sharply contrasting insights into the feel and shape of past experience.*

SIDNEY J. WEINBERG

Senior partner, Goldman-Sachs Company, a leading investment house. He served during Roosevelt's first two Administrations as an industrial adviser.

October 29, 1929—I remember that day very intimately. I stayed in the office a week without going home. The tape was running, I've forgotten how long that night. It must have been ten, eleven o'clock before we got the final reports. It was like a thunder clap. Everybody was stunned. Nobody knew what it was all about. The Street had general confusion. They didn't understand it any more than anybody else. They thought something would be announced.

Prominent people were making statements. John D. Rockefeller, Jr., announced on the steps of J. P. Morgan, I think, that he and his sons were buying common stock. Immediately, the market went down again. Pools combined to support the market, to no avail. The public got scared and sold. It was a very trying period for me. Our investment company went up to two, three hundred, and then went down to practically nothing. As all investment companies did.

Over-speculation was the cause, a reckless disregard of economics. There was a group ruthlessly selling short. You could sell anything and depress the market unduly. The more you depressed it, the more you

From Hard Times: An Oral History of the Great Depression *by Studs Terkel, pp. 72–75. Copyright © 1970 by Studs Terkel. Reprinted by permission of Pantheon Books, a Division of Random House, Inc.*

created panic. Today we have protections against it. Call money went up—was it twenty percent?

No one was so sage that he saw this thing coming. You can be a Sunday morning quarterback. A lot of people have said afterwards, "I saw it coming, I sold all my securities." There's a credibility gap there. There are always some people who are conservative, who did sell out. I didn't know any of these.

I don't know anybody that jumped out of the window. But I know many who threatened to jump. They ended up in nursing homes and insane asylums and things like that. These were people who were trading in the market or in banking houses. They broke down physically, as well as financially.

Roosevelt saved the system. It's trite to say the system would have gone out the window. But certainly a lot of institutions would have changed. We were on the verge of something. You could have had a rebellion; you could have had a civil war.

The Street* was against Roosevelt. Only me and Joe Kennedy, of those I know, were for Roosevelt in 1932. I was Assistant Treasurer of the Democratic National Committee. I did not support him after the first two terms. I had a great argument with him. I didn't think any man should serve any more than two terms. I was getting a little tired, too, of all the New Deal things. When I was asked to work with the War Production Board in 1940, he delayed initialing my employment paper. Later on, we had a rapprochement and were friendly again.

Confidence ended the Depression in 1934. We had a recession in 1937. People got a little too gay on the way up, and you had to have a little leveling of. The war had a great deal of stimulus in 1939.

A Depression could not happen again, not to the extent of the one in '29. Unless inflation went out of hand and values went beyond true worth. A deep stock market reaction could bring a Depression, yes. There would be immediate Government action, of course. A moratorium. But in panic, people sell regardless of worth. Today you've got twenty-odd million stockholders owing stock. At that time you had probably a million and a half. You could have a sharper decline now than you had in 1929.

Most of the net worth of people today is in values. They haven't got it in cash. In a panic, values go down regardless of worth. A house worth $30,000, the minute you have a panic, isn't worth anything. Everybody feels good because the stock they bought at fifty is now selling at eighty. So they have a good feeling. But it's all on paper.

MARTIN DEVRIES

People were speculating. Now who are they gonna blame aside from themselves? It's their fault. See my point? If you gamble and make a mistake, why pick on somebody else? It's your fault, don't you see?

*[Wall Street]

It's like many people on the bread lines. I certainly felt sorry for them. But many of them hadn't lived properly when they were making it. They hadn't saved anything. Many of them wouldn't have been in the shape they were in, if they had been living in a reasonable way. Way back in the '29s, people were wearing $20 silk shirts and throwing their money around like crazy. If they had been buying Arrow $2 shirts and putting the other eighteen in the bank, when the trouble came, they wouldn't have been in the condition they were in.

In 1929, I had a friend who speculated. He'd say, "What's good?" I'd say, "We're selling high-grade first mortgage bonds on Commonwealth Edison." "Oh, hell," he'd say, "five percent. I make ten percent on the stock market." He was buying on margin. He thought he was rich. Know what happened to him? He blew his brains out. The Government had nothing to do with that. It's people.

Most people today are living beyond their means. They don't give a damn. The Government'll take care of them. People today don't want to work. We had a nice colored woman that worked for us fifteen years. She had a grandson. We offered to pay him $2 an hour to take the paper off our bedroom wall. Nothing to it. One coat of paper. We'd provide the bucket and sponge and the ladder. Do you think he'd do it? No. We couldn't get anybody to do it. So I did it myself. Nothing to it.

Do you think the New Deal is responsible . . . ?

Certainly. This huge relief program they began. What do you think brings all the colored people to Chicago and New York?

So When I say F. D. R.—

—my blood begins to boil. The New Deal immediately attacked Wall Street. As far as the country was concerned, Wall Street was responsible for all the upheavals. They set up the Securities and Exchange Commission. That was all right. I know there were some evils. But these fellas Roosevelt put in the SEC were a bunch of young Harvard theorists. Except for old Joe Kennedy. He was a robber baron. These New Dealers felt they had a mission to perform. Roosevelt attacked people—with some reason. But without justice. All people on Wall Street are not crooks.

My friends and I often spoke about it. Especially after his hammy fireside chats. Here we were paying taxes and not asking for anything. Everybody else was asking for relief, for our money to help them out. . . . A certain amount of that is O.K., but when they strip you clean and still don't accomplish much, it's unfair.

They were do-gooders, trying to accomplish something. I give them credit for that. But they didn't listen to anybody who had any sense.

Hoover happened to be in a bad spot. The Depression came on, and there he was. If Jesus Christ had been there, he'd have had the same problem. It's too bad for poor old Herbie that he happened to be there. This was a world-wide Depression. It wasn't Hoover's fault. In

1932, a Chinaman or a monkey could have been elected against him, no question about it.

/   /   /

HARRY TERRELL: A FARMER IN THE 1930s

Three-hundred and twenty acres of farm land, fine land, that my uncle owned and cleared, he lost it. 'Cause they foreclosed the mortgage. Some of the best in the state, and he couldn't borrow a dime.

The farmers didn't have anything they could borrow on. He came down here to see me, because he knew that a fellow that had a job could get credit. He wanted to borrow $850. I knew my banker would give it to me. So I told him I'd get it.

He said, "Harry, I want to give you a mortgage to support this loan." I said I'd never take a mortgage from my mother's brother. But here's what he put up: a John Deere combine and tractor, about sixteen head of cattle, a team of mules and wagons and farm implements. For $850. So you can see how far this had gone. He couldn't get a loan, a man who lived in this state from the time he was two years old.

I was born across the road from the farm of Herbert Hoover's uncle. I knew the Hoover family, distant cousins of the President. My folks sold hogs for 'em, thoroughbred, pure Chester White hogs at two cents a pound. Even people like them, they had times just like the rest of us. That's the way it was going. Corn was going for eight cents a bushel. One county insisted on burning corn to heat the courthouse, 'cause it was cheaper than coal.

This was at the time that mortgaging of farms was getting home to us. So they was having ten cent sales. They'd put up a farmer's property and have a sale and all the neighbors'd come in, and they got the idea of spending twenty-five cents for a horse. They was paying ten cents for a plow. And when it was all over, they'd all give it back to him. It was legal and anybody that bid against that thing, that was trying to get that man's land, they would be dealt with seriously, as it were.

That infuriated all the people that wanted to carry on business as usual. It might be a bank or an implement dealer or a private elevator or something like that. They had their investments in this. The implement dealer, he was on the line, too. The only place he had of getting it was from the fellow who owed him. And they'd have a sheriff's sale.

The people were desperate. They came very near hanging that judge. Because they caught this judge foreclosing farm mortgages, and they had no other way of stopping it. He had issued the whole bunch of foreclosures on his docket.

It all happened in Le Mars. They took the judge out of his court and took him to the fairgrounds and they had a rope around his neck, and they had the rope over the limb of a tree. They were gonna string him up in the old horse thief fashion. But somebody had sense enough to stop the thing before it got too far.

They had marches, just like we have the marches nowadays. They came from all over the state. That was the time of the Farm Holiday. There was a picket line. The Farm Holiday movement was to hold the stuff off the market, to increase the price. It saw its violence, too.

They stopped milk wagons, dumped milk. They stopped farmers hauling their hay to market. They undertook to stop the whole agriculture process. They thought if they could block the highways and access to the packing plants, they couldn't buy these hogs at two cents a pound.

They'd say: we're gonna meet, just east of Cherokee, at the fork of the road, and so on. Now they spread it around the country that they were gonna stop everything from going through. And believe me, they stopped it. They had whatever was necessary to stop them with. Some of 'em had pitchforks. (Laughs.) You can fix the auto tire good with a pitchfork. There were blockades.

The country was getting up in arms about taking a man's property away from him. It was his livelihood. When you took a man's horses and his plow away, you denied him food, you just convicted his family to starvation. It was just that real.

I remember one man, as devout a man as I ever met, a Catholic. He was mixed up in it, too—the violence. His priest tried to cool him down. He says, "My God, Father, we're desperate. We don't know what to do." He was the most old, established man you could find. He was in the state legislature.

I remember in court when they were going to indict a Norwegian Quaker, when they were offering them lighter sentences if they'd plead guilty, his wife said, "Simon, thee must go to jail."

Did they ever talk about changing the society . . . ?

No, the nearer to the ground you get, the nearer you are to conservative. His land is his life. And he's not for anything that might alter the situation. I never found anything in the Iowa farmer to indicate he would accept any form of government but his own. If my family, grandfather, great-grandfather, ever heard my political beliefs, why, they'd turn over in their graves. I don't think that without the Depression this farm country would be anything but McKinley Republican.

You know, Hitler's men were awfully interested that I'd been through a farm strike in northern Iowa. I was in Germany, with my wife, as a tourist in 1937. I had been to Geneva for a disarmament conference. I met Hitler's agricultural attaché in Berlin. They were just putting controls on their farmers. He wanted to know how this violence was handled. He kept getting madder and madder. I said: "What do you do with these people?" He said: "They've got to come to terms with the government or we'll just wipe them out."

LOUIS BANKS: UNEMPLOYED VETERAN

I got to be fourteen years old, I went to work on the Great Lakes at $41.50 a month. I thought: Someday I'm gonna be a great chef. Rough times, though. It was the year 1929. I would work from five in the morning till seven at night. Washing dishes, peeling potatoes, carrying heavy garbage. We would get to Detroit.

They was sleepin' on the docks and be drunk. Next day he'd be dead. I'd see 'em floatin' on the river where they would commit suicide because they didn't have anything. White guys and colored.

I'd get paid off, I'd draw $21 every two weeks and then comin' back I'd have to see where I was goin'. 'Cause I would get robbed. One fella named Scotty, he worked down there, he was firin' a boiler. He was tryin' to send some money home. He'd work so hard and sweat, the hot fire was cookin' his stomach. I felt sorry for him. They killed 'im and throwed 'im in the river, trying to get the $15 or $20 from him. They'd steal and kill each other for fifty cents.

1929 was pretty hard. I hoboed, I bummed, I begged for a nickel to get somethin' to eat. Go get a job, oh, at the foundry there. They didn't hire me because I didn't belong to the right kind of race. 'Nother time I went into Saginaw, it was two white fellas and myself made three. The fella there hired the two men and didn't hire me. I was back out on the streets. That hurt me pretty bad, the race part.

When I was hoboing, I would lay on the side of the tracks and wait until I could see the train comin'. I would always carry a bottle of water in my pocket and a piece of tape or rag to keep it from bustin' and put a piece of bread in my pocket, so I wouldn't starve on the way. I would ride all day and all night long in the hot sun.

I'd ride atop a boxcar and went to Los Angeles, four days and four nights. The Santa Fe, we'd go all the way with Santa Fe. I was goin' over the hump and I was so hungry and weak 'cause I was goin' into the d.t.'s, and I could see snakes draggin' through the smoke. I was sayin', "Lord, help me, Oh Lord, help me," until a white hobo named Callahan, he was a great big guy, looked like Jack Dempsey, and he got a scissors on me, took his legs and wrapped 'em around me. Otherwise, I was about to fall off the Flyer into a cornfield there. I was sick as a dog until I got into Long Beach, California.

Black and white, it didn't make any difference who you were, 'cause everybody was poor. All friendly, sleep in a jungle. We used to take a big pot and cook food, cabbage, meat and beans all together. We all set together, we made a tent. Twenty-five or thirty would be out on the side of the rail, white and colored. They didn't have no mothers or sisters, they didn't have no home, they were dirty, they had overalls on, they didn't have no food, they didn't have anything.

Sometimes we sent one hobo to walk, to see if there were any jobs open. He'd come back and say: Detroit, no jobs. He'd say: they're hirin' in New York City. So we went to New York City. Sometimes ten or fifteen of us would be on the train. And I'd hear one of 'em holler. He'd fall off, he'd get killed. He was trying' to get off the train, he thought he was gettin' home there. He heard a sound. (Imitates train whistle, a low, long, mournful sound.)

And then I saw a railroad police, a white police. They call him Texas Slim. He shoots you off all trains. We come out of Lima, Ohio . . . Lima Slim, he would kill you if he catch you on any train. Sheep train or any kind of merchandise train. He would shoot you off, he wouldn't ask you to get off.

I was in chain gangs and been in jail all over the country. I was in a chain gang in Georgia. I had to pick cotton for four months, for just hoboin' on a train. Just for vag. They gave me thirty-five cents and a pair of overalls when I got out. Just took me off the train, the guard. 1930, during the Depression, in the summertime. Yes, sir, thirty-five cents, that's what they gave me.

I knocked on people's doors. They'd say, "What do you want? I'll call the police." And they'd put you in jail for vag. They'd make you milk cows, thirty or ninety days. Up in Wisconsin, they'd do the same thing. Alabama, they'd do the same thing. California, anywhere you'd go. Always in jail, and I never did nothin'.

A man had to be on the road. Had to leave his wife, had to leave his mother, leave his family just to try to get money to live on. But he think: my dear mother, tryin' to send her money, worryin' how she's starvin'.

The shame I was feeling. I walked out because I didn't have a job. I said, "I'm going' out in the world and get me a job." And God help me, I couldn't get anything. I wouldn't let them see me dirty and ragged and I hadn't shaved. I wouldn't send 'em no picture.

I'd write: "Dear Mother, I'm doin' wonderful and wish you're all fine." That was in Los Angeles and I was sleeping under some steps and there was some paper over me. This is the slum part, Negroes lived down there. And my ma, she'd say, "Oh, my son is in Los Angeles, he's doin' pretty fair."

And I was with a bunch of hoboes, drinkin' canned heat. I wouldn't eat two or three days, 'cause I was too sick to eat. It's a wonder I didn't die. But I believe in God.

I went to the hospital there in Los Angeles. They said, "Where do you live?" I'd say, "Travelers Aid, please send me home." Police says, "O.K., put him in jail." I'd get ninety days for vag. When I was hoboing I was in jail two-thirds of the time. Instead of sayin' five or ten days, they'd say sixty or ninety days. 'Cause that's free labor. Pick the fruit or pick the cotton, then they'd turn you loose.

I had fifteen or twenty jobs. Each job I would have it would be so hard. From six o'clock in the morning till seven o'clock at night. I was fixin' the meat, cookin', washin' dishes and cleaning up. Just like you threw the ball at one end and run down and catch it on the other. You're jack of all trade, you're doin' it all. White chefs were getting' $40 a week, but I was getting' $21 for doin' what they were doin' and everything else. The poor people had it rough. The rich people was livin' off the poor.

'Cause I picked cotton down in Arkansas when I was a little bitty boy and I saw my dad, he was workin' all day long. $2 is what one day the poor man would make. A piece of salt pork and a barrel of flour for us and that was McGehee, Arkansas.

God knows, when he'd get that sack he would pick up maybe two, three hundred pounds of cotton a day, gettin' snake bit and everything in that hot sun. And all he had was a little house and a tub to keep the water. 'Cause I went down there to see him in 1930. I got tired of hoboing and went down to see him and my daddy was all gray and didn't have no bank account and no Blue Cross. He didn't have nothin', and he worked himself to death. (Weeps.) And the white man, he would drive a tractor in there. . . . It seems like yesterday to me, but it was 1930.

'33 in Chicago they had the World's Fair. A big hotel was hirin' colored fellas as bellboys. . . . I worked as a bellhop on the North Side at a hotel, lots of gangsters there. They don't have no colored bellboys at no exclusive hotels now. I guess maybe in the small ones they may have some.

Jobs were doing a little better after '35, after the World's Fair. You could get dishwashin' jobs, little porter jobs.

Work on the WPA, earn $27.50. We just dig a ditch and cover it back up. You thought you was rich. You could buy a suit of clothes. Before that, you wanted money, you didn't have any. No clothes for the kids. My little niece and my little kids had to have hand-down clothes. Couldn't steal. If you did, you went to the penitentiary. You had to shoot pool, walk all night and all day, the best you could make was $15. I raised up all my kids during the Depression. Scuffled . . . a hard way to go.

No kindness. Except for Callahan, the hobo—only reason I'm alive is 'cause Callahan helped me on that train. And the hobo jungle. Everybody else was evil to each other. There was no friendships. Everybody was worried and sad looking. It was pitiful.

When the war came, I was so glad when I got in the army. I knew I was safe. I put a uniform on, and I said, "Now I'm safe." I had money comin', I had food comin', and I had a lot of gang around me. I knew on the streets or hoboing, I might be killed any time.

I'd rather be in the army than outside where I was so raggedy and didn't have no jobs. I was glad to put on a United States Army uniform and get some food. I didn't care about the rifle what scared me. In the army, I wasn't gettin' killed on a train, I wasn't gonna starve. I felt proud to salute and look around and see all the good soldiers of the United States. I was a good soldier and got five battle stars. I'd rather be in the army now than see another Depression.

ANONYMOUS

28 | Down and Out in the Great Depression

Victims of the Great Depression of the 1930s frequently wrote to President Franklin D. Roosevelt, to his wife Eleanor, or to the various agencies and administrators who were responsible for relief. This was largely a new phenomenon in American life. President Herbert Hoover had one secretary answering mail from the public; the Roosevelt White House acquired fifty. The archives of the New Deal era contain tens of millions of letters from ordinary people expressing their concerns and frequently asking for help. This trove of information about the forgotten man and woman of the 1930s reveals attitudes about government, wealth and poverty, opportunity, and patriotism. Unlike many secondary sources for understanding the way events affected everyday people, these letters are not filtered through the perception of some interviewer nor are they time-beclouded memoirs written long after the events.

Robert S. McElvaine, who edited these letters in Down and Out in the Great Depression, *published in 1983, uses them to get closer to the real experience of unemployment and destitution in the 1930s.*

[Oil City, Penna.
December 15, 1930]

Col Arthur Woods
Director, Presidents Committee
Dear Sir:

...I have none of these things [that the rich have], what do they care how much we suffer, how much the health of our children is menaced. Now I happen to know there is something can be done about it and Oil City needs to be awakened up to that fact and compelled to act.

Now that our income is but $15.60 a week (their are five of us My husband Three little children and myself). My husband who is a world war Veteran and saw active service in the trenches, became desperate and applied for Compensation or a pension from the Government and was turned down and that started me thinking.... [There should be]

212

enough to pay all world war veterans a pension, dysabeled or not dysabeled and there by relieve a lot of suffering, and banish resentment that causes Rebellions and Bolshevism. Oh why is it that it is allways a bunch of overley rich, selfish, dumb, ignorant money hogs that persist in being Senitors, legislatures, representitives Where would they and their possessions be if it were not for the Common Soldier, the common laborer that is compelled to work for a starvation wage. for I tell you again the hog of a Landlord gets his there is not enough left for the necessaries if a man has three or more children. Not so many years ago in Russia all the sufferings of poverty (and you can never feel them you are on the other side of the fence but try to understand) conceived a child, that child was brought forth in agony, and its name was Bolshevism. I am on the other side of the fence from you, you are not in a position to see, but I, I can see and feel and understand. I have lived and suffered too. I know, and right now our good old U. S. A. is sitting on a Seething Volcano. In the Public Schools our little children stand at salute and recite a "rig ma role" in which is mentioned "Justice to all" What a lie, what a naked lie, when honest, law abiding citizens, decendents of Revilutionary heros, Civil War heros, and World war heros are denied the priviledge of owning their own homes, that foundation of good citizenship, good morals, and the very foundation of good government the world over. Is all that our Soldiers of all wars fought bled and died for to be sacrificed to a God awful hideous Rebellion? in which all our Citizens will be involved, because of the dumb bungling of rich politicians? Oh for a few Statesmen, oh for but one statesman, as fearless as Abraham Lincoln, the amancipator who died for us. and who said, you can fool some of the people some of the time, But you can't fool all of the people all of the time. Heres hoping you have read this to the end and think it over. I wish you a Mery Christmas and a Happy New Year.

Very Truly Yours
Mrs. M. E. B

Phila., Pa.
November, 26, 1934

Honorable Franklin D. Roosevelt.
Washington, D. C.
Dear Mr. President:

I am forced to write to you because we find ourselves in a very serious condition. For the last three or four years we have had depression and suffered with my family and little children severely. Now Since the Home Owners Loan Corporation opened up, I have been going there in order to save my home, because there has been unemployment in my house for more than three years. You can imagine that I and my family have suffered from lack of water supply in my house for more than two years. Last winter I did not have coal and the pipes burst in my house and therefore could not make heat in the house. Now winter is here again and we are suffering of cold, no water in the house, and we are facing to be forced out of the house, because I have no money to move or pay so much money as they want when after making settlement I am mother of little children, am sick and losing my health, and we are eight people in the family, and where can I go when I don't have money because no one is working in my house. The Home Loan Corporation wants $42. a month rent or else we will have to be on the street. I am living in this house for about ten years and when times were good we would put our last cent in the house and now I have no money, no home and no wheres to go. I beg of you to please help me and my family and little children for the sake of a sick mother and suffering family to give this your immediate attention so we will not be forced to move or put out in the street.

Waiting and Hoping that you will act quickly.

Thanking you very much I remain

Mrs. E. L.

[Cincinnati, Ohio
April 16, 1932]

Department of Labor
Presidents Organization
Washington D. C

... tell me what kind of help can this man [unemployed home-owner] get he is worse off then the real poor, you will help the poor whose has spent all his money in good times now he is the one who gets first aid but the little home owner can get nothing and doesnt know what to become of him ...

[Anonymous]

Lincoln Nebraska.
May 19/34.

Mrs Franklin D. Roosevelt
Washington, D. C.
Dear Mrs Roosevelt;

Will you be kind enough to read the following as it deals with a very important subject which you are very much interested in as well as my self.

In the Presidents inaugral adress delivered from the capitol steps the afternoon of his inauguration he made mention of The Forgotten Man, and I with thousands of others am wondering if the folk who was borned here in America some 60 or 70 years a go are this Forgotten Man, the President had in mind, if we are this Forgotten Man then we are still Forgotten.

We who have tried to be diligent in our support of this most wonderful nation of ours boath social and other wise, we in our younger days tried to do our duty without complaining.

We have helped to pay pensions to veterans of some three wars, we have raised the present young generation and have tried to train them to honor and support this our home country.

And now a great calamity has come upon us and seamingly no cause of our own it has swept away what little savings we had accumulated and we are left in a condition that is imposible for us to correct, for two very prominent reasons if no more.

First we have grown to what is termed Old Age, this befalls every man.

Second as we put fourth every effort in our various business lines trying to rectify and reestablish our selves we are confronted on every hand with the young generation, taking our places, this of corse is what we have looked forward to in training our children. But with the extra ordinary crisese which left us helpless and placed us in the position that our fathers did not have to contend with.

Seamingly every body has been assisted but we the Forgotten Man, and since we for 60 years or more have tried to carry the loan without complaining, we have paid others pensions we have educated and trained the youth, now as we are Old and down and out of no reason of our own, would it be asking to much of our Government and the young generation to do by us as we have tried our best to do by them even without complaint.

We have been honorable citizens all along our journey, calamity and old age has forced its self upon us please donot send us to the Poor Farm but instead allow us the small pension of $40.00 per month and we will do as we have done in the past (not complain)

I personly Know of Widows who are no older than I am who own their own homes and draw $45,00 per month pension, these ladies were born this side of the civil war the same as I, therefore they never experianced war trouble.

Please donot think of us who are asking this assitsnce as Old Broken down dishonorable cotizens, but we are of those borned in this country and have done our bit in making this country, we are folk in all walks of life and businesse.

For example I am an architect and builder I am not and old broken down illiterate dishonorable man although I am 69 years old, but as I put forth every effort to regain my prestage in business I am confronted on every side by the young generation taking my place, yes this is also the case even in the effort of the government with its recovery plan, even though I am qualifyed to suprentend any class of construction but the young man has captured this place also,

What are we to do since the calamity has swept our all away,? We are just asking to be remembered with a small part as we have done to others $40,00 a month is all we are asking.

Mrs. Roosevelt I am asking a personal favor of you as it seems to be the only means through which I may be able to reach the President, some evening very soon, as you and Mr. Roosevelt are having dinner together privately will you ask him to read this. and we American citizens will ever remember your kindness.

Yours very truly.
R. A. [male]

[February, 1936]

Mr. and Mrs. Roosevelt.
Wash. D. C.
Dear Mr. President:

I'm a boy of 12 years. I want to tell you about my family. My father hasn't worked for 5 months. He went plenty times to relief, he filled out application. They won't give us anything. I don't know why. Please you do something. We haven't paid 4 months rent, Everyday the landlord rings the door bell, we don't open the door for him. We are afraid that will be put out, been put out before, and don't want to happen again. We haven't paid the gas bill, and the electric bill, haven't paid grocery bill for 3 months. My brother goes to Lane Tech. High School. he's eighteen years old, hasn't gone to school for 2 weeks because he got no carfare. I have a sister she's twenty years, she can't find work. My father he staying home. All the time he's crying because he can't find work. I told him why are you crying daddy, and daddy said why shouldn't I cry when there is nothing in the house. I feel sorry for him. That night I couldn't sleep. The next morning I wrote this letter to you. in my room. Were American citizens and were born in Chicago, Ill. and I don't know why they don't help us Please answer right away because we need it. will starve Thank you.
God bless you.

[Anonymous]
Chicago, Ill.

Dec. 14—1937.
Columbus, Ind.

Mrs. F. D. Roosevelt,
Washington, D. C.

Mrs. Roosevelt: I suppose from your point of view the work relief, old age pensions, slum clearance and all the rest seems like a perfect remedy for all the ills of this country, but I would like for you to see the results, as the other half see them.

We have always had a shiftless, never-do-well class of people whose one and only aim in life is to live without work. I have been rubbing elbows with this class for nearly sixty years and have tried to help some of the most promising and have seen others try to help them, but it can't be done. We cannot help those who will not try to help themselves and if they do try a square deal is all they need, and by the way that is all this country needs or ever has needed: a square deal for all and then, let each one paddle their own canoe, or sink.

There has never been any necessity for any one who is able to work, being on relief in this locality, but there have been many eating the bread of charity and they have lived better than ever before. I have had taxpayers tell me that their children came from school and asked why they couldn't have nice lunches like the children on relief.

The women and children around here have had to work at the fields to help save the crops and several women fainted while at work and at the same time we couldn't go up or down the road without stumbling over some of the reliefers, moping around carrying dirt from one side of the road to the other and back again, or else asleep. I live along on a farm and have not raised any crops for the last two years as there was no help to be had. I am feeding the stock and have been cutting the wood to keep my home fires burning. There are several reliefers around here now who have been kicked off relief, but they refuse to work unless they can get relief hours and wages, but they are so worthless no one can afford to hire them.

As for the clearance of the real slums, it can't be done as long as their inhabitants are allowed to reproduce their kind. I would like for you to see what a family of that class can do to a decent house in a short time. Such a family moved into an almost new, neat, four-room house near here last winter. They even cut down some of the shade trees or fuel, after they had burned everything they could pry loose. There were two big idle boys in the family and they could get all the fuel they wanted, just for the cutting, but the shade trees were closer and it was taking a great amount of fuel, for they had broken out several windows and they had but very little bedding. There were two women there all the time and three part of the time and there was enough good clothing tramped in the mud around the yard to have made all the bedclothes they needed. It was clothing that had been given them and they had worn it until it was too filthy to wear any longer without washing, so they threw it out and begged more. I will not try to describe their filth for you would not believe me. They paid no rent while there and left between two suns owing everyone from whom they could get a nickels worth of anything. They are just a fair sample of the class of people on whom so much of our hard earned tax-money is being squandered and on whom so much sympathy is being wasted.

As for the old people on beggars' allowances: the taxpayers have provided homes for all the old people who never liked to work, where they will be neither cold nor hungry: much better homes than most of them have ever tried to provide for themselves. They have lived many years through the most prosperous times of our country and had an opportunity to prepare for old age, but they spent their lives in idleness or worse and now they expect those who have worked like slaves, to provide a living for them and all their worthless descendants. Some of them are asking for from thirty to sixty dollars a month when I have known them to live on a dollar a week rather than go to work. There is many a little child doing without butter on its bread, so that some old sot can have his booze and tobacco: some old sot who spent his working years loafing around pool rooms and saloons, boasting that the world owed him a living.

Even the child welfare has become a racket. The parents of large families are getting divorces, so that the mothers and children can qualify for aid. The children to join the ranks of the "unemployed" as they grow up, for no child that has been raised on charity in this community has ever amounted to anything.

You people who have plenty of this worlds goods and whose money comes easy, have no idea of the heart-breaking toil and self-denial which is the lot of the working people who are trying to make an honest living, and then to have to shoulder all these unjust burdens seems like the last straw. During the worst of the depression many of the farmers had to deny their families butter, eggs, meat etc. and sell it to pay their taxes and then had to stand by and see the dead-beats carry it home to their families by the arm load, and they knew their tax money was helping pay for it. One woman saw a man carry out eight pounds of butter at one time. The crookedness, shelfishness, greed and graft of the crooked politicians is making one gigantic racket out of the new deal and it is making this a nation of dead-beats and beggars and if it continues the people who will work will soon be nothing but slaves for the pampered poverty rats and I am afraid these human parasites are going to become a menace to the country unless they are disfranchised. No one should have the right to vote theirself a living at the expense of the tax payers. They learned their strength at the last election and also learned that they can get just about what they want by "voting right." They have had a taste of their coveted life of idleness, and at the rate they are increasing, they will soon control the country. The twentieth child arrived in the home of one chronic reliefer near here some time ago.

Is it any wonder the taxpayers are discouraged by all this penalizing of thrift and industry to reward shiftlessness, or that the whole country is on the brink of chaos?

M. A. H. [female]
Columbus, Ind.

[no address]
Jan. 18, 1937

[Mrs. Roosevelt]

was simply astounded to think that anyone could be nitwit to wish to be included in the so called social security act if they ssibly avoid it. Call it by any name you wish it, in my opinion, of many people I know) is nothing but downright stealing. . . .

Personally, I had my savings so invested that I would have had a satisfactory provision for old age. Now thanks to his [FDR's] desire to "get" the utilities I cannot be sure of anything, being a stockholder, as after business has survived his merciless attacks (if it does) insurance will probably be no good either.

. . . [She goes on to complain about the lack of profits.]

Then the president tells them they should hire more men and work shorter hours so that the laborers, who are getting everything now raises etc. can have a "more abundant life." That simply means taking it from the rest of us in the form of taxes or otherwise. . . .

Believe me, the only thing we want from the president, unless or if you except Communists and the newly trained chiselers, is for him to balance the budget and reduce taxes. That, by the way, is a "mandate from the people" that isn't getting much attention.

I am not an "economic royalist," just an ordinary white collar worker at $1600 per. Please show this to the president and ask him to remember the wishes of the forgotten man, that is, the one who dared to vote against him. We expect to be tramped on but we do wish the stepping would be a little less hard.

Security at the price of freedom is never desired by intelligent people.

M. A. [female]

[Mr. Harry Hopkins
Washington, D. C.]
[Dear Mr. Hopkins:]

Will you please investigate the various relief agencies in many cities of the United States. The cities where there are a large foreign and jewish population. No wonder the cities are now on the verge of bankruptcy because we are feeding a lot of ignorant foreigners by giving them relief. And, they are turning against us every day. I would suggest to deport all foreigners and jews who are not citizens over the United States back to any land where they choose to go and who will admit them. As America is now over crowded with too much immigration and it can not feed even its own citizens without feeding the citizens of other foreign nations. I have found out after careful investigation that we are feeding many foreigners who send out their wives to work and who have money in the bank. While the men drink wine and play cards in saloons and cafes. I have spoken to one Italian whom I met. And I ask him what he was doing for a living. He said me drinka da dago red wine and play cards and send the wife out to work. Isn't a very good thing for us to support them. No wonder the taxpayers are grumbling about taxes. Most of them are a race of black hands murders boot leggers bomb throwers. While most of the sheeney jews as they are called are a race of dishonest people who get rich by swindling, faking and cheating the poor people. Besides the jews are responsible by ruining others in business by the great amount of chisling done. And selling even below the cost prices, in order to get all the others business. The foreigners and jews spend as little as they can to help this country. And, they live as cheap as they can. And, work as cheap as they can, and save all the money they can. And when they have enough they go back to their country. Why don't we deport them under the section of the United States Immigration Laws which relates to paupers and those who become a public charge. The Communist Party is composed mostly by foreigners and jews. The jews are the leaders of the movement and urge the downfall of this government. . . .

A Taxpayer

Hornell, New York
March 7, 1934

My Dear Senator:

It seems very apparent to me that the Administration at Washington is accelerating it's pace towards socialism and communism. Nearly every public statement from Washington is against stimulation of business which would in the end create employment.

Everyone is sympathetic to the cause of creating more jobs and better wages for labor; but, a program continually promoting labor troubles, higher wages, shorter hours, and less profits for business, would seem to me to be leading us fast to a condition where the Government must more and more expand it's relief activities, and will lead in the end to disaster to all classes.

I believe that every citizen is entitled to know the policy of the Government, and I am so confused that I wish you would write me and advise me whether it is the policy of this Administration, of which you are a very important part, to further discourage business enterprise, and eventually set up a program which eliminates private industry and effort, and replaces it with Government control of industry and labor, — call it what you will: socialism, facism, or communism, or by any other name.

I am not addicted to annoying public office holders with correspondence, but if there are any private rights left in this country, then I would appreciate an early reply to this letter, so that I may take such action as is still possible, to protect myself and family.

With kindest personal regards,

Yours truly,
W. L. C. [male]

WLC:JFE
U. S. Senator Robert F. Wagner
Senate Building,
Washington, D. C.

29 | Memories of the Internment Camp

Compared with its record in World War I, America was remarkably careful about protecting civil liberties during World War II. There was, however, one giant exception; the internment of 110,000 Japanese-Americans in concentration camps, euphemistically called "relocation centers." Internment was rationalized by straightforward racism. The military director of the internment program declared, the "Japanese race is an enemy race and while many second and third generation Japanese born on United States soil, possessed of United States Citizenship, have become Americanized, the racial strains are undiluted. . . . It, therefore, follows that along the vital Pacific coast over 112,000 potential enemies, of Japanese extraction, are at large today." These people, 70,000 of them native-born citizens of the United States, were forced to evacuate their homes within forty-eight hours (losing about $500,000,000 in property along with their jobs), and were forced to live in tarpapered barracks behind barbed wire. The Supreme Court of the United States, in two major decisions, supported the constitutionality of internment. Justice Robert Jackson in a dissenting opinion warned that the cases established a precedent that "lays about like a loaded weapon." In 1988, however, Congress appropriated compensation for internees. The following reading, from an interview taken by the writer Archie Satterfield in the 1970s, is about the experiences of two Japanese-Americans who suffered during this tragedy.

BEN YORITA

"Students weren't as aware of national politics then as they are now, and Japanese-Americans were actually apolitical then. Our parents couldn't vote, so we simply weren't interested in politics because there was nothing we could do about it if we were.

"There were two reasons we were living in the ghettos: Birds of a feather flock together, and we had all the traditional aspects of Japanese life—Japanese restaurants, baths, and so forth; and discrimination forced us together. The dominant society prevented us from going elsewhere.

"Right after Pearl Harbor we had no idea what was going to happen, but toward the end of December we started hearing rumors and talk of the evacuation started. We could tell from what we read in the newspapers and the propaganda they were printing—guys like Henry McLemore, who said he hated all Japs and that we should be rounded up, gave us the idea of how strong feelings were against us. So we were expecting something and the evacuation was no great surprise.

"I can't really say what my parents thought about everything because we didn't communicate that well. I never asked them what they thought. We communicated on other things, but not political matters.

"Once the evacuation was decided, we were told we had about a month to get rid of our property or do whatever we wanted to with it. That was a rough time for my brother, who was running a printshop my parents owned. We were still in debt on it and we didn't know what to do with all the equipment. The machines were old but still workable, and we had English type and Japanese type. Japanese characters had to be set by hand and were very hard to replace. Finally, the whole works was sold, and since nobody would buy the Japanese type, we had to sell it as junk lead at 50¢ a pound. We sold the equipment through newspaper classified ads: 'Evacuating: Household goods for sale.' Second-hand dealers and everybody else came in and bought our refrigerator, the piano, and I had a whole bunch of books I sold for $5, which was one of my personal losses. We had to sell our car, and the whole thing was very sad. By the way, it was the first time we had ever had a refrigerator and it had to be sold after only a few months.

"We could take only what we could carry, and most of us were carrying two suitcases or duffel bags. The rest of our stuff that we couldn't sell was stored in the Buddhist church my mother belonged to. When we came back, thieves had broken in and stolen almost everything of value from the church.

"I had a savings account that was left intact, but people who had their money in the Japanese bank in Seattle had their assets frozen from Pearl Harbor until the late 1960s, when the funds were finally released. They received no interest.

"They took all of us down to the Puyallup fairgrounds, Camp Harmony, and everything had been thrown together in haste. They had converted some of the display and exhibit areas into rooms and had put up some barracks on the parking lot. The walls in the barracks were about eight feet high with open space above and with big knotholes in the boards of the partitions. Our family was large, so we had two rooms.

"They had also built barbed-wire fences around the camp with a tower on each corner with military personnel and machine guns, rifles, and searchlights. It was terrifying because we didn't know what was going to happen to us. We didn't know where we were going and we were just doing what we were told. No questions asked. If you get an order, you go ahead and do it.

"There was no fraternization, no contact with the military or any Caucasian except when we were processed into the camp. But the treatment in Camp Harmony was fairly loose in the sense that we were free to roam around in the camp. But it was like buffalo in cages or behind barbed wire.

"There was no privacy whatsoever in the latrines and showers, and it was humiliating for the women because they were much more modest then than today. It wasn't so bad for the men because they were accustomed to open latrines and showers.

"We had no duties in the sense that we were required to work, but you can't expect a camp to manage itself. They had jobs open in the kitchen and stock room, and eventually they opened a school where I helped teach a little. I wasn't a qualified teacher, and I got about $13 a month. We weren't given an allowance while we were in Camp Harmony waiting for the camp at Minidoka to be finished, so it was pretty tight for some families.

"From Camp Harmony on, the family structure was broken down. Children ran everywhere they wanted to in the camp, and parents lost their authority. We could eat in any mess hall we wanted, and kids began ignoring their parents and wandering wherever they pleased.

"Eventually they boarded us on army trucks and took us to trains to be transported to the camps inland. We had been in Camp Harmony from May until September. There was a shortage of transportation at the time and they brought out these old, rusty cars with gaslight fixtures. As soon as we got aboard we pulled the shades down so people couldn't stare at us. The cars were all coaches and we had to sit all the way to camp, which was difficult for some of the older people and the invalids. We made makeshift beds out of the seats for them, and did the best we could.

"When we got to Twin Falls, we were loaded onto trucks again, and we looked around and all we could see was that vast desert with nothing but sagebrush. When the trucks started rolling, it was dusty, and the camp itself wasn't completed yet. The barracks had been built and the kitchen facilities were there, but the laundry room, showers, and latrines were not finished. They had taken a bulldozer in the good old American style and leveled the terrain and then built the camp. When the wind blew, it was dusty and we had to wear face masks to go to the dining hall. When winter came and it rained, the dust turned into gumbo mud. Until the latrines were finished, we had to use outhouses.

"The administrators were civilians and they tried to organize us into a chain of command to make the camp function. Each block of barracks was told to appoint a representative, who were called block managers. Of course we called them the Blockheads.

"When winter came, it was very cold and I began withdrawing my savings to buy clothes because we had none that was suitable for that climate. Montgomery Ward and Sears Roebuck did a landslide business from the camps because we ordered our shoes and warm clothing from them. The people who didn't have savings suffered quite a bit until the camp distributed navy pea coats. Then everybody in camp was wearing outsize pea coats because we were such small people. Other than army blankets, I don't remember any other clothing issues.

"The barracks were just single-wall construction and the only insulation was tar paper nailed on the outside, and they never were improved. The larger rooms had potbellied stoves, and we all slept on army cots. Only the people over sixty years old were able to get metal cots, which had a bit more spring to them than the army cots, which were just stationary hammocks.

"These camps were technically relocation centers and there was no effort to hold us in them, but they didn't try actively to relocate us until much later. On my own initiative I tried to get out as soon as I could, and started writing letters to friends around the country. I found a friend in Salt Lake City who agreed to sponsor me for room and board, and he got his boss to agree to hire me. I got out in May 1943, which was earlier than most. In fact, I was one of the first to leave Minidoka.

"Of course I had to get clearance from Washington, D. C., and they investigated my background. I had to pay my own way from Twin Falls to Salt Lake City, but after I left, the government had a program of per diem for people leaving.

"I got on the bus with my suitcase, all by myself, my first time in the outside world, and paid my fare and began looking for a seat, then this old guy said: 'Hey, Tokyo, sit next to me.'

"I thought, Oh, my God, Tokyo! I sat next to him and he was a friendly old guy who meant well."

Yorita's friend worked in a parking garage across the street from the Mormon tabernacle, and the garage owner let them live in the office, where the two young men cooked their own meals. One nearby grocery-store owner wouldn't let them buy from him, and a barber in the neighborhood hated them on sight. Yorita parked a car once that had a rifle and pair of binoculars in the back seat, and he and his friend took the binoculars out and were looking through them when the barber looked out and saw them studying the Mormon tabernacle. He called the FBI, and two agents were soon in the garage talking to the young men.

Yorita wasn't satisfied with his job in Salt Lake City, and soon left for Cincinnati, then Chicago, which he enjoyed because most Chicago people didn't care what nationality he was. He and a brother were able to find good jobs and a good place to live, and they brought their parents out of the Idaho camp to spend the rest of the war in Chicago.

PHILIP HAYASAKA

Philip Hayasaka was a teen-ager when Pearl Harbor was attacked. Unlike most Japanese-Americans, his parents had been able to find a home in a predominantly Caucasian neighborhood because his father was a wholesale produce dealer and most of his business was conducted with Caucasians. Consequently, when the family was interned, Hayasaka was a stranger to most of the other families.

Still, he and his family understood well the rationale of the Little Tokyos along the West Coast.

"If you could become invisible, you could get along. We were forced into a situation of causing no trouble, of being quiet, not complaining. It was not a matter of our stoic tradition. I've never bought that. We did what we had to do to survive.

"There was a lot of hysteria at the time, a lot of confusion, and the not knowing what was going to happen created such a fear that we became supercautious. We would hear that the FBI was going into different houses and searching, and we would wonder when they were coming to our house. We just knew that they were going to come and knock on the door and that we wouldn't know what to do when they came.

"A lot of people were burning things that didn't need to be burned, but they were afraid suspicion would be attached to those things. All those wonderful old calligraphies were destroyed, priceless things, because they thought someone in authority would believe they represented allegiance to Japan. One time I was with my mother in the house, just the two of us, and there was a knock on the door. My mother had those rosary-type beads that the Buddhists use for prayer, and she put them in my pocket and sent me outside to play and stay out until whoever was at the door left. She was afraid it was the FBI and they would take them away from us. It sounds silly now, but that kind of fear was pervasive then. It was tragic.

"When this happened, my dad's business went to hell. Suddenly all his accounts payable were due immediately, but all the accounts receivable weren't. People knew the guy wasn't going to be around much longer, so they didn't pay him. I knew at one time how much he lost that way—we had to turn in a claim after the war—but I've forgotten now. But it was a considerable amount. Those claims, by the way, didn't give justice to the victims; it only legitimized the government. We got about a nickel on the dollar.

"It was kind of interesting how different people reacted when they came to Camp Harmony to see friends, and how we reacted in return. Friends from Seattle would come down to see me, and we had to talk through the barbed-wire fences. [Note: Nobody was permitted to stand closer than three feet to the fence, which meant conversations were held at least six feet from each other, with people standing and watching].

There was one instance when I saw a close friend from high school just outside the fence, and he had come down to see me. He hadn't seen me inside, so I hid rather than going out to see him. The whole evacuation did funny things to your mind.

"All the leaders of the community were taken away, and my dad was interned before we were and taken to the interrogation camp in Missoula. It was one of the greatest shocks of my life when the FBI came and picked him up. Here was a guy who had followed all the rules, respected authority, and was a leader in the company. And all of the sudden he was behind bars for no reason. He stayed there several months before they let him join us at Minidoka."

/   /   /

When the war ended and the camps were closed, about the only people left in them were young children and the elderly. All who could leave for jobs did so, and the experience had a scattering effect on the Japanese-American communities across the Pacific Coast. Several families settled on the East Coast and in the Midwest, and when those with no other place to go, or who didn't want to migrate away from the Coast, returned to their hometowns, they usually found their former ghettos taken over by other minority groups. Consequently, whether they wanted to or not, they were forced to find housing wherever it was available. It was difficult returning to the cities, however. Everybody dreaded it, and some of the elderly people with no place to go of their own were virtually evacuated from the camps. They had become accustomed to the life there and were afraid to leave.

Some Caucasians, such as Floyd Schmoe and the Reverend Emory Andrews, worked with the returning outcasts to help them resettle as smoothly as possible. A few farms had been saved for the owners, but four years of weeds and brush had accumulated. Schmoe was back teaching at the University of Washington by that time, and he organized groups of his students to go out on weekends and after school to help clear the land for crops again. Some people returning found their former neighbors had turned against them in their absence, and grocery-store owners who had become Jap-haters during the war would not sell them food.

The farmers who did get their crops growing again were often so discriminated against that they could not sell their produce, or get it delivered into the marketplace. Schmoe was able to solve this problem for one farmer by talking a neighbor, a Filipino, into taking the Japanese-American's produce and selling it as his own. Hayasaka's father was able to get back into the wholesale produce business by becoming partners with a young Japanese-American veteran of the famed 442d Regiment, the most highly decorated group in the war. The veteran put up a sign over the office saying the business was operated by a veteran, which made it difficult for buyers to avoid it.

BEN YORITA

"The older people never recovered from the camps. The father was the traditional breadwinner and in total command of the family. But after going into the camps, fathers were no longer the breadwinners; the young sons and daughters were. Most of them couldn't even communicate in English, so all the burdens fell on the second generation. And most of us were just kids, nineteen or twenty. Consequently there was a big turnover of responsibility and authority, and the parents were suddenly totally dependent on their children. When we returned to the cities after the war, it was the second generation again that had to make the decisions and do all the negotiating with landlords, attorneys, and the like."

30 | A Black Officer Remembers the Women's Army Corps

"In another generation," writes Charity Adams Earley in explaining the purpose of her memoir, "young black women who join the military will have scant record of their predecessors who fought on the two fronts of discrimination — segregation and reluctant acceptance by males." In her childhood Earley learned to maintain her dignity against the assault of segregation. Her father was a minister, her mother a former school teacher. She recalled being protected from the harshness of segregation and gradually learning the difficult social skills she called up during her career in the Woman's Army Corps or WAC.

Charity Adams Earley returned to graduate school after the war, served as Dean of Student Personnel Service at several colleges, and later married a medical student. She succeeded in civilian life as she had in the military, serving actively "on committees, task forces, and boards, encompassing the area of human and social services, education, civic affairs, and . . . corporate business." Still, Earley concedes, the problems she faced of discrimination as an Afro-American woman "are still with us."

Graduation day, 29 August 1942, arrived beautiful and hot. The heat was felt early that day, and it dulled our spirits, for we knew how we would look, soggy and damp from perspiration, in our cotton khaki uniforms. However, since we would have open ranks inspection before the ceremony, we did our best to look like the well-groomed soldiers we thought we were. There was excitement and anticipation in the air. . . .

Army ceremonies and services are short and to the point. Our graduation exercises followed this pattern: there was a prayer, followed by greetings, the introduction of the speaker, the address, the oath of office, the awarding of diplomas, the National Anthem, and the benediction. It was over quickly, and we were deeply impressed with the purposes that had motivated our organization. Among the VIPs visiting for the occasion were Maj. Gen. F. E. Uhl, commander of the Seventh Service Command; Col. Oveta Culp Hobby, director of the WAAC; and

From One Woman's Army: A Black Officer Remembers the WAC *by Charity Adams Earley, PT 42–47, 54–63. Published by Texas A& M University Press, 1989. Used by permission.*

Representative Edith Nourse Rogers, sponsor of the bill that created the Women's Army Auxiliary Corps.

/   /   /

I was very happy on that day. The fact that I had been the first Negro woman to receive a commission in the WAAC was nearly as impressive as the fact that we had "arrived." Whatever doubts we might have later, that day we knew ourselves as members of the great fraternity of officers. The only authorized insignia available for us was the gold bars of the second lieutenant, so with obvious disregard for the prescribed manner of wearing insignia, we put on our gold bars and were third officers of the WAAC, comparable to second lieutenants in the U. S. Army.

There was one historic change that took place at our graduation. Traditionally, at Army graduation exercises the candidates are presented according to the company roster, which is the way we were listed in the program. For our graduation the class was presented by platoon, which meant that the Third Platoon, the "colored girls," came last in the First Company. My name was Adams and, alphabetically, I would have been the first WAAC officer to be commissioned. There were four other Negro graduates whose names began with the letter A.

When it was all over and we were free to pursue our own interests for the rest of the day, we realized that now we were in position to have the courtesy of the salute extended to us first. Because we were self-conscious and insecure, three of us, new legal third officers, returned to Barracks 54 right down the middle of the parade ground. We were not sure how we would handle being saluted first—we had not been on that end of a salute before.

One other thing happened to us when we received our commissions. We received new serial numbers; we dropped the A and picked up the L. Mine went from A–50000I to L–50000I.

Classification, or "job assignment" came next. Most of us had heard some strange stories about Army classification; a civilian butcher assigned as a surgeon's assistant, an auto mechanic assigned as a pastry cook, a telephone operator assigned as a typist. These examples were usually offered in jest, but there were a few authentic cases. When I had successfully completed OCS, I believed that I must have learned something that could be used in the service of my country. With that bit of self-confidence I went for my first classification interview on the afternoon following graduation.

I remember that interview quite well. although the only thing I recall about the captain who conducted the interview was that he had beautiful white hair. He hardly looked up from the card on the desk in front of him. When I reported, he said, "You are Charity Adams?"

"Yes, Sir."

"You taught school?"

"Yes, Sir."

"Do you know anything about public relations?"

"No, Sir."

"Are you interested in recruiting?"

"I don't know, Sir."

"Well," the captain said, "we'll see what we can find for you to do. You are too young to be put in charge of people and I don't have any idea what we're going to do with you young women."

"Yes, Sir."

"That's all, Miss."

I was not encouraged by that interview. After the hectic six weeks of OCS, I did not feel so young, although I was among the youngest members of our class. I later found out that all the younger women had been told the same thing, so we rather felt that we would not have a chance to do anything worthwhile, that we might be the people stuck with all the assignments no one else wanted.

In the meantime, after graduation we had moved from our training barracks, 54, into various officers quarters. Some of us moved into houses on Officers Row, and others into more temporary quarters while awaiting assignments. Eleven of us from the Third Platoon moved into Quarters 1, a large double house on the circle around the bandstand. In the other side of the house, Quarters 2, were eleven white third officers who had graduated with us that morning. We had some trouble understanding why we were assigned to Quarters 1, but we finally realized that we were on the end of Officers Row. To put us in any other house on the circle would have mixed us in, and that would have been integration.

/   /   /

Those of us in training to be company officers were assigned to the Third Company, Third Training Regiment. This company was similar to our OC company in that there were two platoons of white women and one of Negro women. The only Negro auxiliaries then at the Training Center were in this company. At the time that we began our assignment with Company 3, there were fewer than forty Negro women at the TC. As a result there were almost as many officers as there were enlisted women.

/   /   /

Here began the confusion as to what third officers would be called. It was agreed that we could no longer use civilian terms of address because we were now definitely part of the military. "Third officer" was certainly a cumbersome title to use, as would be "second officer" and "first officer" at such time as some of us would be promoted to those ranks. For non-commissioned officers the titles were even worse: "auxiliary," "leader," "junior leader," "staff leader," "first leader." It was finally agreed, since we had grades equivalent to Army grades, that we would use the Army titles when addressing each other but that we would sign our names with official WAAC titles. I rather liked being addressed as "Lieutenant Adams" and, except for my signature, I referred to myself that way.

/ / /

Two weeks after we were commissioned, we received the assignments we had wanted. Two Negro companies were formed—a Basic Training Company and a Specialist Training Company. This latter company was in the Second Training Regiment and would be housed in hotels in downtown Des Moines. The Basic Training Company was part of the Third Training Regiment and was located in Boomtown, the new part of the post. My assignment was as company commander of the Basic Training Company, and, since the specialist group would not be operative for a while, the commander of the unit and the other officers were detailed to work with those of us assigned to the first all-Negro company.

/ / /

As could be expected, new WAAC officers knew very little about what their duties were when they received their assignments. Actually, they knew only those things that they had observed in the OC companies and what classroom knowledge that might apply. For this reason a male officer was assigned to each company to show us how to succeed. Our company had for its tactical adviser the same officer with whom we had been associated when we were assigned to Company 3. I am indebted to Captain Wagner for all the help he gave me as I learned to be a company commander, although a great part of his help was in letting me do the job as I wanted. He believed in learning by doing.

For several months we had a full cadre of male officers assigned to each company. As the months passed, these officers were gradually reassigned away from the Training Center until there were no male officers left except the battalion commander.

/ / /

I was very fortunate to have gotten along with all the officers with whom I worked, and I actually became friends with some of them. Besides Captain Stillman, CO of our OCS company, I think our regimental commander, Maj. Joseph Fowler, most influenced my success as an Army officer. He was military to the letter of the regulations, tolerated no foolishness, and gave none. He demanded the best of every member of his command and as a result kept all of us in a state of fear. "The Major," as we usually referred to him, was about six feet, three inches tall, slender, blond, extremely well groomed, and he was a striking figure in his Cavalry uniform. We never saw him without his riding crop, and I always wished that I could have carried one.

After what was to us a terrible struggle getting supplies, beds, sheets, pillowcases, pillows, blankets, office supplies, and the like, we were ready to receive our first basic training group. In those early days the training schedule was issued from the Headquarters Training Section, so we did not have to worry about what to teach, who would teach it, or where it would be taught. The instructors and classrooms were assigned. Our job was the administration of the company, the housing and feeding, and getting the troops to the right place at the right time.

The day came when we received our first auxiliaries for training. There were twenty-two of them for the twenty-seven officers in the company. The women had already had some training because they had been members of Company 3, where we had been assigned as trainees. In spite of their previous training, we went at our jobs with determination and set out to make real soldiers of them.

There were no WAAC noncommissioned officers when we started, so we used commissioned officers in those spots. All the jobs from first sergeant to squad leader were filled by third officers. In our case there were so many officers and so few troops that we had to change the duties frequently so that everyone had a chance to perform. There were so few Negro women coming in for training that we were rather depressed about being in excess so early in the service of our country. Along with this was the ever-present concern for our chances for success. We did not know whether our progress was to be in an all-Negro world or in the all-WAAC world.

/   /   /

Because we had some difficulty getting uniforms in the correct sizes for our troops, sometimes the company made a strange appearance when in formation. It was required that any part of the uniform that fitted would be worn so it was not unusual to see a woman in a WAAC hat, khaki shirt, and plaid skirt. Many of the officers had not received their complete uniforms, and we were still without insignia. On 25 September 1942 there was a sudden snowstorm, and we were wearing summer uniforms. There were no winter uniforms available; snow had not been expected so early in the season. We put on our civilian clothing along with the uniform, anything to keep warm. By this time there were several thousand women at the TC and, with all the bright civilian clothing being worn, we were a strange army, which precipitated prompt action "at the highest level." Every woman in the service was issued an enlisted man's overcoat. We soon found out what was meant by the saying that GI clothing came in two sizes—too large and too small. I was five feet, eight inches, and although my coat reached my knees, the sleeves struggled to approach my wrists. The small people were completely lost in their coats, which reached the ankles and covered the hands.

In a short time these overcoats became standard issue for new recruits, along with knitted wool caps, brown leather gloves, and arctics.

With these, any woman could lose her identify. Of course, the women were also issued the standard WAAC items and equipment, but none of that was visible under the coat. We third officers wore those coats for a long time and proudly pinned our shiny gold bars on the shoulders. We complained about the coats, but we made many jokes about them and made pictures of ourselves in them. Second to the enlisted man's overcoat was the enlisted man's raincoat, which was also issued. The raincoat came in the same two sizes as the overcoat but was lighter weight and easier to carry when walking. The raincoats were uglier because they were constantly wrinkled and creased from the custom of rolling them in the hood for carrying.

After several weeks running the company, we began to feel rather secure in our jobs. The second OC class graduated two weeks after we had, and by the time they were assigned to Boomtown we felt that we were in a position to teach them a great deal. Though all our neighbors were white, we had established excellent rapport, for we were all learning our way at the same time. We had little equipment to use in our activities, so we shared and borrowed from each other without hesitation. We created a friendly rivalry that spurred enthusiasm and work, and when our company was on the drill field along with other companies, each company tried to outdo the others.

/   /   /

Finally, there were enough jobs for us so that all Negro officers had real assignments. The time had come when we had to have real noncommissioned officers to handle the duties that third officers had taken on. A few of the women who had completed their training in the clerks company were sent back to Company 8 for housing and administration until they were given assignments in the field.

When we received the orders sending the clerical school graduates back to us, my officers and I looked over the list and, without knowing the women, picked a group to serve as noncommissioned officers. When they arrived, we put them right to work. Most of those we chose that day remained with us for many months and became the first group of Negro WAACs to become noncommissioned officers and wear stripes. They gradually worked up the ranks until they had the appropriate stripes for the jobs we gave them. We selected as company first sergeant Margaret Charity, who became the best there was. First sergeants from other companies would call her for information and advice. Adding to the general confusion was the fact that my first name was the same as her last name. There were times when callers were unsure to whom they should ask to speak.

Early in December of 1942 the first group of WAACs was assigned to various Army posts where the post commanders had been convinced that the women could be effective by relieving the men from certain duties so that they could take on the more rigorous ones. Among this first group to leave was a detachment of Negro WAACs assigned to

Fort Huachuca, Arizona. The women of this group had been trained as drivers, cooks, bakers, clerks, and basics. This last group had no special training.

As the Negro women graduated from the specialist companies, most of them returned to our company to await assignment, while a few were waiting in the downtown hotel quarters. We had looked forward to the day when we would finally see the trained personnel leave for duty, so the day that the group left for Fort Huachuca was busy and exciting. I was choked with pride as I watched the women leave. Some of them had received all of their basic training under my command in Company 8, and all of them had received a few days' training with me.

Even if the America of 1942 had not embraced formal segregation, it probably would have been practiced at the First WAAC Training Center to accommodate the color prejudice. We were different in color and therefore hated or feared because of this difference. The routine schedule for WAAC recruits was one week in the reception center to receive equipment and orientation, followed by basic training, from which trainees were sent to the specialist companies to develop skills, followed by assignment to a staging company to await assignment in the field. Because there were not many Negro WAACs, all of their routine schedules were done in Company 8 except for the specialist training. The result was that I commanded a receiving company, a basic training company, and a staging company. My officers and I learned in one company, in a short time, what other officers learned over long periods of time.

I did not let these adverse circumstances affect my desire to be a good officer. I was hardly aware of how much I was learning. My satisfaction came from watching a group of civilian women arrive in my company and seeing them leave six weeks later as well-trained soldiers. I knew there were no better trained troops at the Training Center than those who left Company 8.

It was probably during my tour of duty as a company commander that I developed what I later came to call my "lightly attached shoulder chip." I had been raised in the South, and I knew that there was no such thing as separate but equal, but I had become determined to see that any troops I commanded would have every opportunity that was afforded others. I knew that there was no such thing as personal success, that success came only if we all succeeded together.

/   /   /

There had also been promotions for members of the first class. I was really surprised when on 23 December 1942, all members of that class were promoted to second officer except twenty-four of us who were promoted to first officer, over four hundred promotions. At the time there must have been at least a thousand third officers in the corps, and it was necessary to make promotions for the purpose of organization, discipline, and command structure. There were four Negro officers among those promoted to first officer: Alexander, Donaldson, West, and Adams. We would call ourselves captain, although we would sign our names with the official title of first officer. In anticipation of promotions at some point, some of my officers and civilian friends had supplied me with silver bars, the insignia for second officer or first lieutenant. I even had a pair given to me by Captain Wagner, our company adviser, when he had been promoted to captain from first lieutenant. With all my collection of "promotion gear" I was unable to find any captain's bars. There were so many new promotions that the post exchange had exhausted its supply. One of my company officers had to go into the city to secure my first captain's bars.

After graduation I had looked forward to going home for a visit, but my assignment had kept me so busy that I had not had a chance. When, on 10 December 1942 I did get a leave, I was still a relatively new "spit and polish" second lieutenant, and I wanted my family to be proud to me. The visit was very pleasant, and it eliminated any fears my parents may have had about my venture into the unknown. I was feted as the "hometown girl who had made good."

There were, however, several unpleasant events associated with my first visit back to my hometown. The Carolina Special, of the Southern Railway system, was segregated, as were all trains and other accommodations in the South. There were sometimes provisions made, such as they were, for Negro passengers to eat in the dining car in a small curtained-off section. I had boarded the train at night in Cincinnati, and the following morning I went to the dining car and joined the line of people waiting for a seat. When the lined moved, I moved, and I finally made it to the door of the dining car when the steward put his arm across the door and announced that the car was full. I stood there in front of the line and waited. After a rather long time the steward called, "All persons in uniform first." I stepped forward. He thrust his arm across the door again and said, angrily, "I said all persons in uniform first." Before I could answer, I heard a voice behind me.

"Well, what in the hell do you think that is that she has on? Get your _____ _____ arm down before I break it off for you."

The voice was so obviously southern that I turned around in surprise. That voice belonged to a very tall, very blond second lieutenant, and he was so angry that his face was quite red. He continued to talk, and loudly. "What in the world are we fighting this damned war for? She's giving her service, too, and can eat anywhere I can. And, by Jesus, I am going to eat with her in this diner."

By this time I was rather alarmed and wondered what would happen next. When I looked at the steward, he had stepped aside and was waiting to show me to my seat. I followed him to the middle of the diner where he seated me at a table for four. The lieutenant came right behind and sat down opposite me. The dining room was absolutely quiet until we were seated, and when people resumed eating there was only the sound of flatware being used. We did have breakfast together, and as we ate, the officer kept up in his tirade against "crackers" and "cheap whites" and "what this war is all about." He did all the talking, and when the meal was over, he escorted me back to my seat, bowed, and left. I never saw him again, but I still think of him as a southern gentlemen.

The Negro Ministerial Alliance and the NAACP (National Association for the Advancement of Colored People) had been very active in Columbia, especially about the mistreatment of Negro soldiers by white military police stationed at Fort Jackson. The pressure forced authorities to put Negro MPs on the streets, but they were unarmed and subject to the same mistreatment that other enlisted personnel received. To even things up, the Negro ministers armed themselves and patrolled the streets, one minister for each Negro MP. There were never any incidents with this system, and finally the military armed the Negro MPs, which, of course, did not go over very well with many of the more bigoted citizens.

As it happened, my first visit home was in December 1942, and while I was there the NAACP chapter had its annual meeting. My father was president of the branch and was presiding at the meeting, which was also attended by the state president of the NAACP. As I sat listening to the proceedings in a church auditorium, I heard someone whisper my name. I looked toward the side door, where a man whom I had known all my life beckoned me to come to him, which I did. He wanted to make sure that my father knew before we left the meeting to go home that the Ku Klux Klan had surrounded our house, as well as that of the Reverend Hinton, the state president. With great difficulty I refrained from rushing up to deliver the message. As soon as the meeting was over, I told my father and asked what we were going to do. We went home, to find a line of cars parked in the street in front of the house. It was not possible to surround the house without entering private property, but the Klan was lined up, in the hoods, in considerable strength along the street. Daddy got out his double-barreled shotgun and shells, gave instructions to Mamma, my sister who was home from college for the weekend, my younger brother, and me, and then he left to join Mr. Hinton because his family was out of the city and he was alone. We sat in darkness following our instructions, which were to make sure that we did nothing that could be considered provocation. It had been just dusk when we came home, and we could see the men clearly. They had made no move when we came in and none when Daddy left, but they continued to sit in front of the house as the night passed. We could peep through the slats of the venetian blinds and would occasionally see one of the men light a cigarette. About dawn the cars left. It must have been a prearranged time, for they left Mr. Hinton's house about the same time. The whole thing had been reported to the police, but they "couldn't do anything about men parked on the street."

Questions for Part III

1 Explain "honest graft" as Plunkitt defines it. What are the worthy functions of political machines according to him? What is your opinion of his view?

2 What did Sinclair expect *The Jungle* to accomplish? Did it do so? How did the novel affect the populace?

3 Sometimes, as in the case of the Triangle Fire, terrible disasters lead to much-needed reforms. Can you think of any other examples? Report on one or two, describing the tragedy and the resulting reform.

4 While Zabriskie was concentrating on the technologies being developed at the beginning of the twentieth century, he was unaware of some problems they would create. What are some of these problems? What has been done about them, if anything?

5 What values did Dick O'Neill fight for? How does he feel about his wartime experiences? How do you think he would have viewed Emma Goldman?

6 Why did Goldman oppose the draft? What values did she support that caused her to risk prison or deportation?

7 What do the letters from the "great migration" tell you about what life was like for blacks in the South? What were some consequences of the population shift?

8 What points did Calkins make in his defense of advertising? What were some of the criticisms of advertising?

9 What were some of the problems faced by Afro-Americans in the U. S. Army? How did they contrast with life in Harlem after the First World War?

10 Based on your reading of the *Klansman's Manual*, what aspects of the Klan would appeal to a struggling lower-class white man of the 1920s? What aspects appeal to you? What do you find repugnant?

11 If possible, talk to elderly people you know—perhaps your grandparents or other relatives—about their memories of the 1930s. Compare what they say with the comments of the people Terkel interviewed.

12 What were the motives for writing these letters to the president and other officials? What do you think was accomplished?

13   In your library look up the Supreme Court decisions concerning
     the internment of Japanese-Americans during World War II. How
     did the majority of the justices explain their decisions? What is
     your opinion on this issue?

14   How does Earley contrast her acceptance by the mostly male mil-
     itary and by the Southern population of her hometown? Which
     do you think was more difficult for her, and why?

PART *IV* | *AMERICA SINCE 1945*

Victory in World War II planted seeds both of hope and of anxiety. Americans feared that economic depression would return once industries stopped producing tanks, jeeps, and planes. Uncertainties about the future of America were accompanied by ideological quarrels with the Soviet Union. And the frightening new atomic bomb haunted a generation's imagination.

But as always people were determined that the years ahead be "the best years of our lives." Susan Allen Toth's family exemplified a style of life devoted to certain perceived eternal truths. Jo Ann Gibson Robinson, an Alabama college teacher, anticipated and worked for a better world for the Montgomery black community.

As the 1950s ended, young people, dissatisfied with the placid suburban dream, and Afro-Americans, shut out of the dream, found new ways of asserting their rights and needs. New lifestyles were suddenly undermining American attitudes toward money and toward family behavior. Many young people who read Kerouac's On the Road *took to the road or to drugs. Americans went into debt and experimented with new ways of experiencing their personal lives even while public figures reaffirmed traditional values.*

The black struggle for equality, unrest among young people, and the reawakening of a vocal movement on the political Right (led by Barry Goldwater) were prominent in the growing ferment of the late 1950s. John F. Kennedy captured these trends in the rhetoric of the 1960 presidential campaign and, in his Inaugural Address, issued an urgent call for action. Responses to that call are obvious in many a manifesto of the 1960s, among them the "Port Huron Statement" by the influential Students for a Democratic Society. We see the idealism of the 1960s in the letters from Mississippi. But overshadowing all American lives was the growing cancer of the nation's longest and strangest war, personalized in the testimony of Dave Baker and Clarence Fitch.

The fight for civil liberties continued past the 1960s, most notably in the attempts to pass a constitutional amendment explicitly guaranteeing equal rights and freedom from discrimination for women. However, beginning in the early

1970s, at least a segment of society was calling for order, consolidation, and traditional values.

Although to some people the 1980s seemed to be a time of 1920s-style affluence and growth, to others it was a time when husband and wife both had to work simply to maintain their standard of living. The number of millionaires increased considerably, but poor female-headed households increased yet more dramatically, and homelessness became a national issue. Economic pressures brought into focus the problems women faced as they felt pressure to choose between new-found economic opportunities and their interest in roles as spouses or parents.

Although the administration of Ronald Reagan was able to intertwine American hopes and memories in a way that no popular critic seemingly could disentangle, and that of George Bush continued in a similar path, not all citizens were optimistic about the future. The toxic waste problem at Love Canal was repeated at Times Beach and elsewhere across the nation. All this was less significant, however, to a new generation of immigrants, who like José and Rosa, left political and economic instability in their homelands to come to a new land in renewal of the American dream of prosperity and good fortune. To them, America still represented the best hope for a secure future.

31 | "The Parties Were Enormous"

Unlike major events in politics, diplomacy, or war, those in the history of a culture usually occur unheralded by trumpets, protocol, or news reporters. The publication of Jack Kerouac's On the Road *in 1957 marked the advent of a new sensibility. Kerouac's novel describes the netherworld of the "beat" generation, which sought redemption and a sense of community in drugs and sex, exotic religion, mystical inspiration, poetry, and jazz, and rejected the materialism and mass culture of American society in the 1950s. Jack Kerouac's prose and Allen Ginsberg's poetry (Ginsberg is the "Carlo Marx" of* On the Road*) influenced a generation of restless and daring young people in the 1960s to experiment with new ways of living and of viewing the world. "Beat" and its condescending derivative "beatnik" rapidly entered the language as the mass media took up the phenomena. The beat lifestyle was parodied and commercialized, the literary works were scorned by professional critics, and the drug culture was attacked by moralists and the police.*

Setting a tone that would continue over the next two decades, America in the 1950s greeted the new challenge to its conventions with curiosity, disdain, and ambivalence. Time Magazine *described beatniks as a "pack of oddballs who celebrate booze, dope, sex, and despair," and in California a hostess could rent a beatnik to add color and surprise to her parties.*

The parties were enormous; there were at least a hundred people at a basement apartment in the West Nineties. People overflowed into the cellar compartments near the furnace. Something was going on in every corner, on every bed and couch—not an orgy but just a New Year's party with frantic screaming and wild radio music. There was even a Chinese girl. Dean ran like Groucho Marx from group to group, digging everybody. Periodically we rushed out to the car to pick up more people. Damion came. Damion is the hero of my New York gang, as Dean is the chief hero of the Western. They immediately took a dislike to each other. Damion's girl suddenly socked Damion on the jaw with a roundhouse right. He stood reeling. She carried him home. Some of our mad newspaper friends came in from the office with bottles. There was a tremendous and wonderful snowstorm going on outside. Ed Dunkel met Lucille's sister and disappeared with her; I forgot to say that Ed Dunkel is a very smooth man with the women. He's six foot four, mild, affable, agreeable, bland, and delightful. He helps women on with their coats. That's the way to do things. At five o'clock in the morning we were all rushing through the backyard of a tenement and climbing in through a window of an apartment where a huge party was going on. At dawn we were back at Tom Saybrook's. People were drawing pictures and drinking stale beer. I slept on a couch with a girl called Mona in my arms. Great groups filed in from the old Columbia Campus bar. Everything in life, all the faces of life, were piling into the same dank room. At Ian MacArthur's the party went on. Ian MacArthur is a wonderful sweet fellow who wears glasses and peers out of them with delight. He began to learn "Yes!" to everything, just like Dean at this time, and hasn't stopped since. To the wild sounds of Dexter Gordon and Wardell Gray blowing "The Hunt," Dean and I played catch with Marylou over the couch; she was no small doll either. Dean went around with no undershirt, just his pants, barefoot, till it was time to hit the car and fetch more people. Everything happened. We found the wild, ecstatic Rollo Greb and spent a night at his house on Long Island. Rollo lives in a nice house with his aunt; when she dies the house is all his. Meanwhile she refuses to comply with any of his wishes and hates his friends. He brought this ragged gang of Dean, Marylou, Ed, and me, and began a roaring party. The woman prowled upstairs; she threatened to call the police. "Oh, shut up, you old bag!" yelled Greb. I wondered how he could live with her like this. He had more books than I've ever seen in all my life—two libraries, two rooms loaded from floor to ceiling around all four walls, and such books as the Apocryphal Something-or-Other in ten volumes. He played Verdi operas and pantomimed them in his pajamas with a great rip down the back. He didn't give a damn about anything. He is a great scholar who goes reeling down the New York waterfront with original seventeenth-century musical manuscripts under his arm, shouting. He crawls like a big spider through the streets. His excitement blew out of his eyes in stabs of fiendish light. He rolled his neck in spastic ecstasy. He lisped, he writhed, he flopped, he moaned, he howled, he fell back in despair. He could hardly get a word out, he was so excited with life. Dean stood before him with head bowed, repeating over and over again, "Yes . . . Yes . . . Yes." He took me into a corner. "That Rollo Greb is the greatest, most wonderful of all. That's what I was trying to tell you—that's what I want to be. I want to be like him. He's never hung-up, he goes every direction, he lets it all out, he knows times, he has nothing to do but rock back and forth. Man, he's the end! You see, if you go like him all the time you'll finally get it."

"Get what?"

"IT! IT! I'll tell you—now no time, we have no time now." Dean rushed back to watch Rollo Greb some more.

George Shearing, the great jazz pianist, Dean said, was exactly like Rollo Greb. Dean and I went to see Shearing at Birdland in the midst of the long, mad weekend. The place was deserted, we were the first customers, ten o'clock. Shearing came out, blind, led by the hand to his keyboard. He was a distinguished-looking Englishman with a stiff white collar, slightly beefy, blond, with a delicate English-summer's-night air about him that came out in the first rippling sweet number he played as the bass-player leaned to him reverently and thrummed the beat. The drummer, Denzil Best, sat motionless except for his wrists snapping the brushes. And Shearing began to rock; a smile broke over his ecstatic face; he began to rock in the piano seat, back and forth, slowly at first, then the beat went up, and he began rocking fast, his left foot jumped up with every beat, his neck began to rock crookedly, he brought his face down to the keys, he pushed his hair back, his combed hair dissolved, he began to sweat. The music picked up. The bass-player hunched over and socked it in, faster and faster, it seemed faster and faster, that's all. Shearing began to play his chords; they rolled out of the piano in great rich showers, you'd think the man wouldn't have time to line them up. They rolled and rolled like the sea. Folks yelled for him to "Go!" Dean was sweating; the sweat poured down his collar. "There he is! That's him! Old God! Old God Shearing! Yes! Yes! Yes!" And Shearing was conscious of the madman behind him, he could hear every one of Dean's gasps and imprecations, he could sense it though he couldn't see. "That's right!" Dean said. "Yes!" Shearing smiled; he rocked. Shearing rose from the piano, dripping with sweat; these were his great 1949 days before he became cool and commercial. When he was gone Dean pointed to the empty piano seat. "God's empty chair," he said. On the piano a horn sat; its golden shadow made a strange reflection along the desert caravan painted on the wall behind the drums. God was gone; it was the silence of his departure. It was a rainy night. It was the myth of the rainy night. Dean was popeyed with awe. This madness would lead nowhere. I didn't know what was happening to me, and I suddenly realized it was only the tea that we were smoking; Dean had bought some in New York. It made me think that everything was about to arrive—the moment when you know all and everything is decided forever.

/ / /

It was drizzling and mysterious at the beginning of our journey. I could see that it was all going to be one big saga of the mist. "Whooee!" yelled Dean. "Here we go!" And he hunched over the wheel and gunned her; he was back in his element, everybody could see that. We were all delighted, we all realized we were leaving confusion and nonsense behind and performing our one and noble function of the time, *move*. And we moved! We flashed past the mysterious white signs in the night somewhere in New Jersey that say *SOUTH* (with an arrow) and *WEST* (with an arrow) and took the south one. New Orleans! It burned in our brains. From the dirty snows of "frosty fagtown New York," as Dean called it, all the way to the greeneries and river smells of old New Orleans at the washed-out bottom of America; then west. Ed was in the back seat; Marylou and Dean and I sat in front and had the warmest talk about the goodness and joy of life. Dean suddenly became tender. "Now dammit, look here, all of you, we all must admit that everything is fine and there's no need in the world to worry, and in fact we should realize what it would mean to us to UNDERSTAND that we're not REALLY worried about ANYTHING. Am I right?" We all agreed. "Here we go, we're all together... What did we do in New York? Let's forgive." We all had our spats back there. "That's behind us, merely by miles and inclinations. Now we're heading down to New Orleans to dig Old Bull Lee and ain't that going to be kicks and listen will you to this old tenorman blow his top" — he shot up the radio volume till the car shuddered — "and listen to him tell the story and put down true relaxation and knowledge."

We all jumped to the music and agreed. The purity of the road. The white line in the middle of the highway unrolled and hugged our left front tire as if glued to our groove. Dean hunched his muscular neck, T-shirted in the winter night, and blasted the car along. He insisted I drive through Baltimore for traffic practice; that was all right, except he and Marylou insisted on steering while they kissed and fooled around. It was crazy; the radio was on full blast. Dean beat drums on the dashboard till a great sag developed in it; I did too. The poor Hudson — the slow boat to China — was receiving her beating.

"Oh man, what kicks!" yelled Dean. "Now Marylou, listen really, honey, you know that I'm hotrock capable of everything at the same time and I have unlimited energy — now in San Francisco we must go on living together. I know just the place for you — at the end of the regular chain-gang run — I'll be home just a cut-hair less than every two days and for twelve hours at a stretch, and man, you know what we can do in twelve hours, darling. Meanwhile I'll go right on living at Camille's like nothin', see, she won't know. We can work it, we've done it before." It was all right with Marylou, she was really out for Camille's scalp. The understanding had been that Marylou would switch to me in Frisco, but I now began to see they were going to stick and I was going to be left alone on my butt at the other end of the continent. But why think about that when all the golden land's ahead of you and all kinds of unforeseen events wait lurking to surprise you and make you glad you're alive to see?

JO ANN GIBSON ROBINSON

32 Launching the Montgomery Bus Boycott

In March 1954, two months before the United States Supreme Court announced its historic ruling in Oliver Brown v. Board of Education of Topeka, Kansas, *which declared segregated schools to be unconstitutional, the Women's Political Council of Montgomery, Alabama, remonstrated with the City Commission to end abusive practices against Afro-Americans on the city's buses. Shortly after, this organization of Afro-American women, modeled after the League of Women Voters (whose Montgomery chapter had refused them membership), threatened to join with other black community organizations to boycott the buses citywide. On December 5, 1955, four days after Mrs. Rosa Parks had been arrested for refusing to surrender her bus seat, the WPC did just that.*

Mrs. Robinson's careful narrative explains the role of her organization in beginning the boycott, as well as her personal part in writing, mimeographing, and distributing over 50,000 flyers urging the black community to boycott the buses on December 5. Their plan for a one-day boycott grew wondrously into nearly a year of walking, carpooling, and facing down all the intimidation that Jim Crow (state codes of segregation in public transport) could devise until the leadership of the Reverend Martin Luther King, Jr., and a Supreme Court decision brought them victory. This long-neglected story of the Women's Political Council is a major part of the first significant victory of the civil rights movement and the emergence of its greatest leader, Mrs. Robinson's minister at the Dexter Avenue Baptist Church, the Reverend Martin Luther King, Jr.

In the afternoon of Thursday, December 1, a prominent black woman named Mrs. Rosa Parks was arrested for refusing to vacate her seat for a white man. Mrs. Parks was a medium-sized, cultured mulatto woman; a civic and religious worker; quiet, unassuming, and pleasant in manner and appearance; dignified and reserved; of high morals and a strong character. She was—and still is, for she lives to tell the story—

respected in all black circles. By trade she was a seamstress, adept and competent in her work.

Tired from work, Mrs. Parks boarded a bus. The "reserved seats" were partially filled, but the seats just behind the reserved section were vacant, and Mrs. Parks sat down in one. It was during the busy evening rush hour. More black and white passengers boarded the bus, and soon all the reserved seats were occupied. The driver demanded that Mrs. Parks get up and surrender her seat to a white man, but she was tired from her work. Besides, she was a woman, and the person waiting was a man. She remained seated. In a few minutes, police summoned by the driver appeared, placed Mrs. Parks under arrest, and took her to jail.

It was the first time the soft-spoken, middle-aged woman had been arrested. She maintained decorum and poise, and the word of her arrest spread. Mr. E. D. Nixon, a longtime stalwart of our NAACP branch, along with liberal white attorney Clifford Durr and his wife Virginia, went to the jail and obtained Mrs. Parks's release on bond. Her trial was scheduled for Monday, December 5, 1955.

The news traveled like wildfire into every black home. Telephones jangled; people congregated on street corners and in homes and talked. But nothing was done. A numbing helplessness seemed to paralyze everyone. Very few stayed off the buses the rest of that day or the next. There was fear, discontent, and uncertainty. Everyone seemed to wait for someone to *do* something, but nobody made a move. For that day and a half, black Americans rode the buses as before, as if nothing had happened. They were sullen and uncommunicative, but they rode the buses. There was a silent, tension-filled waiting. For blacks were not talking loudly in public places—they were quiet, sullen, waiting. Just waiting!

Thursday evening came and went. Thursday night was far spent, when, at about 11:30 P.M., I sat alone in my peaceful single-family dwelling on a quiet street. I was thinking about the situation. Lost in thought, I was startled by the telephone's ring. Black attorney Fred Gray, who had been out of town all day, had just gotten back and was returning the phone message I had left for him about Mrs. Parks's arrest. Attorney Gray, though a very young man, had been one of my most active colleagues in our previous meetings with bus company officials and Commissioner Birmingham. A Montgomery native who had attended Alabama State and been one of my students, Fred Gray had gone on to law school in Ohio before returning to his home town to open a practice with the only other black lawyer in Montgomery, Charles Langford.

Fred Gray and his wife Bernice were good friends of mine, and we talked often. In addition to being a lawyer, Gray was a trained, ordained minister of the gospel, actively serving as assistant pastor of Holt Street Church of Christ.

Tonight his voice on the phone was very short and to the point. Fred was shocked by the news of Mrs. Parks's arrest. I informed him that I already was thinking that the WPC should distribute thousands of notices calling for all bus riders to stay off the buses on Monday, the day of Mrs. Parks's trial. "Are you ready?" he asked. Without hesitation, I assured him that we were. With that he hung up, and I went to work.

I made some notes on the back of an envelope: "The Women's Political Council will not wait for Mrs. Parks's consent to call for a boycott of city buses. On Friday, December 2, 1955, the women of Montgomery will call for a boycott to take place on Monday, December 5."

Some of the WPC officers previously had discussed plans for distributing thousands of notices announcing a bus boycott. Now the time had come for me to write just such a notice. I sat down and quickly drafted a message and then called a good friend and colleague, John Cannon, chairman of the business department at the college, who had access to the college's mimeograph equipment. When I told him that the WPC was staging a boycott and needed to run off the notices, he told me that he too had suffered embarrassment on the city buses. Like myself, he had been hurt and angry. He said that he would happily assist me. Along with two of my most trusted senior students, we quickly agreed to meet almost immediately, in the middle of the night, at the college's duplicating room. We were able to get three messages to a page, greatly reducing the number of pages that had to be mimeographed in order to produce the tens of thousands of leaflets we knew would be needed. By 4 A.M. Friday, the sheets had been duplicated, cut in thirds, and bundled. Each leaflet read:

> Another Negro woman has been arrested and thrown in jail because she refused to get up out of her seat on the bus for a white person to sit down. It is the second time since the Claudette Colvin case that a Negro woman has been arrested for the same thing. This has to be stopped. Negroes have rights, too, for if Negroes did not ride the buses, they could not operate. Three-fourths of the riders are Negroes, yet we are arrested, or have to stand over empty seats. If we do not do something to stop these arrests, they will continue. The next time it may be you, or your daughter, or mother. This woman's case will come up on Monday. We are, therefore, asking every Negro to stay off the buses Monday in protest of the arrest and trial. Don't ride the buses to work, to town, to school, or anywhere on Monday. You can afford to stay out of school for one day if you have no other way to go except by bus. You can also afford to stay out of town for one day. If you work, take a cab, or walk. But please, children and grown-ups, don't ride the bus at all on Monday. Please stay off of all buses Monday.

Between 4 and 7 A.M., the two students and I mapped out distribution routes for the notices. Some of the WPC officers previously had discussed how and where to deliver thousands of leaflets announcing a boycott, and those plans now stood me in good stead. We outlined our routes, arranged the bundles in sequences, stacked them in our cars, and arrived at my 8 A.M. class, in which both young men were enrolled, with several minutes to spare. We weren't even tired or hungry. Just like me, the two students felt a tremendous sense of satisfaction at being able to contribute to the cause of justice.

After class my two students and I quickly finalized our plans for distributing the thousands of leaflets so that one would reach every black home in Montgomery. I took out the WPC membership roster and called the former president, Dr. Mary Fair Burks, then the Pierces, the Glasses, Mrs. Mary Cross, Mrs. Elizabeth Arrington, Mrs. Josie Lawrence, Mrs. Geraldine Nesbitt, Mrs. H. Councill Trenholm, Mrs. Catherine N. Johnson, and a dozen or more others. I alerted all of them to the forthcoming distribution of the leaflets, and enlisted their aid in speeding and organizing the distribution network. Each would have one person waiting at a certain place to take a package of notices as soon as my car stopped and the young men could hand them a bundle of leaflets.

Then I and my two student helpers set out. Throughout the late morning and early afternoon hours we dropped off tens of thousands of leaflets. Some of our bundles were dropped off at schools, where both students and staff members helped distribute them further and spread the word for people to read the notices and then pass them on to neighbors. Leaflets were also dropped off at business places, storefronts, beauty parlors, beer halls, factories, barber shops, and every other available place. Workers would pass along notices both to other employees as well as to customers.

During those hours of crucial work, nothing went wrong. Suspicion was never raised. The action of all involved was so casual, so unconcerned, so nonchalant, that suspicion was never raised, and neither the city nor its people ever suspected a thing! We never missed a spot. And no one missed a class, a job, or a normal routine. Everything was done by the plan, with perfect timing. By 2 o'clock, thousands of the mimeographed handbills had changed hands many times. Practically every black man, woman, and child in Montgomery knew the plan and was passing the word along. No one knew where the notices had come from or who had arranged for their circulation, and no one cared. Those who passed them on did so efficiently, quietly, and without comment. But deep within the heart of every black person was a joy he or she dared not reveal.

Meanwhile, at the college, one of the women teachers who was not a member of the Women's Political Council, nor even a resident of Montgomery (she lived in Mobile), took a leaflet as I and my two seniors got into my car to leave the campus on our delivery route. She carried that leaflet straight to the office of the president of Alabama State College, Dr. H. Councill Trenholm.

Dr. Trenholm was president of Alabama State College for a total of thirty-eight years. When I first came to teach at ASC, a number of long-time teachers there told me that when Dr. Trenholm became president of ASC, following in the footsteps of his father, H. Councill Trenholm, Sr., who had been president for five years before him, he was a young man, brilliant, easygoing, and friendly with his colleagues, many of whom were twice or more his age. He made them feel comfortable during individual conference periods. Even when he criticized or found fault with a teacher's work, what he said was more of a suggestion or recommendation for a better method than a blunt criticism. And nobody but the two of them, he and that teacher, ever knew what the conference was all about. The teachers loved him for that!

He was a diligent worker, a stickler for perfection—a "work ox," somebody labeled him. The institution was a junior college when he first took over, with a few students, limited grounds, and even fewer teachers. He immediately began to go out, meet people, introduce himself, and give scholarships to the very poor and deserving students who wanted to go on but had no money to matriculate. Being a young, ambitious man, he began visiting the immediate communities and talking with parents and young people who were hoping for a college education. In a very short time, he had a large number of students matriculating. He was in a tough position because state funds for "black" college students were limited, and in some places there was no appropriation at all for black students. However, Dr. Trenholm talked with state officials, plus local financiers, and things began to change. Enrollments increased; parents became involved. The junior college became a senior college, and seniors graduated. The state purchased more land, added more space, and the student body grew.

During the Depression, when funds were limited, Dr. Trenholm had helped fund the institution with money from his own savings and from money-raising projects. He gave his youth, his intellect, his *all* to ASC. In so doing, he built an institution that was an intellectual light to the city of Montgomery and the state of Alabama. Thousands of graduates are rendering service to mankind all over the United States and even in other parts of the globe.

When I returned to the campus that Friday for my two o'clock class, after delivering the notices, I found a message from Dr. Trenholm, asking me to come to his office immediately. Very angry and visibly shaken, the president showed me the leaflet and demanded to know what the movement was about and what *my* role was. I informed Dr. Trenholm of the arrest of Mrs. Rosa Parks and of how in the past others had been arrested for the same thing, for refusing to give up their seats to white people.

"Were there other seats?" he asked. I assured him there were not. I informed him that there were many adults who had been arrested for the same thing, and that because the college had no direct connection with the persons, college personnel often had no way of knowing about it. I stressed the fact that black people, innocent black people young and old, were suffering, and that they could not help themselves.

"What are they being arrested for?" he asked. And I did not hesitate to inform him. For all of a sudden, I remembered that time when I was made to get up from a seat in the fifth row from the front of a bus, when there were only three people riding the entire bus.

"I have sent for a teacher; she will be here soon to take charge of your class," he said, in a voice which was not conciliatory. "Sit down and tell me about this situation."

In this powerful man's presence I felt fear for the first time, a fear that penetrated my entire being. He had a frown on his face; his voice revealed impatience. For the first time I felt that he might fire me. But at that moment, I did not care if he did! I breathed a silent prayer for guidance and felt a wave of peace inundate me. I knew then that if he fired me, I would stay right there until the right was won.

I described the frequent repetition of these outrages, how many children, men, and women, old and middle-aged people, had been humiliated and made to relinquish their seats to white people. I told him of Claudette Colvin and of Mrs. Rosa Parks, both of whom had been jailed. He stopped me several times to ask questions; then I would proceed.

As I talked, I could see the anger slowly receding from his face and heard his tone of voice softening. Concern began to show in his expression, as he settled in his chair. I relaxed a bit. Then I told him of the three hundred black women who had organized the WPC to fight any inhumane impositions upon black people. I assured him that the WPC would never involve the college, that ASC had not been mentioned nor would it ever be. I convinced him also that if some intelligent, organized group did not take the initiative and seek improvements from the city hall power structure, angry hot-heads would resort to other means. We would choose to fight not with weapons, but with reason. When I told him that somebody, or some organization, had to fight this assault on blacks' rights, and that the WPC was prepared to do it, I felt that I had said enough. I sat with my eyes cast downward breathing a prayer while I waited for his response. His anger gone, deep sympathetic concern spread over his face; his eyes seemed to penetrate the walls of his office; he sat for a moment, pondering, lost in thought. He seemed to have aged years in the brief span of our conversation, and he leaned on his desk as he talked to me. He seemed so tired.

Then he said: "Your group must continue to press for civil rights." He cautioned me, however, to be careful, to work behind the scenes, not to involve the college, and not to neglect my responsibilities as a member of the faculty of Alabama State College. Then he stood up to indicate the discussion was ended.

After thanking him for his understanding and encouragement, I hurried toward the outer door of his office, filled with happiness that he had understood and given us his support. My talk with him had been a wonderful experience.

But before the door closed completely, he called me back.

"Jo Ann," he said, smiling now.

"Yes, Dr. Trenholm?" I responded hesitatingly, realizing he had not yet finished.

"I called Mr. John Cannon's office after receiving this notice of the boycott. Mr. Cannon confirmed my suspicion that you ran off these boycott notices on school paper."

"Yes, sir, that is correct," I admitted. "Let me see, sir. We used thirty-five reams of paper at 500 sheets per ream. That made 17,500 sheets, cut into thirds, for a total of 52,500 leaflets distributed. So by my count, sir, the Women's Political Council owes Mr. Cannon's office for thirty-five reams of paper. We will find out the cost from Mr. Cannon and pay that bill immediately, sir." Actually, the WPC *had no treasury!* I paid that bill out of my own pocket.

As we will see, once the battle was begun, the bus company and city officials would request Dr. Trenholm to sit on a board with them to help arrive at a satisfactory conclusion of the boycott.

Dr. Trenholm did not participate personally in the boycott. But he was mentally and spiritually involved—and deeply so! He was financially involved, too, and often contributed to the collections for people who were suffering because of the loss of their jobs. He never went onto the housetop and screamed of what his contributions had been, but his actions, his constant advice, his donations, and his guidance amounted to much more than dollars and cents.

Dr. Trenholm's wife, Portia, was a brilliant, talented, highly-trained lady, an accomplished pianist who taught music at ASC. She and I were good friends. Although Portia was not a member of the WPC or, later, the Montgomery Improvement Association, she played a key role in the bus boycott ordeal. Like all faculty members at the college, she gave rides to pedestrians during her free periods between classes and contributed funds to help keep the station wagons in operation. She was just as sympathetic to the boycott cause as the rest of the faculty. But most important, she was my "information passport" to Dr. Trenholm's office, day or night, early or late. I had promised Dr. Trenholm that I would "keep him informed," and with Portia's help I kept that promise throughout the boycott. He knew in advance what the WPC's plans were; he neither advised nor protested the plans. Many people sympathized with the president and his wife and kept them informed. Because Portia relayed the messages to her husband, Dr. Trenholm knew more of the facts of the boycott than many of those who were "walking for the cause."

I could not just telephone Dr. Trenholm's office and talk to him directly. According to the protocol of the black intellectual arena, faculty members respect their leaders. And when I had, of necessity, to consult with Dr. Trenholm at night about the boycott, a matter which was practically alien to the college jurisdiction, I could not simply call him at his office. I called his home, and talked with his wife first. She would buzz him to see if he could speak with me, and then I would be connected. Or if he was busy, I talked with her. I explained to her everything I wanted conveyed to him, and she would relay the message when he was in a position to receive it.

I called Portia each night to report the progress made on bus authorities' attitude or other facts. She could get ideas from Dr. Trenholm, who was a brilliant man, and she would pass them along to me; I in turn would relay them to the relevant organization, which would carry on from there. No matter the hour, if the wPC needed advice, I as president would call Portia, and she would relay the message to Dr. Trenholm and give me his answer. Many times I went to him for advice for the wPC, and he never sent me away without submitting workable solutions to almost insoluble problems. Each answer he gave took consideration of the students, the college, and the masses who walked the streets daily for a better way of life, for he loved them all. His answers were in line with those of the ministers, for all we were demanding was justice on the buses. The Trenholms' concern reached out to the entire body of teachers, students, workers, and all that touched the college family. They were involved!

Thus I worked on the boycott with Dr. Trenholm's approval. Even so, I never missed a class! Or if I did, I made up the time. It wasn't easy. I had ten minutes' break to change classes, a thirty-minute morning break, forty-five minutes for lunch, and then back to class for the rest of the day. All crucial meetings pertaining to the boycott were scheduled during my off periods, evenings, and Saturdays. Nobody complained. But if I had to leave a class, I gave the students work to do, for I never, in thirty years of teaching, went to a class without a lesson plan. I worked and got paid for my service, both in terms of finance and students' gratitude. Students knew that I was asked to serve, and they were proud, for they would have an opportunity to speak their opinion, and they had excellent ideas. I taught white and black students and never saw color. I was pleased that I had such support for my involvement in the planning and subsequent day-to-day activities of the Montgomery Bus Boycott.

THE BOYCOTT BEGINS

On Friday morning, December 2, 1955, a goodly number of Montgomery's black clergymen happened to be meeting at the Hilliard Chapel A.M.E. Zion Church on Highland Avenue. When the Women's Political Council officers learned that the ministers were assembled in that meeting, we felt that God was on our side. It was easy for my two students and me to leave a handful of our circulars at the church, and those disciples of God could not truthfully have told where the notices came from if their very lives had depended on it. Many of the ministers received their notices of the boycott at the same time, in the same place. They all felt equal, included, appreciated, needed. It seemed predestined that this should be so.

One minister read the circular, inquired about the announcements, and found that all the city's black congregations were quite intelligent on the matter and were planning to support the one-day boycott with or without their ministers' leadership. It was then that the ministers decided that it was time for them, the leaders, to catch up with the masses. If the people were really determined to stage this one-day protest, then they would need moral support and Christian leadership. The churches could serve as channels of communication, as well as altars where people could come for prayer and spiritual guidance. Since the ministers were servants of the people and of God, and believed in the gospel of social justice, and since the churches were institutions supported by the people, the clerics could serve as channels through which all the necessary benefits could flow. Thus, for the first time in the history of Montgomery, black ministers united to lead action for civic improvement. There was no thought of denomination. Baptists, Presbyterians, Episcopalians, Lutherans, Congregationalists, and others joined together and became one band of ministerial brothers, offering their leadership to the masses. Had they not done so, they might have alienated themselves from their congregations and indeed lost members, for the masses were ready, and they were united!

The black ministers and their churches made the Montgomery Bus Boycott of 1955–1956 the success that it was. Had it not been for the ministers and the support they received from their wonderful congregations, the outcome of the boycott might have been different. The ministers gave themselves, their time, their contributions, their minds, their prayers, and their leadership, all of which set examples for the laymen to follow. They gave us confidence, faith in ourselves, faith in them and their leadership, that helped the congregations to support the movement every foot of the way.

Under the aegis of the Interdenominational Ministerial Alliance a meeting was called for that Friday evening at the Dexter Avenue Baptist Church, of which the Reverend Dr. Martin Luther King, Jr., was pastor. To this meeting were invited all the ministers, all club presidents and officers, all church organization heads, and any interested persons.

In the meantime, domestic workers who worked late into the day toyed with the slips of paper carrying the important information of the protest. Most of them destroyed the evidence, buried the information in their memories, and went merrily on their way to work. However, one lone black woman, a domestic loyal to her "white lady," in spite of her concern over the plight of her black peers and without any sense of obligation to her people, carried the handbill to her job and did not stop until the precious paper was safe in her "white lady's" hands. It was only a matter of minutes before the bus company, the City Commission, the chief of police, and the press knew its contents. The *Alabama Journal*, Montgomery's afternoon newspaper, ran a story on Saturday. Another article appeared in the *Montgomery Advertiser* on Sunday. The two local television stations and the four radio stations completed the coverage. The secret was out.

In recalling this particular incident later, the leaders of the boycott wondered if that woman's action had been providential, part of a divine plan to make the boycott succeed. If this was the case, she was not disloyal to her people, but rather was following the dictates of a higher authority!

The original intention had been that the whole affair would come as a complete surprise to whites. Then if all the darker set did not cooperate, no one would be the wiser. But now the news was out, and some misgivings and fear among blacks followed. Southern blacks, who had never been known to stick together as a group, to follow leadership, or to keep their mouths shut from exposing secrets, were on the spot!

One good thing, however, came from the revelation: the few black citizens in remote corners of the city who might not have gotten the news of the boycott, knew it now. The news that circulated through the newspapers, radio, television, and other channels of communication covered every possible isolated place not reached by the leaflets.

Publicity given the Monday boycott probably accounted, too, for the very large attendance which turned out for the Friday night meeting at Dexter Avenue Baptist Church. More than one hundred leaders were present.

There the organization of the boycott began. Special committees were set up. The main one focused on transportation. To help the walking public, volunteer cars had to be pooled, taxis had to be contacted, and donations had to be determined through cooperative means. Routes had to be mapped out to get workers to all parts of the city. Regular bus routes had to be followed so that workers who "walked along" the streets could be picked up. This committee, headed by Alfonso Campbell and staffed by volunteer workers, worked all night Friday to complete this phase of the program. The pickup system was so effectively planned that many writers described it as comparable in precision to a military operation.

What the ministers failed to do at that meeting was to select one person who would head the boycott. Those present discussed it, pointing out the leadership preparation of various individuals, but no definite decision was made. That had to wait until Monday afternoon, when the ministers realized that the one-day boycott was going to be successful. Then they met again, and Dr. Martin Luther King, Jr., agreed to accept the leadership post.

33 | Blooming: A Small-Town Girlhood

The germination of Blooming *was a question from Susan Allen Toth's four-year-old daughter Jennifer: "What was it like in the old days, Mommy? Did you wear long dresses? Did you ever ride in a covered wagon?" Writing in the 1970s, Toth recognized that the world of the 1950s was in fact the "old days" even if covered wagons were long past. Divorced, under stress, and ambivalent about how her childhood prepared her for the adult world, Toth recorded these vivid recollections of a world that seems both familiar and lost. There is no way to avoid, she notes, the "painful reassessments that have made us question the kinds of assumptions upon which we so confidently based our lives." Yet she asks of her childhood and adolescence in Ames, Iowa: "Was such innocence constricting, or did it give me shelter and space to grow?" And what substitutes, we must ask, has American culture provided for the old innocence of childhood as the basis for an adult life?*

Girlfriends were as essential as mothers. I could survive weeks, even months, without a boyfriend, although I did need to be able to produce one in those endless circular conversations of "Who do you like best?" "Do you think he likes me or Celia better?" "Don't you agree with us that Herb is a nerd?" "Would you ever sit next to Jim if you didn't have to?" But I always had to have a best friend.

A set of girlfriends provided a sense of security, as belonging to any group does. But having a best friend was more complicated: using a friend as a mirror or as a model, expanding your own knowledge through someone else's, painfully acquiring social skills. What little we learned about living with another person in an equal relationship, outside our own families, we learned from our girlfriends. It certainly wasn't a full preparation for marriage, but it was the only one some of us ever got.

My earliest memory of a best friend is a humiliating one. After spending a year in California in third grade, I returned to Ames to skip a grade and suddenly enter fifth. We had just moved to a new house in a different neighborhood, so I also had to switch to the other elementary school on the campus side of town. Both schools joined at Welch Junior High, where we children remained together, a relatively unchanging group, until we moved downtown to merge with Central Junior High in Ames High School. By then our social alliances had been firmly forged.

My year away had erased a lot, and I was a new kid in fifth grade, suspiciously smart and a year too young. I felt lost and lonely, and the only girl who would consent to spend any time with me on the playground or after school was Margie Dwyer. Margie, though rather pretty, was shy and awkward. Her dark hair was twisted in old-fashioned braids on top of her head, emphasizing her sallow skin. I seem to remember she wore one dark plaid jumper all the time. Her father was a janitor somewhere at the college, and they lived in a basement apartment in an old building not far from our house. I don't remember visiting there, or her parents, but I do remember how grateful I was to hold hands with Margie, who smiled at me as we skipped in unison down the sidewalk. But I clearly knew then and remembered with shame later that Margie, like me, was a social pariah. She had no set of friends, no status. After we stopped being best friends the next year, she became best friends with "Sappy" Strickland, the dumbest girl in class. Years later Margie dropped out of high school and married an older man, an auto mechanic. No one noticed.

What humiliates me about my memory of Margie is how quickly I dropped her when, in sixth grade, I was suddenly adopted into an acceptable set of friends. There weren't, in fact, many sets to choose from. With two sections of each grade, about thirty students in each, we had a "pool" of sixty; roughly half of those were boys; so thirty girls had to divide themselves into appropriate groups. Six formed the elite, a group so tight, so deliberately exclusive, that they earned themselves the name of "the Society Six." They were the prettiest, most sophisticated, and stylish girls and naturally included all the ninth-grade cheerleaders. They chose the boyfriends they wanted from the homeroom presidents, athletes, and other "neat" boys.

Needless to say, with my plumpness, brains, wicked tongue and awkward uncertainties, I did not belong to the "Society Six." Years later, so many years I had not heard of or seen any of the "Society Six" for two decades, I was talking at dinner to a psychiatrist about our junior-high social groups. I had never been a cheerleader, I told him self-effacingly, but then I added, "You know, they didn't end up all that well. One of them, Delaney Deere, lost all her popularity when she got to high school. She started going with an older man from Des Moines, quit school, and left town. I wonder what ever happened to her." He smiled with that knowing look a psychiatrist acquires, and said quietly, "Still hurts, doesn't it?" "What?" I said. "I mean, your not getting to be a cheerleader. Not being one of that High Society, or whatever-you-call-it. Why do you still take such satisfaction in what happened to that Delaney girl?" He smiled again and went to find another rumaki, while I stared speechless at my plate.

But if I couldn't be a member of the Society Six, I was delighted to be accepted into the next group on the social scale, a larger and more fluid one, ten or fifteen girls, democratic enough at least to be nameless. One of its leaders was Kristy Harbinger, whose parents were good friends of my mother's. On the day Kristy asked me to come over to her house after school to play "Sorry," I knew I had made it. Kristy and the other girls in this group were from various backgrounds, some with faculty parents, others with fathers who included an insurance salesman, a banker, a plumber, an oil-company representative who toured the state for Mobil. What your father did wasn't important, though you needed to have a house where you could bring friends home without embarrassment.

Most of us attended the nearby Presbyterian, Methodist or Baptist churches, but by ninth grade, when parochial schools ended, we had two Catholic friends as well. I'm not sure on what grounds we admitted others as friends, how we made up the guest lists for our slumber parties or Valentines or birthdays, how we knew whom to call to go to the movies. Most of us went on to college, but we certainly didn't base our friendship on intellectual merit. Most of us were moderately attractive, but one or two of us didn't date at all for years. Most of us were "popular," but I don't know exactly why. Perhaps we merely defined ourselves in relation to the Society Six and to all the other girls below us, the loners, the stupid ones, the fat ones. We had absorbed already by sixth grade a set of careful and cruel distinctions.

Whatever the sociology of our group, it was large enough to absorb newcomers and to permit trading best friends. When Kristy Harbinger asked me to her house to play "Sorry," I was already involved with Joyce Schwartz. For almost a year Kristy, Joyce and I uneasily maneuvered to see who would be whose best friend. I liked Joyce because she was more mature than I. Her body already rounded nicely, and when she wore a sweater, it had real bumps. When she turned a corner, Joyce flounced, her skirt swirling in a flutter of pleats. Even her hair seemed bouncier than mine, a neat cap of natural waves, while mine hung relentlessly straight in a long ponytail. Though I knew a little about teasing boys, Joyce actually flirted, her eyes flashing and her sparkly teeth dazzling the bewildered boy who would lean his bike awkwardly on the sidewalk while he tried to keep up with her jokes and jibes. To me Joyce represented self-confidence; my mother, who didn't like her much, said she though Joyce was "tough" and "a little mean." We were probably talking about the same thing.

Although Joyce hadn't started to date then in sixth grade—no really nice girl did till seventh or eighth—she seemed to me to know more about boys, about life, than I did. For one thing, her parents fought. Since my mother had been widowed when I was just seven, I couldn't remember much about my parents' marriage, though my mother said they had been very happy and she still wept when she spoke of my father. None of my other friends' parents ever argued in front of me, except in brief, unthreatening exchanges of mild displeasure: "Oh, George, I *told* you to pick that up!" "How can we be out of beer *again*?" "No, I do *not* want to go out to dinner." But the Schwartzes really fought, yelling loudly and banging doors. At least Mr. Schwartz did. He was a large, flabby man with quick, shifty eyes—like Joyce's, only hers were set in a pretty face—and he had a quick, loud temper. When he came home, he always had a few pleasant words for us—Joyce openly flirted with him, as she did with the boys on the streets—but then he would ask us to leave, go outside, play upstairs, and soon we would hear his booming voice as he argued with his wife. Joyce's mother was pale, brown-haired, washed-out, with so little personality that I wondered if Mr. Schwartz shouted at her just to get some response. I never heard her answers from behind the closed doors. Sometimes, Joyce said matter-of-factly, her father hit her mother. "Not real hard," she added. I was shocked, not only by this disclosure of violence but by my knowledge that Mr. Schwartz was a leading deacon in his church. I was sure my own Collegiate Presbyterian wouldn't have stood for it.

Visiting the Harbingers' after school with Kristy was a complete change. Mrs. Harbinger, who was warm, friendly, and still poignantly beautiful, presided over a house filled with comforting sounds and smells: chocolate-chip cookies fresh from the oven, a ringing phone, the padding of active feet, shouts and laughter from Kristy's older brother and his friends. Doors slammed, but the sound was a happy one of activity, not the warning prelude it was at the Schwartzes'. Joyce Schwartz liked to come to the Harbingers' too, but she preferred to be asked by herself, not with me. Kristy Harbinger, understandably flattered by our jealous attentions, played us against each other. I remember dragging home heartsick, running to my room to cry, because Kristy and Joyce, whispering and giggling together at recess, had hurried off after school before I could catch up with them. Once I asked Joyce if she wanted to go to a Saturday-afternoon movie, only to be told, snippily, that she was already going with Kristy. "But if you want," she said, with a wide smile that made me seethe, "I'll find out if you can go with us." Whenever Joyce had something particularly nasty to say, she smiled. Her self-control always enraged me. Speechless, I turned away. We both knew that the three of us couldn't go together. Who would sit next to whom in the theatre? Who would get the prized middle seat? Whose house would we go to afterward? If we went to Schwartzes', would Joyce ignore me? If we went to Harbingers', though, couldn't Kristy join with Joyce in playing Ping-Pong while I waited disconsolately on the sidelines? If we played "Sorry" and I lost, wouldn't Joyce smile widely? And if we went to my house, didn't I know for sure that Joyce would complain there was nothing to do and leave early, probably with Kristy, so I couldn't follow?

Exactly how this triangle of tension sagged and lost one side I cannot now recall. But by the end of sixth grade, with subtle shifts in the social quicksands, I had risen and Joyce had fallen. Her flirtatiousness had come to seem brazen, her stylishness a bit cheap. She had begun to date, a sluggish, heavy football player who had almost flunked fifth grade; despite his athletic skills, he wasn't a boyfriend many of us wanted. Joyce's choice seemed to confirm a growing sense that she wasn't, in fact, quite the right sort. Meanwhile I had been elected homeroom secretary and probably shown other signs of promise. When Kristy showed me her latest list of friends, I had moved to the top. I quickly put her at the top of my list, too, and we were finally best friends.

Most memories of girlfriends lose their bitterness after sixth grade. Though Kristy and I did not remain best friends, I settled comfortably for the next six years into her gang. When I remember my desperate scrabbling in fifth-grade darkness, clinging to Margie Dwyer, and contrast it to my sailing with relative ease through junior high and high school in a convoy of friends, I am frightened for my own daughter. What will be her source of support? If she has to hang onto the edges of a group longer than I did, can I help her? Should I? What can I do about the other little girls, the ones *she* rejects, won't ask to her birthday parties, doesn't want to play with? Would life at the edges develop qualities I missed? If she doesn't have the girlfriends I did, will she be content? Will I?

Once the relentless search for a "best friend" merged into group acceptance, the tenor of my life depended not so much on family or on boyfriends as it did on girlfriends. My mother was always there in the background, of course, a quiet support. Boyfriends drifted across my skies, dreamy clouds, fierce thunder, dramatic lightening: they passed, and the weather changed. But my girlfriends filled my days with the steady pulse of constant companionship. When I remember what I actually *did*, outside of school and evenings at home, I always see myself with one or more girlfriends.

What did we do? Mostly, I think, we talked. We talked on the buses, in the halls, at our lockers, in the classrooms, between classes in the toilets, after school at the bus stop. Once home, we called each other up almost instantly and talked on the phone until some parent couldn't stand it any longer. Then we hung up for a while with promises to call back later. What on earth, our parents asked us, did we find to talk about? But it wasn't so much the topics we found engrossing, I think, the boys, teachers, clothes, gossip. All that talking built up a steady confidence that the trivia of our lives were worth discussion, that our *lives* were worth discussing, that we as individuals were worth someone's attention. "Do you think I ought to get my hair cut?" was a question that asked not only "How would I look with my hair shorter?" but "Do you *care* how I look?" Teachers snapped and lectured; parents discussed and argued; boys teased and muttered; but the steady hum of girlfriends, punctuated by laughter and whispers, was a reassuring continuo.

Besides talking, girlfriends went places with each other. No self-respecting boy would ever be seen shopping with a girl. We girls usually shopped in twos or threes, after school or on Saturday afternoons, not only to approve new purchases, but for the sheer fun of trying on new clothes. We were all known in Younkers, and although Mrs. Corter, the no-nonsense saleswoman, would tell us firmly to leave if someone else wanted the dressing room, until she did we could use the store as though it were a costume shop and we were actresses trying on different roles. Some afternoons we slipped into formals, very carefully, while Mrs. Corter hovered disapprovingly nearby, eagle-eyed for any rip or tear. We floated before the mirrors in layers of pink tulle or swooshes of yellow satin, admiring how much older we looked with bare shoulders and boned-in strapless bodices. We tried on the new cotton spring dresses as soon as they arrived in midwinter, assuring Mrs. Corter that we were already "looking for an Easter dress." She wasn't fooled and whipped the dresses back to the racks as fast as we slipped them off. We giggled to each other, crowded into the tiny dressing room together, knowing her irritation.

Drifting up and down Main Street, we had regular rounds. We'd browse quickly through Penney's and Ward's, if we were really killing time, and maybe pause at Marty's, a collegiate sportswear shop. We didn't feel right yet in the Shetland sweaters and matching pleated skirts that Marty's sold in Iowa State Girls. But we stroked the cashmeres, sorted through cocktail dresses, and tried to imagine ourselves older and shapelier. We would only "look in" at Carole's, not daring to stay too long under the snooty, hard stares of the two saleswomen with pouffed lacquered hair, bright lipstick and shiny nails. Then we'd wander toward the library, or stop at Edith's Gift Shoppe to see whose new wedding patterns of silver and china were on display, maybe drink a Coke at the Rainbow Cafe before catching the bus home. And all the time we talked, talked, talked.

On weekends we went to the movies. By high school many of us dated, and sometimes we'd go with our boyfriends. But, with the bolstering company of two other girls—one wasn't enough—we'd go in a gang together, not caring whether we had dates or not. Sometimes the boys would come in their gangs, too, and we carefully arranged to sit so there'd be an empty row behind us for them. Couples migrated toward the back or the balcony, detached from our noisy, laughing, poking crowd, and we pretended not to notice them as we streamed down the aisles.

Since I was easily embarrassed on movie dates, fidgeting when a boy and I had to stare at a love scene side-by-side, I was happiest going to the movies with the girls. Then I could whisper whatever I wanted, unafraid of sounding foolish, surrounded by friendly elbows and nudging knees. Engulfed in the comforting blackness of the theatre, we could sometimes ask each other questions that would have been impossible elsewhere. One Sunday afternoon at the movies I briefly glimpsed the limits of my knowledge about sex. We girls had gone to see *The Barefoot Contessa*, a murky but dramatic love story in which Ava Gardner, a sexpot who verges on nymphomania, eventually marries mysterious but handsome Rossano Brazzi. On their wedding night, however, he appears at their bedroom door and announces that he cannot sleep with her. The words escape me after all these years, but not their doom-laden import. I vaguely remember Rossano telling Ava, who lay there visibly panting, that he was "wounded in the war." What I acutely remember is the dialogue that then took place in the New Ames Theater. Seated next to me was Leslie Gerard, a girl who was, everyone agreed, thoroughly nice. Her pleasant personality had led her to the presidency of Y-Teens, leadership in her church youth group, membership on Student Council. Sturdy and forthright, she would have been our captain if we'd had any girls' athletic teams. But Leslie did not date yet, and her mother did not let her stay overnight at slumber parties. So perhaps I shouldn't have been surprised when Leslie leaned over to me, puzzled, and said, "What does that mean, he was wounded in the war?" While I paused, one of the boys in the row behind us guffawed loudly. He had heard Leslie's question too. Leaning forward, he stuck his face between our heads and stage-whispered so that both rows could hear, "He had his balls shot off!" The boys collapsed in laughter, while a few of the bolder girls giggled and the rest blushed and looked straight ahead. Under cover of the laughter, Leslie still undaunted, leaned toward me again and, barely audible, whispered in my ear, "What are balls?" "Tell you later," I hissed back quickly. But the fact was I didn't know. Someone else came to Leslie's and my rescue after the show was over.

Besides shopping and going to movies together, we girls herded together to attend dances and parties, those where you didn't need dates, as well as football and basketball games and track meets. Small towns in Iowa had girls' basketball, but Ames was too sophisticated for such pastimes. Girls who liked sports could swim or play tennis. But otherwise we watched the boys, cheering and caring so intensely whether they won or lost that we regularly wept or shouted ourselves hoarse. When the Ames High football team swept down the field, or a center dunked a difficult jump shot, we shared the boys' triumph; it was one of the few times we thought of us all belonging together and working for a common goal. Since I was a clumsy athlete, I was perfectly happy to sit in my black skirt and orange jacket, blending into the cheering section, a small but vital part of the whole. Even Leslie Gerard, whose skill at basketball amazed our gym teacher, and who regularly pleaded, usually vainly, for one of us girls to "shoot a few baskets after school," never murmured the wish that we could have a girls' team. She sat in the front of the section, captain of the Pep Squad, and cheered more loudly than all of us.

Even when we had boyfriends in high school, we spent our spare afternoons and weekend daytimes with girls. Boys had jobs, cars, athletics. Mostly we saw them at night under artificial lights. Boys were dates; girls were friends. We girls went sledding or skating together in the winter; swam, roller-skated and rode bikes in the summer. With other girls we took dancing, swimming, tennis lessons; we accompanied each other on family picnics and even vacations. A girlfriend was as close as the nearest telephone.

A girlfriend wasn't someone for whom you had to plan activities. My closest friend in high school, Peggy O'Reilly, and I always knew what the other felt like or wanted to do, and we usually wanted to do the same thing. Sometimes during our Saturday morning down-town, one of us would always ask the other, "What about going into Eschbach's?" In the late fifties, few of us could afford the expensive new long-playing records. Eschbach's Music Store, with two small glass-enclosed listening booths, tolerantly allowed us to take one l.p. at a time into a booth, sit on the floor, and lose ourselves in the music. Plugging one ear and holding the other close to the speaker, you could almost get the sensation of hi-fi. We never had any doubt about what records to lis-ten to, since Peggy and I shared a terrible crush on Frank Sinatra. Those were his revival years, when his lean face, slouched hat, and hunched shoulders proclaimed on album after album, "How I need someone to watch over me!" Peggy and I felt he was singing to us, discerning our inarticulate fears of being lonely and rejected. Frank Sinatra knew that we weren't always sure life was going to be wonderful. We didn't know whether anyone would ever love us. He understood, and he told us how we felt. So we mooned and dreamed in Eschbach's glass booth, until, like Mrs. Corter in Younkers, an impatient clerk tapped at the window and motioned us out. Sighing, we left our melancholy in the stuffy little room and wandered out into the sunshine. "You know," I said to Peggy, "when I'm twenty-one he'll only be forty-six. Don't you think that would be all right?" Peggy smiled, nodded reassuringly, and linked her arm with mine. She was sure it would be all right. She was, after all, my best friend.

The spring we graduated from high school, we girls began to feel the first twinges of separation. Though some of us were planning to go to Iowa State, many of us were scattering east and west, to New York, Pennsylvania, Massachusetts, California. We couldn't believe that we wouldn't still keep in touch, stay close and spend our vacations to-gether; but we also knew that something was ending. More deliberately than usual, we organized "girl parties," after-school and weekend get-togethers where we tried to pretend that nothing had changed. During the summer, while we sewed and shopped for college, we even prac-ticed giving "luncheons," baking casseroles from our mother's cook-books and entertaining each other with tunafish and noodles, deviled eggs in white sauce, and almost anything based on cream-of-mushroom soup. We "dressed up" and came at twelve-thirty for grape juice and ginger ale. Our mothers looked on tolerantly, helping in the kitchen, tactfully disappearing when "guests" arrived. Perhaps they could see what was happening. They may have remembered their own gradua-tions and losses, old friends who had married and disappeared forever under other names in other towns.

34 | *"Agenda for a Generation"*

During the 1960s, Students for a Democratic Society (SDS) came closer than did any other organization to being the leader of the politically left student movement. The organization emerged when two activists at the University of Michigan, Al Haber and Tom Hayden, coordinated groups at numerous campuses and organized a national meeting in 1962. This meeting, held at a United Auto Workers center in Port Huron, Michigan, approved the following manifesto, which was drafted by Hayden. Tentative in its assertions and written in the language of social science, The Port Huron Statement *nonetheless touched on most of the themes of 1960s radicalism, giving an "agenda for a generation." And that generation, when pressure from the Vietnam War was added to the idealism and political assertion of the Kennedy era, took its agenda into the streets.*

INTRODUCTION: AGENDA FOR A GENERATION

We are people of this generation, bred in at least modest comfort, housed now in universities, looking uncomfortably to the world we inherit.

When we were kids the United States was the wealthiest and strongest country in the world; the only one with the atom bomb, the least scarred by modern war, an initiator of the United Nations that we thought would distribute Western influence throughout the world. Freedom and equality for each individual, government of, by, and for the people — these American values we found good, principles by which we could live as men. Many of us began maturing in complacency.

As we grew, however, our comfort was penetrated by events too troubling to dismiss. First, the permeating and victimizing fact of human degradation, symbolized by the Southern struggle against racial bigotry, compelled most of us from silence to activism. Second, the enclosing fact of the Cold War, symbolized by the presence of the Bomb, brought awareness that we ourselves, and our friends, and millions of abstract "others" we knew more directly because of our common peril, might die at any time. We might deliberately ignore, or avoid, or fail to feel all other human problems, but not these two, for these were too immediate and crushing in their impact, too challenging in the demand that we as individuals take the responsibility for encounter and resolution.

While these and other problems either directly oppressed us or rankled our consciences and became our own subjective concerns, we began to see complicated and disturbing paradoxes in our surrounding America. The declaration "all men are created equal . . ." rang hollow before the facts of Negro life in the South and the big cities of the North. The proclaimed peaceful intentions of the United States contradicted its economic and military investments in the Cold War status quo.

We witnessed, and continue to witness, other paradoxes. With nuclear energy whole cities can easily be powered, yet the dominant nation-states seem more likely to unleash destruction greater than that incurred in all wars of human history. Although our own technology is destroying old and creating new forms of social organization, men still tolerate meaningless work and idleness. While two-thirds of mankind suffers undernourishment, our own upper classes revel amidst super-fluous abundance. Although world population is expected to double in forty years, the nations still tolerate anarchy as a major principle of international conduct and uncontrolled exploitation governs the mapping of the earth's physical resources. Although mankind desperately needs revolutionary leadership, America rests in national stalemate, its goals ambiguous and tradition-bound instead of informed and clear, its democratic system apathetic and manipulated rather than "of, by, and for the people."

Not only did tarnish appear on our image of American virtue, not only did disillusion occur when the hypocrisy of American ideals was discovered, but we began to sense that what we had originally seen as the American Golden Age was actually the decline of an era. The world-wide outbreak of revolution against colonialism and imperialism, the entrenchment of totalitarian states, the menace of war, overpopulation, international disorder, supertechnology—these trends were testing the tenacity of our own commitment to democracy and freedom and our abilities to visualize their application to a world in upheaval.

/   /   /

Some would have us believe that Americans feel contentment amidst prosperity—but might it not better be called a glaze above deeply felt anxieties about their role in the new world? And if these anxieties produce a developed indifference to human affairs, do they not as well produce a yearning to believe there *is* an alternative to the present, that something *can* be done to change circumstances in the school, the work-places, the bureaucracies, the government? It is to this latter yearning, at once the spark and engine of change, that we direct our present ap-peal. The search for truly democratic alternatives to the present, and a commitment to social experimentation with them, is a worthy and fulfilling human enterprise, one which moves us and, we hope, others today. On such a basis do we offer this document of our convictions and analysis: as an effort in understanding and changing the conditions of humanity in the late twentieth century, an effort rooted in the ancient, still unfulfilled conception of man attaining determining influence over his circumstances of life.

VALUES

Making values explicit—an initial task in establishing alternatives—is an activity that has been devalued and corrupted. The conventional moral terms of the age, the politician moralities—"free world," "people's democracies"—reflect realities poorly, if at all, and seem to function more as ruling myths than as descriptive principles. But neither has our experience in the universities brought us moral enlightenment. Our professors and administrators sacrifice controversy to public relations; their curriculums change more slowly than the living events of the world; their skills and silence are purchased by investors in the arms race; passion is called unscholastic. The questions we might want raised—what is really important? can we live in a different and better way? if we wanted to change society, how would we do it?—are not thought to be questions of a "fruitful, empirical nature," and thus are brushed aside.

/   /   /

Men have unrealized potential for self-cultivation, self-direction, self-understanding, and creativity. It is this potential that we regard as crucial and to which we appeal, not to the human potentiality for violence, unreason, and submission to authority. The goal of man and society should be human independence: a concern not with image of popularity but with finding a meaning in life that is personally authentic; a quality of mind not compulsively driven by a sense of powerlessness, nor one which unthinkingly adopts status values, nor one which represses all threats to its habits, but one which has full, spontaneous access to present and past experiences, one which easily unites the fragmented parts of personal history, one which openly faces problems which are troubling and unresolved; one with an intuitive awareness of possibilities, an active sense of curiosity, an ability and willingness to learn.

This kind of independence does not mean egotistic individualism—the object is not to have one's way so much as it is to have a way that is one's own. Nor do we deify man—we merely have faith in his potential.

Human relationships should involve fraternity and honesty. Human interdependence is contemporary fact; human brotherhood must be willed, however, as a condition of future survival and as the most appropriate form of social relations. Personal links between man and man are needed, especially to go beyond the partial and fragmentary bonds of function that bind men only as worker to worker, employer to employee, teacher to student, American to Russian.

Loneliness, estrangement, isolation describe the vast distance between man and man today. These dominant tendencies cannot be overcome by better personnel management, nor by improved gadgets, but only when a love of man overcomes the idolatrous worship of things by man. As the individualism we affirm is not egoism, the selflessness we affirm is not self-elimination. On the contrary, we believe in generosity of a kind that imprints one's unique individual qualities in the relation to other men, and to all human activity. Further, to dislike isolation is not to favor the abolition of privacy; the latter differs from isolation in that it occurs or is abolished according to individual will.

We would replace power rooted in possession, privilege, or circumstance by power and uniqueness rooted in love, reflectiveness, reason, and creativity. As a *social system* we seek the establishment of a democracy of individual participation, governed by two central aims: that the individual share in those social decisions determining the quality and direction of his life; that society be organized to encourage independence in men and provide the media for their common participation. . . .

THE STUDENTS

In the last few years, thousands of American students demonstrated that they at least felt the urgency of the times. They moved actively and directly against racial injustices, the threat of war, violations of individual rights of conscience and, less frequently, against economic manipulation. They succeeded in restoring a small measure of controversy to the campuses after the stillness of the McCarthy period. They succeeded, too, in gaining some concessions from the people and institutions they opposed, especially in the fight against racial bigotry.

The significance of these scattered movements lies not in their success or failure in gaining objectives—at least not yet. Nor does the significance lie in the intellectual "competence" or "maturity" of the students involved—as some pedantic elders allege. The significance is in the fact the students are breaking the crust of apathy and overcoming the inner alienation that remain the defining characteristics of American college life.

If student movements for change are still rarities on the campus scene, what is commonplace there? The real campus, the familiar campus, is a place of private people, engaged in their notorious "inner emigration" It is a place of commitment to business-as-usual, getting ahead, playing it cool. It is a place of mass affirmation of the Twist, but mass reluctance toward the controversial public stance. Rules are accepted as "inevitable," bureaucracy as "just circumstances," irrelevance as "scholarship," selflessness as "martyrdom," politics as "just another way to make people do what you want, and an unprofitable one, too."

Almost no students value activity as citizens. Passive in public, they are hardly more idealistic in arranging their private lives: Gallup concludes they will settle for "low success, and won't risk high failure." There is not much willingness to take risks (not even in business), no setting of dangerous goals, no real conception of personal identity except one manufactured in the image of others, no real urge for personal fulfillment except to be almost as successful as the very successful people. Attention is being paid to social status (the quality of shirt collars, meeting people, getting wives or husbands, making solid contacts for later on); much, too, is paid to academic status (grades, honors, the med school rat race). But neglected generally is real intellectual status, the personal cultivation of the mind.

"Students don't even give a damn about the apathy," one has said. Apathy toward apathy begets a privately constructed universe, a place of systematic study schedules, two nights each week for beer, a girl or two, and early marriage; a framework infused with personality, warmth, and under control, no matter how unsatisfying otherwise . . .

The academic life contains reinforcing counterparts to the way in which extracurricular life is organized. The academic world is founded on a teacher-student relation analogous to the parent-child relation which characterizes *in loco parentis*. Further, academia includes a radical separation of the student from the material of study. That which is studied, the social reality, is "objectified" to sterility, dividing the student from life—just as he is restrained in active involvement by the deans controlling student government. The specialization of function and knowledge, admittedly necessary to our complex technological and social structure, has produced an exaggerated compartmentalization of study and understanding. This has contributed to an overly parochial view, by faculty, of the role of its research and scholarship, to a discontinuous and truncated understanding, by students, of the surrounding social order; and to a loss of personal attachment, by nearly all, to the worth of study as a humanistic enterprise.

There is, finally, the cumbersome academic bureaucracy extending throughout the academic as well as the extracurricular structures, contributing to the sense of outer complexity and inner powerlessness that transforms the honest searching of many students to a ratification of convention and, worse, to a numbness to present and future catastrophes. The size and financing systems of the university enhance the permanent trusteeship of the administrative bureaucracy, their power leading to a shift within the university toward the value standards of business and the administrative mentality. Huge foundations and other private financial interests shape the under-financed colleges and universities, not only making them more commercial, but less disposed to diagnose society critically, less open to dissent. Many social and physical scientists, neglecting the liberating heritage of higher learning, develop "human relations" or "morale-producing" techniques for the corporate economy, while others exercise their intellectual skills to accelerate the arms race.

/   /   /

35 | Letters to Home

In the summer of 1964, after nearly a decade of civil rights demonstrations, more than a thousand people, most of them white Northern college students, volunteered to go to Mississippi to help Afro-Americans register to vote, and to conduct "freedom schools." The Mississippi Summer Freedom Project was both a high point and nearly the end of the integrated, nonviolent civil rights movement of the 1950s and 1960s. It was a hard summer. One could consider this macabre "score": at least one black and two white civil rights workers were killed, not including an uncertain number of black Mississippians who died mysteriously; more than eighty were wounded; more than a thousand were arrested; thirty-five Afro-American churches were burned; and thirty homes and other buildings were bombed. Twelve hundred new Afro-American voters registered in the state.

National attention focused on the deaths of three young volunteers who were murdered in Philadelphia, Mississippi: James Chaney, Michael Schwerner, and Andrew Goodman. The letters below, from participants in the project (some supplied without attribution), testify to the intensity of the volunteers' experiences that summer.

Mileston, August 18

Dear folks,

One can't move onto a plantation cold; or canvas a plantation in the same manner as the Negro ghetto in town. It's far too dangerous. Many plantations—homes included—are posted, meaning that no trespassing is permitted, and the owner feels that he has the prerogative to shoot us on sight when we are in the house of one of *his* Negroes.

Before we canvas a plantation, our preparation includes finding out whether the houses are posted, driving through or around the plantation without stopping, meanwhile making a detailed map of the plantation.

We're especially concerned with the number of roads in and out of the plantation. For instance, some houses could be too dangerous to canvas because of their location near the boss man's house and on a dead end road.

In addition to mapping, we attempt to talk to some of the tenants when they are off the plantation, and ask them about conditions. The kids often have contacts, and can get on the plantation unnoticed by the boss man, with the pretense of just visiting friends.

Our canvassing includes not only voter registration, but also extensive reports on conditions—wages, treatment by the boss man, condition of the houses, number of acres of cotton, etc. Much more such work needs to be done. The plantation system is crucial in Delta politics and economics, and the plantation system must be brought to an end if democracy is to be brought to the Delta. . . .

Love,
Joel

July 18

. . . Four of us went to distribute flyers announcing the meeting. I talked to a woman who had been down to register a week before. She was afraid. Her husband had lost his job. Even before we got there a couple of her sons had been man-handled by the police. She was now full of wild rumors about shootings and beatings, etc. I checked out two of them later. They were groundless. This sort of rumorspreading is quite prevalent when people get really scared. . . .

At 6 P.M. we returned to Drew for the meeting, to be held in front of a church (they wouldn't let us meet inside, but hadn't told us not to meet outside). A number of kids collected and stood around in a circle with about 15 of us to sing freedom songs. Across the street perhaps 100 adults stood watching. Since this was the first meeting in town, we passed out mimeoed song sheets. Fred Miller, Negro from Mobile, stepped out to the edge of the street to give somebody a sheet. The cops nabbed him. I was about to follow suit so he wouldn't be alone, but Mac's policy [Charles McLaurin, SNCC—a civil rights group—project director] was to ignore the arrest. We sang on mightily "Ain't going to let no jailing turn me around." A group of girls was sort of leaning against the cars on the periphery of the meeting. Mac went over to encourage them to join us. I gave a couple of song sheets to the girls. A cop rushed across the street and told me to come along. I guess I was sort of aware that my actions would get me arrested, but felt that we had to show these girls that we were not afraid. I was also concerned with what might happen to Fred if he was the only one.

. . . The cop at the station was quite scrupulous about letting me make a phone call. I was then driven to a little concrete structure which looked like a power house. I could hear Fred's courageous, off-key rendition of a freedom song from inside and joined him as we approached. He was very happy to see me. Not long thereafter, four more of our group were driven up to make their calls . . .

The Drew jail consists of three small cells off a wide hall. It was filthy, hot and stuffy. A cop came back to give us some toilet paper. We sang songs for a while, and yelled greetings to Negroes who drove by curiously. One of the staff workers had been in jail 106 times. I asked the cop if he could open another cell as there were not enough beds accessible to us. He mumbled something about how that would be impossible and left. They hadn't confiscated anything and one of the guys had a battered copy of *The Other America*, so we divided up the chapters. I got the dismal one on the problems of the aged ... To be old and forgotten is certainly a worse sentence than mine (I wouldn't recommend that book for those planning to do time) ...

Well, the night was spent swatting mosquitoes. An old Negro couple walked by in front of the jail and asked how we were doing. They said they supported us and the old lady said, "God bless you all." This, in the context of a tense town with a pretty constant stream of whites in cars driving by. . . .

Holly Spring

Dear Mom and Dad:

The atmosphere in class is unbelievable. It is what every teacher dreams about—real, honest enthusiasm and desire to learn anything and everything. The girls come to class of their own free will. They respond to everything that is said. They are excited about learning. They drain me of everything that I have to offer so that I go home at night completely exhausted but very happy. . . .

I start out at 10:30 teaching what we call the Core Curriculum, which is Negro History and the History and Philosophy of the Movement, to about fifteen girls ranging from 15 to 25 years of age. I have one girl who is married with four children, another who is 23 and a graduate from a white college in Tennessee, also very poorly educated. The majority go to a Roman Catholic High School in Holly Springs and have therefore received a fairly decent education by Mississippi standards. They can, for the most part, express themselves on paper but their skills in no way compare to juniors and seniors in northern suburban schools.

In one of my first classes, I gave a talk on Haiti and the slave revolt which took place at the end of the eighteenth century. I told them how the French government (during the French Revolution) abolished slavery all over the French Empire. And then I told them that the English decided to invade the island and take it over for a colony of their own. I watched faces fall all around me. They knew that a small island, run by former slaves, could not defeat England. And then I told them that the people of Haiti succeeded in keeping the English out. I watched a smile spread slowly over a girl's face. And I felt the girls sit up and look at me intently. Then I told them that Napoleon came to power, reinstated slavery, and sent an expedition to reconquer Haiti. Their faces began to fall again. They waited for me to tell them that France defeated the former slaves, hoping against hope that I would say that they didn't. But when I told them that the French generals tricked the Haitian leader Toussaint to come aboard their ship, captured him and sent him back to France to die, they knew that there was no hope. They waited for me to spell out the defeat. And when I told them that Haiti did succeed in keeping out the European powers and was recognized finally as an independent republic, they just looked at me and smiled. The room stirred with a gladness and a pride that this could have happened. And I felt so happy and so humble that I could have told them this little story and it could have meant so much.

We have also talked about what it means to be a Southern white who wants to stand up but who is alone, rejected by other whites and not fully accepted by the Negroes. We have talked about their feelings about Southern whites. One day three little white girls came to our school and I asked them to understand how the three girls felt by remembering how it feels when they are around a lot of whites. We agreed that we would not stare at the girls but try to make them feel as normal as possible.

Along with my Core class I teach a religion class at one every afternoon and a class on non-violence at four-fifteen. All my classes are approximately an hour. Both these classes are made up of four to six girls from my morning class and about four boys of the same age group. In religion they are being confronted for the first time with people whom they respect who do not believe in God and with people who believe in God but do not take the Bible literally. It's a challenging class because I have no desire to destroy their belief, whether Roman Catholic or Baptist, but I want them to learn to look at all things critically and to learn to separate fact from interpretation and myth in all areas, not just religion.

Every class is beautiful. The girls respond, respond, respond. And they disagree among themselves. I have no doubt that soon they will be disagreeing with me. At least this one thing that I am working towards. They are a sharp group. But they are under-educated and starved for knowledge. They know that they have been cheated and they want anything and everything that we can give them.

I have a great deal of faith in these students. They are very mature and very concerned about other people. I really think that they will be able to carry on without us. At least this is my dream . . .

Love,
Pam

Indianola, August 17

I can see the change. The 16-year-old's discovery of poetry, of Whitman and Cummings and above all, the struggle to express thoughts in words, to translate ideas into concrete written words. After two weeks a child finally looks me in the eye, unafraid, acknowledging a bond of trust which 300 years of Mississippians said should never, could never exist. I can feel the growth of self-confidence . . .

Biloxi, Aug. 16

In the Freedom School one day during poetry writing, a 12-year-old girl handed in this poem to her teacher:

What Is Wrong?

What is wrong with me everywhere I go
    No one seems to look at me.
Sometimes I cry.

I walk through woods and sit on a stone.
    I look at the stars and I sometimes wish.

Probably if my wish ever comes true,
    Everyone will look at me.

Then she broke down crying in her sister's arms. The Freedom School here had given this girl the opportunity of meeting someone she felt she could express her problems to . . .

Ruleville

To my brother,

Last night, I was a long time before sleeping, although I was extremely tired. Every shadow, every noise—the bark of a dog, the sound of a car—in my fear and exhaustion was turned into a terrorist's approach. And I believed that I heard the back door open and a Klansman walk in, until he was close by the bed. Almost paralyzed by the fear, silent, I finally shone my flashlight on the spot where I thought he was standing . . . I tried consciously to overcome this fear. To relax, I began to breathe deep, think the words of a song, pull the sheet up close to my neck . . . still the tension. Then I rethought why I was here, rethought what could be gained in view of what could be lost. All this was in rather personal terms, and then in larger scope of the whole Project. I remembered Bob Moses saying he had felt justified in asking hundreds of students to go to Mississippi because he was not asking anyone to do something that he would not do . . . I became aware of the uselessness of fear that immobilizes an individual. Then I began to relax.

"We are not afraid. Oh Lord, deep in my heart, I do believe. We Shall Overcome Someday" and then I think I began to truly understand what the words meant. Anyone who comes down here and is not afraid I think must be crazy as well as dangerous to this project where security is quite important. But the type of fear that they mean when they, when we, sing "we are not afraid" is the type that immobilizes. . . . The songs help to dissipate the fear. Some of the words in the songs do not hold real meaning on their own, others become rather monotonous — but when they are sung in unison, or sung silently by oneself, they take on new meaning beyond words or rhythm . . . There is almost a religious quality about some of these songs, having little to do with the usual concept of a god. It has to do with the miracle that youth has organized to fight hatred and ignorance. It has to do with the holiness of the dignity of man. The god that makes such miracles is the god I do believe in when we sing "God is on our side." I know I am on that god's side. And I do hope he is on ours.

Jon, please be considerate to Mom and Dad. The fear I just expressed, I am sure they feel much more intensely without the relief of being here to know exactly how things are. Please don't go defending me or attacking them if they are critical of the Project. . . .

They said over the phone "Did you know how much it takes to make a child?" and I thought of how much it took to make a Herbert Lee (or many others whose names I do not know) . . . I thought of how much it took to be a Negro in Mississippi twelve months a year for a lifetime. How can such a thing as a life be weighed? . . .

With constant love,
Heather

Greenwood, June 29

We have heard rumors twice to the effect that the three men were found weighted down in that river. Both stories, though the same, were later completely dropped in an hour or so. How do you like that guy Gov. Johnson saying that they might be hiding in the North or maybe in Cuba for all he knew . . .

Tchula, July 16

Yesterday while the Mississippi River was being dragged looking for the three missing civil rights workers, two bodies of Negroes were found — — — one cut in half and one without a head. Mississippi is the only state where you can drag a river any time and find bodies you were not expecting. Things are really much better for rabbits — there's a closed season on rabbits.

Como, August 3

About three weeks ago there was a flying rumor that they had been found in a rural jail. Tonight it was said that three graves had been found near Philadelphia. How the ghosts of those three shadow all our work! "Did you know them?" I am constantly asked. Did I need to?

/   /   /

Meridian, August 4

Last night Pete Seeger was giving a concert in Meridian. We sang a
lot of freedom songs, and every time a verse like 'No more lynchings'
was sung, or 'before I'd be a slave I'd be buried in my grave,' I had
the flash of understanding that sometimes comes when you suddenly
think about the meaning of a familiar song . . . I wanted to stand up and
shout to them, "Think about what you are singing—people really have
died to keep us all from being slaves." Most of the people there still
did not know that the bodies had been found. Finally just before the
singing of "We Shall Overcome," Pete Seeger made the announcement.
"We must sing 'We Shall Overcome' now," said Seeger. "The three boys
would not have wanted us to weep now, but to sing and understand
this song." That seems to me the best way to explain the greatness of
this project—that death can have this meaning. Dying is not an ever-
present possibility in Meridian, the way some reports may suggest. Nor
do any of us want to die. Yet in a moment like last night, we can feel
that anyone who did die for the Project would wish to be remembered
not by tributes or grief but by understanding and continuation of what
he was doing . . .

As we left the church, we heard on the radio the end of President
Johnson's speech announcing the air attacks on Vietnam . . . I could only
think "This must not be the beginning of a war. There is still a freedom
fight, and we are winning. We must have time to live and help Mississippi to be alive." Half an hour before, I had understood death in a new
way. Now I realized that Mississippi, in spite of itself, has given real
meaning to life. In Mississippi you never ask, "What is the meaning of
life?" or "Is there any point to it all?" but only that we may have enough
life to do all that there is to be done. . . .

Meridian, August 5

At the Freedom school and at the community center, many of the
kids had known Mickey and almost all knew Jimmy Chaney. Today we
asked the kids to describe Mickey and Jimmy because we had never
known them.

"Mickey was a big guy. He wore blue jeans all the time" . . . I asked
the kids, "What did his eyes look like?" and they told me they were
"friendly eyes" "nice eyes" ("nice" is a lovely word in a Mississippi
accent). "Mickey was a man who was at home everywhere and with
anybody," said the 17-year-old girl I stay with. The littlest kids, the 6,
7, 8 years olds, tell about how he played "Frankenstein" with them or
took them for drives or talked with them about Freedom. Many of the
teen-age boys were delinquents until Mickey went down to the bars
and jails and showed them that one person at least would respect them
if they began to fight for something important . . . And the grownups
too, trusted him. The lady I stay with tells with pride of how Mickey
and Rita came to supper at their house, and police cars circled around

the house all during the meal. But Mickey could make them feel glad to take the risk.

People talk less about James Chaney here, but feel more. The kids describe a boy who played with them—whom everyone respected but who never had to join in fights to maintain this respect—a quiet boy but very sharp and very understanding when he did speak. Mostly we know James through his sisters and especially his 12-year-old brother, Ben. Today Ben was in the Freedom School. At lunchtime the kids have a jazz band (piano, washtub bass, cardboard boxes and bongos as drums) and tiny Ben was there leading all even with his broken arm, with so much energy and rhythm that even Senator Eastland would have had to stop and listen if he'd been walking by. . . .

/ / /

Meridian, August 8

. . . The service was preceded by several silent marches beginning at churches throughout Meridian and converging on the First Union Baptist Church. I have been on a large number of walks, marches, vigils, pickets, etc., in my life, but I can't remember anything which was quite like this one. In the first place, it was completely silent (at least, the march I was on), even though it lasted over 50 minutes, and even though there were a fair number of children involved. . . .

Meridian, August 11

. . . In the line I was in, there were about 150 people—white and Negro—walking solemnly, quietly, and without incident for about a mile and half through white and Negro neighborhoods (segregation is like a checkerboard here). The police held up traffic at the stoplights, and of all the white people watching only one girl heckled. I dislike remembering the service—the photographers with their television cameras were omnipresent, it was really bad. And cameras when people are crying . . . and bright lights. Someone said it was on television later. I suppose it was.

Dave Dennis spoke—it was as if he was realizing his anger and feeling only as he spoke. As if the deepest emotion—the bitterness, then hatred—came as he expressed it, and could not have been planned or forethought . . .

Laurel, August 11

Dear Folks,

. . . The memorial service began around 7:30 with over 120 people filling the small, wooden-pew lined church. David Dennis of CORE [a civil rights group], the Assistant Director for the Mississippi Summer Project, spoke for COFO [an amalgam of civil rights organizations]. He talked to the Negro people of Meridian—it was a speech to move people, to end the lethargy, to make people stand up. It went something like this:

"I am not here to memorialize James Chaney, I am not here to pay tribute—I am too sick and tired. Do YOU hear me, I am S-I-C-K and T-I-R-E-D. I have attended too many memorials, too many funerals. This has got to stop. Mack Parker, Medgar Evers, Herbert Lee, Lewis Allen, Emmett Till, four little girls in Birmingham, a 13-year old boy in Birmingham, and the list goes on and on. I have attended these funerals and memorials and I am SICK and TIRED. But the trouble is that YOU are NOT sick and tired and for that reason YOU, yes YOU, are to blame. Everyone of your damn souls. And if you are going to let this continue now then you are to blame, yes YOU. Just as much as the monsters of hate who pulled the trigger or brought down the club; just as much to blame as the sheriff and the chief of police, as the governor in Jackson who said that he 'did not have time' for Mrs. Schwerner when she went to see him, and just as much to blame as the President and Attorney General in Washington who wouldn't provide protection for Chaney, Goodman and Schwerner when we told them that protection was necessary in Neshoba County... Yes, I am angry, I AM. And it's high time that you got angry too, angry enough to go up to the courthouse Monday and register—everyone of you. Angry enough to take five and then other people with you. Then and only then can these brutal killings be stopped. Remember it is your sons and your daughters who have been killed all these years and you have done nothing about it, and if you don't do nothing NOW baby, I say God Damn Your Souls. . . ."

Mileston, August 9

Dear Blake,

. . . Dave finally broke down and couldn't finish and the Chaney family was moaning and much of the audience and I were also crying. It's such an impossible thing to describe but suddenly again, as I'd first realized when I heard the three men were missing when we were still training up at Oxford [Ohio], I felt the sacrifice the Negroes have been making for so long. How the Negro people are able to accept all the abuses of the whites—all the insults and injustices which make me ashamed to be white—and then turn around and say they want to love us, is beyond me. There are Negros who want to kill whites and many Negros have much bitterness but still the majority seem to have the quality of being able to look for a future in which whites will love the Negroes. Our kids talk very critically of all the whites around here and still they have a dream of freedom in which both races understand and accept each other. There is such an overpowering task ahead of these kids that sometimes I can't do anything but cry for them. I hope they are up to the task, I'm not sure I would be if I were a Mississippi Negro. As a white northerner I can get involved whenever I feel like it and run home whenever I get bored or frustrated or scared. I hate the attitude and position of the Northern whites and despise myself when I think that way. Lately I've been feeling homesick and longing for pleasant old Westport and sailing and swimming and my friends. I don't quite know what to do because I can't ignore my desire to go home and yet I feel I am a much weaker person than I like to think I am because I do have these emotions. I've always tried to avoid situations which aren't so nice, like arguments and dirty houses and now maybe Mississippi. I asked my father if I could stay down here for a whole year and I was almost glad when he said "no" that we couldn't afford it because it would mean supporting me this year in addition to three more years of college. I have a desire to go home and to read a lot and go to Quaker meetings and be by myself so I can think about all this rather than being in the middle of it all the time. But I know if my emotions run like they have in the past, that I can only take that pacific sort of life for a little while and then I get the desire to be active again and get involved with knowing other people. I guess this all sounds crazy and I seem to always think out my problems as I write to you. I am angry because I have a choice as to whether or not to work in the Movement and I am playing upon that choice and leaving here. I wish I could talk with you 'cause I'd like to know if you ever felt this way about anything. I mean have you ever despised yourself for your weak conviction or something. And what is making it worse is that all those damn northerners are thinking of me as a brave hero. . . .

Martha

36 | The War in Vietnam

The war in Vietnam was the first war to be broadcast on television into American homes. Constant exposure to the details of the war did not, however, translate into enduring public support for American participation. The justification of the war on grounds other than that of an immediate threat to American security, the strangeness of its setting, and the scope of its violence (its extensive involvement of children and civilians) made the war in Vietnam a particularly disquieting event in the nation's history.

The Americans for whom the Vietnam war was a most personal experience are, of course, those who fought in overseas combat. The readings that follow are from two soldiers: Dave Baker, an Army volunteer, who patrolled a Vietnamese village with a "killer" guard dog; and Clarence Fitch, an Afro-American Marine, who before and after the war maintained an interest in civil rights.

Baker's testimony is an account common to many soldiers who went to Vietnam and faced gradual disillusionment with the American mission in the war. It also documents the pain faced by a soldier who risked his life overseas and returned to a country that treated him as an outcast or a criminal.

It has long been stated that Vietnam was not a war in which all Americans shared the risks of the nation's involvement. Deferments, disqualifications for combat, and alternative service, it has been argued, meant that those most likely to serve overseas were those who were poor, politically unconnected, or black. Fitch's testimony does not directly address questions about the fairness of the draft, but it does argue that Afro-Americans faced the greatest danger of being killed in action (KIA). It also demonstrates that those who fought in Vietnam did not do so in isolation from the greater social discord of the 1960s.

DAVE BAKER

All my life I have hunted. I go deer hunting and I get maybe five or six a year. When I was little, it was squirrels. I think I was twelve years old when my father gave me my first gun. We had about six acres, and behind that there was land that you could hunt and I really enjoyed it.

My father always told me, "If you kill it, you eat it. If you don't want to eat it, don't kill it." Nothing was just shot and dropped on the ground.

When the Vietnam War was going on I thought there was a real need for us, and I wanted to sign up. A bunch of friends of mine, five of us who all went to high school together, were going to join the Marines. We were going to go in at the same time, but by the time I got done with my chores at home, some lawn work and stuff like that, I didn't get down until after they were there. They'd already signed up in the Marines, and the Marine Corps recruiter took them out to lunch.

I started to walk out of the Marine recruiting office, because there was no one there, and this Army sergeant said, "Who are you looking for?" I explained to him what it was, and he said, "Well, why do you want to go in the Marines? Let me show you what the Army has," Then I took this test, and it turned out I had high enough marks that I could do anything I wanted to. He said, "Well, you get your choice," I remembered a guy I'd met who'd been a dog handler in the Army, and I said, "Can I get to be a dog handler?" And he arranged it, and that's what I got into. You had to be a volunteer for dog handler, and you knew that if you went in, you were going to Vietnam. But that's what I wanted to do.

/   /   /

The dogs are trained to be hateful against human beings, really aggressive. I think if the ASPCA ever found out what you did, they'd be at the government's door so fast. . . . Those dogs are hung by the tail, beaten with barbed wires, their ears are sliced with razor blades. Of course, you don't do it to your own dog, okay? Because then they'll hate you. When you go through the course, there's twenty people altogether. Ten people will tie the dogs up, and they'll be agitators for the ten that are holding their dogs. I'll be hitting someone else's dog with barbed wire, and he'll be hitting mine.

Instructors come by and zip the dogs' ears with razor blades. They know just what to do not to go too far. And they switch them and beat them. You want to stop them, but you don't, because you know that the meaner your dog gets, the better the chance of you staying alive when you get over to Vietnam. So you let it happen, because you want to come out of there with the best poodle to keep you alive and do your job. It's like a weapon. Do you want a piece of junk that jams, or do you want something that really works good? My dog was a really good dog—a very, very aggressive dog.

/   /   /

The village I was sent to in Vietnam had been built earlier by the French and had a few cement buildings, but the majority of it was just sticks with tin roofs. When people went to the bathroom, they just came out and did it in the street. It stunk, it stunk. And on a hot day it *really* stunk. But you got so used to it that it was, after a while, you know, like being home. I mean, you know, it was just a normal thing.

Walking down the street any day you'd see two or three kids with elephantiasis—like a pretty little girl with a leg blown up using two sticks to walk with, and she's pulling the worms out of her. And there's nothing you can do to fix her, either. You think to yourself, Oh my God, what should I do? Shoot her and put an end to all her misery or what? If you felt sorry for everybody you saw in that village there, you'd be a blabbering slob by the time you got to the end.

The dog handler's job was to patrol the bush outside the village at night to make sure none of the VC [Viet Cong] could sneak up on us. There were tunnels around our unit, and the VC would use them to get close to the fence. Then they'd come up and get through the fence and get to our main communications center. Tried to blow it up a number of times.

/   /   /

In the village I was in and in the villages around, there were just local VC. They'd have maybe two or three bullets allotted to them to shoot for the night, and they'd come out with their single-shot rifles and go *blinkety-blink*. About every two weeks or so, they'd put on a mortar attack, but primarily it was just snipers. You always had to watch your back, because there was no front line there, and you had women and kids as warriors, too, and you really didn't know who was trustworthy and who wasn't. It was all a battlefield.

There'd be accidents, bad accidents. In one village that I had to go through, the kids would play a game: They would try to touch the killer dogs. If they could touch a killer dog, they were big heroes. But this wasn't known to me when I first got there. A lot of the old-timers don't tell you all the tricks of the trade, you know. So I knew nothing of this game of the kids. One night I was working, cutting through the side of the village, and I'm looking into a shack over there and I see a bunch of eyes. I didn't know whose they were. I just figured to myself, Jesus, somebody in there is going to shoot me just when I get to the right spot.

I had my gun on my side with my hand on it, and my dog was pulling ahead real hard, but I wasn't paying too much attention to him. I was looking at those eyes as I walked. And I was on the ready, because if I saw anything that looked wrong, I was going to start shooting. What I didn't know was that those eyes were all little kids watching their buddy, who had dug a ditch and hidden himself under some weeds right by the path. When I came by, he was going to jump up, touch my dog, and then take off, and he would be a hero. And they were watching for him to do it. So as I went by, he jumped up, touched my dog, and my dog took his head off instantly. [*Sharp snap of fingers.*] Just popped it like that. You know, some of these Vietnam people are very,

very thin, especially the young kids. The neck was like a dog bone to him.

I didn't know what to do. I mean, I'm standing there—the head's sitting over there, spitting and gurgling. Oooooh. . . . I get goose bumps now just thinking about it. It was a real ripper for me. I pulled the dog back quick, and I looked this way and that way, and the kid's mother was coming after me. She had something in her hand, and I thought, "It's a grenade. It's cocked. I'm in real trouble now." So I had to pack her down. I shot her. We can't take a gamble, you know. I just blasted her, and I kept shooting as I backed out.

When I got back to my base, they sent an alert out to see what went on, and it turned out she just had a rock in her hand, but I didn't know that. I just thought, She's going to get me, and I'm going to blast her. . . . That was a rough one.

And, you know, it stays with you. When you're that close to them, and you see it happen—it's not like when you're in the dark, and you're shooting, and the next day you hear that somebody fell down dead. Here, you're with them, and you see it, and it stays with you. I imagine a lot of guys who were there don't mention things like that to anybody. They keep it in, because it's hurting them, and it hurts them to keep it in, too.

/   /   /

I got back to the United States in '68 and there was a lot of antiwar movement going on. It hadn't been like that when I left, so I wasn't expecting it. I got off at Kennedy Airport, and I didn't have any money in my pocket because I'd spent it all on my airplane ticket. So I thought, "Oh, well, I'll go out and hitchhike." I thought that in the uniform, you know, they'd pick me up right away. But no one would touch me. You were the kiss of death in a uniform. So I walked and walked. It took me from early in the morning until late at night to get home. I got a few rides, but most of the time I was walking. One time a fellow I knew came by. I'd been to school with him, and he'd been in one of my classes. He came up and slowed his car and looked at me, called me by my name and everything, but when he saw the uniform, he just [cursed] and drove away and left me there. And I thought to myself, Boy, some howdy-do this is.

When I got into my hometown, they were burning the American flag at the monument in front of the police station. One of the cops saw me and saw the medals on my uniform and ran down the street and grabbed me and brought me away. He said, "Dave, you don't want to see what's going on here. You don't want to see it." He told me, "The kids don't really know what's going on. It's not aimed directly at you." And, of course, I understood it wasn't, okay? So I went on my way.

When I was about a mile away from home, my next-door neighbor drove by. She slowed down and looked at me, and then *zoom*, she took off. I was tired as hell, you know, walking all this way and carrying a big duffel bag, but she took right off and left me. And this was a lady I'd shoveled the driveway for when it snowed. I was really pissed. Everybody had this stereotype of a Vietnam veteran coming home either a murderer or a cuckoo.

Why did they shun me? I went to do what they wanted to be done, and now, all of a sudden, they change their mind, and they don't want what is being done to be done, and it's my fault. . . .

I didn't feel like getting a job right away when I came back, so I went out to the California, rented a house on the beach, and drank all night and slept all day. I wasn't ready for anything else yet. People back home bothered me. You'd hear them complain about the silliest little thing, like "It's too hot," if it's ninety-two degrees and a little humid. Think about 130 degrees for three or four months at a time, and ninety-eight in the shade. That's tough.

They would complain about everything. There was a water shortage on, and they were complaining about maybe only taking a bath every two days, or a shower just once a day . . . over there we were lucky if we got to take a shower every two weeks or a month. And during the monsoon season, we would go through a month wearing the same clothes, until they rotted off. You couldn't wash, you couldn't change your clothes, it was pouring rain, everything was wet and mucky. And here people complain, "Oooh, it's raining out." Tough, Get an umbrella. Live with it. I just hated people in general. I don't know why. I just hated everybody.

My mother said a different person came back than what went over to Vietnam, different as night and day, and it changed me, no question about it. When my father died, it seemed I could care less, you know. I was standing right there, my mother was crying, and my brother and everybody else was crying, and I could only see that he was dead. Big deal, you know, I've seen that before. What's next?

/   /   /

I have a very thick wall around me now. I don't let anyone come too close. They know a little bit about me, but nobody knows the inside me. I have a girlfriend living with me now. She's been with me for four years, but I don't even let her come that close. I think being over there made me very cold to people.

And yet, you know, I'd go back today to Vietnam if the people wanted help, and we could help them. Because that's what I thought we were going for in the beginning. I would like to give them a good staple food. So much of the inland water has been ruined there, because of the bombing and defoliation, and a lot of the areas where they were raising fish before are history. I'd like to do that, give something to the people. That was supposed to be the reason we were there anyway. I felt cheated after the war, that what the government said we were going over for we weren't doing.

/   /   /

You know, my sport is to kill. And when I go hunting or fishing now, I can't eat all the stuff I get, so I put it in plastic baggies, and I give it away to my Vietnamese friends here. I might get five or six deer a year, and they can't afford to go hunting, so I give them the meat. I stop off at their houses, and I give it to them. And if I go fishing for bluefish, I'll come back with maybe thirty bluefish, and I'll give it to them. Not for thanks, or to make my head swell, you know, but just to see a smile on their faces.

Am I doing it because of what I did over there? Making up for it in my own noodle? It's nothing that I think about. Maybe subconsciously there is something in there telling me to do it, because of what I did over there. Who the hell knows?

CLARENCE FITCH

We weren't living in no vacuum in Vietnam. There was a certain growing black consciousness that was happening in the States, and also over there in Vietnam. People was aware of what was going on. One of the characteristics of this war was that people didn't come over there together. People just had tours of duty, and so every day somebody was going home and you had somebody coming from home, bringing information. And guys that would leave Vietnam would send stuff back. You know, "Okay, send us all the *Ebonys* and *Jets* and black publications you can get your hands on." Like I sent stuff when I got back to guys I left over there.

The militancy really grew after Martin Luther King got killed in '68. It made black people really angry. You remember the riots after Dr. King's death was some of the fiercest, and the brothers took that up in Vietnam. People changed after that. People were saying it doesn't pay to be nonviolent and benevolent. There were a lot of staff NCOs, the type of so-called Negro that would be telling you to be patient, just do your job, pull yourself up by the bootstraps. So we called them Uncle Toms and that was that. People were saying, "I'm black and I'm proud. I'm not going to be no Uncle Tom."

There was a whole Black Power thing. There was Black Power salutes and handshakes and Afros and beads. It was a whole atmosphere. All that was a way of showing our camaraderie, like brothers really hanging together. When a new brother came into the unit, we used to really reach out for the guy, show him the ropes and tell him what's happening. It was like a togetherness that I ain't never seen since.

I think people really listened to Martin Luther King. We didn't hear his speech about Vietnam until much later, but somehow or another we got a copy of the speech, and we was really impressed. He talked about how blacks were dying in Vietnam at a greater rate, and he was the first person we really ever heard say that, even though it was something we knew.

We saw what was going on. I was there for the Tet Offensive of '68, and I was at this aid station. The place was always getting hit, and I got wounded there. It was like ten miles from the DMZ. I saw a lot of blood and a lot of death, and we would be bumping stretchers for all the casualties from all the units operating in the area.

It would still be more Caucasian bodies coming back than black bodies, but what Dr. King said was that blacks was at the time ten percent of the population and thirty percent of the KIAs. It was like more white guys was in the rear with the easy jobs. They were driving trucks and working in the PX and . . . we're out there in the bush, and that's why we was dying. A lot of the line companies over there were mostly black. There were white grunts, too, assigned to infantry units, but there was a *lot* of black grunts.

And then, as jobs became available in the rear, they would pull people back for jobs like company driver, stuff like that. You know, after so much time in the field, they pull you back to rear-area jobs. And we wasn't getting pulled that easy to the rear. Black guys were staying their whole tour in the field. You just looked around you and said, "Well, they're just using us as cannon fodder."

/   /   /

A lot of blacks fought valiantly at points, but a lot of them didn't see the sense dying in this war. It was more honorable to go to jail. People were refusing to go to the field anymore, just refusing and getting locked up. This was a hell of a thing to do, because brig time didn't count on your tour in Vietnam. They called it "bad time." You did your six months in jail, and then you still had to serve your time in the field. But guys did it. Guys were sitting in the Marine brig for long periods of time. I guess they were hoping the war would just end while they're sitting in jail. . . .

/   /   /

There were people that would go so far as to hurt themselves enough to get out of going into the bush. I seen people shoot themselves in the arm or the foot or the legs to get one of those Stateside wounds. I seen people fake injuries. I had this friend of mine, a brother from Birmingham, Alabama, he broke his ankle three different times to stay in the rear. Every time they took the cast off, he would get a hammer and whack it again, and it would swell up, and they'd put another cast on it. He'd be in the rear playing cards for another month or two, and then they would take the cast off, and he couldn't walk. He would play it right out to the max.

The powers that be knew it, but they couldn't prove it. He caught a lot of flak. They would call him a traitor and all this crap. And he said,

"Well. . . . I'm not going out there." And that's the way it went down until his rotation date. It wasn't like World War II, where you stayed for the duration. You did have a date, and the thing was to survive until that date and that's what people did. The other brothers supported him.

We didn't put him down or ridicule him. We respected him. We knew we was dying at a higher rate, so we felt very much justified not to add to this . . . figure.

There were fragging incidents for the same reason. It didn't happen every day, but after a while it got to be an unwritten rule. A lot of times you get these boot-camp second lieutenants, just out of Quantico, the officer training school, no field experience, and they just give them a platoon. The smart ones would come over and take suggestions, use their NCOs and squad leaders—guys that have been in the bush six, seven, eight months and really know what's going on—to show them until they get the ropes. But you get these guys that want to come over with schoolbook tactics, and they might want to do something that's detrimental to the company. Then you're talking about people's lives. Well, hey, the first firefight you get in, somebody takes him out. "Killed in action."

I seen one fragging incident up close: a new lieutenant, fresh out of Quantico. He was an asshole, very gung-ho. He would run patrols and set up ambushes, and he wasn't very careful. He took a lot of chances, and people didn't like it. They were trying to take him out, but they didn't get in the right kind of firefight that they could fire on him.

One night we were stationed on this bridge to keep Charlie from blowing the bridge up, and I was on radio, monitoring communications. About four or five in the morning, just before dawn, I seen this brother come out with this hand grenade, and he said, "Hey, Fitch, don't say nothing, man." The lieutenant's bunker was maybe ten yards from the bridge, and this guy went over, pulled the pin on the grenade, held it for a couple of seconds, and rolled it into the bunker. I said, "Oh, shit. I don't want to see this."

Then I heard *boom*, and the lieutenant came staggering out of the bunker. They got a medevac helicopter and medevacked him out of there. He was hurt pretty bad, but he survived it. Went back to the States, I guess . . .

/   /   /

I saw a lot of craziness there. In retrospect, the reason I think so much of it happened was that everyone was just living a violent way of life. It was a world where everyone carried a gun and had access to all the ammunition they wanted. There would be fights between GIs that might begin over a card game, and one guy would just pull out a rifle and slap in a a magazine and say, "I'm going to lock and load on you." I think this must be the way it was in the Wild West when everyone carried a gun.

I left Vietnam in January '69, came home, and got stationed in Camp Lejeune, North Carolina. It was all Vietnam vets there, and people just wasn't into that Stateside regimentation no more. People were tired of the whole military scene. There was a lot of discipline problems. It was pretty hard to keep up haircut regulations in Vietnam, and some brothers hadn't had haircuts in a year. When we returned, they wanted you to get a military haircut. I think Marine Corps regulations said your hair can't be longer than three inches. For a white guy, if his hair is longer than three inches, it looks like a lot of hair. Very seldom does an Afro go higher than three inches, but they still wanted to make us get a haircut. So it was a lot of struggle around the Afros.

/   /   /

It was a pretty nasty time between blacks and whites. Blacks tended to stick together in groups, and there were whites going the other extreme. There were Ku Klux Klan chapters. I was glad I was getting out, because things really got bad. Any small disagreements would be blown out of proportion. I remember these rednecks started a fight because a black guy was dancing with a white girl. Then other guys jumped in, and somebody got stabbed and killed. There were riots.

The media got ahold of it, and I remember the Commandant of the Marine Corps getting on television and making this big announcement that Marines would be able to wear Afro haircuts, that there would be more black music on the jukebox in the enlisted clubs.

But they were still disciplining . . . people, and a lot of black people got really hurt. People got in a lot of trouble, trouble that they're probably going to have to live with the rest of their lives. The facts show that blacks got bad discharges—dishonorable or bad conduct or undesirable—that are proportionately higher than white GIs. Guys were getting kicked out of the service left and right and not really caring, because when you're young you tend to live for the day. Since then all that bad paper is coming back to haunt people, because now, if the employer knows, it can hurt you.

GLORIA STEINEM AND
MARGARET HECKLER

37 | Testimony in Favor of the ERA

*In recent decades, there has been a growing awareness that women do not share
equally with men the rewards that American society has to offer. Indeed, some
feminists go further and maintain that American women—although comprising
a majority of the population—are treated like a persecuted ethnic or racial minority. The current revival of the movement for women's rights in the United
States may be said to have begun with the publication of Betty Friedan's* The
Feminine Mystique *in 1963. It marked a turnaround after a period of about
forty years during which the gains of an earlier feminist movement had been
trivialized by a seemingly unquestioned consensus that women's proper roles
were mother, homemaker, teacher, or nurse.*

*In fact, by the 1960s the percentage of women working outside the home in
"nontraditional" occupations had been increasing for several decades—however,
these women worked for substandard wages. Thus, with so many other groups
re-evaluating their places in American society in the 1960s, a revival of feminism
was inevitable. It is quite possible that the women's movement may turn out to
be the most permanent and sustained of all manifestations of cultural radicalism
of recent years, the one that has the largest impact on American values and that
has the greatest likelihood of continuing to change the way the nation lives.*

*The following excerpts are from hearings held in 1970 by a committee of the
U. S. Senate to consider the proposed Equal Rights Amendment (ERA) to the
Constitution. Although passed by Congress, the ERA was not ratified by the
required three-fourths of the states and did not go into effect. Some opponents of
the ERA argued that it would force on the nation a social revolution for which it
was ill-prepared and which it did not desire. More moderate opponents argued
that existing legal statutes protected women in the workplace.*

*The response to the first argument has been that there is no explicit or
implicit language in the ERA calling for a legally mandated reorganization of
male and female roles in society. To the second argument the response has been
that differences in pay between men and women performing similar jobs persist,
despite general antidiscrimination laws. Supporters of the ERA maintain that,
in any event, preexisting legislation is no reason in itself to deny women a
constitutional reaffirmation of their full rights as human beings.*

From "The Equal Rights" Amendment: Hearings Before the Subcommittee on Constitutional Amendments of the Committee on the Judiciary of the United States Senate, *91st
Congress, May 5, 6, and 7, 1970 (Washington, D.C., Government Printing Office, 1970) pp.
331–335, 38–41. 575–578.*

STATEMENT OF GLORIA STEINEM, WRITER AND CRITIC

My name is Gloria Steinem. I am a writer and editor, and I am currently a member of the policy council of the Democratic committee. And I work regularly with the lowest-paid workers in the country, the migrant workers, men, women, and children both in California and in my own State of New York.

/   /   /

During 12 years of working for a living, I have experienced much of the legal and social discrimination reserved for women in this country. I have been refused service in public restaurants, ordered out of public gathering places, and turned away from apartment rentals; all for the clearly-stated, sole reason that I am a woman. And all without the legal remedies available to blacks and other minorities. I have been excluded from professional groups, writing assignments on so-called "unfeminine" subjects such as politics, full participation in the Democratic Party, jury duty, and even from such small male privileges as discounts on airline fares. Most important to me, I have been denied a society in which women are encouraged, or even allowed to think of themselves as first-class citizens and responsible human beings.

However, after 2 years of researching the status of American women, I have discovered that in reality, I am very, very lucky. Most women, both wage-earners and housewives, routinely suffer more humiliation and injustice than I do.

As a freelance writer, I don't work in the male-dominated hierarchy of an office. (Women, like blacks and other visibly different minorities, do better in individual professions such as the arts, sports, or domestic work; anything in which they don't have authority over white males.) I am not one of the millions of women who must support a family. Therefore, I haven't had to go on welfare because there are no day-care centers for my children while I work, and I haven't had to submit to the humiliating welfare inquiries about my private and sexual life, inquiries from which men are exempt. I haven't had to brave the sex bias of labor unions and employers, only to see my family subsist on a median salary 40 percent less than the male median salary.

I hope this committee will hear the personal, daily injustices suffered by many women—professionals and day laborers, women housebound by welfare as well as by suburbia. We have all been silent for too long. But we won't be silent anymore.

The truth is that all our problems stem from the same sex based myths. We may appear before you as white radicals or the middle-aged middleclass or black soul sisters, but we are all sisters in fighting against these outdated myths. Like racial myths, they have been reflected in our laws. Let me list a few.

That woman are biologically inferior to men. In fact, an equally good case can be made for the reverse. Women live longer than men, even when the men are not subject to business pressures. Women survived Nazi concentration camps better, keep cooler heads in emergencies currently studied by disaster-researchers, are protected against heart attacks by their female sex hormones, and are so much more durable at every stage of life that nature must conceive 20 to 50 percent more males in order to keep the balance going.

Man's hunting activities are forever being pointed to as tribal proof of superiority. But while he was hunting, women built houses, tilled the fields, developed animal husbandry, and perfected language. Men, being all alone in the bush, often developed into a creature as strong as women, fleeter of foot, but not very bright.

However, I don't want to prove the superiority of one sex to another. That would only be repeating a male mistake. English scientists once definitively proved, after all, that the English were descended from the angels, while the Irish were descended from the apes; it was the rationale for England's domination of Ireland for more than a century. The point is that science is used to support current myth and economics almost as much as the church was.

What we do know is that the difference between two races or two sexes is much smaller than the differences to be found within each group. Therefore, in spite of the slide show on female inferiorities that I understand was shown to you yesterday, the law makes much more sense when it treats individuals, not groups bundled together by some condition of birth.

/   /   /

Another myth, that women are already treated equally in this society. I am sure there has been ample testimony to prove that equal pay for equal work, equal chance for advancement, and equal training or encouragement is obscenely scarce in every field, even those—like food and fashion industries—that are supposedly "feminine."

A deeper result of social and legal injustice, however, is what sociologists refer to as "Internalized Aggression." Victims of aggression absorb the myth of their own inferiority, and come to believe that their group is in fact second class. Even when they themselves realize they are not second class, they may still think their group is, thus the tendency to be the only Jew in the club, the only black woman on the block, the only woman in the office.

Women suffer this second class treatment from the moment they are born. They are expected to be, rather than achieve, to function biologically rather than learn. A brother, whatever his intellect, is more likely to get the family's encouragement and education money, while girls are often pressured to conceal ambition and intelligence, to "Uncle Tom."

I interviewed a New York public school teacher who told me about a black teenager's desire to be a doctor. With all the barriers in mind, she suggested kindly that he be a veterinarian instead.

The same day, a high school teacher mentioned a girl who wanted to be a doctor. The teacher said, "How about a nurse?"

Teachers, parents, and the Supreme Court may exude a protective, well-meaning rationale, but limiting the individual's ambition is doing no one a favor. Certainly not this country; it needs all the talent it can get.

Another myth, that American women hold great economic power. Fifty-one percent of all shareholders in this country are women. That is a favorite male-chauvinist statistic. However, the number of shares they hold is so small that the total is only 18 percent of all the shares. Even those holdings are often controlled by men.

Similarly, only 5 percent of all the people in the country who receive $10,000 a year or more, earned or otherwise, are women. And that includes the famous rich widows.

The constantly repeated myth of our economic power seems less testimony to our real power than to the resentment of what little power we do have.

Another myth, that children must have full-time mothers. American mothers spend more time with their homes and children than those of any other society we know about. In the past, joint families, servants, a prevalent system in which grandparents raised the children, or family field work in the agrarian systems—all these factors contributed more to child care than the labor-saving devices of which we are so proud.

The truth is that most American children seem to be suffering from too much mother, and too little father. Part of the program of Women's Liberation is a return of fathers to their children. If laws permit women equal work and pay opportunities, men will then be relieved of their role as sole breadwinner. Fewer ulcers, fewer hours of meaningless work, equal responsibility for his own children: these are a few of the reasons that Women's Liberation is Men's Liberation too.

As for psychic health of the children, studies show that the quality of time spent by parents is more important than the quantity. The most damaged children were not those whose mothers worked, but those whose mothers preferred to work but stayed home out of the role-playing desire to be a "good mother."

Another myth, that the women's movement is not political, won't last, or is somehow not "serious."

When black people leave their 19th century roles, they are feared. When women dare to leave theirs, they are ridiculed. We understand this; we accept the burden of ridicule. It won't keep us quiet anymore.

Similarly, it shouldn't deceive male observers into thinking that this is somehow a joke. We are 51 percent of the population; we are essentially united on these issues across boundaries of class or race or age; and we may well end by changing this society more than the civil rights movement. That is an apt parallel. We, too, have our right wing and left wing, our separatists, gradualists, and Uncle Toms. But we are changing our own consciousness, and that of the country. Engels noted the relationship of the authoritarian, nuclear family to capitalism: the father as capitalist, the mother as means of production, and the children as labor. He said the family would change as the economic system did, and that seems to have happened, whether we want to admit it or not. Women's bodies will no longer be owned by the state for the production of workers and soldiers; birth control and abortion are facts of everyday life. The new family is an egalitarian family.

Gunnar Myrdal noted 30 years ago the parallel between women and Negroes in this country. Both suffered from such restricting social myths as: smaller brains, passive natures, inability to govern themselves (and certainly not white men), sex objects only, childlike natures, special skills, and the like. When evaluating a general statement about women, it might be valuable to substitute "black people" for "women"—just to test the prejudice at work.

And it might be valuable to do this constitutionally as well. Neither group is going to be content as a cheap labor pool anymore. And neither is going to be content without full constitutional rights.

Finally, I would like to say one thing about this time in which I am testifying.

I had deep misgivings about discussing this topic when National Guardsmen are occupying our campuses, the country is being turned against itself in a terrible polarization, and America is enlarging an already inhuman and unjustifiable war. But it seems to me that much of the trouble in this country has to do with the "masculine mystique;" with the myth that masculinity somehow depends on the subjugation of other people. It is a bipartisan problem; both our past and current Presidents seem to be victims of this myth, and to behave accordingly.

Women are not more moral than men. We are only uncorrupted by power. But we do not want to imitate men, to join this country as it is, and I think our very participation will change it. Perhaps women elected leaders—and there will be many of them—will not be so likely to dominate black people or yellow people or men; anybody who looks different from us.

After all, we won't have our masculinity to prove.

/ / /

STATEMENT OF HON. MARGARET M. HECKLER, A REPRESENTATIVE IN CONGRESS FROM THE 10TH DISTRICT OF THE STATE OF MASSACHUSETTS*

Thank you very much, Mr. Chairman and distinguished members of the subcommittee.

It is assumed today by many persons that women were granted equality with the passage of the 14th amendment, ratified in 1868. Only

*Margaret Heckler was defeated in her 1982 bid for reelection. In 1983, she began a term as Secretary of Health and Human Services in the Reagan administration. President Reagan and many of his major officials were opposed to the ERA.

50 years later, however, was woman suffrage guaranteed by the ratification of the 19th amendment. Half a century of waiting for the vote
required a great deal of patience. In the temper of these turbulent times,
I do not believe that total equality of opportunity for women can be further postponed.

Thus I speak out in support of the equal rights amendment—a
measure that has been before each Congress since 1923. The fast pace of
life in the world today fosters impatience. And when much is promised,
failure to deliver becomes a matter of critical importance.

I am sure that every woman who has been in the position of "job
seeker" identifies in some small measure with the fundamental complaints that have generated the crusade for equality in employment for
women. The 42 percent of working women who are heads of household
takes a serious economic interest in fair job opportunity, a basic goal in
the cause for women's rights. And the women who have contributed
their full share to social security, yet who receive the sum allotted widows, certainly have cause for contemplation.

The average woman in America has no seething desire to smoke
cigars or to burn the bra—but she does seek equal recognition of her
status as a citizen before the courts of law, and she does seek fair and
just recognition of her qualifications in the employment market. The
American working woman does not want to be limited in advancement
by virtue of her sex. She does not want to be prohibited from the job she
desires or from the overtime work she needs by "protective" legislation.

These types of discrimination must be stopped, and the forthright
means of halting discrimination against women is passage of the equal
rights amendment at the earliest possible time. In fact, I have heard it
said quite often that the only discrimination that is still fashionable is
discrimination against women.

Perhaps, as some say, it is derived from a protective inclination
on the part of men. But women seek recognition as individual human
beings with abilities useful to society—rather than shelter or protection
from the real world.

John Gardner has said that our Nation's most underdeveloped resource is womanpower. The old saying "you can't keep a good man
down" might well serve as a warning. It is safe to say, I think, that
women are unlikely to stay down and out of the field of competition
for much longer.

Legal remedies are clearly in order, and the equal rights amendment is especially timely. Although changes in social attitudes cannot
be legislated, they are guided by the formulation of our Federal laws.
This constitutional amendment must be passed so that discriminatory
legislation will be overturned. That custom and attitude be subject to a
faster pace of evolution is essential if we are to avoid revolution on the
part of qualified women who seek equality in the employment world.

Time and again I have heard American men question the fact of discrimination against women in America. "American women," they say,
"enjoy greater freedom than women of any other nation." This may be

true with regard to freedom from kitchen labor—because the average American housewife enjoys a considerable degree of automation in her kitchen. But once she seeks to fill her leisure time gained from automated kitchen equipment by entering the male world of employment, the picture changes. Many countries we consider "underprivileged" far surpass America in quality and availability of child care available to working mothers, in enlightened attitudes about employment leave for pregnancy, and in guiding women into the professions.

Since World War II, nearly 14 million American women have joined the labor force—double the number of men. Forty percent of our Nation's labor force is now comprised of women. Yet less than 3 percent of our Nation's attorneys are women, only about 7 percent of our doctors, and 9 percent of our scientists are women. Only a slightly higher percentage of our graduate students in these fields of study are women, despite the fact that women characteristically score better on entrance examinations. The average woman college graduate's annual earnings ($6,694) exceed by just a fraction the annual earnings of an average male educated only through the eighth grade ($6,580). An average male college graduate, however, may be expected to earn almost twice as much as the female—$11,795. Twenty percent of the women with 4 years of college training can find employment only in clerical, sales, or factory jobs. The equal pay provision of the Fair Labor Standards Act does not include administrative, executive, or professional positions—a loophole which permits the talents and training of highly qualified women to be obtained more cheaply than those of comparable qualified men.

Of the 7.5 million American college students enrolled in 1968, at least 40 percent were women. American parents are struggling to educate their daughters as well as their sons—and are sending them to the best colleges they can possibly afford. As many of these mothers attend commencement exercises this summer, their hearts will swell with pride as their daughters receive college degrees—and these mothers may realize their daughters will have aspirations far exceeding their own horizons.

Few of the fathers or mothers, enrolling their daughters in college several years ago, were at the time aware of the obstacles to opportunity their daughters would face. But today they are becoming aware that opportunity for their daughters is only half of that available to their sons. And they are justifiably indignant. Young women graduating with degrees in business administration take positions as clerks while their male counterparts become management trainees. Women graduating from law school are often forced to become legal secretaries, while male graduates from the same class survey a panorama of exciting possibilities.

To frustrate the aspirations of the competent young women graduating from our institutions of higher learning would be a dangerous and foolish thing. The youth of today are inspired with a passion to improve the quality of life around us—an admirable and essential goal, indeed. The job is a mammoth one, however; and it would be ill-advised to assume that the role of women in the crusade of the future will not be a significant one. To the contrary, never before has our Nation and our world cried out for talent and creative energy with greater need. To deny full participation of the resources of women, who compose over half the population of our country, would be a serious form of neglect. The contributions of women have always been intrinsic in our national development. With the increasing complexity of our world, it becomes all the more essential to tap every conceivable resource at our command.

The time is thus ripe for passage of the equal rights amendment. The women of American are demanding full rights and full responsibilities in developing their individual potential as human beings in relationship to the world as well as to the home and in contributing in an active way to the improvement of society.

In this day of the urban crisis, when we seem to be running out of clean air and water, when the quantity of our rubbish defies our current disposal methods, when crime on the streets is rampant, when our world commitments seem at odds with our obligations here at home, when breaking the cycle of ongoing poverty requires new and innovative approaches, when increased lifespan generates a whole new series of gerontological problems—in these complicated and critical times, our Nation needs the fully developed resources of all our citizens—both men and women—in order to meet the demands of society today.

Women are not requesting special privilege—but rather a full measure of responsibility, a fair share of the load in the effort to improve life in America. The upcoming generation is no longer asking for full opportunity to contribute, however—they are demanding this opportunity.

The equal rights amendment is necessary to establish unequivocally the American commitment to full and equal recognition of the rights of all its citizens. Stopgap measures and delays will no longer be acceptable—firm guarantees are now required. The seventies mark an era of great promise if the untapped resource of womanpower is brought forth into the open and allowed to flourish so that women may take their rightful place in the mainstream of American life. Both men and women have a great deal to gain.

Thank you, Mr. Chairman.

LOIS GIBBS

38 | A Toxic Neighborhood

When the environmental movement first gained momentum in the 1960s, some of its goals—the protection of endangered species of animals and plants, overpopulation in Third Word nations—seemed esoteric and distant to large segments of the American public. In more recent years, however, environmental issues have begun to hit home. To those injured as a result of exposure to chemicals at their jobs, to those who have had to abandon their houses because of environmental hazards inside or nearby, the argument that economic self-interest is in harmony with an acrid smell in the air no longer makes sense.

Love Canal was the first toxic waste dump-site to be identified as a major environmental hazard. The Environmental Protection Agency has estimated that there are tens of thousands of such dumps in the United States. Located in the center of the town of Niagara Falls, New York, this long trench is part of an unfinished canal begun in 1892 by William T. Love. In 1920, the Hooker Chemical Corporation, along with the City of Niagara Falls and the U.S. Army, began to use Love Canal as a disposal site for chemical wastes.

In 1953, the Hooker Company filled in the canal and sold it to the Niagara Falls Board of Education for $1.00, stipulating that, if buried wastes there caused any physical harm, the corporation would not be responsible. During the suburban boom of the 1950s, houses and an elementary school were built on the site. Despite complaints about odors, corrosive substances, and black sludge, only in the late 1970s did the State of New York begin to investigate the environmental problem.

A series of steps involving the relocation, first of people living closest to the canal and then of people farther away, began on August 2, 1978. Finally, on October 1, 1980, President Jimmy Carter signed a bill evacuating all families permanently from the canal.

What follows is the bare outline of the beginning of community awareness of the dangers of Love Canal. Lois Gibbs was a major force in mobilizing citizens in the face of what seemed to be bureaucratic indifference or outright callousness.

Such issues as toxic waste dumps, the greenhouse effect, and nuclear waste disposal promise to be important factors in local, national, and international politics well into the next century. With the publication in 1906 of The Jungle, Americans began to fear what might be contained in the processed food that lay

Reprinted from Love Canal: My Story by Lois Marie Gibbs, as told to Murray Levine, pp. 9–19, 22–26, by permission of the State University of New York Press. Copyright © 1982 by Lois Marie Gibbs.

on their dining table. In the 1990s, along with reports of trace contaminants in what they eat, Americans living in or near industrial areas face disheartening information about the air they breathe, the water they drink, the cars they drive, and the soil on which they build their homes with disturbing frequency.

MY SON ATTENDING THAT SCHOOL

Love Canal actually began for me in June 1978 with Mike Brown's articles in the Niagara Falls *Gazette*. At first, I didn't realize where the canal was. Niagara Falls has two sets of streets numbered the same. Brown's articles said Love Canal was between 99th and 97th streets, but I didn't think he meant the place where my children went to school or where I took them to play on the jungle gyms and swings. Although I read the articles, I didn't pay much attention to them. One article did stand out, though. In it, Mike Brown wrote about monkeys subjected to PCB's having miscarriages and deformed offspring.

One of his later articles pointed out that the school had been built over the canal. Still, I paid little attention. It didn't affect me, Lois Gibbs. I thought it was terrible; but I lived on the other side of Pine Avenue. Those poor people over there on the other side were the ones who had to worry. the problem didn't affect me, so I wasn't going to bother doing anything about it, and I certainly wasn't going to speak out about it. Then when I found out the 99th Street School was indeed on top of it, I was alarmed. My son attended that school. He was in kindergarten that year. I decided I needed to do some investigating.

I went to my brother-in-law, Wayne Hadley, a biologist and, at the time, a professor at the State University of New York at Buffalo. He had worked on environmental problems and knew a lot about chemicals. I asked him to translate some of that jibber-jabber in the articles into English. I showed Wayne Mike Brown's articles listing the chemicals in the canal and asked what they were. I was really alarmed by his answer. Some of the chemicals, he said, can affect the nervous system. Just a little bit, even the amount that's in paint or gasoline, can kill brain cells. I still couldn't believe it; but if it *were* true, I wanted to get Michael out of that 99th Street School.

I went down to the offices of the *Gazette* and was surprised to learn how many articles there were on Love Canal. It not only surprised me, it panicked me! The articles listed the chemicals and described some reactions to them. One is damage to the central nervous system. (Michael had begun having seizures after he started school.) Another is leukemia and other blood diseases. (Michael's white blood cell count had gone down.) The doctor said that might have been caused by the medication he took for his epilepsy, but now I wasn't so sure. Michael had started school in September and had developed epilepsy in December; in February his white blood count dropped.

All of a sudden, everything seemed to fall into place. There's no history of epilepsy in either my family or my husband's. So why should Michael develop it? He had always been sensitive to medication. I could never give him an aspirin like a normal baby because he would get sick to his stomach or break out in a rash. I couldn't give him *anything* because of that sensitivity. If it were true that Michael was more sensitive than most other children, then whatever chemicals were buried under the school would affect him more than they did other children in the school, or even more than my daughter Missy, who has always been a strong, lively child. The chemicals probably would not affect Missy, at least not right away. I wasn't thinking then about long-term effects. (A year and a half later, Missy was hospitalized for a blood-platelet disorder, but later she was fine.)

I went over all the articles with Wayne, and decided Michael definitely should not attend that school—nor, for that matter, should any child. They shouldn't even play on that playground. Wayne was worried about his son Eric. He and my sister Kathy used to leave Eric for me to baby-sit while they were at work.

I was stunned that the school board had allowed a school to be built on such a location. Even today, it doesn't seem possible that, knowing there were dangerous chemicals buried there, someone could put up a *school* on the site. The 99th Street School had over 400 children that year, one of its lowest annual enrollments. . . .

/   /   /

I was furious. [Her son could not be transferred to another school.] I wasn't going to send my child to a place that was poisoned. The thoughts that can go through a person's head. I thought that I, as a person, had rights, that I ought to have a choice, and that one of those choices was not to send my child to school in a contaminated place. Like many people, I can be stubborn when I get angry. I decided to go door-to-door and see if the other parents in the neighborhood felt the same way. That way, maybe something could be done. At the time, though, I didn't really think of it as "organizing."

It wasn't just the phone call with the superintendent that convinced me I had to do something. I called the president of the 99th Street School PTA and asked her if she could help me, or if she could at least tell me whom to go to or what to do. She said she was about to go on vacation. I got the feeling she wasn't interested. She seemed to be pushing me away, as if she didn't want to have anything to do with me.

I was disappointed and angry. School would open again in two months, and I wasn't going to let my child go back to that school. I didn't care what I had to do to prevent it. I wasn't going to send him to a private school, either. First of all, we couldn't afford it; and second, I thought parents had the right to send their children to schools that were safe.

KNOCKING ON DOORS

As I said, I decided to go door-to-door with a petition. It seemed like a good idea to start near the school, to talk to the mothers nearest it. I had already heard that a lot of the residents near the school had been upset about the chemicals for the past couple of years. I thought they might help me. I had never done anything like this, however, and I was frightened. I was afraid a lot of doors would be slammed in my face, that people would think I was some crazy fanatic. But I decided to do it anyway. I went to 99th and Wheatfield and knocked on my first door. There was no answer. I just stood there, not knowing what to do. It was an unusually warm June day and I was perspiring. I thought: *What am I doing here? I must be crazy. People are going to think I am. Go home, you fool!* And that's just what I did.

It was one of those times when I had to sit down and face myself. I was afraid of making a fool of myself, I had scared myself, and I had gone home. When I got there, I sat at the kitchen table with my petition in my hand, thinking. *Wait. What if people do slam doors in your face? People may think you're crazy. But what's more important—what people think or your child's health? Either you're going to do something or you're going to have to admit you're a coward and not do it.* I decided to wait until the next day—partly to figure out exactly how I was going to do this but more, I think, to build my self-confidence.

/   /   /

At first, I went to my friend's houses.* I went to the back door, as I always did when I visited a neighbor. Each house took about twenty or twenty-five minutes. They wanted to know about Love Canal. Many of the people who lived farther from the canal than 97th or 99th streets didn't even know the canal existed; they thought the area was a field. Some had heard about Love Canal, but they didn't realize where it was, and they didn't pay much attention to the issue—just as I hadn't. So I spent a lot of time giving them the background, explaining what Love Canal was. Something began to happen to me as I went around talking to these people. It was hot and humid that summer. My mother kept saying I was crazy to do it. I was losing weight, mainly because I didn't have much time to eat. My house was a mess because I wasn't home. Dinner was late, and Harry sometimes was upset. Between the kids and the heat, I was getting very tired. But something drove me on. I kept going door-to-door, still on my own street. When I finished 101st, I did 102d; when I finished those two streets, I felt ready to go back to 99th Street, where I had begun by running home afraid of looking foolish.

*In this book I am going to write as though people were actually saying certain things, because that's the way I remember what was said. I can't guarantee that they used exactly those words, but what they did say was similar to the way I have written it, and the meaning is the same.

Just before going back to 99th Street, I called a woman who lived on 97th Street. Her backyard abutted the canal. I had read about her in the newspaper. She was one of the people who had been organizing others. She said she would be willing to help, but nothing ever happened. Somehow something about her voice didn't sound right. Although I didn't realize it at the time, I was getting another lesson: even though we all have common problems, we don't always work together.

I shouldn't have been too surprised when I discovered later that emergencies like this bring out the best and the worst in people. Sometimes people have honest differences about the best way to solve a problem. Sometimes, however, people have big egos; it's more important for them to be up front and draw attention to themselves than cooperate with others in working for a cause. I really did have a lot to learn. At the time, there were a lot of small groups organizing. Tom Heisner and Karen Schroeder, who lived right on the canal, had started getting people together, and they were doing a good job, though we later had our differences.

/   /   /

A SICK COMMUNITY

As I proceeded down 99th Street, I developed a set speech. I would tell people what I wanted. But the speech wasn't all that necessary. It seemed as though every home on 99th Street had someone with an illness. One family had a young daughter with arthritis. They couldn't understand why she had it at her age. Another daughter had had a miscarriage. The father, still a fairly young man, had had a heart attack. I went to the next house, and there, people would tell me *their* troubles. People were reaching out; they were telling me their troubles in hopes I would do something. But I didn't know anything to do. I was also confused. I just wanted to stop children from going to that school. Now look at all those other health problems! Maybe they were related to the canal. But even if they were, what could I do?

As I continued going door-to-door, I heard more. The more I heard, the more frightened I became. This problem involved much more than the 99th Street School. The entire community seemed to be sick! Then I remembered my own neighbors. One who lived on the left of my husband and me was suffering from severe migraines and had been hospitalized three or four times that year. Her daughter had kidney problems and bleeding. A woman on the other side of us had gastrointestinal problems. A man in the next house down was dying of lung cancer and he didn't even work in industry. The man across the street had just had lung surgery. I though about Michael; maybe there *was* more to it than just the school. I didn't understand how chemicals could get all the way over to 101st Street from 99th; but the more I thought about it, the more frightened I became—for my family and for the whole neighborhood.

Everything was unbelievable. I worried that I was exaggerating, or that people were exaggerating their complaints. I talked it over with Wayne. Luckily, he knew someone who might be able to help us—a Dr. Beverly Paigen, who is a biologist, geneticist, and cancer research scientist at the Roswell Park Memorial Institute, a world-famous research hospital in Buffalo. We went to see Dr. Paigen. She is a wonderful, brave person who, like Wayne, had been involved in environmental-pollution fights. She asked us to bring some soil samples so she could do an Ames test. The Ames test is a quick way of determining potentially dangerous effects of chemicals. When bacteria are exposed to mutagenic chemicals, Dr. Paigen told us, they reproduce abnormally.

I continued to go door-to-door. I was becoming more worried because of the many families with children who had birth defects. Then I learned something even more frightening: there had been five crib deaths within a few short blocks. . . .

/   /   /

A REAL PROBLEM?

The New York State Health Department held a public meeting in June 1978. It was the first one I attended. Dr. Nicholas Vianna and some of his staff explained that they were going to do environmental and health studies. They wanted to take samples—of blood, air, and soil, as well as from sump pumps. They wanted to find out if there really was a problem. They would study only the first ring of houses, though, the ones with backyards abutting Love Canal. Bob Matthews, Niagara Falls city engineer, was there to explain the city's plan for remedial construction. They all sat in front of a big, green chalkboard on the stage in the auditorium of the 99th Street School.

I didn't understand everything that was said, especially about determining whether there was a problem. A pretty young woman carefully dressed, with a lovely scarf, spoke articulately. Her dog's nose had been burned when it sniffed the ground in her yard. She kept asking Dr. Vianna: "What does this mean? How did he burn his nose?" She said the dog was suffering, that her children loved the dog and loved playing with him; but she was willing to have the dog put away if Dr. Vianna would first test the dog.

That was a new reaction to me, one I hadn't come across in my canvassing. How *did* the dog burn his nose? Did that mean chemicals were on the surface? I knew there were health problems, and I felt the school should be closed; but I hadn't actually *seen* any chemicals. I felt a chill. This was a new danger, and a more ominous one. A man got up and said he couldn't put his daughter out in his own backyard because if he did, the soles of her feet would burn. The man thought chemicals were causing it. His daughter was with him. She was a cute little thing, only eighteen months old, with curly dark hair. Imagine he couldn't let her play in his own backyard, and he didn't know why!

/   /   /

I asked Dr. Vianna if the 99th Street School was safe. He answered that the air readings on the school had come back clean. But there we were sitting in the school auditorium, smelling chemicals! I said: "You are telling me there are chemicals there.... But you also tell us we can't eat the vegetables. How can these kids be safe walking on the playground? How can it be safe?" "Have the children walk on the sidewalk," Dr. Vianna said. "Make sure they don't cut across the canal or walk on the canal itself."

I couldn't believe what I was hearing. I asked again: "How can you say all that when the playground is on the canal?" He didn't have an answer. He just said: "You are their mother. You can limit the time they play on the canal." I wondered if he had any children.

By now the audience was really frustrated, and so was I. People began walking out, muttering, furious. There were no answers. They didn't understand, and they were becoming frightened.

RAPIDLY LOSING MY FAITH

Every time I went to another house, I learned something new. In one home, I met a graying heavyset man with a pitted face. He couldn't walk very well. He had worked for Hooker at one time, and now he had chloracne, a condition that results from exposure to certain chemicals. I didn't know it then but chloracne is also a symptom of dioxin poisoning. Dioxin is toxic in parts per trillion. Later we learned that it was in Love Canal. The man was as nice and pleasant as he could be, but his face looked awful. It was all I could do to look at him. He wanted to go ahead with a class-action suit; but he was afraid to jeopardize his pension from Hooker.

I thought to myself: *How could you be so concerned about your pension? The law will protect you. Who cares about Hooker? Look what they've done to you in the plant, let alone what they've done to your family living here on one of their dump sites.* It was hard to understand why people were so afraid of Hooker, of what the company might do to them. Why weren't they angrier?

There were so many unbelievable things about the situation. In one house, a divorced woman with four children showed me a letter from the New York State Health Department. It was a thank-you letter, and a check was enclosed. I asked the woman what the check was for. She said the health department had contacted her and asked if her son would go onto Love Canal proper, find two "hot" rocks, and put them in the jars they sent her. She had been instructed to give the rocks to Dr. Vianna or to someone at the 99th Street School headquarters of the health department. The so-called hot rocks were phosphorus rocks that the children would pick up and throw against cement, and, in the process, burn themselves. The rocks would pop like firecrackers.

It amused the kids; but some had been burned on the eyes and skin. I just couldn't understand how a supposedly responsible agency would send an eleven-year-old child into a potentially dangerous area such as Love Canal and ask him to pick up something there that could harm him. To get the rocks, he had to climb a snow fence put there to keep children out. It amazed me that the health department would do such a thing. They are supposed to protect people's health, and here they were jeopardizing an innocent child. I used to have a lot of faith in officials, especially doctors and experts. Now I was losing that faith—fast!

/   /   /

I wanted Harry [my husband] to be tested also. I was worried that we were being affected even over there on 101st Street. Some of my neighbors thought it was silly to think we could be affected that far from the canal; but it was only a block and a half farther away. Most people on 101st said they wouldn't take the blood test. If I wanted to shut down the school, fine; but let's not carry it too far. "There's no problem over here," some said. "You have no business going over there. You're not a resident of 97th or 99th. Why don't you stay home and behave yourself!" Some of the women in the neighborhood would get together at a neighbor's house and gossip. "She's just doing it for publicity." But the gossip didn't bother me much. I was developing a pretty thick skin.

After weeks of carrying the petition door-to-door, one door *was* slammed in my face. It wasn't as bad as I had feared, though. The woman who answered my knock recognized me immediately. She really laid it on: "What are you out here for? Why are you doing this? Look what you're doing to property values. When did you put your house up for sale?" She was a bitter woman, but her attack wasn't on me personally. She was just letting me know how she felt. She wouldn't sign my petition. That was the worst encounter I had with a neighbor. By then, such a rebuff made almost no difference. I was disappointed that she wouldn't sign, but I didn't lose any sleep over it.

/   /   /

One woman, divorced and with three sick children, looked at the piece of paper* with numbers and started crying hysterically: "No wonder my children are sick. Am I going to die? What's going to happen to my children?" No one could answer. The health department didn't even give her the OSHA standards provided by the Occupational Safety and Health Administration. I went over to calm her down. I told her that, based on what I had learned from Dr. Paigen and from Wayne, it might be a good idea for her to stay with a relative until the health department

---

*Containing air-sample results for her home.

finished evaluating the area. She calmed down somewhat, but she was already very nervous and this uncertainty didn't help.

The night was very warm and humid, and the air was stagnant. On a night like that, the smell of Love Canal is hard to describe. It's all around you. It's as though it were about to envelop you and smother you. By now, we were outside, standing in the parking lot. The woman's panic caught on, starting a chain reaction. Soon, many people there were hysterical.

/ / /

The meeting had one good effect: it brought people together. People who had been feuding because little Johnny hit little Billy were now talking to each other. They had air readings in common or a dead plant or a dead tree. They compared readings, saying, "Hey, this is what I've got. What have you got?" The word spread fast and the community became close-knit. Everywhere you looked, there were people in little groups talking and wondering and worrying.

AL SANTOLI

39 | Crossing the Rio Grande

Throughout American history waves of immigration have shaped the nation's life. Only in the period from 1924 to 1965, when federal law set racial and ethnic quotas, did migration become somewhat less influential. Since the mid-1960s the historic American pattern has reasserted itself, with migrants—particularly from Asia, the Caribbean, and Latin America—strongly affecting American social, economic, and cultural life.

The new Americans are at least as varied as the old: Mexican, Central American, Filipino, Korean, Indian, Iranian, Jamaican, Taiwanese, Vietnamese, and others fill the stream of legal immigrants. In addition, a large number of illegal aliens from Mexico and elsewhere in Latin America have swelled the populations of Florida, Texas, Arizona, New Mexico, and southern California. All have different stories, motives, and prospects in the society they enter. Some have been viewed as essential labor; others as potential welfare cases; and still others as entrepreneurs who will fuel a rebirth of economic growth. The United States government has recognized the value of this new immigration by granting citizenship to those who have resided in this country for a number of years—the "amnesty" José Luis mentions in his interview. The interviews collected in Al Santoli's New Americans: An Oral History, *published in 1988, suggest that we are still a nation of immigrants.*

Rosa María Urbina, age thirty-five, crossed the muddy Rio Grande in 1984 with the hope that she could earn enough money as a housecleaner in El Paso to take her three children out of an orphanage. A widow, she had to place her children in an institution because the $14 a week she earned on a factory assembly line in Juárez was not enough to feed them.

Each morning she joined hundreds of other young to middle-aged women from the hillside colonias, *who walked down to the concrete riverbank and paid men called* burros *to ferry them across the river on their shoulders—and back to the squalor of Juárez in the evening. On one of these excursions, she met a handsome farm worker, José Luis, age twenty-six, with dark mestizo features. It was fate, they believe. Within months, Rosa's children joined them in a two-room apartment on the American side of the river.*

I was introduced to José and Rosa during a tour of overcrowded tenement buildings in South El Paso that house many of the city's fifty thousand illegal residents. In Mexican slang, they are called mojados, *or "wets," the river people.*

My guide, Julie Padilla, a public-health nurse from the Centro de Salud Familiar La Fe clinic, visits the Urbinas to give their two-month-old baby, José Luis, Jr., a post-natal checkup. We walked up a dark stairwell to a dimly lit landing decorated with a colorful gold-framed mural of Our Lady of Guadalupe, the religious patron of all Mexican Catholics. There are sixteen apartments with ripped screen doors along a narrow graffiti-covered corridor. On the back fire-escape is a closet-sized communal toilet. Julie said, "There used to be one bathtub that every family on the corridor shared. But in the past year, that's been taken out. I don't know where they bathe now."

Rosa María, José, and the children have the luxury apartment. Half of the 12-foot-square room is taken up by a bed covered by a magenta Woolworth blanket. On the wall, above a calendar of the Good Shepherd, is a portrait of Pope John Paul II. A Winnie the Pooh blanket serves as a makeshift closet door. On a miniature two-tiered nightstand, alongside baby bottles and a green plant, are metal-framed elementary-school photos of the children. Their seven-year-old daughter's Honor Roll certificate is proudly displayed on a mirror above an all-purpose foldout table.

During winter months, José Luis is out of farm work. The baby is Rosa's full-time chore. They survive on $58 a month in food stamps earmarked for the baby, who is an American citizen by virtue of his birth in El Paso. And WICC, the Women, Infant and Children Care program, provides a bag of groceries each week. Although the children attend public school, José and Rosa seldom leave the apartment. They fear that border patrolmen will send them back across the river to the squalor of Juárez.

JOSÉ: The majority of the people in our apartment building have the same problem as my family. All of us are in El Paso without legal papers. I have been living here since 1981.

ROSA: I came in 1984, to find work. After José and I were married and we found a place to live, I brought my children from a previous marriage. We lived across the river, in Juárez. But I was born further south, in Zacatecas.

JOSÉ: My hometown is Juárez. Since I was nine years old, I've been coming to El Paso to work. At first I did gardening in people's yards, but I have stayed in El Paso constantly since 1981, going out to the fields to do farm work. I used to go to Juárez to visit my relatives at least one day each month. But in the last year, I haven't gone, because of the immigration law. To visit Juárez I have to swim across the river. I can't cross the bridge or the *"migra"* [Border Patrol officers] can catch me right there.

    During the past few months, the river has been very high and fast. That's one reason why not so many people have been crossing lately. I am not working now, because it isn't the growing or harvesting season on the big farms. On February 15, we usually begin to plant onions. That is when the main agricultural season begins. But during a three-month period between planting and harvesting, there is no work.

We haven't paid our rent since December. If we're lucky, I can find some part-time work to pay for food. Our baby, José Luis, is two months old. Because he was born in El Paso, he is an American citizen. We can only get food assistance for him. Once in a while, I find a job as a construction laborer, house painter, whatever is available. We use the money to buy food for the baby and the other three children first.

ROSA: I haven't been able to work lately, because the baby is so small. My other children are all in school. Lorenzo is twelve years old, José Rubén is ten, and Miriam is seven. From the time I came to El Paso, I have worked as a housekeeper and minding homes for people. I am not used to staying in the apartment every day, but I have no other choice, because of my small baby.

I have known many changes in my life. I moved to Juárez from a farm in Zacatecas when I was seven years old. My mother and father were split up. After mother remarried, my stepfather took us to Juárez. We lived in an adobe house in the colonias [ramshackle housing projects] up in the hills.

When I was a teenager, I worked as a hairdresser in a beauty salon, cutting hair. My first husband was a mechanic, fixing cars. We made a good living. But my husband spent the money he made drinking in the cantinas. And after a while, he wouldn't let me work, because I had young children to take care of. When he died in 1984, he left me nothing at all. He drank too much and died from cirrhosis of his liver. I had no money . . . nothing. My children were nine, seven, and three years old. I had to find a way to pay rent and feed them.

At that time, the economy in Mexico had become horrible. Inflation was going crazy. The peso jumped to 500 per dollar. Today it is still climbing at 1,000 per dollar. I found a job working on an assembly line at a factory. We produced rubber gloves for hospitals and medical supplies like little caps for syringes. I would go into work at 4:30 in the afternoon and stay until 2:00 A.M. I was paid only 7,000 pesos [$14] each week. that was not enough to feed my kids. And I didn't have any relatives or friends to watch the kids while I worked. So I had no other choice but to put them in a special institution, like an orphanage, for children without parents. This upset me very much. But with my husband dead, and no other form of support, there was nothing I could do.

My only hope was to cross the river to the United States. If I could find a job that paid enough money, my children could join me. I wanted them to have an education and a proper life . . . to be someone.

After I made up my mind to cross the river, I met José Luis. It was like fate—we just found each other. You could say it was love at first sight. [Laughs] I had two young boys who needed a good man to learn from. When he asked me to live with him, I said yes.

JOSÉ: Before I met Rosa, I lived with my grandmother in Juárez. I would go back and forth across the river to work in El Paso or the farms in New Mexico. After Rosa and I fell in love, we decided to rent this apartment in El Paso and live together.

ROSA: Before I met José, I crossed back and forth across the river five days each week to my housekeeping jobs in El Paso. On weekends, I took my children out of the orphanage. Then I had to reluctantly return them to the orphanage on Sunday evenings and prepare to go back across the river.

For a while, I traveled alone, which can be dangerous. But after I met José Luis, we crossed together. There are men who carry people across the river on their shoulders. The water is kind of rough, but that's what these men do to make a living. They charge passengers 1,500 to 2,000 pesos [$1.50 to $2.50]. The water is up to their chests, but they manage to hold us up on their shoulders so we can get to work dry.

JOSÉ: Crossing the river can be very dangerous, especially if you cross alone. There are fast water currents, and sometimes the water is quite high. If you don't know how to swim, the undercurrents can pull you right down. And in places the bottom of the river is like quicksand that can trap you. The water turns into kind of a funnel that can drag you down. Some friends of mine have died.

ROSA: I don't know how to swim. I relied on José Luis, who is a good swimmer. We were both very lucky. I can clearly remember an incident where we almost drowned. It began on a Sunday evening, which is a customary time for crossing. At the time, a man was running loose who was raping and killing women who crossed alone. So there were a lot of American border patrolmen and Mexican police along both banks.

After the sun went down and it became quite dark, José and I waited for a while near the riverbank, but it seemed hopeless to try to cross the river undetected. We waited until the next morning to try again.

When the sun came up, we saw that the men who carried people across on their shoulders weren't working, because of all the police. When we noticed that the border patrolmen had left the area, we decided to try to cross by ourselves. That was a big mistake. The current was very fast that day. In the middle of the river, we lost our balance and began to be dragged downstream. I felt helpless and began to panic. Fortunately, another man who was a strong swimmer came to our rescue. He pulled us to the shore.

After José and I began living together in El Paso, I decided to bring my children across the river. The water was too high and swift to risk men carrying them on their shoulders. So I had the children taxied across on a rubber raft.

JOSÉ: Another danger for people who cross the river is crime. Packs of men hang around the riverbank like wolves. They try to steal people's knapsacks or purses. Sometimes they demand that you give your wallet or wristwatch. If you don't obey them, they will knife you.

Were we ever caught by the *migra* when we crossed the river together? Oh, yes. [Laughs] Lots of times. But the patrolmen are really okay people. They arrest you, ask the usual questions. If you get rough, they will get rough, too. Otherwise they are fine. It all depends on the person who arrests you. If he has a mean personality, he will treat you rudely, whether you are impolite or not. But most of the time, it is a routine procedure.

When the *migra* catch us, they just put us in their truck and take us to their station. They ask our name, address, where we were born. They keep us in a cell maybe three or four hours. Then they put us in a bus and drive us back to Juárez. They drop the women off very near the main bridge. The men are taken a little further away from town.

Our favorite place to cross the river is close to the Black Bridge, which is not far from downtown El Paso. Many of us would stand on the Juárez riverbank and wait for the change of Border Patrol shifts. Each morning, the shift changes between seven-thirty and eight-thirty, sometimes nine-thirty. We learn by observing over long periods of time. And all of our friends have been held in the immigration station. We observed certain patrolmen coming in to work and others checking out after their shifts.

Experienced river crossers pass this information to new people who are just learning the daily routines. Over a period of time, we learn the shift changes by recognizing different officers' faces. Some Mexican people even know the *migra* by name.

ROSA: Suppose I am caught by the patrolmen at seven-thirty in the morning. They will take me to the station and hold me for a few hours, then bus me back to Juárez. I would walk back to a crossing point and try once again. It is like a game. I think the most times I was ever caught by the *migra* was six times in one day. No matter how many times they catch me, I keep coming back.

The majority of the people in the *calonia* where I lived in Juárez worked in El Paso, mostly as housekeepers, construction workers, or helpers in the fields. In the United States there is a lot of work, but in Mexico we have nothing.

JOSÉ: The men, like myself, who work in the fields come across the river at around 2:30 A.M. to meet the buses that take us to the fields from El Paso. The transportation is owned by the *padrone* of the farms, or by the labor-crew chiefs who hire and pay the workers. In the evenings, we ride the buses back to the river. Sometimes I work twelve hours in a day and earn $20. I've learned to check around to see which farms pay the best. Some pay up to $35 a day.

Farm-labor jobs are not very steady. We just grab whatever is open at the moment. I accept anything, any time, as long as it is work. But suppose I take a job that only pays me $12 a day. It would only be enough to cover my transportation and meals in the field. I must find jobs that pay enough to feed my family.

In order to make $25, I must pick seventy-two buckets of chili peppers. That could take me four or five hours; it depends on how fast my hands are. The total amount of buckets we pick depends upon the amount contracted by the big companies in California. For a big contract, we work as long as necessary to complete the order. But the most I can earn in a day is $35.

During the summer, it gets very hot in the fields, up to 110 degrees. We work for eight hours with a half-hour break for lunch. To save money, I bring my lunch from home. The companies usually provide us with a thermos bottle of cold water. The farthest we travel from El Paso is to Lordsburg, New Mexico. That is around three and a half hours by bus. We leave El Paso at 3:00 A.M. For Las Cruces we leave at 5:00 or 5:30 A.M.

ROSA: To my housekeeping jobs I can take a regular El Paso city bus at 7:00 or 8:00 A.M. I usually come home around 3:30 or 4:00 P.M. each day. For a long while, I worked at one house — a Mexican-American family. They started me at $20 a day. Eventually they increased my wages to $25. They live near a large shopping center in the eastern part of town. The job was a little bit easier than working in the factory in Juárez, and paid much better.

In the factory, a whistle blows to let us know when to start, when to stop, when to eat dinner, and when to resume work. Doing housecleaning, I can rest a little when I need to take a short break.

To compare our apartment in El Paso with where I lived in Juárez, I prefer it a little better over there, because in the *colonia* I had a place to hang my clothes after I washed them. The bathroom was outside of the house. But we don't have a bathroom in our apartment here, either. All of the apartments in this part of the building share a toilet on the back stairwell. But in this apartment we have electric appliances, which makes life better than my previous home.

JOSÉ: The landlord who owns this building is very generous. He lets us owe him rent for the months that I am not working. He understands how tough our life is. We pay whatever we can, even if it's only $50. And he knows that, if the day comes where we are raided by immigration officers, we will run.

The rent for this apartment is $125 a month plus electricity. We all live and sleep in this one room. The two boys sleep on the couch. Our daughter, Miriam, sleeps with us on the bed. And the baby sleeps in a crib next to our bed. Fortunately, we have a kitchen, and a closet in this room. Living conditions in Juárez were better, but there was no work at all.

If it is possible, Rosa and I would like to become American citizens. I would have my documents, and the government wouldn't be after us. All we want is to be able to work in peace.

Our dream is to be able to give our children the best of everything. We know that, for them to have a better future and purpose in life, they need a good education. Of the three children in school now, Miriam is the fastest learner. She received an award for being an honor student, the best in her classroom.

We hope the children can finish high school and have the career of their choice. We are going to sacrifice for them, so that they can have the profession that they desire.

I was only allowed to finish grammar school. I am the oldest in my family, of five sisters and two boys. I had to stop going to school when I was twelve, to work with my father to support the family. I would have liked to finish school, but my parents needed me to work. They chose my sisters to study. So I gave up my studies to support my sisters.

At first, I liked working better than going to school. But after a while, I wanted to attend junior high school. But my mother told me that the family couldn't afford for me to go, and she said my sisters seemed to like the books better than I did. So I continued working. My father had a fruit-and-vegetable business. We sold from a pushcart in downtown Juárez, and I came across the river to do some gardening.

Even though I've come to work in Texas and New Mexico for many years, I've never learned to speak much English. I would like to learn, but I've never had the chance to study. I have a lot of responsibility now to provide for the children. It is more important that they have school, so I must work.

The dreams that Rosa Maria and I had of living in the U.S. and reality are not the same. We hoped to find a job and live comfortably. Now that we are here, our main purpose is to survive.

I worry about our status under the new immigration law. In the previous place where I lived, I paid the rent all the time, but the landlord threw away all of the receipts. So we have no proof that we have been living here enough years to qualify for amnesty.

On the farms where I worked, my employers or crew bosses didn't keep pay records, because I only worked temporarily at each place. And, besides, I was illegal. So what was the use? If the police showed up, we would be in trouble whether or not the employer had a record. And the employers wanted to protect themselves. They didn't pay us with checks; it was always cash.

Fortunately, the last farmer I worked for took taxes and Social Security out of our wages. He is sending me a W-2 form as proof. I am waiting for it now. But things are getting worse, because the immigration police are putting pressure on people who hire undocumented workers. If the police catch illegals on a job site, the boss can be arrested under the new law. So most places have stopped hiring illegals. For example, my last job in El Paso, I was fired because the *migra* would raid the construction site every day. We would have to stop working and run.

When the planting season begins on the farms, I hope the immigration police don't show up. They raid a farm with a truck and four or five police cars. They position themselves outside the entrance to the farm and wait for us to walk by. They ask us for identification. If we cannot show proof that we are legal, we've had it. They'll take us away.

On the farms where I work, some people are legal and others aren't. If you drive your own car, the police usually won't question you. But if you come to work in the employer's bus, they'll take you away.

ROSA: In town, we don't feel comfortable walking on the street. If the immigration officers see us, they will grab us. We are not afraid for ourselves, because we are accustomed to it. But I worry about the children. They have just begun studying in school here in El Paso. They like it very much. My sons are in the sixth and fifth grades, and Miriam is in second grade. They are learning English very quickly. My oldest boy, Lorenzo, likes social studies and mathematics; he would like to be a doctor. My other son likes the army a lot. He could probably be a good soldier.

JOSÉ: If we become citizens and the United States government asks them to spend time in the army, we would be honored if they are chosen to serve. We would be very proud of our children for doing their duty for their country.

ROSA: My daughter, Miriam, received a certificate from her teacher. You can ask her what she would like to do when she finishes school.

MIRIAM: [Big grin] I like to study English and mathematics. Some day I would like to be a teacher.

ROSA: In the buildings on this block, the majority of the people are families. In each apartment there are three or four children. This is the only area we found where the landlords don't mind renting to families with kids. The kids play outside, in the alley behind our building. Not many cars pass on this street at night, so it is pretty quiet. But other neighborhoods are more active and there is more crime on the streets.

We would like to have an ordinary life, but our problems with the *migra* are nothing new. If they catch me again and send me back to Juárez, I will just come back across the river.

SYLVIA ANN HEWLETT

40 | Painful Choices

In the 1970s and 1980s, economic realities converged with feminist efforts to move more women into the workplace in a full range of white-collar and blue-collar occupations.

Whether they worked out of necessity (because real family income in the 1970s and 1980s suffered a gradual decline) or to achieve independence and a new self-respect, women faced difficult choices as they attempted to balance their professional and personal lives. The following selection, from Sylvia Ann Hewlett's book, A Lesser Life, relates the experiences of several women who tried to exercise the best options available to them. (To document that men's and women's choices in the 1980s are not based on equality, Hewlett considers whether women, more frequently than men, feel that success in their careers means they must forgo the option to have children. She refers to an October 30, 1984, Wall Street Journal article that cites a study showing that 52% of high-level women executives are childless, compared with 7% of their male counterparts.)

Studies of American society in the 1970s and 1980s have examined the impact of the high-income, dual-wage-earner family; the family in which both spouses must work in order to break even; and the single-parent household, created by accident, choice, or divorce. The long-term impact of these phenomena on the nation's social structure and economy has yet to be fully evaluated. Meanwhile, conflicts over traditional versus modern values are played out in the lives of millions of contemporary Americans.

At 8:00 P.M. on September 21, 1984, my apartment filled with excited young women greeting long-lost classmates.* They ranged in age from twenty-three to thirty-three, and half were married. Some were self-consciously businesslike in skirted suits, little string ties, and cropped hair. But even the more feminine members of the group, in elegant dresses and clever makeup, carried bulging briefcases. Most of them had come straight from work, two brought spouses, and one woman was conspicuously pregnant. After an hour of eating, drinking, gossip-

*[of Barnard College]

From A Lesser Life *by Sylvia Ann Hewlett, pp. 384–389. Copyright © 1986. Used by permission of William Morrow and Company, Inc./Publishers, New York.*

ing, and cuddling my children (my third child, Adam, was just five months old and particularly popular, despite a tendency to dribble down silk blouses) the serious business of the evening began. We sat around in a big circle, and after some encouragement (I, after all, was an old hand at conducting seminars) everyone started to talk. The first topic these women gravitated toward was how to combine careers with children (a rather surprising choice, for although one of these women was pregnant, *none* had yet had children).

Marion,* age twenty-four, class of '81, one of the most able students of her year, now holds an entry-level position at an investment banking firm, a job she took after completing a master's degree in economics. Marion likes her work and looks forward to building a career in international finance. Marion is getting married in the spring, and her one great worry is: "Can I make room in this career for children?" She recognizes that she has chosen a very time-intensive profession: "Ten to twelve hours a day plus a lot of travel. Not only does my job require me to travel abroad ten days of each month, but I have a ninety-minute commute, which means that I never get home until eight in the evening." Marion particularly regrets that there are no role models in her field. "In my firm there are a hundred partners, only three of them are women, and none of these are in my department, so I don't know them." In a larger financial world Marion has found some women, "but if they are married, they tend to be childless."

Marion does not see herself attempting to have children for at least five years, yet, as she freely admits, "it is a question I think about a lot." Her great hope is that by them "I will be in control of my career and have much more ability to dictate my terms to it."

At this point Marion was interrupted by Laura,** age twenty-nine, class of '77, who said quietly but with conviction, "It's not as easy as that. Things don't resolve themselves. In some ways the choices get harder."

"My situation is typical. I'll be thirty in July and am beginning to feel enormous pressure to have a child. I read somewhere that infertility problems begin to mount in your early thirties, and I would very much like to avoid that kind of trouble. Besides, I've been married for seven years, and both of us want a child quite badly. The other day Michael told me that he 'needed' a child. Yet I cannot decide how to reconcile a family with my work. The basic problem is that my career cannot be put on hold for a few years. If I were to take time out, there would be no way of picking up the threads two or three years down the line."

Everyone in the room was listening very closely to Laura. She was seen by her classmates as an immensely efficient woman thoroughly

*Pseudonym.

**Pseudonym.

in control of her life. If she was encountering problems, they were surely significant ones. Marion pushed Laura to be more explicit. "I don't understand. I thought it was OK to slow down once your career was established."

Laura decided to tell of her experience in some detail, and as she talked, her voice rose and became filled with emotion. Clearly her dilemma was causing considerable pain.

"Professional careers do not become easier or plateau out in your late twenties or early thirties. At these critical early stages there is always *the next step*. I work in a commercial bank. When I started seven years ago, my first goal was to become an officer. Then I wanted to become a higher-level officer, then assistant vice-president. And now I am waiting for my vice-presidency.

"I put in twelve- to fourteen-hour days. I have taken only four sick days in seven years, and I have earned my medals; but that does not mean that I can relax a whole lot now. There just isn't much flexibility in my career. Citibank thinks it has a decent maternity policy—three months' leave—but the kid is not even sleeping through the night by then. The bank will not tolerate part-time work or flextime and has no child-care facilities. Besides, as soon as you get pregnant, people at work start viewing you differently. They assume your priorities have changed and you will have less energy for your job.

"We bought a house in the suburbs a year and a half ago, and since my husband wants to be a neurosurgeon and has four years of specialized training in front of him, there is no way we could keep the house if I stopped work.

"So you see, despite the fact that I have launched my career, delayed childbearing, and done all the things I was supposed to do, I face some very tough choices.

"When we have a child, I can do one of three things. I can continue my career by hiring enough help for full-time coverage at home. I have priced it out; it would cost twenty thousand dollars a year. The snag is I would have to resign myself to seeing my baby only an hour or two a day. Or I can opt out of my banking career and work part time for my father (who has a small business). This way I can make enough money to pay the mortgage and still have time to see my child and manage the house. Or, finally, we could sell the house, move into an apartment, and I can take time out of the work force and become a traditional homemaker.

"All three options entail huge costs for me. I can already visualize the massive guilt I would feel if I took option number one. I had a very traditional upbringing, and an important part of me believes that mothers should be with their children. I have nightmares about my child forgetting that I am its mother, preferring the baby-sitter to me. I can deal with hard work and crazy hours, I would even get up at five A.M. to spend some quality time with my child, but can I cope with the guilt? I don't think so.

"Option number two would kill my career—at least any ambitious version of my career. If I took even a few years out of banking, there is no way I could get back on the fast track in my mid or late thirties. In other words, if I opted to work part time for my father, I would have to permanently lower my expectations of money, status, and power.

"Option number three is the least attractive to me. I would not like losing the house; I have worked hard for my creature comforts and value them. But more than that, if I were to stay at home all day, I would more than likely go crazy. I thrive on stimulus and love my work. I am now a formed person and cannot change my personality or temperament because it's convenient to do so." . . .

/   /   /

Debbie,* class of '80 and an associate editor at a top women's magazine, was six months pregnant. She tried to rise to the challenge that had been thrown her and said with some irony, "I wish I did have some solutions, but in many ways my options are more limited than Laura's. You see we face a Catch-twenty-two situation. Both John and I work in low-paying fields, so I need to earn money for us to survive. And I mean, survive. We rent a small apartment in Brooklyn, we don't own a car, yet we barely get by on our two salaries. Despite this need to earn money, which will become more acute when we have a child, it will be impossible for me to keep my job. My maternity benefits are far from good—four weeks of partially paid leave before the birth and four weeks afterward. But even if I could cope with so little time off, full-time high-quality child care would consume all my salary. So my solution (if you can call it that) is to leave my job after the birth of my child and become a free-lance writer. This way I can do a large part of the child care myself and continue to earn at least some money.

"But it's scary. I'm afraid of becoming isolated and unproductive— at home all day with a tiny child. And I'm afraid that John and I will lose the equality we have so carefully built up. If he begins to earn much more than I, it will obviously be difficult to maintain an equal division of household tasks, and I think I will become resentful if I end up with all the cooking and cleaning."

Debbie paused and then added reflectively, "You know, there are a lot of women on the creative, editorial side of the company [the Hearst organization, which owns several magazines including the one Debbie works for], but in management, upper management, I don't think there is one woman, and it is in management that the high salaries are. Even Helen Gurley Brown has no clout; she is not even on the board. All these women's magazines are supposedly setting up role models for women, but good role models don't exist at the source."

*Pseudonym.

Debbie had one final comment: "This past summer I have been troubled by the fact that I could not work up much enthusiasm for Geraldine Ferraro.* Somehow I felt guilty about not giving her more support. I think the problem is that her life has been so unreal. She took thirteen years off to have her children and then was able to jump back into the work force and get back on track as a lawyer and a politician. I guess I don't believe that you can do that unless you are married to a wealthy man and have great political connections. Most of us need to earn money in order to survive, and many of us are in competitive professions, where it just isn't possible to take a few years off to have a family, let alone thirteen years off. Ferraro talks a lot about her hard life, but she really hasn't faced the toughest issue—rearing children and building a career at one and the same time. I suppose that makes it hard for me to see her as a role model."

/   /   /

*The 1984 vice-presidential nominee of the Democratic Party.

JONATHAN KOZOL

41 | A Welfare Hotel

Homelessness is not new. There have always been hobos, many of them victims of alcohol and other drugs; and the temporarily unemployed have often wandered without a home base. In recent years the numbers of homeless people swelled with the deinstitutionalizing of the mentally ill. And in the last two decades a persistent stratum of permanent poverty, the so-called underclass, has been added.

In the 1980s American cities witnessed the growth of a new group: homeless children, members of families who could not afford housing. As housing came to consume a higher percentage of family income, an increasing number of families found themselves unable to maintain any kind of residence at all.

Jonathan Kozol wrote Rachel and Her Children: Homeless Families in America, *published in 1988, based on interviews with people whose luck has run out: Industries closed and they lost their jobs; family illness overwhelmed their finances; a fire pushed them out of cheaper housing and they could not afford the fees, deposits, or simply the rising rents around them. Cumbersome policies often trapped them in seedy hotels at enormous public expense. They are an underclass created by a lack of affordable housing.*

There are families in this building whose existence, difficult though it may be, still represents an island of serenity and peace. Annie Harrington's family has a kind of pained serenity. Gwen and her children live with the peace of resignation. I think of these families like refugees who, in the midst of war, cling to each other and establish a small zone of safety. Most people here do not have resources to create a zone of safety. Terrorized already on arrival, they are quickly caught up in a vortex of accelerating threats and are tossed about like bits of wood and broken furniture and shattered houses in an Arkansas tornado. Chaos and disorder alternate with lethargy and nearly absolute bewilderment in face of regulations they cannot observe or do not understand.

Two women whom I meet in the same evening after Christmas, Wanda and Terry, frighten me by their entire inability to fathom or to govern what is going on inside and all around them.

Terry is pregnant, in her ninth month. She's afraid that, when she gives birth, she may not be able to bring home her baby from the hospital because she is not legally residing here.

Wanda, curled up like a newborn in a room no larger than a closet, is three months pregnant, planning an abortion.

Would doctors say these women are emotionally unwell? They might have no choice. Were these women sick before they came here? I don't see how we could possibly find out. What startles me is not that they have difficulty coping but that neither yet has given up entirely.

Terry: twenty-eight years old. She has three kids. She graduated from a school in Flushing and has worked for eight years as a lab assistant. Burnt out of her home, she stayed for two years with her sister's family: three adults, eight children, crowded into four unheated rooms. Evicted by her sister when the pressure on her sister's husband and their kids began to damage their own marriage, she had to take her children to the EAU* at Church Street in Manhattan. Refusing to accept a placement at a barracks shelter, she's been sleeping here illegally for several nights in a small room rented to her cousin.

When we meet, she's in the corridor outside the crisis center, crying and perspiring heavily. She sits on a broken chair to talk to me. She's not on Medicaid and has been removed from AFDC. "My card's being reprocessed," she explains, although this explanation explains nothing. She's not on WIC. "I've got to file an application." Her back is aching. She is due to have her child any day.

This is the reason for her panic: "If I can't be placed before the baby's born, the hospital won't let me take the baby. They don't let you take a newborn if you haven't go a home." As we will see, this is not always so; but the possibility of this occurrence is quite real. Where are her kids? "They're here. I've got them hidden in the room."

She takes me to her cousin Wanda's room. I measure it: nine feet by twelve, a little smaller than the room in which I store my files on the homeless. Wanda's been here fifteen months, has four kids, no hot plate, and no food in the refrigerator. She's had no food stamps and no restaurant allowance for two months. I ask her why. (You ask these questions even though you know the answer will be vague, confused, because so many of these women have no possible idea of why they do or don't receive the benefits they do or don't deserve.) She's curled up in a tattered slip and a torn sweater on a mattress with no sheet. Her case was closed, she says. Faintly, I hear something about "an application." Her words are hard to understand. I ask her whether she was here for Christmas. The very few words she speaks come out in

*Emergency Assistance Unit—offices open at night and on weekends for emergency placement into shelters.

small reluctant phrases: "Where else would I go?" She says her children got some presents from the fire department. There's a painting of Jesus and Mary on the wall above the bed. "My mother gave it to me."

A week later I stop by to visit. She's in the same position: drowsy and withdrawn. I ask her if she celebrated New Year's Eve. "Stayed by my lonesome" is all that I understand. She rouses herself enough to ask me if I have a cigarette. In the vacuum of emotion I ask if she ever gets to do something for fun. "Go to a movie . . . ' But when I ask the last time she's been to a movie she says: "1984." What was the movie? *"Dawn of the Living Dead."*

When she says she's pregnant and is planning an abortion I don't care to ask her why, but she sits up halfway, props herself against a pillow, looks at Terry, shrugs, and mumbles this: "What you want to bring another baby into this place for? There ain't nothin' waitin' for them here but dirty rooms and dyin'."

Her children, scattered like wilted weeds around her on the floor, don't talk or play or move around or interrupt. Outside in the corridor I ask her cousin if the kids are sick. Terry says: "They're okay. They just didn't have no food to eat today." So I ask: "Did you?" She shakes her head. I go down to Herald Square, buy french fries and chicken at a fast-food store, milk and cookies at a delicatessen, and return. The minute I walk in Wanda sits up, clearheaded and alert. Her kids wake from their stupor. Fifteen minutes later, every bit of chicken, all the french fries, cookies, milk have been consumed. There is a rush of energy and talking in the room. The kids are pestering the adults, as they ought to.

"I have a problem," Wanda says. "My blood sugar goes down. It is called [pronounced very precisely] hypoglycemia."

I meet Terry one year later by sheer chance outside Grand Central Station. She's in a food line for the sandwiches distributed by a charitable group at 10:00 P.M. Her kids are with her. She's holding a baby in her arms. She tells me she's in another hotel near the Martinique. "Don't have no refrigerators there . . . "

I lose her in the crowd of people waiting for a meal.

In the subway station under Herald Square a woman who has seem me coming from the Martinique follows me and stops me by the stairs. Her hair is disheveled. Words spill from her mouth. She says that she was thrown out of the Martinique. Her children were sick with diarrhea. Someone "reported" her; for what I do not ask. After the Martinique she says that she was in a place I've never heard of called the Brooklyn Arms. Her youngest child, one year old, became much sicker there. City workers finally persuaded her to give up all three kids to foster care. She's living now in a crowded women's shelter where, she says, there are twelve women in a room. She shrieks this information at me on the platform not far from the shrieking trains.

"There's no soap, no hygiene. You go to the desk and ask for toilet paper. You get a single sheet. If you need another sheet you go back down and ask them for some more. I sleep on an army cot. The bathroom's flooded."

Is she telling me the truth? Is she on drugs? Is she unwell? Why did she elect to tell me this? Why do the words come out so fast? I feel unkind to cut her off, but I am frightened by her desperation. I leave her there, pouring out her words into the night.

The nurse in the Martinique says this: "A mother gave birth last week to a baby that weighed just over a pound. She was in her seventh month. Her children rubbed her belly while she cried. I called the ambulance."

The nurse is kind, compassionate, and overwhelmed. "People are fractured by this system. I'm responsible for 500 families, here and in another building. Custody cases. Pregnant women. Newborn children. I can get them into WIC. I'm snowed . . . " She's on the telephone, buried in papers, talking with women, hearing their questions, trying to come up with answers. There are others like her in the crisis center who create a tiny zone of safety in the larger zone of fear. But twenty-five hardworking nurses like this woman would be scarcely equal to the miseries that flood across her desk out of this factory of pain and tears.

Far from any zone of safety lives a man named Mr. Allesandro. He's six feet tall and weighs 120 pounds—down 20 pounds from late September. When he came to the hotel a year ago he weighed 165. I first met him in the ballroom before Christmas when I handed him an apple. One bright apple. One week later he does not forget and, when he sees me in the lobby, asks me if I have some time to talk.

His two daughters are asleep. Christopher, his nine-year-old, is lying on the top bunk, fully dressed and wrapped beneath a pile of blankets, but he is awake and vigilant and almost belligerently alert. It's a cold night and the room appears to be unheated. Mr. Allesandro shows me a cracked pane of glass that he has covered over with a sheet of garbage plastic and Scotch tape. The two coils of the hot plate offer a symbolic reassurance ("heat exists") But they do not provide much warmth. He's wearing a coat and woolen hat. His mother, who is seventy-three, lives with them; for some reason, she's not here.

There aren't many men as heads of households in this building; this fact, I think, adds to his feeling of humiliation. His story, quickly told, remains less vivid for me later on than certain details like his trembling hands, the freezing room, the strange sight of his watchful boy, unsleeping on the bed. The boy reminds me of a rabbit staring from a thicket or caught in the headlights of a car.

These, as Mr. Allesandro tells me, are the facts: He was one of several maintenance workers in a high-rise building in Manhattan owned by one of the well-known developers. It was early autumn and his wife, for reasons I don't learn until much later, just picked up one day and disappeared. He tried to keep his job and home by rising early, feeding the children, bringing them to school, then rushing to his job. But his shift required him to be on duty very early. He was reprimanded and, when he explained his problem, was permitted to stay on but cut back to a half-time job. Half-time work was not enough to pay the rent. He was evicted. In the subsequent emergency he had to take leave from his job.

"My mother went with me to the EAU. We asked them if we could be placed together. That way, she could get the kids to school and I could keep my job." Instead, they put him in a barracks shelter with the children but would not allow his mother to go with them. As best he understands, this is because she drew a Social Security check and was on a different budget from his own. Eligibility rules are difficult to fathom; but even where the consequences are calamitous and costly, they are faithfully observed.

"So I'm alone there in this place with about 200 cots packed side by side. Men and women, children," he says, "all together. No dividers. There's no curtains and no screens. I have to dress my kids with people watching. When my girls go to the toilet I can't take them and they're scared to go alone. A lot of women there are frantic. So I stand and wait outside the door."

He went back to the EAU and begged once more. "In my line of work," he says, "you don't earn much of your money from the salary. The people in the building get to know you and you do them favors and they give you money in return. Christmas is the time you get your tips. They'll hand you an envelope. Twenty dollars. Fifty dollars. Some give you a hundred. These are very wealthy people..." So this disappointment was intensified by recognition of the fact that he could not get back his job in time to benefit from the expected generosity of people whom he'd known: "Some of those people knew me well. They liked me." He seems desperate to be assured that he was liked, remembered, missed, by people who had frequently befriended him.

The use of barracks shelters as deterrence to the homeless is not absolute. Assignments are made "on an ad hoc basis," as one social worker states it. But nothing that Mr. Allesandro said could bring the EAU to place his mother with him. His former boss, he says, had told him he would take him back if he could start the day at 5:00 A.M. "There's no way that I could do it. Would you leave your kids alone within a place like that at 5:00 A.M.? I couldn't do it."

The upshot is this: He loses the chance to go back to his job a few weeks before Christmas. Although he's worked for many years, he hasn't been on *this* job long enough to have accumulated pension benefits. Dispossession from his home has left him unemployed; unemployment now will render permanent his homelessness.

Having finally lost everything he had, he returns a few weeks later to the EAU. This time, having undergone "deterrence" and still being homeless, he is granted "temporary" placement at the Martinique. His mother can join him now. But he is no longer a wage earner; he's an AFDC father, broken in spirit, mourning for those lost tips which he will obsessively recall each time we talk. His job has been assigned to someone else. He loses self-control. He thanks God for his mother. This strikes me as a gruesome and enormously expensive instance of municipal assault upon a man's work ethic and familial integrity at the same time.

How does he feel not working?

"It's a nightmare. I'm Italian. You know—I don't mean this to sound prejudiced"—all of the white people here, I notice, are extremely careful and apologetic on this score—"my people work. My father and grandfather worked. My mother worked. I can do construction, carpentry. I can repair things. I'm somebody who's mechanically inclined. I would make beds, I would clean toilets. I'd do anything if I could have a decent job."

He searches the ads, walks the pavement, rides the subway; but he cannot find a job that pays enough to rent a home and feed three children. His rent allowance is $281. He's seen apartments for $350 and $400. If he takes an apartment over his rent limit he will have to make the difference up by cutting back on food and clothes. His mother's pension is too small to offer them a safety margin. "I wouldn't risk it. I'm afraid to take a chance. Even if I got a job, what if I lost it? I'd be back there with the children in the barracks."

So, like everybody else, he's drowning in the squalor of the Martinique Hotel but dreads the thought of being forced to leave.

"My mother helps to make it like a home. She tries. We got the kids a kitten, which is something that is not allowed. I don't like to break the rules, but you have got to give them something to remember that they're children."

Thinking of his hunger, I ask how he feeds the cat.

"We don't need to. We have never bought one can. She eats better than we do—on the mice and rats."

Around midnight I notice that Christopher is wide awake and watching from the bed: blue eyes, pale skin, blondish hair. Mrs. Allesandro cuts the children's hair.

Where is Mrs. Allesandro?

Mr. Allesandro calls her "grandma" and he speaks of her as if she were *his* grandmother as well. Grandma fell in the stairwell Friday afternoon. There had been a fire and the stairs were still slick from the water left there by the fire hoses. She's in the hospital for an examination of her hip. He tells me that she has a heart condition. "If anything happens to her [pauses] . . . I'd be dead. She's the one that's holding us together."

Other people in this building speak of Mrs. Allesandro in almost identical words. They count on her perhaps even a little more than on the nurse or on the other people in the crisis center. Unlike the crisis workers she is here around the clock. As short of food and money as the Allesandros are, I am told that she is often in the hallways bringing food to neighbors, to a pregnant woman, a sick child living somewhere on the floor. A man who knows her but does not live on this floor speaks of Mrs. Allesandro in these words: "Here she is, an old Italian lady. Here are all these women. Most of them Puerto Rican, black... You will see them holding onto her, crying to her as if she was their mother."

Mrs. Allesandro, however, is not here tonight. Her son is on his own—a skeleton of hunger, disappointment, fear. I look at him, at the two girls, asleep, and at the boy—awake, alert. The boy's persistent gaze unsettles me. I ask him: "Are you sleepy?" He just shakes his head. His father is too proud to tell me that the boy is hungry. I feel embarrassed that it's taken me so long to ask. At my request he opens the refrigerator door. There is one packaged dinner, smuggled out of the lunch program. "There was something wrong with it," he says. It has a rancid smell. "It's spoiled." There's a gallon tin of peanut butter, two part-empty jars of apple sauce, some hardened bread. That's it.

Mr. Allesandro takes the $20 that I hand him to the corner store. Christopher sits up halfway and talks with me. He lists for me the ten largest cities of America. I ask him whether he likes school. He does not give the usual perfunctory affirmative response. "I hate it," Christopher says. I ask him what he does for fun. He plays ball on the sidewalk at the corner of the street across from the hotel.

"Is there room to play ball on the sidewalk?"

He explains: "We play against the building of the bank—against the wall."

He falls asleep after I think of giving him a candy bar. His father returns in twenty minutes with a box of Kellogg's Special K, a gallon of juice, half-gallon of milk, a loaf of bread, a dozen eggs, a package of sausages, a roll of toilet paper. He wakes his son. The boy has a bowl of cereal with milk. His father stands before the counter where he placed the food. He looks like a man who has been admitted to an elegant buffet.

Is Mr. Allesandro laden with anxiety? Is Christopher depleted, sick, exhausted? Yes, I suppose both statements are correct. Are they candidates for psychiatric care? Perhaps they are; but I should think a more important observation is that they are starving.

A few months after my evening with the Allesandros, President Reagan meets a group of high school students from New York. Between government help and private charity, he says, "I don't believe there is anyone that is going hungry in America simply by reason of denial...." The president says there is a problem of "people not knowing where or how to get this help." This is what he also says of those who can't find space in public housing that he has stopped building.

His former counselor and now attorney general, Edwin Meese, concedes that people have been turning to soup kitchens but refuses to accept that they are in real need. They go to soup kitchens "because the food is free," he says, and adds, "that's easier than paying for it."

Marian Wright Edelman of the Children's Defense Fund makes this interesting calculation: If Defense Secretary Caspar Weinberger were to give up just a single Pentagon budget item, that which pays for him to have a private dining room, one million low-income school children could get back their morning snack—a snack denied them by administration cuts.

Hundreds of miles from Christopher's bedroom in the Martinique, a reporter describes an underground limestone cave near Kansas City: the largest surplus-food repository in the nation. In this cave and in some other large facilities, in the winter of 1986, the government was storing some 2 billion pounds of surplus food. To a child like Christopher, the vision of millions of pounds of milk and cheese and butter secreted in limestone caves might seem beyond belief. Storage of this surplus food costs taxpayers $1 million a day.

Getting surplus food from limestone caves to children's tables calls the modest but essential transportation costs. In an extraordinary action, termed illegal by the General Accounting Office, the president preferred funds allocated by the Congress for transporting food to homeless people. The sum involved, $28 million, is a small amount beside the $365 million spent to store this food in limestone caves and other warehouse areas. The withholding of such funds may possibly make sense to an economist. I do not know whether it would make much sense to Christopher.

November 1986: I'm in New York and visit with the Allesandros. Grandma's back. She says her health is good. But Christopher looks frighteningly thin. Food was scarce before. The situation's worsened since I was here last. Families in the homeless shelters of New York have been cut back on their food-stamp allocations. The White House has decided to consider money paid for rental to the hotel owners as a part of family income. By this standard, families in the Martinique are very rich. "Tightening of eligibility requirements" has an abstract sound in Washington. On the twelfth floor of the Martinique what does it mean?

I study the computerized receipts that Mr. Allesandro has received. In June, his food-stamp allocation was $145. In August, the first stage in government reductions lowered this to $65. In October: $50. As of December it will be $33.

Mrs. Allesandro does not speak in ambiguities about the lives of her grandchildren. I ask her what the cuts will mean. "They mean," she says, "that we aren't going to eat." New York announces it will help make up the difference but, at the time I visit, no supplemental restaurant allowances have been received.

Questions for Part IV

1 How does Jack Kerouac describe the culture represented by the narrator of *On the Road*? How are women depicted in the reading? Who or what, if anything, in today's America seems closely related to Kerouac's "beatniks"?

2 Can you describe what might have been Rosa Parks's emotions when she refused to move her seat on the bus. Describe how you might feel if you decided to do something similar.

3 How did Toth and her friends feel about each other's social acceptability? Is such clannishness damaging to a spirit of individuality? Did you have similar experiences as a teenager or are Toth's memories dated? Describe your emotions about a particular incident that happened to you.

4 What is the agenda set forth in the Port Huron statement? How much of it has been realized?

5 Many of the volunteers in the Mississippi Project had great courage. What other participants in the civil rights movement were notably courageous? Why do you think there was such strong—at times violent—opposition to this movement?

6 How did the attitudes of Baker and Fitch about the Vietnam war change as a result of their experiences overseas? How were their views changed by their awareness of events that were taking place in the United States?

7 What injustices are cited by the women testifying in favor of the Equal Rights Amendment? What were the main issues in the "human nature" argument against the ERA? How did Gloria Steinem and Margaret Heckler respond to the claims of their opponents?

8 What were the essential elements in Gibbs's success as a grass-roots organizer? What other issues have developed into causes for popular organizing in the 1970s, 1980s, and 1990s?

9 Considering how they are treated once they reach the United States, why would an illegal immigrant want to come here?

10 What are the major trade-offs faced by the women in Hewett's book?

11 Discuss the use of the word "underclass." Do you think it is an accurate way to describe poor and homeless people? Or is does it exemplify prejudice toward these groups?